THE HANDBOOK OF EXOTIC OPTIONS

Instruments, Analysis, and Applications

THE HANDBOOK OF EXOTIC OPTIONS

Instruments, Analysis, and Applications

Edited by Israel Nelken

Chicago • London • Singapore

Trademark Acknowledgments:

IBM AND IBM PC are registered trademarks of International Business Machines Corporation.

Microsoft and Windows are registered trademarks of Microsoft Corporation.

DISCLAIMER

Richard D. Irwin, Inc., makes no warranties, either expressed of implied, regarding the enclosed computer software package, its merchantability or its fitness for any particular purpose. The exclusion of implied warranties is not permitted by some states. The exclusion may not apply to you. This warranty provides you with specific legal rights. There may be other rights that you may have which may vary from state to state.

This publication is designed to provide accurate and authoritative information in regard to the subject matter covered. It is sold with the understanding that neither the author or the publisher is engaged in rendering legal, accounting, or other professional service. If legal advice or other expert assistance is required, the services of a competent professional person should be sought.

From a Declaration of Principles jointly adopted by a Committee of the American Bar Association and a Committee of Publishers.

Irwin Professional Book Team

Publisher: *Wayne McGuirt*
Associate publisher: *Michael E. Desposito*
Executive editor: *Kevin Commins*
Managing editor: *Kevin Thornton*
Marketing manager: *Kelly Sheridan*
Project editor: *Beth Cigler*
Production supervisor: *Laurie Kersch/Carol Klein*
Jacket designer: *Tim Kaage*
Compositor: *Weimer Graphics, Inc.*
Typeface: *11/13 Times Roman*
Printer: *Buxton Skinner Printing Company*

Library of Congress Cataloging-in-Publication Data

The handbook of exotic options: instruments, analysis and applications / edited by Israel Nelken.
p. cm.
Includes bibliographical references and index.
ISBN 1-55738-904-7
1. Derivative securities. 2. Options (Finance) I. Nelken, Israel.
HG6024,.A3H358 1996
332.63′228—dc20 95–25296

Printed in the United States of America
4 5 6 7 8 9 0 BS 2 1 0 9 8 7

Dedicated to my late mother,
Dr. Edith Nelken-Sussmann

Preface

An option is a financial instrument which gives its holder the right to receive certain cash payoffs under certain conditions. For this privilege the holder pays a premium to the writer of the option. Therefore, it is of paramount importance that both parties understand the exact nature of the transaction, including their rights and obligations.

Traditional options have been traded for hundreds of years and are fairly well understood. Whether European or American expiry, they are sometimes called "vanilla" options. In contrast, exotic options such as Asian, Chooser, Compound, Barrier, Binary, Lookback, Quanto, and Two Color Rainbow are much newer innovations. While a vanilla option pays off depending on the price of the underlying asset, the payoff of an exotic option typically depends on some function of the price of the underlying asset, or on a relationship between several underlying assets.

Recently, derivatives have been in the news in connection with well-advertised losses by institutions such as Barings Bank, Gibson Greetings, Orange County California, and the State of Wisconsin Investment Board. While the details of each of these incidents may be different, it seems that the top managers did not understand the precise nature of the instruments being traded. Instead, they allowed positions to be built up and accumulated—positions that eventually led to disaster.

In this book, we have assembled the leading experts in the field and asked them to write about exotic options. In addition, we've included a sample software disk so that each reader can personally experiment with a wide variety of portfolios of options. A deliberate effort was made to choose authors with a wide range of backgrounds. Some are from the financial industry, while others are from academia. However, they do have a common denominator, and that is their vast knowledge and their willingness to share it. Indeed, we are very grateful to all of our authors for their time and dedication.

I would like to thank both Robert Klein and Jess Lederman for their tireless efforts. We also owe our appreciation to the people at Irwin Professional Publishing who made this book a reality.

Israel "Izzy" Nelken

About the Contributors

Dr. Eric Berger is the founder of Berger Financial Research, Ltd. (BFR), a company specializing both in the development of valuation models for derivative securities and in financial engineering. Mr. Berger and BFR work in close association with Bloomberg Financial Markets, and he is a contributing editor to *Bloomberg Magazine*. Previously, Mr. Berger was an associate director in the fixed income strategies group at Bear Stearns & Company. Dr. Berger has a PhD in pure mathematics from Harvard University.

Dr. Phelim P. Boyle holds the J. Page R. Wadsworth Chair in the School of Accountancy at the University of Waterloo and is the director of the Centre for Advanced Studies in Finance. He is an active researcher in the valuation of derivative securities and specializes in numerical valuation methods and computational finance. Dr. Boyle has been widely published and is an associate editor of several journals, including *Mathematical Finance*. Dr. Boyle holds degrees from Queen's University and Trinity College.

Dr. Robin J. Brenner is a vice president in the trading research group at Merrill Lynch, where he has developed pricing formulas for bond options, exotic bond options, FX options, and exotic FX options. He has published numerous articles in industry journals. Previously, he was an assistant professor in the finance department at the University of Arizona. Dr. Brenner received a PhD from Cornell University, an MS in finance and an MBA from Cornell, and a BS in accounting from the University of Illinois—Urbana.

Dr. Emmanuel Derman is head of the quantitative strategies group at Goldman Sachs, where he directs the valuation modeling and the production of risk-management systems for equity derivative products. Previously, he worked for Bell Laboratories and held a number of academic positions in which he did research in particle physics. He is a co-author of the well-known Black-Derman-Toy interest-rate model. Dr. Derman has a PhD in theoretical physics from Columbia University.

Dr. Robert Geske is professor of financial economics at the University of California, Los Angeles, and is a founding principal of LOR/Geske Bock Associates. He has published numerous articles on the subjects of option pricing, volatility estimation, interest-rate risk, and inflation in financial journals, and has been the recipient of a Woodrow Wilson Fellowship and a Fullbright Fellowship. Dr. Geske has consulted for a number of public and private clients, including numerous commercial and investment banking institutions. Dr. Geske received his PhD in financial economics from the University of California—Berkeley.

Dr. J. P. Hunziker is a vice president with Winterthur Insurance Group, where he is responsible for central risk management in the finance department. He has been instrumental in the development of the equity-linked life insurance market in Switzerland and has co-authored several articles on the topic. Previously, he worked for Swiss Re and Ecofin, a research and consulting company based in Zurich. Dr. Hunziker holds a degree in physics from the Swiss Federal Institute of Technology and a PhD in economics from the University of Zurich.

Mr. Richard C. Kleinberg is a director of global derivatives at D.E. Shaw & Co. He was previously director of research at the New York Commodity Exchange and has worked extensively with users of equity and commodity derivatives worldwide to structure hedging and proprietary trading schemes. Mr. Kleinberg did his graduate work in economics at New York University, where he later served on the faculty.

Dr. P. Koch-Medina is an assistant vice president with Winterthur Insurance Group, where he is in charge of the development of insurance products involving derivatives at Winterthur-Life. He has been instrumental in the development of the equity-linked life insurance market in Switzerland and has co-authored several articles on the topic. Previously, Dr. Koch-Medina has worked for J.P. Morgan. Dr. Koch-Medina holds a PhD in mathematics from the University of Zurich.

Dr. Jeffrey L. McIver, director of financial engineering for Infinity Financial Technology, Inc., is active in the research and development of financial analytic tools for Infinity's object-oriented class library, Fin++. Dr. McIver has worked at Bank of America, where he contributed to the development of an advanced probabilistic credit-evaluation system, and at the Federal Home Loan Bank in San Francisco, where he was engaged in all aspects of the U.S. mortgage market. Dr. McIver holds a PhD in mathematics from the University of California—Berkeley. He is a member of the FMA and the AMA.

Dr. Jack W. Mosevich is a senior partner and manager of analytics and systems at Harris Investment Management, Inc. He has eight years experience in fixed income analytics and derivatives research. Previously, Dr. Mosevich was a professor of computer science at the University of Waterloo and earlier served as manager of operations research at Air Canada. He has published research in mathematics, computer science, and finance. Dr. Mosevich holds a BSc from the University of Illinois, an MSc from Northern Illinois University, and a PhD in mathematics from the University of British Columbia.

Dr. Israel (Izzy) Nelken is the founder of Super Computing Consulting Corporation, which provides services to the financial community. He has developed new methodologies and software for pricing and evaluating exotic options and convertible bonds. Previously, Dr. Nelken served on the faculty of the department of computer science at the University of Toronto. He has published numerous articles, and is a frequent lecturer on topics such as credit derivatives, exotic options, and equity swaps. Dr. Nelken received his BSc in mathematics and computer science from Tel Aviv University, and his PhD in computer science from Rutgers University.

Dr. Anthony Neuberger is S.G. Warburg Group Research Fellow at the Institute of Finance and Accounting at the London Business School. He teaches and does research on the use of derivatives, particularly in investment management, and on corporate finance. Before joining LBS, he worked for the UK Department of Energy. Dr. Neuberger received his BS in mathematics and MS in philosophy at Trinity College, Cambridge. He earned an MBA and PhD from the London Business School.

Dr. Michael K. Ong is head of the market risk analysis unit of First Chicago Bank, where he is involved in global risk management, assessment of trading models and hedging strategies, and oversight of the corporation's overall involvement in market risk. He also serves as chair of the research council of First Chicago, and as adjunct professor at the Stuart School of Business of the Illinois Institute of Technology. Previously, Dr. Ong was responsible for quantitative research at Chicago Research and Trading Group (now NationsBanc CRT), and served as assistant professor of mathematics at Bowdoin College, with research specialty in mathematical physics. Dr. Ong holds a BS in physics from the University of the Philippines, an MA in physics, and both MS and PhD degrees in applied math from the the State University of New York at Stony Brook.

Dr. K. (Ravi) Ravindran is the head of the customized solutions group at TD Securities Institute and is an adjunct professor in the department of statistics and actuarial science at the University of Waterloo. He is the author of numerous articles in professional journals and is a member of the editorial board of the *Journal of Derivatives Use, Trading and Regulation*. Dr. Ravindran holds a PhD in probability theory.

Dr. David C. Shimko is vice president, commodity derivatives research and derivatives sales research, for J.P. Morgan, Inc. He specializes in corporate risk-management strategy and derivative structuring for commodity firms. Previously, he was assistant professor of finance at the University of Southern California. Dr. Shimko's work has been published in numerous industry journals, and he currently writes a column for *Risk Magazine*. Dr. Shimko received his BA and PhD from Northwestern University.

Dr. Ton C. F. Vorst is a full professor of finance and business econometrics at Erasmus University. He has been a consultant for major financial institutions in the United States and Europe. Dr. Vorst is an associate editor of the *Journal of Derivatives*, the *Review of Derivatives Research*, and the *International Review of Financial Analysis*, and he has published in numerous journals. He is currently a director of the Erasmus Center for Financial Research and of the Econometric Institute of Erasmus University. Dr. Vorst holds a PhD in mathematics from the University of Utrecht and a masters degree in econometrics from Erasmus University, Rotterdam.

Dr. Eran Yehudai is head of risk management for the global derivatives group at D.E. Shaw & Co., a quantitative finance boutique. His team is responsible for structuring, pricing, and hedging derivatives positions. Dr. Yehudai received his PhD in physics from Stanford University and a BSc in physics and mathematics from Tel Aviv University.

Contents

PART I

INTRODUCTION TO EXOTIC OPTIONS

Chapter One

Exotic Options: The Market and Their Taxonomy*

Michael Ong
Vice President and Head of Market Risk Analysis
First Chicago Corporation

INTRODUCTION

Vanilla options, as we now call them, have been in existence for a long time. The earliest recorded account of options can be traced to the philosopher/mathematician Thales of ancient Greece, who negotiated (during winter when there was very little demand) for the use of olive presses for the following spring. The demand was, of course, contingent on having a great harvest the following spring. During the first half of the seventeenth century, options were also used in Holland during the tulip bulb craze. In the United States, options first appeared in the 1790s during the humble beginnings of the New York Stock Exchange. The concept of "put-call" parity, originally known as conversion, was understood during the late nineteenth century by Russell Sage, a great railroad speculator who is considered by many to be the grandfather of modern option trading. Although the words "put" and "call" were used around this time, the word "option" is a relatively new coinage.

Exotic options have also been in the market for quite a number of years—almost 30 years to date. Down-and-out call options, members of

*The author wishes to thank Art Porton for the outstanding graphics work and his careful reading of the manuscript. In addition, Chris Hansen and Mark Kolas' critique of the first draft substantially helped improve this paper.

the barrier options family, have been sporadically available in the U.S. over-the-counter market since as early as 1967. The up-and-out put began to emerge as a significant OTC product in the late 1980s when Nikkei-linked bonds embedded with short European up-and-out puts were very attractive to Japanese investors. Given the long history of vanilla options, the relatively long history of exotic options is hardly surprising.

In spite of its history, the word "exotic" is quite new. When the first barrier options were introduced in the 1960s, words like "boutique" options and "designer" options were used to describe them. The word "exotic" can perhaps be traced to the November 1990 monograph entitled *Exotic Options* and originally authored by Mark Rubinstein. This collection of short articles contained, for the first time, a series of simple pricing models (most of which are in closed form) of these boutique/designer options based on the Black-Scholes framework. While incomplete, the monograph underwent several revisions (current version May 1992) and was widely circulated, first within academic circles and subsequently to researchers in the industry. For the most part, the closed-form formulas presented in the monograph are very seldom used in actual trading. The reasons are clear. Most of the formulas are generic in nature and often cannot fit neatly into the customized OTC markets. But perhaps more important, because most of the OTC requirements tend to have longer maturities and predefined monitoring frequencies of the underlying movements, the assumption of constant variance (and interest rates) and the continuous nature of the Black-Scholes framework may lead to significant mispricings of long-dated and path-dependent options.

Even before the 1990 exotic options exposition, the pricing of some exotic options already appeared in the literature. The most notable are:

1. 1973: **Down-and-Out Call**
   R. Merton, "Theory of Rational Option Pricing," *Bell Journal of Economics and Management Science,* 4 (1973) 141–183.
2. 1978: **Exchange Option**
   W. Margrabe, "The Value of an Option to Exchange One Asset for Another," *Journal of Finance,* 33 (March 1978) 177–186.
3. 1979: **Compound Options**
   R. Geske, "The Valuation of Compound Options," *Journal of Financial Economics,* 7 (1979) 63–81.

4. 1979: **Lookback Options**
   B. Goldman, H. Sosin, and M. A. Gato, "Path-Dependent Options: Buy at the Low, Sell at the High," *Journal of Finance,* 34 (Dec. 1979) 1111–1127.
5. 1982: **Performance Options**
   R. Stulz, "Options on the Minimum or Maximum of Two Assets," *Journal of Financial Economics,* 10 (1982) 161–185.
6. 1986: **Average (or Asian) Options**
   J. Ingersoll, *Theory of Financial Decision Making* (Totowa, NJ: Rowman and Littlefield, 1987).
   Remark: In his book, Ingersoll derived the partial differential equation for an average (continuous) strike option but did not come up with an explicit closed-form solution. He taunted his readers, indicating that a closed-form solution is possible, "but since the option in question is an artificial example it would be of little use." Currently, averaging-type options are popular, and we know that an exact closed-form solution for the arithmetic case is not possible.

Through the landmark publication of the seminal paper by F. Black and M. Scholes entitled "The Pricing of Options and Corporate Liabilities" in the July 1973 *Journal of Political Economy* and, later in the same year, R. Merton's article on the rigorous theoretical framework for vanilla options, the option-trading community quickly embraced the simplicity and intuitiveness of the Black-Scholes formula. Prior to 1973, there was no acceptable standard for determining what an option is worth. The large variation of prices and the wide bid-asked spread contributed to the illiquidity of the market and this made options very expensive to trade. Until 10:00 a.m. on April 26, 1973, when the Chicago Board Options Exchange officially opened for business (as an SEC "pilot" program!) for the first time, the stock options market was largely controlled by put-call dealers who advertised their prices each morning in *The Wall Street Journal.* A trade was consummated with an actual written contract prepared with the details of the transaction granting the option buyer the legal right to buy or sell the security as specified on the document. What fair price the buyer should pay for the option was anyone's guess.

In 1995 we celebrated the 22nd anniversary of this historic breakthrough in valuation. While the details have changed a bit, largely regarding the stochastic behavior of volatility and the dynamic behavior across strikes, the fundamental valuation of contingent claims still remains to this date inherently Black-Scholes in nature. Exotic options, being a second-generation derivative product of vanilla options, are not exempt from this generalization.

EVOLUTION TOWARD EXOTIC OPTIONS

The market for exotic options was inevitable. Exotic options, by construction, necessarily give more flexibility than their vanilla counterparts. Before 1973, the option market was strictly over-the-counter. The newly established option exchanges quickly corralled the market, and as soon as the vanilla market became mature in the late 1980s, the market had no choice but to spill back over the counter again. It was only a matter of time before people would start demanding customized payoffs. In the meantime, more "quants" from the hard sciences arrived at the scene. More and more, the market was being populated by quants and the market became more quantified—and options became more exotic.

Furthermore, as the vanilla market matures and options pricing theory becomes more transparent and accessible, specialized structures dictated by dynamic hedging and portfolio insurance strategies used to control investment risk in equity, fixed-income, and foreign-exchange portfolios place more demand for customizing specific payoffs. Originally, the payoffs could be replicated synthetically by linear combinations of vanilla options, but often, replicating the payoffs could prove to be expensive. Eventually, as the required payoffs become more complex, new products have to be engineered—there is no other way. Many of these newly engineered products have never existed before.

From a hedging perspective, whether acting singly or constructed as a judicious combination, these new products provide guaranteed returns in very volatile markets and enhanced yields when prevailing rates are low. Very often, the new products not only exhibit extreme flexibility, they are also relatively inexpensive when compared to a combination of the vanilla varieties. All of the specialized characteristics mentioned above guarantee the rapid proliferation of exotic options in the financial markets. The range of exotica now being offered in the market is very wide and truly phenomenal. Indeed, if there is a willing counterparty requiring more inventive designs, an array of exotic products can always be invented and financially engineered.

Based on our discussions above, we can summarize the following reasons for the evolution of the vanilla market into the exotica market and the associated motivation for the use of exotic options:

1. The increasing ability of many firms to construct complicated payoff structures because of the presence of more *high-powered quants.*
2. It is *sometimes cheaper* to consider an exotic structure instead of replicating the exotic structure by a linear combination of vanilla options.
3. Since customization means *more flexibility,* exotic options are indeed very flexible. If one doesn't exist, it can always be invented or "financially engineered."
4. Increased *understanding and sophistication* of the potential users—e.g., corporate hedgers and funds managers—contributed to more widespread use of exotic products.
5. Increased *competition* in the marketplace over the past few years spurred the creation of more exotica, some of which were constructed mainly for *"show-off"* purposes. This "peacock syndrome" forces the trading desks in competing firms to respond with "if they can do it, so can we."
6. Pure *greed*—in low-yield environments, users of exotica were attracted to these products not simply because of the usually lower costs associated with their use, but because of the possibility of above-market yields if the users' views of the market were correct. In many instances, exotic products promising higher payoffs are embedded with "bet" options that requires the users to make specific bets on the direction or range of the market.
7. *Charlatanism and ego trip* on the part of many users who think they understand the structures and their underlying risks but actually don't—the mirror image of the show-off in item 5 but, this time, from the end users' perspectives.

Exotica Temere

The current fear of derivatives loaded with exotic options is not totally unfounded. The last three items above, in addition to the hysteria surrounding some recent derivatives blowups—such as the Showa Shell Sekiyu $1.58BB foray in yen/dollar futures (1992); the Metallgesellschaft AG (1993) $1.8BB hoopla in oil futures/forward contracts; Chile's Codelco $200MM "coppergate" scandal at the London Metals Exchange (1993); the Gibson Greetings multi-million-dollar "hello-and-goodbye" to a leveraged LIBOR-squared, a periodic floor, two spread-locks, a knock-out call, and a time swap, among other exotic smorgasbord (1994); the Procter and Gamble $157MM gamble in leveraged DM/dollar spreads (1994); the Barings over $1BB lone-ranger-cum-trader-triggered collapse (1995); Orange County's perhaps not-so-creative $1.7BB worth of writing on a pile of structured notes (1995); other so-called major hedge funds' tippy-toeing in the derivatives boutique shops; and other less-publicized exotic derivatives debacles—have contributed significantly to the recent intense scrutiny of exotic products by various regulatory bodies. The current brouhaha on derivatives in general, however, does not address the issue of the usefulness of many of these exotic products, if and when used judiciously and prudently. It is equally irresponsible, in my opinion, to be betting on derivatives as it is to not use the proper instruments to manage the risk in a complex exposure. One of the goals of this chapter is to promote greater understanding and transparency of the whole universe of exotic options so that they can be used to properly risk-manage exposures that would otherwise be difficult or impossible using vanillas alone.

The fear of exotic options, due to either misunderstanding or a lack of understanding, is deeply rooted in the original fear surrounding vanilla options. Vanilla options have a somewhat dark and troubled history. The tulip bulb craze in the first half of the seventeenth century caused average citizens to mortgage their homes and sell their businesses in order to participate in the secondary market. When the bubble finally burst and the Dutch economy collapsed (partially due to the speculators' failure and disavowal to comply with their options obligations), options trading was stigmatized in Europe. A century later in England, the collapse of the options market for the shares of The South Sea Company (ca. 1711) rendered options trading virtually illegal in London. Across the Atlantic, following the panic of 1929 and the demise of the option-pool operators—until the subsequent creation of the Securities and Exchange Commission (1934)—Congress all but declared that the options business was manipulative in nature. It was not until 1973, with the establishment of the CBOE, that options trading was put in a more favorable light.

MARKET FOR EXOTIC OPTIONS

In 1991, the Chicago Board Options Exchange (CBOE) introduced a new type of option on the OEX and the SPX indexes, called a CAP. The Standard & Poor's 100 (OEX) and the S&P 500 (SPX) are two of the most popular indexes tracked in U.S. markets. A CAP call is issued at-the-money, with a cap level set 30 index points above the strike level. Unlike a vanilla call, if the underlying index closes at or above the cap level on any trading day up to and including the last day, the option is automatically exercised. The holder of the CAP then receives a payout of $30 times 100—the size of the contract. In today's *lingua exotica*, we say the option has been *knocked out*. Indeed, the CAP is one of the 16 members of the barrier option family. It is interesting to note, however, that in the announcement heralding the arrival of the new CAP option, the CBOE mistakenly compared the CAP call to a vertical call spread, where the buyer is long a vanilla call on the index with strike K and short a vanilla index call with a strike of $K + 30$. This, of course, is only true at the expiry of the CAP call. The knock-out feature, providing for the option's early exercise once the cap level is breached, is not a rational one—it assigns the short position a value lower than it would have in a real vertical call-spread. The CAP call is, therefore, worth more than a vanilla call-spread. In retrospect, it is quite disconcerting to note how such a misconception could arise even as late as 1991.

Following the introduction of the CAP on the exchange, in February 1993 the CBOE again introduced a new product called FLEX (*Fl*exible *Ex*change) Options, which were developed to enable institutional investors to implement large-scale portfolio hedges. The customization of the FLEX includes an American, a European, or a capped exercise. The exchange-traded story on exotic options pretty much ends here.

Much earlier in the OTC market, the Macotta Metals Corporation of New York began trading lookback options on gold, silver, and platinum on March 16, 1982. On April 22, 1982, Manufacturers Hanover

Corporation transacted a convertible note wherein, at maturity, the securities would be converted into shares of the company's common stock. The conversion price would be the lower of $55.55 or the average closing price of the common stock for the 30-day period immediately preceding the note's maturity. This is theoretically a *performance option* (i.e., choose the best of A or B), with an embedded *average rate* optionality, in which one of the choices is dependent on the path taken by the stock price over a 30-day period before the maturity of the note.

We are now in the second half of the 1990s. Where is the market for exotic options?

Currently, the OTC market's interest in exotic options centers on average-rate options, barrier options, basket options, digital options, and rainbow-type options. Their applicability can be found across the board in the commodities, foreign-exchange, equities (single issues and indexes), interest-rate, energy, fixed-income (Treasuries, agencies, corporates, and LDC debt), and other lesser markets. In the commodities and energy markets, the exotic-options markets are concentrated in crude, natural gas, precious metals, and base metals, with the bulk in barrier-type or averaging-type exotic products. In the foreign-exchange market, the interest in exotic products is in averaging, barrier, and digital types of options in the major currencies, and basket options on both major and minor currencies. Spread options between two different indexes are popular in the fixed-income and interest-rate sectors; however, on a much broader scale, any kind of exotic options can be embedded in structured notes and other debentures. We list a few of them in the embeddos section of the taxonomy. In addition to these popular ones, performance-type exotics are common in the equities market and indexes.

TAXONOMY OF EXOTIC OPTIONS

The plethora of exotic options can be classified according to the following distinct characteristics:

- Payoff structures
- Severity of singularity
- Curvilinearity or degree of leverage

- Degree of path-dependency
- Codependency and multivariate features
- Timing of choice or exercise
- Kinds of embeddings in the structure

The characteristics delineated above also provide a good perspective on the different risk characteristics of each kind of exotic option, thereby enabling us to determine the appropriate risk exposures embedded in each product.

We list below the taxonomy of exotica and their associated etymology:

- Path-Dependent
  - Extremum-Dependent
    - Barrier
      - Partial
      - Outside
      - Multiple
      - Curvilinear
    - Lookback
      - Partials
      - Modified
    - Ladder
      - Modified
      - Step-Lock
    - Ratchet
    - Shout
      - Simple
      - Modified
  - Average
    - Average Rate
    - Average Strike
    - Inverse Average Rate
    - Partial Average
    - Flexible Average
    - Geometric
  - Capped Options
  - Caps and Floors
- Singular Payoffs
  - Contingent Premium

- Digitals
  - Cash-or-Nothing
  - Asset-or-Nothing
  - Correlation Digitals
- Digital Barriers

Time-Dependent or Preference
- American
- Quasi-American
- Chooser
  - Simple
  - Complex
- Forward Start
- Ratchets

Multivariate
- Basket
- Rainbow
  - First-Order Correlation Products
    - Best/Worst of n Assets or Cash
    - Min or Max of n Assets
    - Portfolio Options
    - Multi-Strike
    - Pyramid
    - Madonna
    - Spread
    - Exchange
    - Generalized Rainbow
  - Second-Order Correlation Products
    - FX-Linked Options
      - Cross-Currency Options
      - Quantos
        - Fixed
        - Flexible
      - Compos
        - Type A
        - Type B

Nested or Compounded
- Chooser
  - Simple or Complex
- Compound
  - Simple or Complex
- Caption
- Floortion

- Leveraged
    - Power
    - Curvilinear
    - Inverse Floaters
- Embeddos
    - Implicitly Embedded
        - Delevered Floater
        - Dual-Index Floater
        - Levered Inverse Floater
        - Index-Linked Floater
        - Hi-Lo Floater Reverse
        - Principal FX-Linked Bond
        - Stepped Cap/Floor Floater
        - Index Principal Swap
        - Miscellaneous
    - Explicitly Embedded
        - Range Floater
        - Range Rover
        - Ratchet Floater

TERMINAL PAYOFF FUNCTIONS

The most intuitive approach to describing exotic options is to observe their respective payoff functions at maturity time T. For a vanilla call, the terminal payoff is

$$\max\,[0, S_T - K]$$

where S_T is the stock price at time T and K is the strike price. The terminal payoff for a vanilla put is max $[0, K - S_T]$. The terminal payoff functions act as one of the fundamental boundary conditions in the contingent claim. The two other boundary conditions are when the underlying price goes to either zero or infinity, for times at and away from the inception time. Together, these three boundary conditions determine the unique payoff of the contingent claim for all other times. The terminal payoff function of an option, therefore, reveals a lot of information about the behavior of the option at all other times. For the purpose of this exposition, understanding the terminal payoffs of the claims is sufficient to comprehend the underlying risks embedded in the structures.

Following we list the payoff functions for exotic options:

Path-Dependent

Unlike the vanilla variety, path-dependent options have claims that are contingent on the price path taken by the underlying asset. There are three subclassifications, namely, *extremum-dependent, average type*, and *capped.*

Extremum-dependent

These are path-dependent options that depend not only on the path taken by the underlying asset but also depend on either the maximum or minimum point achieved during the life of the option. In other words, this type of option depends on the *extreme* points traversed by the underlying asset over the life of the option, and is hence classified as an extremum-dependent option.

Barrier

One example of a barrier option is a *knock-out* call that ceases to exist if, at any time prior to maturity T, the underlying price S touches or falls below the level H. The payoff function for the knock-out call is

$$\begin{array}{ll} \max\,[0, S_T - K], & \textit{if } S(t) > H, \textit{ for all time } t \leq T \\ \textit{rebate or zero,} & \textit{if } S(t) \leq H, \textit{ for some time } t \leq T. \end{array}$$

At the time the option gets knocked out, one either gets nothing or is compensated with a *rebate* consisting of a fixed amount of cash. More specifically, the option described above is a *"down-and-out"* knock-out call—when the underlying price goes down and breaches the barrier level, the option gets extinguished.

There are eight possible combinations for the knock-out variety and another eight for the *knock-in* variety. The knock-in option comes alive as soon as the threshold H is breached, however, at any time prior to breaching the level H, the option doesn't exist. Other nomenclatures are *extinguishing* or *disappearing options* for the knock-outs and *appearing options* for the knock-ins.

Note: In the absence of rebate payments, the following decomposition *always* holds:

vanilla = knock-out + knock-in, *when rebate is zero*.

This obviates the need to price both knock-out and knock-in options. Once either one is known, the other one can be obtained via decomposition.

Variations of barrier options:

1. **Partial Barriers:** The period for monitoring the movement of the underlying asset is a subset of the tenor of the option. For example, a 6-month partial-barrier option could have the monitoring period be specified between the 3rd and the 5th month during the life of the option. If the barrier level H is breached during this time frame, the option either gets knocked in or knocked out. Outside this time frame, nothing happens.

2. **Outside Barriers:** A second variable determines whether the option is knocked out or knocked in. For example, suppose the payoff of the option is a function of \$/DM, but the level of gold price triggers whether the option on \$/DM gets knocked in or knocked out.

Example: Let S be the *payoff variable* (i.e., \$/DM) and R the *knock-out variable* (i.e., gold price), then the payoff function for an *"outside" down-and-out* call is

$$\begin{array}{ll} \max\,[0, S_T - K], & \textit{if } R(t) > H, \textit{ for all time } t \leq T \\ \textit{rebate or zero,} & \textit{if } R(t) \leq H, \textit{ for all time } t \leq T \end{array}$$

where K is the strike price of the option and H is the barrier level for gold.

Note: In principle, the outside barriers belong to the *multivariate* class of exotic options, since the correlation between S and R is necessary to value the options.

3. **Multiple Barriers:** In this case, there are two or more barrier levels H_i, $i = 1, 2, 3, \ldots, n$. The most commonly traded in the market are the *double barrier* options on the Nikkei index. The upper and lower thresholds can either be knock-in or knock-out or a combination of both.

4. **Curvilinear Barriers:** Unlike ordinary barrier options, the barrier level H is not a constant but is a function of both time and the underlying asset. The most common ones are the *exponential barriers* where the barrier level decreases (or increases) exponentially through time.

Example: For example, the upper and lower barriers are given by

$$\begin{aligned} H_{lower} &= H_L\, e^{\delta_L \tau} \\ H_{upper} &= H_U\, e^{\delta_U \tau}, \qquad t \leq \tau \leq T \end{aligned}$$

where H_L, H_U, δ_L, δ_U are constants and τ is the time between inception t and maturity T. The optionality at either barrier level can either be an "in" or an "out."

Note: All of the variations mentioned above have closed-form formulas derived under the usual Black-Scholes assumption of nonstochastic (i.e., constant) volatility and interest rates. The outside barrier, being a correlation product, requires a *bivariate cumulative normal distribution* function, in contrast to the univariate case of the other barriers.

Lookback

The lookback option gives the holder the right to purchase or sell the underlying asset at the best possible price attained over the life of the option. The payoff functions are

lookback call

$\max\,[0, S_T - \min\,(S_0, S_1, S_2, \ldots, S_T)]$

lookback put

$\max\,[0, \max\,(S_0, S_1, S_2, \ldots, S_T) - S_T]$

where $S_0, S_1, S_2, \ldots, S_T$ is the sequence of underlying prices observed during the life of the option. These lookback options are also known as *floating-strike options.*

Variations of lookback options:

1. **Partial Lookback 1:** Similar to the partial barrier, the monitoring period of the movement of the underlying asset is any subset of the tenor of the option. For instance, a 1-year partial lookback call can have the observation be allowed only during the last four months of the option.

2. **Partial Lookback 2:** The "partial" in this variation refers to some percentage over the observed maximum or minimum. For example, the payoff function for the partial lookback 2 call is

$$\max\,[0, S_T - \lambda \min\,(S_0, S_1, S_2, \ldots, S_T)], \qquad 0 < \lambda < 1.$$

For obvious reasons, this particular option is also known as a *variable floating-strike* option.

3. **Modified Lookbacks:** Unlike the regular lookbacks, which have floating strikes, the modified lookbacks have *fixed* strikes K, viz.,

modified lookback call

$\max\,[0, \max\,(S_0, S_1, S_2, \ldots, S_T) - K]$

modified lookback put
$\max\,[0, K - \min\,(S_0, S_1, S_2, \ldots, S_T)]$.

Of course, the modified lookbacks can also be made either partial or variable as needed.

Ladder

Ladder options look back on the path traversed by the underlying asset, as do lookbacks. Unlike lookbacks, ladders have payoffs that "lock in" at some preset levels. The ladder option is really a variation of the lookback option with one little twist—the lookback mechanism is effective only for a set of predetermined levels achieved by the underlying asset. Suppose there are n such ladder levels, denoted by $L_1, L_2, L_3, \ldots, L_n$, then the payoff functions are

ladder call
$\max\,[0, S_T - \min\,(L_1, L_2, L_3, \ldots, L_n, S_T)]$

ladder put
$\max\,[0, \max\,(L_1, L_2, L_3, \ldots, L_n, S_T) - S_T]$

Also, notice that the strikes for either the ladder call or put are not determined at the inception of the option. Thus, another name for this type of ladder is the *floating-strike ladder.*

Variations of ladder options:

1. **Modified Ladder:** Unlike the regular ladders, which have floating strikes, the modified ladders have *fixed* strikes K, viz.,

modified-ladder call
$\max\,[0, \max\,(L_1, L_2, L_3, \ldots, L_n, S_T) - K]$

modified-ladder put
$\max\,[0, K - \min\,(L_1, L_2, L_3, \ldots, L_n, S_T)]$

2. **Step-Lock Ladder:** Similar to the ordinary ladder, there are predetermined levels, except for the provision that the intrinsic value is locked in and a new strike level is established at that level. There are many variations. For example, if cash is paid out immediately upon reaching two successively *higher* rungs of the ladder, namely L_1 and L_2, at times t_1 and t_2 , respectively, then the payoff function for this particular call ladder, with initial strike K, is

$$\max\,[0, S_T - \max\,(L_i \mid S_T > L_i)] + (L_1 - K)\,e^{r(T-t_1)} + (L_2 - L_1)\,e^{r(T-t_2)}.$$

The first term shows that the strike resets itself at the highest rung breached, while the next two terms are the future values (to maturity of the option) of the cash amount locked in at the two rungs breached by the underlying asset.

Ratchet

The locking-in mechanism of the ratchet option is similar to the step-lock ladder option. The ratchet option behaves initially as a vanilla option with a fixed strike, but as time moves on, the strike is reset to the price attained by the underlying asset on predetermined dates. When the strike is reset, the intrinsic value is automatically locked in. If the underlying asset price is below the previous level at the next reset date, no intrinsic value is locked in. Rather, the strike price will be reset to the current price attained by the underlying asset. The intrinsic value will be locked in again if the underlying asset price exceeds the current level at the next reset date.

Given a series of underlying prices $S_0, S_1, S_2, \ldots, S_T$ at times $t_0, t_1, t_2, \ldots, t_T$, the ratchet option is simply a string of forward-starting options, viz.,

$$\max\,[S_{t_0} - K, 0]\;e^{r(T-t_0)} + \max\,[S_{t_1} - S_{t_0}, 0]\;e^{r(T-t_1)} + \ldots + \max\,[S_T - S_{t_{n-1}}, 0].$$

The ratchet option was first developed in France and was based on the CAC 40 index. It is also known as the *cliquet option.*

Shout

The shout option is a hybrid of the lookback, ratchet, and ladder options. For the ladder option, the strike is reset once predetermined levels are breached. With the ratchet option, the strike is reset at predetermined dates. In contrast, the shout option resets its strike neither by predetermined levels or dates. Instead, the owner of the shout option can reset its strike to equal the current level of the underlying by simply "shouting" the new level. The shouting is presumably done at a level the owner feels is the most advantageous to do so. Assuming that the shouting is done rationally at the most optimal time, the payoff is simply

$$\max [S_T - K, S_{t_{shout}} - K, 0] = \max [S_T - S_{t_{shout}}, 0] + [S_{t_{shout}} - K].$$

The decomposition above shows that the shout option is composed of a spread option between the terminal time T and the shouting time t_{shout} plus the intrinsic part, which is locked in upon shouting.

Variations of shout options:

1. **Simple Shout:** The simple shout call has a *floating strike* with payoff function given by

$$\max [S_T - \min (S_T, S_{t_{shout}}), 0].$$

2. **Modified Shout:** The modified shout call has a *fixed strike K* with payoff function given by

$$\max [\max (S_T, S_{t_{shout}}) - K, 0].$$

Average

These are path-dependent options, which take into account the mean or average path traversed by the underlying asset. The mean in this context is taken to be either the simple arithmetic average or the weighted arithmetic average. Another name for the average option is *Asian option*, a coinage that apparently originated in the Tokyo office of Bankers Trust, which was the first to offer this type of product. Strictly speaking, the term "average" refers only to those whose payoffs depend on the simple arithmetic average. Consider the most general case where the underlying asset prices over a period of time are $S_1, S_2, S_3, \ldots, S_n$ and with weights $\omega_1, \omega_2, \omega_3, \ldots, \omega_n$ (in percentage). The weighted arithmetic average is

$$A = \sum_{i=1}^{n} \omega_i S_i$$

where the weights ω_i sum to one.

Variations of average options:

1. **Average Rate:** The average rate option is simply a vanilla option where the underlying price is replaced by the average prices observed during the entire life of the option. The payoff function for the average rate call option is $\max [A - K, 0]$.

2. **Average Strike:** Instead of the underlying price, it is the strike price of the call option that is replaced by the average prices observed during the entire life of the option, viz., $\max [S_T - A, 0]$.

3. **Inverse Average-Rate:** Particularly when applied to the foreign-exchange markets, the counterparty could have an exposure denominated in a currency opposite to that of the quoting convention. In this case, the counterparty may wish to have an inverse average-rate option, whose payoff function is max $[A^{-1} - K, 0]$.

Of course, the strike price K and the inverse average A^{-1} must be denominated in the same currency. For instance, if the exchange rates S_i are denominated in \$/yen, then A^{-1} will be denominated in yen/\$.

Another possibility for the inverse average is max $[\tilde{A}^{-1} - \tilde{K}, 0]$ where the inverse average is calculated as

$$\tilde{A}^{-1} = \frac{1}{\frac{1}{n}\sum_{i=1}^{n}\frac{1}{S_i}}.$$

The quantities $\tilde{A}^{-1}$ and $\tilde{K}$ must be denominated in the same currency units. For instance, if the exchange rates S_i are denominated in \$/DM, then $\tilde{A}^{-1}$ will also be denominated in \$/DM.

4. **Partial Average:** In the previous variations, the average of A is taken over the entire life of the option. For partial-average options, the averaging period could be any subset of time during the life of the option. Furthermore, the monitoring frequencies can be daily, weekly, monthly, etc.

5. **Flexible Average:** All of the averages obtained above have flexible weights ω_i and are therefore classified as flexible-average options.

Suppose there are n observations that make up the average A, and each observation is equally weighted, i.e., $\omega_i = 1/n$, then the average becomes a simple arithmetic average, viz.,

$$\bar{A} = \frac{1}{n}\sum_{i=1}^{n} S_i.$$

This is commonly referred to as the Asian option.

6. **Geometric Average:** Instead of an arithmetic sum, it could be the geometric average given by

$$G = \left\{\prod_{i=1}^{n} S_i\right\}^{1/n}.$$

The geometric average can also be made with flexible weights. The geometric-average option has a closed-form formula under the normal Black-Scholes assumptions; the arithmetic-average options do not.

Although the geometric case is not the average of choice in the OTC markets, it is interesting to note that the U.S. Dollar Index (USDX) futures contract, listed in the FINEX division of the New York Cotton Exchange, is calculated from a formula that is a geometric mean of the spot quotations from Reuters Information Services on the dollar index of ten major exchange rates. The index is defined as

$$USDX = 1000 \prod_{i=1}^{10} \left(\frac{B_i}{S_i}\right)^{\omega_i}$$

where ω_i is the weight on currency i, B_i is the base value of the currency i quoted on March 1973, and S_i is the spot exchange rate for currency i quoted in American convention (i.e., U.S. dollars per one unit of foreign currency). Technically, an option structured on the USDX is a geometric option, therefore geometric average options do exist in the market, contrary to popular belief.

Capped options

We have discussed capped options earlier. These exchange-traded capped options, introduced by the CBOE, trade off the S&P 100 and 500 indexes, while the capped options on the Amex trade off of the Major Market and Institutional Indexes. Capped options are path-dependent because ceilings are imposed on the payoff functions. These ceilings could be breached any time during the life of the options. If the capped option fails to reach the ceiling during its lifetime, the option expires worthless. However, upon breaching the ceiling, the seller must pay the option holder the difference between the index level and the ceiling but no more than a fixed cap value. Capped options are therefore, in many ways, members of the barrier-options family.

Caps and Floors

Not to be confused with capped options, caps and floors are over-the-counter interest-rate derivatives that trade off of interest rates, e.g., LIBOR, instead of indexes. *Caps* are designed to provide insurance against the interest rate of a floating-rate instrument rising above a certain level, known as the cap rate R_{cap}. In general, a cap consists of a string of *caplets*. Each caplet has a payoff of

$$[\textit{periodic notional}] * \max\,[R_\tau - R_{cap}, 0]$$

where R_τ is the value of the interest rate at the end of the caplet period and the periodic notional is the fraction of the notional amount of the entire cap applicable for the particular caplet. The payoff function of the caplet is identical to a vanilla call on an interest rate, with the strike price replaced by the cap rate applicable for the caplet period.

A *floor* is simply a string of *floorlets* whose payoffs are identical to vanilla puts on interest rates, with the strike price again replaced by the floor rate R_{floor}.

Both caps and floors are classified as path-dependent options, since the payoffs of these options depend on the path traversed by the relevant interest rates. Because they are nearly identical to vanilla puts and calls, interest-rate caps and floors are technically not exotic options. However, since the cap level or the floor level can be reset either at the end or the beginning of each period, resettable caps and floors behave very much like ladder options.

Singular Payoffs

Exotic options with singular payoffs exhibit discontinuities or sudden jumps in the payoff functions. The jumps usually take the form of abrupt steps. For instance, the digital option pays either something or nothing. Options with singular payoffs, while easy to value, are quite difficult to hedge, since changes in the option values are usually pronounced and rapid. We have already encountered an option with a singular payoff. The barrier option, which pays a rebate upon getting knocked out, exhibits such a jump. The magnitude of the jump is the difference between the current value of the option and the rebate amount. The larger the difference, the more severe the singularity will be. Figure 1–1 illustrates the jump in the payoff function.

The following are examples of options with singular payoffs.

Contingent premium

Contingent-premium options are also known as *COD* (cash-on-delivery) and *pay-later options*. They are also known as *zero-premium options* because the buyer pays nothing for them initially. As the name implies, there is a contingency clause attached during the life of the option—the premium of the option is payable as soon as the option is exercised. Furthermore, as soon as the underlying asset price touches or exceeds the strike price at any time during the life of the option, the contingency clause requires that the option be exercised. In contrast, the premium for a vanilla option is payable at the inception of the option, regardless of whether the option is exercised or not. The contingent-premium option is much more expensive than a vanilla option so that there is really nothing gratuitous about it. Contingent-premium options originated in the

FIGURE 1–1
Knock-Out Put with Rebate

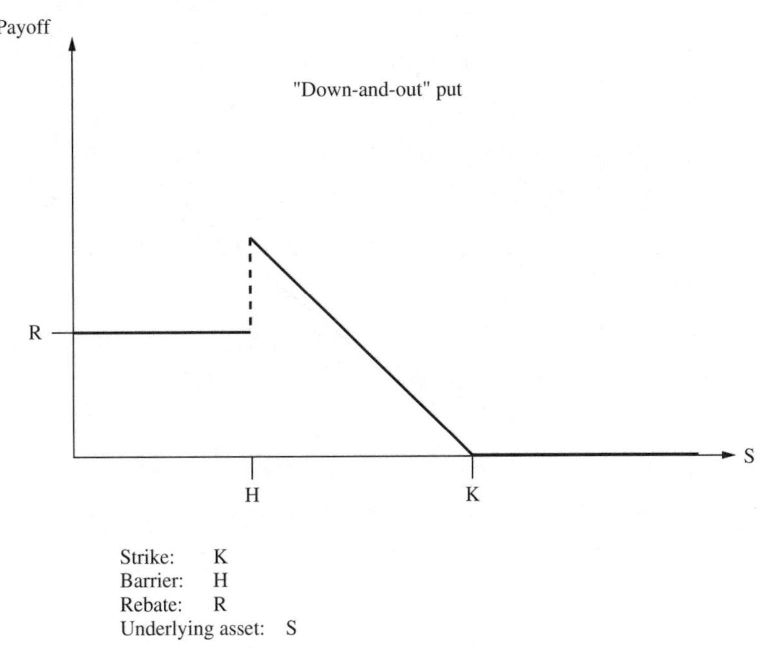

commodity markets, became very popular among investors betting on the Nikkei 225 index and ultimately attracted people in the foreign-exchange markets. Figure 1–2 shows that there is an abrupt jump right at the strike price of the option. This points to the fact that the premium is not paid unless the option is exercised. The payoff function for a COD call is

$$S_T - K - premium, \qquad if\ S_T \geq K$$

$$0, \qquad if\ S_T < K.$$

where "premium" is the value of the continent-premium option.

Variations of contingent premium options:

1. **Reverse Contingent Option:** This option requires no initial payment of premium, but a premium must be paid if, at expiration, the option finishes *out-of-the-money*. The payoff function is obviously the reverse of the COD we saw earlier, viz.,

FIGURE 1–2
Contingent-Premium Option

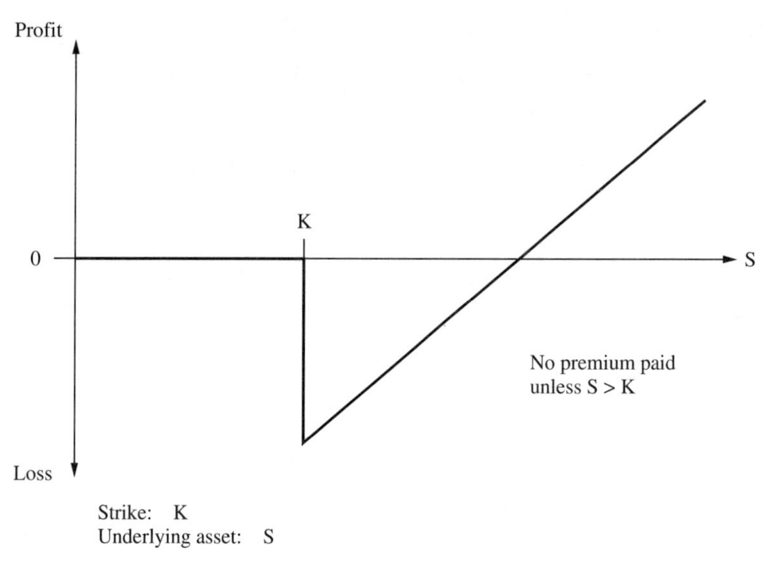

$S_T - K - premium, \qquad if\ S_T < K$

$0, \qquad if\ S_T \geq K$

2. **Money-Back Option:** This option gives back the initial premium paid if and when the option finishes in-the-money.

Note: Both of these variations on contingent-premium options can be easily valued using the standard Black-Scholes argument. The contingency on the payment or payback of the premium can also be made even more complex by stipulating other "if-and-when" clauses into the claim.

Digitals

Digital options pay either something or nothing. Other names for the digital option are *all-or-nothing option, binary option*, or *bet option.* The payoff can be either cash or the underlying asset itself.

Variations of digitals:

1. If the payout is cash, the digital is called a Cash-or-Nothing option.

FIGURE 1–3
Digital Option

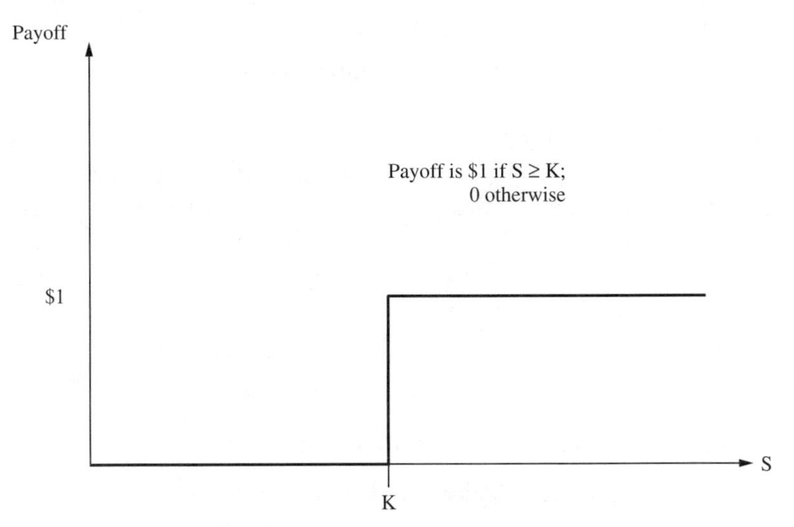

2. If the payout is the underlying asset, the digital is called an Asset-or-Nothing option.

The payoff function for a *generic digital-call* option is

1, $\quad$ *if* $S_T \geq K$

0, $\quad$ *if* $S_T < K$.

For a cash-or-nothing option that pays \$5, replace 1 by \$5. For an asset-or-nothing option, simply replace 1 by the underlying price at expiry, i.e., S_T. Closed-form formulas for both cases can be easily derived. Figure 1–3 shows the payoff for the digital option. Notice that the digital option exhibits a singularity more severe (i.e., more abrupt) than the pay-later option.

Note: A COD option can be decomposed into long a vanilla option and short a digital option, both of which have the same strike and expiration date, i.e.,

COD = vanilla − digital

with same strike and tenor.

3. **Correlation Digital Option:** This option has a payoff based on a variable but the "trigger" is based on another variable. For instance,

consider a digital option that pays at a certain level of the DAX index only if, at the option's maturity, the U.S. dollar is at a certain prescribed level against the DM. The correlation digital is similar to the *outside-barrier* option encountered earlier. Like the outside barrier, an index different from the payoff index determines whether a certain threshold is breached.

The payoff function for a correlation digital-call option on the index S, with strike K and trigger H, which pays *$1* if the other index $\tilde{S}$ touches or exceeds the threshold H, and pays *zero* otherwise, is given by $\max\,[(S_T - K, 0) \mid \tilde{S}_T > H]$.

The symbol $\max\,[\ldots \mid \tilde{S}_T > H]$ is another way of saying "provided that $\tilde{S}_T > H$. Because there are two stochastic variables in the payoff function, the value of this option will depend on the correlation between these two indexes.

> *Variations of options with singular payoffs:*
>
> Options with singular payoffs can either be path-dependent or path-independent. The COD and digital are both path-independent. An example of a singular payoff with path-dependency is the digital barrier.

Digital barriers

A digital barrier option is a hybrid between a digital and a barrier. It is, in fact, a digital embedded with a barrier option. There are many possible combinations—28 of them to be precise. For a complete taxonomy of digital barriers, please refer to the Exotic Options Monograph by Rubinstein. As an example, consider the *down-and-out digital* (DOD) call with a payoff function of

$$
\begin{array}{lll}
1, & \text{if } S_t \geq H, & \text{for all } t \leq T \\
0, & \text{if } S_t < H, & \text{for some } t \leq T
\end{array}
$$

From the payoff function, we see that the DOD call pays $1 if, for *all* time t before maturity T, the underlying asset price S_t is always above the barrier H. However, if for any time before maturity, the underlying asset price falls below the barrier, the option pays nothing. The digital can either pay out a dollar amount or the underlying asset at the time of first breaching the barrier. The other 27 combinations are easy to construct.

Time-Dependent or Preference

While all options are explicitly dependent on time, some have a more subtle preference or dependence on time than others. The European option's dependence on time is very rigid—the option can only be exercised at maturity. At the other extreme, we have the American-style option, which can be exercised at any time prior to maturity, whether rationally or not.

American-style options

These options require no further discussion. They can be exercised at any time prior to the maturity of the option.

Quasi-American

Also known as *Bermuda* or *Mid-Atlantic options*, these options are somewhere between American and European options. A quasi-American option allows exercise only on specific dates during the life of the option. The window for exercise can be a specific day or a range of days specified at the inception of the option contract. There can also be several windows of opportunity during the life of the option. If during the first opportunity, the option is not exercised, the option can still be exercised at later time periods. Clearly, as the number of exercise opportunities during the life of the option approaches infinity, the option becomes more and more like the American-style option.

Chooser

The chooser option is also known as the *pay-now-choose-later option.* It allows the buyer a choice between a vanilla call and a put at some time in the future.

There are two variations:

1. **Simple Chooser:** The *simple chooser* option allows the buyer of the option to choose between a vanilla call-option and a vanilla put-option of the same prespecified strike and maturity date at some predetermined time in the future. The payoff function is

$$\max\,[C(K, T - t), P(K, T - t); t]$$

where T is the time to maturity of the two option choices and t is the time to choose.

2. **Complex Chooser:** In contrast, the *complex chooser* allows the buyer a choice between a vanilla call with strike K_1 and time to maturity T_1 and vanilla put with strike K_2 and time to maturity T_2, at some predetermined time in the future. In other words, a complex chooser allows

a choice of two options with two different strikes and different times to maturity. The payoff function is

$$\max\ [C(K_1, T_1 - t), P(K_2, T_2 - t); t]$$

where t is the time to choose.

Note: Only the simple chooser has a closed-form formula. The value of the complex chooser, however, can be expressed as a double integral, which can then be integrated numerically.

Forward start

The forward-start option grants the holder, at the option's expiry, another option with the strike price set equal to the underlying asset price at that future date. This implies that the value of the forward-starting at-the-money call option on that future point in time is

$$C(S_t, S_t, T)$$

where t is some known elapsed time in the future ("grant date") and T is the term to maturity of the call option to be granted at time t. From the *homogeneity property* of options in option pricing theory, we can rewrite

$$C(S_t, S_t, T) = S_t\ C(1, 1, T)$$

where the call $C(1, 1, T)$ is known in advance since it is the current value of an at-the-money option with the underlying asset price set to 1 and with expiration time T. Another name for the forward start option is the *delayed option.*

Ratchets

The ratchet option we discussed earlier can also be classified as a time-preference option since the strike is reset at some predetermined dates in the future.

Shout

We discussed earlier that the owner of the shout option can reset its strike to equal the current level of the underlying asset by simply "shouting" the new level. The shouting time is controlled by the holder and the shout option, therefore, has a time-preference feature.

Multivariate

Options that are classified in this category are usually dependent on two or more underlying assets. In addition to volatilities, the co-movements of the different underlying assets, as embodied in their mutual correlation coefficients, also have to be taken into consideration when valuing these options. Other names for the multivariate options are *multifactor options* and *correlation products.*

Earlier in the family of barrier options, we encountered the *outside barrier,* whose payoff is dependent on one variable but the knock-out or knock-in mechanism is triggered by a different variable. The co-movement of these two variables, represented by the correlation coefficient, is an example of the multivariate feature of this type of option. Another example encountered earlier is the *correlation digital* option.

Basket

The basket option is one of the most popular correlation products. As the name implies, the basket is made up of a variety of underlying assets, e.g., stocks and currencies, and the option is then structured on the basket. If S_1^T, S_2^T, S_3^T, . . . , S_n^T represents the terminal values of *n different* stocks and ω_1, ω_2, ω_3, . . . , ω_n are the weights in percentage denoting the relative composition of the basket, the payoff function of the basket option is

$$\max\left[\sum_{i=1}^{n} \omega_i \; S_i^T - K, 0\right].$$

The strike price is usually chosen to be a numerical value based on (1 ± some percentage) of the numerical value of the weighted basket.

Rainbow

The most general rainbow option is a rainbow with *n* colors. The contingent claim can come in a variety of flavors. It can range from an option that delivers the best or worst of *n* assets to an option that delivers either the call or put on the maximum (or minimum) of *n* risky assets.

Variations of rainbow options:

1. **Best/Worst of n Assets or Cash:** The payoff function at terminal time is simply

Best:

$$\max\,[S_1^T, S_2^T, S_3^T, \ldots, S_n^T, K]$$

Worst:

$$\min\,[S_1^T, S_2^T, S_3^T, \ldots, S_n^T, K]$$

where K represents the fixed cash amount potentially received at expiration. These simple options deliver the best performing (largest) or worst performing (smallest) of either n assets or a cash amount K upon exercise. For this reason, these options are also known as *best/worst performance options.*

2. **Option on the Max or Min of n Assets:** For a call option on the max, the payoff function is max [max $(S_1^T, S_2^T, S_3^T, \ldots, S_n^T) - K, 0]$, whereas for a put option on the min, the payoff is max $[K -$ min $(S_1^T, S_2^T, S_3^T, \ldots, S_n^T), 0]$.

Note: There are some very natural decompositions. For instance, a *call on the max* can be rewritten as

$$\max [\max (S_1^T, S_2^T, S_3^T, \ldots, S_n^T) - K, 0]$$

$$= \max [S_1^T, S_2^T, S_3^T, \ldots, S_n^T, K] - K$$

$$= \textit{Best of n Assets or Cash} - \text{cash amount } K$$

so that a *call on the max* is equivalent to the *Best of n Assets or Cash less* the cash amount K. By a similar argument, the *put on the max* is equivalent to the *Best of n Assets or Cash plus* the cash amount K.

The earliest performance option was formulated by Stulz in 1982. The paper published at that time was on options on the minimum or maximum on *two* assets, i.e., a two-color rainbow.

3. **Portfolio Options:** Portfolio options are very similar to basket options except that the weights for the portfolio options are the number of units of the respective assets. For instance, a call portfolio option on stocks has a payoff function given by

$$\max \left[\sum_{i=1}^{n} n_i S_i^T - K, 0 \right]$$

where n_i is the *number of shares* of the stock S_i and not the percentage composition of the basket.

4. **Multi-Strike Options:** A multi-strike option has many strikes. The call option has the obvious payoff function, max $[S_1^T - K_1, S_2^T - K_2, \ldots, S_n^T - K_n, 0]$.

The put option is just the reflection.

5. **Pyramid Options:** The pyramid option is so named because the payoff looks like a pyramid in n-dimensions, viz.,

$$\max [|S_1^T - K_1| + |S_2^T - K_2| + \ldots + |S_n^T - K_n| - K, 0].$$

Again, the put counterpart is simply the reflection, viz.,

$$\max [K - (|S_1^T - K_1| + |S_2^T - K_2| + \ldots + |S_n^T - K_n|), 0].$$

6. **Madonna Options:** The madonna call has a payoff function given by

$$\max\,[\sqrt{(S_1^T - K_1)^2 + (S_2^T - K_2)^2 + \ldots + (S_n^T - K_n)^2} - K, 0].$$

Again, the put counterpart is simply the reflection.

7. **Spread Options:** The most popular of the two-color rainbow options is the spread option, i.e., the option on the difference in either prices or yields between two underlying assets, viz.,

$$\max\,[(S_1^T - S_2^T) - K, 0].$$

The spread option can be written on the difference between the yields of a Treasury or mortgage-backed security, the difference in price of two different grades of oil, etc. If the spread is allowed to be negative, the spread (treated as one single asset) has to be modeled using a normal distribution assumption. Otherwise, the regular Black-Scholes assumptions hold. The spread option is also called the *outperformance option.*

8. **Exchange Options:** The exchange option was originally formulated by Margrabe in 1978. The exchange option is a two-color rainbow, since it allows the holder to exchange one risky asset for another. The payoff function for the exchange of asset B for asset A is $\max\,[A_T - B_T, 0]$.

The subscript T denotes terminal values at expiry.

9. **Generalized Rainbow:** The exchange option, portfolio option, and the multi-strike option are all special cases of the generalized rainbow. The generalized payoff function can be written as

$$\max\,[c_1 S_1^T + c_2 S_2^T + \ldots + c_n S_n^T + c_o, 0]$$

where the constants c_i are either positive or negative.

Note: The options delineated above in the rainbow category are collectively known as *first-order correlation products,* since each one of these options is explicitly dependent on the correlation coefficients among the different assets. In contrast, the FX-Linked options below are classified as *second-order correlation products,* since the contingent claim is really one underlying asset. The price of the option is greatly affected by the co-movements of the foreign-exchange rate and the underlying asset, although the foreign-exchange component is not the subject of the contingent claim.

FX-linked options

This class of options invariably involves a foreign-exchange component whose main function is to act as a *numeraire*, i.e., a conversion factor used to change the units from one denomination to another. The most familiar example is a *cross-currency option*. Cross-currency options are puts and calls whose premiums are quoted in a third currency. There are three currencies involved: the deliverable currency, the strike currency, and the currency that is used to quote the option's price. The covariance relationship, embodied in the correlation coefficient between the deliverable and the strike currencies, plays a very important role in the pricing of cross-currency options.

Variations of FX-linked options:

1. **Cross-Currency Options:** Consider, for instance, the *cross exchange-rate* S_X denominated in units of [yen/mark], *deliverable currency* S_A denominated in [dollar/mark], and the *strike currency* S_K denominated in units of [dollar/yen]. Then, clearly $S_X = \frac{S_A}{S_K}$.

Using the technique of Margrabe's exchange option for a change in *numeraire*, one can show that if both S_A and S_K follow diffusion processes, then the variance of the cross rate S_X is equal to

$$var\,[S_X] = \sigma_X^2 = \sigma_A^2 + \sigma_K^2 - 2\,\rho\sigma_A\sigma_K$$

where ρ is the correlation between the stochastic elements of the two diffusion processes for S_A and S_K. The option on the cross exchange rate S_X can now be easily modeled using the usual Black-Scholes assumptions but with the volatility replaced by σ_X. The payoff function for a call is

$$\max\,[S_X^T - S_K^T, 0]$$

where the superscript T denote terminal values. Notice that the payoff function is that of an *exchange option* and the cross-currency option can therefore be valued like an option to exchange one risky asset for another.

2. **Quantos:** The term "quanto" option is an abbreviation for *quantity-adjusted option*. The payoff depends on both the underlying asset price and the size of the exposure as a function of the underlying price. The contingent claim is therefore on the asset and not on the size of the exposure. Most applications of quantos center on the purchase of an asset in a currency different from the purchaser's home currency. Because the purchaser is required to convert the purchase into the home currency, the quantity of the purchase must be adjusted correspondingly.

There are two possibilities: (a) fixed exchange rate, or (b) flexible exchange rate.

Variations of quantos:

1. **Fixed Exchange Rate:** Suppose the purchaser of an option on a foreign equity wants the option to be struck in the foreign currency but prefers that the final payoff be converted to the home currency *at a prespecified exchange rate*. The quantity of the purchase must be adjusted correspondingly to a *fixed* foreign-exchange rate S_o^{fixed} at time zero (denoted by the zero subscript). Let us consider the following notation:

$S^{foreign}$ = stock price denominated in a foreign currency

$K^{foreign}$ = strike price denominated in a foreign currency

S_X is the *current* exchange rate in units of [home/foreign].

S_X^T is the *prevailing* exchange rate in units of [home/foreign] at time T.

S_o^{fixed} is the *fixed* exchange rate in units of [home/foreign] prespecified at time 0.

Then, the payoff of a quanto call with fixed exchange rate on the foreign-denominated stock and struck at the same foreign currency, with the option payable in the home currency at a fixed exchange rate S_o^{fixed}, is

$$S_o^{fixed} * \max\,[S_T^{foreign} - K^{foreign}, 0].$$

The value of this *fixed quanto call*, surprisingly, depends on the correlation between the foreign equity price and the exchange rate. Since, in reality, exchange rates are not fixed and can deviate significantly from the fixed rate at the option's expiry, the pricing of the fixed quanto requires an adjustment to the forward price of the foreign equity by a factor proportional to the accumulated interest-rate differential over the life of the option. In addition, since the exchange rate and the equity are correlated, an extra factor needs to be introduced into the forward price.

The fixed quanto is the original quanto developed at Goldman Sachs and is now known as the *true quanto*.

2. **Flexible Exchange Rate:** In contrast to the fixed (true) quanto, suppose the exchange rate is not fixed, but is allowed to be the prevailing exchange rate at the option's expiry. This *flexible quanto call* obviously allows the holder to participate in the foreign equity but with no protection against foreign-exchange risk. At the final payoff, the proceeds will

simply be converted to the holder's home currency at the then prevailing exchange rate S_X^T. The valuation is extremely simple—Black-Scholes formula on $S^{foreign}$ with strike $K^{foreign}$ and multiply the result by S_X^T, the prevailing exchange at the option's expiry T. The *flexible quanto call* therefore has a payoff function given by $S_X^T * \max [S_T^{foreign} - K^{foreign}, 0]$.

3. **Compos:** Compos *(composite options)* are, in contrast to quantos, options on foreign equity (denominated in either home or foreign currencies) and struck in either the home or foreign currency. They also constitute the class of options where the optionality is based on the foreign-exchange component, but the foreign equity is delivered in the final payoff. There are, therefore, two variations. In either case, it is the foreign equity that is delivered upon exercise.

Variations of Compos:

1. **Compos A: Option on Foreign Equity Struck in Domestic Currency**

The payoff function for a Compo A call is

$$\max [S_X^T S_T^{foreign} - K, 0]$$

where the strike K is denominated in the home currency. Observe that the payoff is denominated in the home currency since the price of the foreign equity is converted to the home currency at the prevailing exchange rate S_X^T at the option's expiry T. Since the underlying asset in this case is the product $S_X^T S_T^{foreign}$, the option will depend on the correlation between the exchange rate and the foreign equity. This structure therefore provides some protection against foreign-exchange risk, since the correlation effect is *explicitly* taken into account during the valuation of the option. The valuation of this option is simple. Treating the product $S_X^T S_T^{foreign}$ as one asset, this is simply Margrabe's option to exchange some amount of home currency K with some shares of foreign stock denominated in the home currency $S_X^T S_T^{foreign}$.

2. **Compos B: Equity-Linked Foreign-Exchange Option**

This compo is an option that delivers the foreign equity but the option is structured on the foreign exchange, with a strike denominated in the home currency. The payoff function for the call is

$$S_T^{foreign} * \max [S_X^T - K, 0]$$

where the subscript T on the foreign equity denotes that once the option is exercised, some shares of the foreign equity, at the option's expiry T, are delivered. This option is really a foreign-exchange option that places a floor on the exchange-rate exposure of the investor. The investor is, of course, exposed to the rise and fall of the foreign stock. Hence, the investor is exposed to the downside risk of the equity although completely protected against the downside risk of the foreign exchange because of the floor.

Other examples of quantos:

1. **Differential Swaps:** A swap is structured in one currency but the payout is denominated in another currency.
2. **Quanto Hybrids:** Quantos can be combined in a variety of ways with other exotic options. Typical combinations are with spreads, performance-type, and barrier-type options. The combination depends on the investor's specific trading view and the degree of foreign-exchange protection desired. For this reason, quantos are also known as *currency-protected size options* or *percentage-change options.* Since the correlation coefficient is not a traded quantity and is difficult to estimate, the pricing of FX-Linked options tends to have relatively wide bid-ask spreads.

Nested or Compounded

The usual contingent claim is normally structured on one or more underlying risky assets. In some circumstances, either due to hedging requirements or specific market views, the contingent claim is structured on options. These options are collectively known as the nested type. Earlier, we encountered a classic example from the time-preference class—the chooser option. The chooser option allows the holder of the option, at some specified time in the future, to choose between a call option and a put option. There are other examples.

Chooser

Please refer to earlier discussions in the class of time-dependent or preference options.

Compound

Compound options allow the holder the right but not the obligation to buy another underlying option. In essence, there are two options involved, a mother option and a daughter option. The mother can be a call or a put, and the same is true for the daughter. The simplest case has four possible combinations:

call on a call (or put)

put on a call (or put)

Like the choosers, the combinations can either be *complex* or *simple.*

Variations of compound options:

1. **Simple Compound:** Both mother and daughter have the same strike and time to expiry.

2. **Complex Compound:** Mother and daughter have different strikes and different time to expiry. In the most complex case, mother and daughter also have different volatilities.

For example, the payoff function for a *complex call* (with strike K_M and time to maturity t) *on a put* (with strike K_D and time to maturity T) is

$$\max\,[0, PV_t\{\max\,(0, K_D - S_t \mid T > t)\} - K_M \mid t].$$

Explanation: The daughter is a put with payoff

$$\max\,(0, K_D - S_t \mid T > t)$$

where S_t is the underlying asset price at time t, i.e., the asset price at the expiry of the mother option. The extra notation $T > t$ is a reminder that the expiry of the daughter T is after the expiry of the mother t. The notation PV_t { } denotes that the payoff of the daughter put has to be present valued back from time T to the terminal time t of the mother call. The complex call therefore has a payoff given by the largest of zero or the difference between the daughter put and the mother strike K_M, viz.,

$$\max\,[0, PV_t\{daughterput\} - K_M \mid t].$$

Of course, as usual, the timing of the present value of the daughter put coincides with the terminal time of the complex call.

The payoff functions of the other three combinations of the compound option are simple reflections and images of the one given above. Closed-form formulas for simple compounds were first derived by Geske in 1979. Complex compounds do not exhibit closed-form formulas but can be numerically calculated using double integrals.

Most compound options are found in the currency and interest-rate markets, and to some extent, in the equity market. Compound options are also traded on U.S. Treasury securities. Because the most important inputs to a compound option are the mother and daughter volatilities, compound options are used by some to bet on increases in volatility by risking a relatively small amount of money.

Note: Other interest-rate-related compound options include calls (or puts) on caps or floors, which are used generally when the interest-risk exposure is uncertain or unknown.

1. **Caption (Option on a Cap):** Captions provide a good way to express a view on both the shape and volatility of the interest-rate swap curve. A steep USD LIBOR curve implies rising short-term interest rates in the near future, so a cap buyer would pay a lot of forward intrinsic value. A hedger who believes that the yield curve will flatten and volatility will decrease would expect to pay less if the cap were purchased in the future. The hedger could monetize her view by buying a caption today and protect the future cash outlay should the opposite scenario occur. The coinage "caption" is a Marine Midland trademark name.
2. **Floortions or Floptions:** These are options on a floor.

Leveraged

Leveraged options refer to those claims whose payoffs are not the usual straight-line "hockey sticks" of vanilla options. These options are leveraged and do not move either one-to-one or in a linear fashion with the underlying asset movement, unlike vanilla options.

Power

The general power option has a payoff function given by an nth order polynomial, viz.,

$$\max\left[\sum_{i=1}^{n} c_i S_T^i - K, 0\right]$$

where c_i are constants and the subscript T denotes terminal values. Another name for power options is *polynomial options*. The simplest leveraged call-option pays off a *multiple*, say c, of the underlying asset, viz.,

$$\max\,[c\,S_T - K, 0]$$

where the constant c can be 1, 2, 3, ...

Another example is the *"squared" power option,* which has a payoff of $\max\,[S_T^2 - K, 0]$.

This payoff attracts investors whose preference is to maximize their gamma exposure to the underlying asset. Figure 1–4 is a graph of the "Squared" Power Option.

FIGURE 1–4
"Squared" Power Option

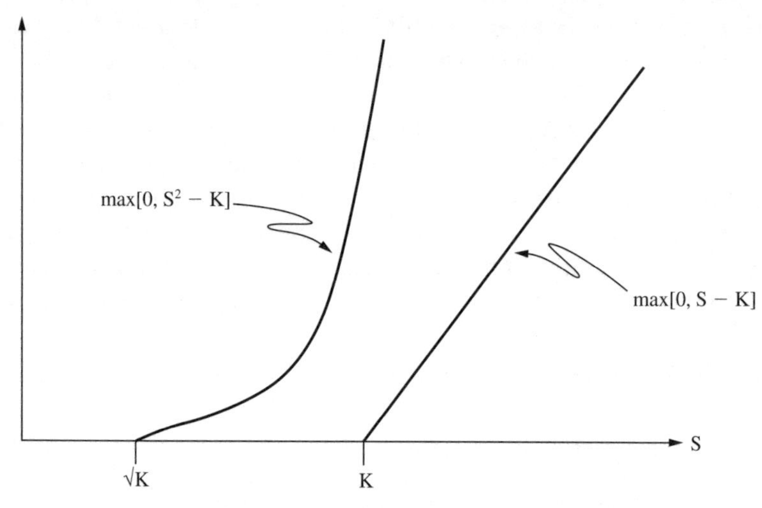

The pricing of power options is trivial. If S is lognormally distributed with the diffusion $dS = \mu S dt + \sigma S dz$, then S^n is also lognormally distributed with diffusion given by

$$d(S^n) = \left[n\mu + \frac{1}{2}\sigma^2 n(n-1) \right] S^n dt + [n\sigma]\, S^n dz.$$

For instance, when n = 2, we have

$$d(S^2) = (2\mu + \sigma^2)S^2 dt + (2\sigma)S^2 dz$$

so that we simply need to replace the drift by $2\mu + \sigma^2$ and the volatility by 2σ in the Black-Scholes formula. Clearly, we can see that the "squared" power option has a much exaggerated payoff not only because of the square in the underlying asset price, but also because the volatility is increased twofold.

Curvilinear

Curvilinear options are hybrids of options with linear payoffs and power options. The combination of straight lines and curves can result in a variety of intricate payoffs, many of which may find no use in the market. Furthermore, in many cases, hedging may be difficult.

Inverse floaters

Inverse floaters are interest-rate derivatives whose payoff varies inversely with changes in the general interest-rate levels. For example, consider a bond that pays out as follows

fixed coupon of 5.25% through July 1995
and thereafter max [9.75% − 6-month LIBOR, 0].

It is clear that, beyond July 1995, once 6-month LIBOR reaches the level of 4.50 percent or higher, the coupon payment will start to decrease from the fixed rate of 5.25 percent. Six-month LIBOR rates higher than 9.75 percent will result in no payout at all. The provision that beyond July 1995 the coupon payout is

max [9.75% − 6*mo LIBOR*, 0]

introduces an embedded optionality into the payout structure of the bond. More precisely, the provision is a put option on 6-month LIBOR struck at 9.75 percent.

Theoretically, inverse floaters are not options; they are embedded with optionality. In fact, technically they are bonds. An inverse floater is, in reality, a combination of a swap, an issue, and a cap/floor. In addition, because the inverse floaters can be optioned, the payoff for these options can be quite interesting.

Many LDC ("less developed countries") debt issues are structured with embedded floating-rate optionalities. Inverse floaters are normally used by banks and fund managers as alternative floating-rate instruments and are usually highly structured and customized. Variations of inverse floaters include those that can be denominated in one currency and paid out in another, requiring the use of quanto options. In the following section on embeddos, we will present some more examples of floaters.

Embeddos

Embeddos are a very large class of options that don't exist independently in and of themselves, but are normally *emdebbed* in other complex structures.

The embeddings are usually of two types:

1. **Explicit Embeddos:** In this case, the exotic options are *explicitly* embedded into a complex structure. The embedded options are full-fledged options, which can be valued independently of the structure. Common embeddings are digitals, spreads, certain kinds of rainbows, baskets, and averages. The *range floater note*, which pays an above-market coupon rate if and only if the index lies within a prespecified range, is a classic example of an explicit embeddo. The embeddos in this case are two digitals—one on either end of the chosen index range.

2. **Implicit Embeddos:** The embeddings here are more subtle than in the explicit case. There is no "real" option in the complex structure, although the payoff of the structure behaves in a curvilinear fashion just like an option. For example, the prepayment optionality embedded in mortgage-backed securities is not a real option and does not exist independently of the security. Using options theory, however, one can approximate the value of the embedded option. The *index principal swap* is an example of an implicit embeddo. The embeddo in this example is the paydown of the principal as stipulated in the amortization schedule.

Most of the embeddos are embedded in structured notes. Many of these embeddos exhibit floater characteristics, since the underlying asset is usually an interest-rate index.

Some examples of implicit *embeddos:*

1. **Delevered Floater:** A bond that pays the investor an interest rate that incorporates a spread over a fractional percentage *decrease* in the index.

Example: *(0.5 * 10-year CMT) + 1.25%.*

Note: This bond is delevered by 0.5 times the 10-year CMT yield.

2. **Dual-Index Floater:** A bond whose coupon rate is determined by the spread between *two different indexes.* The bond normally has a "teaser" fixed rate for the first period of the bond's life, after which the interest rate floats according to a pre-determined formula.

Example: fixed rate at 6 percent to Aug. 95 and thereafter coupon is

max [(10-year CMS + 3.1%) − 3-month USD LIBOR, 0].

Note: The embedded optionality in this example is a *two-color rainbow option* so that the correlation between the 10-yr CMS and the 3-month USD LIBOR has to be taken into account.

3. **Levered Inverse Floater:** A bond whose coupon varies inversely with changes in the general interest rates and applies a multiplier greater than 1 to the specified index in its calculation of interest payment.

Example: fixed rate at 6 percent up until June 1997 and thereafter the coupon is *max [14.55% − (2.5 * 3-month USD LIBOR), 0]*.

Note: The embedded optionality is a *leveraged* (2.5 times) *put option* on the 3-month USD LIBOR, struck at 14.55 percent.

4. **Index-Linked Bond:** A bond whose interest rate is derived from the differential between *current* and *forward* index values. This is a variation of the dual-index floater.

Example: accrues at 3.0 percent up to maturity, but with an additional interest payment to be made prior to maturity based on the formula *1.5 * max [S&P 500 closing on 01/03/00 − S&P 500 closing on 01/03/95, 0]*.

Note: The optionality embedded here is a *time-preference* type of exotic option.

5. **Hi-Lo Floater:** This bond pays an interest rate stated as the *higher* or *lower* of two formulas.

Example: floats at 3-month $LIBOR + 0.35 percent up to July 1995; thereafter pays out at *min [3-mo $LIBOR + 0.35%, 18.26% − (2 * 3-mo $LIBOR)]* to maturity.

Note: The optionality embedded here is a *worst-of-two asset option*. If min were replaced by max, the embedding would be a *best-of-two asset option*.

6. **Reverse Principal FX-Linked Bond:** A bond that pays a fixed or floating rate in one currency, but whose principal repayment is denominated in another currency.

Example: Principal payment will equal, in USD equivalents, *(1,500 CAD $ + 1,300.5 AUD $ + 150,000 Yen)*, as determined by the appropriate FX spot rates on Sept. 3, 1997.

Note: The embedded optionality is a *flexible quanto*.

7. **Stepped Cap/Floor Floater:** This bond pays a floating rate, subject to a scheduled cap and/or floor.

Example: Initially floats with *3-month $LIBOR + 1.2%*; thereafter pays out at *3-month $LIBOR + 1.35%*. Caps will *step from 6% to 7.75%, in 25 bp increments with quarterly resets* up to Aug. 1997; thereafter *cap max at 8.25%*.

Note: The embedded optionality here is a *ladder* and a series of *ratchets* with resettable strikes.

8. **Index Principal Swap:** Also known as an *index amortizing swap,* this is a swap whose notional amount is either reduced or increased according to a prespecified amortization schedule. The schedule specifies the reduction or increase in the notional amount as a function of index ranges. Table 1–1 is an illustration of such a schedule. In some cases, the schedule is not a fixed one.

9. **Miscellaneous:** *multi step-ups* or *step-downs, variable step-ups,* etc.

All of the structures discussed above are implicitly embedded with exotic options, which are part of the structures themselves. Below we discuss some common embeddos whose optionality can be isolated and detached from the structures.

Some examples of explicit *embeddos:*

1. **Range Floater:** This bond normally pays an attractive above-market rate for each day that the reference index stays within a prespecified range chosen by the investor; otherwise, the payoff is either zero or below market rates. A standard range floater is embedded with true digitals, which either pay something or nothing.

Example 1: the payout is locked in at 6 percent for *every day* that the 3-month $LIBOR is between 4.5 percent and 5.5 percent. Outside this range, the bond will accrue daily at 0 percent.

Note: The embedded optionality here consists of a *digital option* on either end of the range, for each trading day. There are twice as many digitals as there are days in the life of this bond. The embedding is explicit, since the bond has to be structured by actually pricing these digitals over the life of the range floater.

Example 2: the bond accrues interest at the rate *[(3-mo $LIBOR + 2.07%) * 1.0753] + 2.01%* for each day that the JPY/USD spot exchange rate is greater than or equal to 97.70. For every day outside that range, the bond will accrue at 2.01 percent.

A *range rover* is a variation of the range floater wherein at every reset date (quarterly, semiannually, etc.) the holder of the bond has the right to change the range of the index. In essence, the range is roving from one reset date to the next. The range rover is generally more expensive than a range floater because of the additional flexibility on the part of the holder to choose the desired index range.

2. **Ratchet Floater:** This bond pays out a floating rate and has an adjustable cap and/or floor, which moves in sync with each new reset rate.

Table 1–1
Index Principal Swap

Notional Amount: US$100MM
Fixed Rate: 5.50% (2-yr. U.S. Treasury @ 4.50% + 100bp).
Maturity: 5 years
Index: 3-month LIBOR
Initial Base Rate: 5.60% (to be set by customer).
Lock-out: No paydown of principal for the first 2 years.
Amortization Schedule:

Index Change (bp)	*Index (%)*	*Annual Amort. Rate (%)*
−300 or lower	2.60	0
−200	3.60	25
−100	4.60	50
0	5.60	100
+100	6.60	100
+200	7.60	100
+300 or higher	8.60	100

Clean-up Provision: The swap matures if the outstanding notional amount reaches 10% or less of the original notional amount.

Example: The bond pays out 3-month $LIBOR + 50 bp. In addition to having a lifetime cap of 7.25 percent, the coupon will be *collared* each period between the previous coupon or the previous coupon + 25 bp.

PRICING EXOTIC OPTIONS AND STRUCTURES

Our rather lengthy foray into the taxonomy of exotic options reveals a phenomenally large collection of options, which has mushroomed over a relatively short period of time. These financially engineered exotic options, whether individually engineered or embedded in complex structures, can be found in various markets ranging from commodities, foreign-exchange, equities (single issues and indexes), interest-rate, energy, fixed-income (Treasuries, agencies, corporates, and LDC debt), and other lesser markets. The more amazing observation is that the bulk of them have been invented within the past few years. The taxonomy presented earlier is quite complete—the rest of the exotica are either minor variants or subtle combinations of those listed above.

All of these exotic options exhibit, one way or the other, varying degrees of *path-dependency* or *co-dependency*, different levels of severity in *singularity*, relative degrees of *leverage* or *curvilinearity* in their payoff structures, and various *time dependencies* or *preferences*. Each level of complication translates to different issues in hedgeability that must be addressed during the modeling or financial engineering of the exotic structure.

Pricing these exotic options is no longer an issue. The majority, if not all of them, can be valued quite easily using a variety of mathematical methods, such as:

1. Direct integration of the expectation of the terminal payoff
   a. single integrals for univariate
   b. multiple integrals for multivariate options or certain time-dependent ones
   c. numerical integration of above
2. Monte Carlo simulation
3. Finite difference methods (on the Black-Scholes partial differential equation)
   a. explicit
   b. implicit
   c. Crank-Nicholson's algorithms
4. Lattice methods
   a. binomial
   b. trinomial
   c. trees
5. Equivalent semi-Martingale measures (compact versions of integration methods).

The issue, therefore, is not the valuation but the *risk management* of these exotic options.

EPILOGUE

"Life insurance" or "keno pits"—the new generation of exotic options allows the end users even greater flexibility and a greater abundance of choices than their vanilla counterparts for the possible use or abuse of these innovative products. Whether one likes it or not, the exotic market is here and will continue to develop and evolve. For as long as there are technically talented people to structure them and either charlatans or well-informed end users to use them, exotic options and their associated complex structures will continue to thrive—for better or for worse.

Chapter Two

Exotic Options: The Basic Building Blocks and Their Applications*

K. Ravindran
Head of the Customized Solutions Group,
TD Securities Inc.
Adjunct Professor
Department of Statistics and Actuarial Science,
University of Waterloo

INTRODUCTION

Since the early 1970s, derivatives have been the most widely used hedging and investment vehicles in many financial markets. Due to the increasing level of sophistication in the financial markets, these vanilla-type derivatives, also known as first-generation derivatives, have led to a steady development of another generation of derivatives known as the exotic derivatives.

As the derivatives market is a very large one, this chapter will focus only on the options segment of derivatives. Starting with a brief description of vanilla options, the first section of this chapter describes the limitations of such options and how exotic options better address the complexity of modern-day risk exposure. The basic building blocks of these options and their practical use are described in the second section, keeping the amount of mathematics to a bare minimum. Although most of this chapter's discussion is restricted to either the currency or the interest-rate asset class, there is nothing that prevents us from extending any part of the discussion to other asset classes such as equity, commodity or credit.

TABLE 2–1
Payoffs of the European-Style Option

Type Of Option	*Payoff at Expiry Time* T
$C_E\,(X, 0, T, S_0)$	$\max\,[-P^*_{T,C}, S_T - X - P^*_{T,C}]$
$P_E\,(X, 0, T, S_0)$	$\max\,[-P^*_{T,P}, X - S_T - P^*_{T,P}]$

where $C_E\,(X, 0, T, S_0)$ and $P_E\,(X, 0, T, S_0)$ represent the vanilla European-style call and put option respectively when the strike rate is X, the current time is 0, the option maturity time is T, and the current spot rate is S_0, $P^*_{T,C}$ and $P^*_{T,P}$ represent the call and put option premiums respectively that are future valued to the option expiry date; and *max [a,b]* represents the maximum value of a and b.

VANILLA OPTIONS AND THEIR LIMITATIONS

The term "vanilla options," as described in the introduction, refers to the basic European- and American-style call and put options. More precisely, a European call (put) currency option buyer pays a premium at the inception of the option contract for the right to buy (sell) currency at a specified rate (also known as the strike rate) at the time of the option expiration. Letting T, X, and S_T denote the life of the option, the strike rate of the currency option and the value of the spot rate at time T, respectively, the buyer of a European-style call (put) option will only exercise the option at time T if $S_T > X$ $(S_T < X)$. Throughout this chapter, the spot exchange rate represents the number of foreign currency units per U.S. dollar. The payoff to the buyer of the currency option at time T is shown in Table 2–1. These payoffs are depicted in Figures 2–1 and 2–2.

Unlike the buyer of an option who can choose to walk away from the contract, the seller (or writer) of the option is always obligated to perform his or her end of the contract if the option is exercised. See Hull (1993) for an excellent introduction to the fundamentals of options and Ravindran (1993) for a recreational approach to option pricing.

In addition to possessing the properties of a European option, the American-style option allows the buyer to exercise at any time during the life of the option. Since the European option has only one exercise time, known as a decision node, at time T and the American option has infinite decision nodes in the time interval 0 to T, it would be intuitively

FIGURE 2–1
Call Option Buyer's Payoff at Maturity

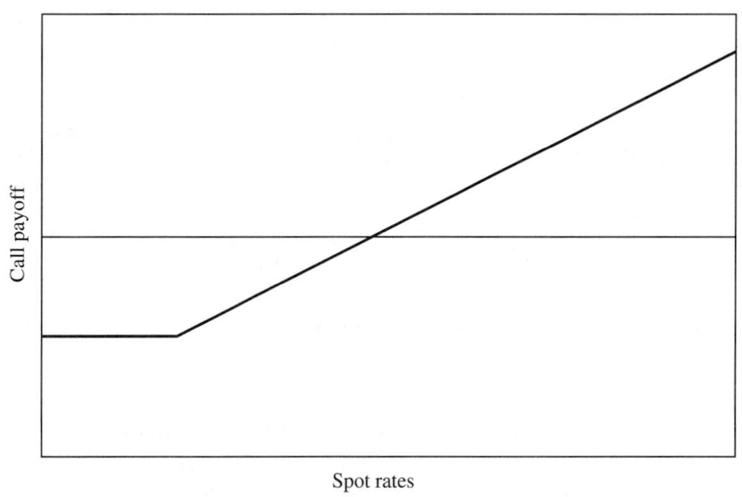

FIGURE 2–2
Put Option Buyer's Payoff at Maturity

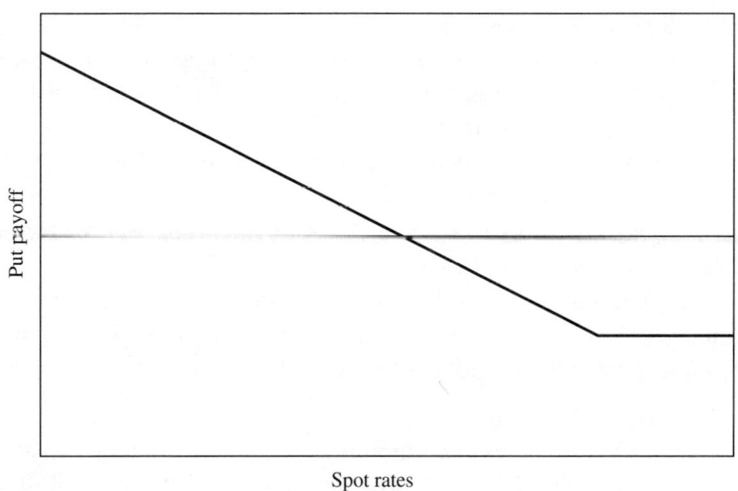

TABLE 2–2
Payoffs of the American-Style Option

Type of Option	*Payoff at Time* t	*Payoff at Expiry Time* T
$C_A\ (X, 0, T, S_0)$	$\max\ [S_t - X - P^*_{t,C}, C_{A,t} - P^*_{t,C}]$	$\max\ [-P^*_{T,C}, S_T - X - P^*_{T,C}]$
$P_A\ (X, 0, T, S_0)$	$\max\ [X - S_t - P^*_{t,P}, P_{A,t} - P^*_{t,P}]$	$\max\ [-P^*_{T,P}, X - S_T - P^*_{T,P}]$

where $C_A(X, 0, T, S_0)$ and $P_A(X, 0, T, S_0)$ represent the American-style call and put options respectively when X is the strike rate, the current time is *0*, the life of the option is T, the current spot rate is S_0, and t lies in the time interval $[0,T]$; $P^*_{t,C}$ and $P^*_{t,P}$ represent the call and put option premiums respectively that are future valued to time t; $C_{A,t}$ and $P_{A,t}$ represent the values of the American call and put options respectively at time t when the strike rate is X, the current time is t, the option expiry time is T, and the current spot rate is S_t.

reasonable to expect the value of an American option to be at least as large as that of its European counterpart. The payoff to the buyer of an American-style currency option is given in Table 2–2.

It is important to note that any currency option can be analogously viewed as an option on a stock that pays a continuous dividend. Furthermore, for a non-dividend-paying stock, the value of a European-style vanilla call stock-option can be shown to be the same as that of its American counterpart. An intuitive reason for this feature is that by exercising an American-style call option early, the buyer of the option has to pay up a strike value of X for a stock that does not pay any dividend. Due to the accrued interest on the strike that is foregone if the option is exercised before time T, it is optimal for the buyer of the option to delay exercising as much as possible.

Although we have only discussed vanilla currency-options, offering vanilla options on other asset classes—such as equity, interest rate, commodity or credit—is also possible. Despite the type of insurance or yield-enhancing opportunities that vanilla options can provide, clients more often than not require solutions that manage their risk or monetize their market view more effectively and, if possible, at a lower cost. As examples, consider the following three scenarios:

1. An investor has bought a new issue of a five-year semiannual bond with a 10 percent coupon that is callable at par by its issuer on any of its coupon dates after three years of its issue. To hedge against the issuer's call, the investor could buy five European-

style bond options, each of which expires on every one of the callable dates and exercises into a par value synthetic bond with 10 percent coupon that matures on the same date as the callable bond.

Alternatively, the investor could buy a quasi-American-style bond option with both the option and the synthetic bond maturing in five years. The exercise of the option on any one of the coupon dates after three years would allow the investor to pay a par value for the synthetic 10 percent coupon bond. This solution, which would provide a cheaper and more effective means of insurance, is also known as a Mid-Atlantic/Bermudian option and is described in the section on Mid-Atlantic options.

2. An importer of Canadian goods has to make payments in Canadian dollars on prespecified future dates. The importer could either lock into a sequence of forward contracts on the Canadian dollar/U.S. dollar exchange rate or convert U.S. dollars into Canadian ones on the actual payment dates. If the U.S. dollar currently appears to be weaker than what the exchange rate has historically been, the latter alternative would seem the better choice. The only risk encountered in the latter alternative is when the U.S. dollar gets even weaker. Here, the buying of put options on the U.S. dollar appears to be a good form of insurance because the put options would finish in-the-money when the U.S. dollar weakens. However, buying a series of put options for various option maturities may get expensive. A method of cheapening this cost would be to embed within the put options an extinguishing feature so that if the U.S. dollar strengthens during the life of the option past a certain level (called a barrier), the put option is extinguished. This type of insurance, which is also known as a knock-out option, is described in the section on sudden birth/death options.
3. Based on the current shape of the yield curve, an asset manager believes that the spread between the five-year bond yield and the three-year bond yield would widen in three months (i.e., the yield curve would get steeper). Instead of buying a duration-weighted amount of each of the underlying bonds and then unwinding the positions in three months, which would involve huge cash positions and a large possible downside, he could alternatively buy a European option that pays off the maximum of the difference of the two bond yields (i.e., five-year bond yield less three-year bond yield) and zero at the end of the three months. To enter into such an option, the asset manager only needs to

pay an up-front premium to monetize his view. This option, also known as a spread option, is discussed in the section on spread options.

The above examples describe just three of the numerous single and multivariate path-dependent risks that investors and risk managers may wish to speculate on or hedge. In each instance, the vanilla European- and American-style options are totally ineffective, thereby clearly demonstrating the need for the use of nontraditional derivatives. In the next section, we will describe and use the various building blocks of exotic options.

DEMYSTIFYING EXOTIC OPTIONS THROUGH EXAMPLES

This section attempts to demystify the whole concept of exotic options by describing the characteristics of the basic building blocks of exoticland, which can be very effectively combined to produce a complex but efficient financial instrument. In addition, the section will also discuss how these instruments are used in the marketplace either as yield enhancements or disaster insurances. Although the building blocks have been presented in alphabetical order, it is very important to realize that marrying these products across asset classes to arrive at hybrid instruments could result in more-effective and cost-efficient solutions.

Average-Rate Options

A Canadian exporting company is exposed to the exchange-rate risk between the Canadian and U.S. dollar every week. The treasurer of the company, in preparing a quarterly budget, has to forecast the cash inflows and outflows from the existing contracts of the company and state the company's expected net profit or loss for the upcoming quarter in Canadian funds. To do the conversion to Canadian funds, the treasurer picks an average exchange rate of Can$1.29/U.S.$1.00 Clearly, the treasurer does not have to worry about anything if the U.S. dollar gets stronger and the average of the weekly Canadian dollar/U.S. dollar exchange rates over the next quarter exceeds the Can$1.29/U.S.$1.00 level. However, if the Canadian dollar gets stronger over the next quarter, she will not be able to meet her budget. In order to hedge herself—or more precisely, her budget—she would need a currency put-option on the U.S. dollar that is based on the weekly averaging of exchange rates for the next quarter and struck at Can$1.29/U.S.$1.00. This type of option is called an averaging put-option.

An averaging put-option, also known as an Asian put option, is a derivative security that gives the buyer at the maturity date of the option a payoff that is the greater of zero and the difference between the strike rate and the average value of the exchange rates realized during the averaging period. The following example better illustrates the sequence of events depicting the nature of the transaction:

Time 0 mo: The Canadian dollar is currently trading at Can$1.33/U.S.$1.00. A treasurer, who has just submitted his quarterly budget, is worried about the Canadian dollar strengthening and pays a premium to buy an averaging put-option on the U.S. dollar that is struck at Can$1.29/U.S.$1.00 and matures in four months. To do the averaging, the exchange rates are monitored once a week (also called a weekly sampling period) at noon starting from today's spot rate of Can$1.33/U.S.$1.00 until and including the exchange rate at the expiry date of the option. An arithmetic average is calculated for all these observed rates and then compared with a strike rate of Can$1.29/U.S.$1.00.

Time 4 mo: *Case 1.* The Canadian dollar is currently trading at Can$1.30/U.S.$1.00. The arithmetic average of the weekly observed exchange rates (inclusive of the exchange rate on the option maturity date) turns out to be Can$1.2850/U.S.$1.00. The option finishes in-the-money and the payoff to the treasurer is $(1.29 - 1.2850 - P^*_{4\,mo,\,PA})$ Canadian dollar/U.S. dollar, where $P^*_{4\,mo,\,PA}$ represents the premium of the average-rate put-option future valued to four months.

Case 2. Currency is trading at Can$1.30/U.S.$1.00. The arithmetic average of the observed exchange rates turns out to be Can$1.2950/U.S.$1.00. The option goes out-of-the-money and the treasurer loses his premium.

There are four important observations that should be made from the above example. First, in dealing with vanilla currency-options, it is not uncommon to see the terms U.S. dollar/Canadian dollar and Canadian dollar/U.S. dollar used interchangeably. Since a call option on the U.S.

dollar is equivalent to a put option on the Canadian dollar, this interchangeability does not pose any problem. To extend this nomenclature to the averaging option, it is crucial to note that for a call or put (put or call, respectively) option on the U.S. (Canadian) dollar the averaging must be done on Canadian dollar/U.S. dollar (U.S./Canadian). This is due to the fact that the reciprocal of an average may not necessarily be equal to the average of the reciprocal. To understand this statement better, consider, for example, the exchange-rate triplet (1.28, 1.30, 1.32) Canadian/U.S., whose arithmetic average can easily be shown to be Can$1.28/U.S.$1.00. When these exchange rates are expressed in U.S./Canadian, the triplet (1.28, 1.30, 1.32) becomes (1/1.28, 1/1.30, 1/1.32), whose arithmetic average of 0.7828 U.S./Canadian is not a reciprocal of the average 1.28 Canadian/U.S. This sort of ambiguity, however, does not exist in other asset classes.

Second, the type of averaging discussed in the above example is of the arithmetic type (i.e., the arithmetic average of the numbers 2, 3, 4 is $(2 + 3 + 4)/3 = 3$). The treasurer could have alternatively bought a put option, whose payoff on the option maturity date is based on a geometric average of the weekly observed rates, where the geometric average of the numbers 2, 3, 4 is defined to be $(2 \times 3 \times 4)^{1/3} = 2.88$. Furthermore, it can be concluded in general that an arithmetic average-rate put option can never be more expensive than a structurally similar geometric average-rate put option. The converse is, however, true for an average-rate call option.

Third, if the notional sizes of the currency exposure vary over the weekly observed periods, a more customized hedge instrument would be a weighted averaging option on the currency rates. This can be further tailored to entertain either a daily averaging or an infrequent averaging (e.g., observing the daily exchange rates for the first month and then the biweekly exchange rates over the next three months). Finally, although the sampling period for computing the average starts at the inception of the option contract and ends at the option maturity date in the above example, nothing prohibits transacting on an average-rate option whose sampling period is not a subset of the option life.

Letting S_i be the spot rate at time t_i (for $i = 1, 2, \ldots, n$) where the time intervals between the observation periods may not be the same (e.g., $t_n - t_{n-1}$ may not be necessarily equal to $t_{n-1} - t_{n-2}$), and w_i be the weight associated with spot rate S_i where $\Sigma w_i = w_1 + w_2 + \ldots + w_n = 1$, the payoffs of the averaging option can be more generally written as detailed in Table 2–3.

TABLE 2–3
Payoffs of the European-Style Average-Rate Option

Type of Average-Rate Option	*Payoff at Expiry Time* T
$C_{E,A}(X, 0, T, S_0, w_1, \ldots, w_n, t_1, \ldots, t_n)$	$\max\left[-P^*_{T,CA}, \sum_{i=1}^{n} w_i S_{t_i} - X - P^*_{T,CA}\right]$
$P_{E,A}(X, 0, T, S_0, w_1, \ldots, w_n, t_1, \ldots, t_n)$	$\max\left[-P^*_{T,PA}, X - \sum_{i=1}^{n} w_i S_{t_i} - P^*_{T,PA}\right]$
$C_{E,G}(X, 0, T, S_0, w_1, \ldots, w_n, t_1, \ldots, t_n)$	$\max\left[-P^*_{T,CG}, \prod_{i=1}^{n} S_{t_i}^{w_i} - X - P^*_{T,CG}\right]$
$P_{E,G}(X, 0, T, S_0, w_1, \ldots, w_n, t_1, \ldots, t_n)$	$\max\left[-P^*_{T,PG}, X - \prod_{i=1}^{n} S_{t_i}^{w_i} - P^*_{T,PG}\right]$

where $C_{E,A}(X, 0, T, S_0, w_1, \ldots, w_n, t_1, \ldots, t_n)$ and $P_{E,A}(X, 0, T, S_0, w_1, \ldots, w_n, t_1, \ldots, t_n)$ represent the arithmetic weighted averaging European-style call and put options respectively; $C_{E,G}(X, 0, T, S_0, w_1, \ldots, w_n, t_1, \ldots, t_n)$ and $P_{E,G}(X, 0, T, S_0, w_1, \ldots, w_n, t_1, \ldots, t_n)$ represent the geometric weighted averaging European-style call and put options respectively when the strike rate is X, the current time is *0*, the option maturity T, and the current spot rate is S_0; $P^*_{T,CA}$ and $P^*_{T,PA}$ represent the premiums of the weighted arithmetic average-rate call and put option respectively that are future valued to time T; $P^*_{T,CG}$ and $P^*_{T,PG}$ represent the premiums of the weighted geometric average-rate call and put option respectively that are future valued to time T; and $\prod_{i=1}^{n} S_{t_i}^{w_i} = S_{t_1}^{w_1} \ldots S_{t_n}^{w_n}$. When the weights $w_i = 1/n$ and the time intervals $t_{i+1} - t_i$ are all equal (for $i = 1, \ldots, n - 1$), the above payoffs collapse to those of a simple arithmetic and a geometric average-rate option.

The pricing formulae for standard arithmetic and geometric options are given in Levy (1992) and Kemna and Vorst (1990), respectively. Ravindran (1995b) extends these results to include weighted averaging and continuous time averaging.

By the nature of an average-rate option, the contribution of a spot rate toward the averaging of the sampled points usually decreases as the option maturity date draws closer. This implies that the risk characteristics of an averaging option usually diminish as the option decays in time and as such these options can easily be delta-hedged. Figure 2–3 shows the effect of varying the sampling (averaging) frequency of a simple arithmetic averaging call option on the premium of such an option. Despite this, it is not necessarily true that the greater the sampling frequency, the cheaper the options, although these options would, in fact, be cheaper than vanilla options expiring at the same time.

FIGURE 2–3
Effect of Averaging Frequency on Call Premium

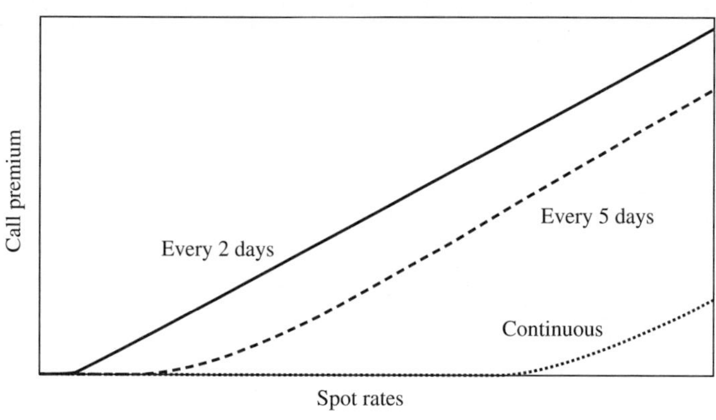

Although the discussion has so far been based on a currency transaction, the concept of averaging options can be effectively used by treasurers to cap their total annual borrowing costs. Averaging options also lend themselves naturally to the commodity markets, where the underlying price of a commodity trades as an average index (or price).

Basket Options

Although the TSE 35, TSE 100, and TSE 300 represent three of the major equity market indices in Canada, none of the industries represented in these indices is biasedly weighted. Thus, an investor with a view on the forest-sector stocks contained in the TSE 300 index cannot effectively monetize her view by simply purchasing any form of derivative on the TSE 300 index. Depending on the type of view or risk she is trying to manage, she would fundamentally need a derivative on the forest-sector stocks, since the 18 stocks in the paper and forest sector contribute only 4.82 percent to the entire index.

Due to economic fundamentals and cyclic trends, suppose, for example, that the investor feels the paper and forest-sector stocks are in general going to increase in value over the next month. To monetize her view, she could purchase a call option on the TSE 300 index. As mentioned earlier, the setback of this strategy is the fact that the paper and forest sector constitute only a meager 4.82 percent of the TSE 300 index. Her second alternative would be to purchase the 18 paper and forest stocks underlying the index, which would give her a large downside if her view turns out to be wrong. To protect herself against this downside risk, she could alternatively choose to purchase 18 at-the-money call options underlying each of the 18 stocks. Given the investor's view that the paper and forest sector, as a whole, should increase in value, purchasing 18 at-the-money call options would be an expensive way of monetizing the view. A cheaper and a more effective way to achieve the same objective would be to purchase an at-the-money call option on the basket of 18 stocks. The cheapness of this strategy is due to the fact that the investor is in essence employing the notion of correlation between the 18 stocks to monetize her view. Options of this sort are known as basket or portfolio options. The following mechanics better illustrate how basket options work in practice.

Time 0 mo: Since the pipeline sector of the TSE 300 index has good economic fundamentals, an investor feels that the three stocks in this sector—symbolized by IPL, TRP, and W—should increase in value in a month. IPL, TRP, and W are currently trading at \$28, \$18, and \$23, respectively. To monetize her view, the investor pays a premium to purchase \$50 million worth of call option on a basket of three stocks that expire in one month. In purchasing this basket option, the investor desires each stock to be weighted by an amount that is proportional to the value of the stock. More precisely, each stock price would be weighted by an amount of $\frac{1}{28+18+23} = \frac{1}{69}$ and the strike price of the at-the-money option would be $\left(\frac{1}{69} * 28\right) + \left(\frac{1}{69} * 18\right) + \left(\frac{1}{69} * 23\right) = 1.$

Time 1 mo: *Case 1.* The values of IPL, TRP, and W are \$35, \$16, and \$25, respectively, which implies that the index value of the basket is $\left(\frac{1}{69} * 35\right) + \left(\frac{1}{69} * 16\right) + \left(\frac{1}{69} * 25\right) = 1.1.$ Hence, the option finishes in-the-money and the investor gets a net payoff of \$50 * (1.1 − 1 1 − $P^*_{1mo,\,C}$), where $P^*_{1mo,\,C}$ represents the basket-option premium per dollar notional amount future valued to one month, and the payoff is in millions of dollars.

TABLE 2–4
Payoffs of the European-Style Basket Option

Type of Basket Option	*Payoff at Expiry Time*
$C_E(X, 0, T, S_{10}, \ldots, S_{n0}, w_1, \ldots, w_n)$	$\max\left[-P^*_{T,C}, \sum_{i=1}^{n} w_i S_{iT} - X - P^*_{T,C}\right]$
$P_E(X, 0, T, S_{10}, \ldots, S_{n0}, w_1, \ldots, w_n)$	$\max\left[-P^*_{T,P}, X - \sum_{i=1}^{n} w_i S_{iT} - P^*_{T,P}\right]$

where $C_E(X, 0, T, S_{10}, \ldots, S_{n0}, w_1, \ldots, w_n)$ and $P_E(X, 0, T, S_{10}, \ldots, S_{n0}, w_1, \ldots, w_n)$ represent the European-style call and put basket options respectively when the strike rate is X, the current time is *0*, the option maturity T and the current spot rates are $S_{10}, \ldots, S_{n0}$ whose respective weights are $w_1, \ldots, w_n$; $P^*_{T,C}$ and $P^*_{T,P}$ represent the premiums of the call and put basket options respectively that are future valued to time T; $\sum_{i=1}^{n} w_i = 1$.

Case 2. The values of IPL, TRP, and W are \$30, \$16, and \$20, respectively, which implies that the index value of the basket is $\left(\frac{1}{69} * 30\right) + \left(\frac{1}{69} * 16\right) + \left(\frac{1}{69} * 20\right) = 0.95$, which is less than 1. The option finishes out-of-the-money and the investor loses the premium.

Although the above example illustrated the use of an option on a basket of three stocks, the payoffs of an option on a basket of n stocks, where $n \geq 2$, can be more generally written as detailed in Table 2–4.

It is important to note that the illustration discussed above is just one of the many variations that could be structured to suit the client's objective. Due to liquidity constraints, suppose that the client alternatively monetized her view by requesting instead that the stocks IPL, TRP, and W have contributing weights of 50 percent, 30 percent, and 20 percent, respectively, to the basket. Since the at-the-money strike value works out to be $(0.5*28) + (0.3*18) + (0.2*23) = 24$ dollars, it would make sense for the purchaser to have an in-the-money payoff that is equal to the amount of the "in-the-moneyness" of the option multiplied by the number of option contracts, instead of simply multiplying the amount of the "in-the-moneyness" of the option by the notional principal amount of the trade, as illustrated in the above example.

From Tables 2–3 and 2–4, it can be seen that the payoffs of a basket option resemble those of an arithmetic average-rate option closely. The only distinguishing feature between these two payoffs is that for an arithmetic average-rate option, one asset is monitored n times during the life of the option, and hence we can think of the average-rate option as an option on n autocorrelated assets, which are monitored sequentially at different points in time, where the autocorrelation coefficient can many times be implicitly calculated. On the other hand, for a basket option, n assets are monitored simultaneously on the expiry date of the option, which implies that the correlation between these asset prices can only be calculated historically. It is this observation that allows us to value a basket option using the methods developed for pricing an arithmetic average-rate option. Although this was the spirit of the methodology that was discussed by Huynh (1994), there does exist a simpler variation of the pricing formula produced by Huynh. More precisely, we could modify the algorithm of Levy (1992) to effectively and efficiently arrive at good approximate solutions for many practical situations.

Although basket options can be valued by modifying the arithmetic average-rate option pricing formulae, the risk characteristics of a basket option are totally different from those of an averaging option, which was shown in the previous section to typically diminish in magnitude as the option nears its maturity date. Furthermore, since there is only one variable or asset underlying the option, there is no element of correlation risk present in an averaging option. Unlike the averaging option, the risk characteristics of a basket option do not diminish as the option nears its maturity date, and the historical correlation coefficients between the underlying assets are crucial inputs to valuing the option. Furthermore, for an option written on a basket of n assets, the value of the option will be dependent on $\frac{n(n-1)}{2}$ historical correlation coefficients. Among these coefficients, it is intuitively reasonable to expect the correlation coefficient contribution from any two assets to be high as long as their individual contributing weights to the basket is large. Thus, in addition to delta-hedging a basket option, the correlation risk component should be carefully managed, with special consideration given to heavily weighted stocks.

Basket options can also be effectively used by foreign investors with views on specific sectors. Suppose, for example, that a Japanese investor has a view that the utility component of the TSE 300 index is going to drop in value over the next two weeks. Since the Canadian dollar has been weakening relative to the Japanese yen, assume that the investor does not want his view to be affected by any currency movements. As in the above example, we can structure a put option on a basket of stocks that make up the utility component of the TSE 300 index. This option should be a yen-denominated put on a basket of utility stocks, which if it finishes in-the-money, would also pay out in yen. Options of this sort allow the investor to take a view on a subindex of any foreign market without being subjected to the currency risk.

Binary Options

Based on current market conditions, an asset manager feels that the three-month LIBOR is at its all-time low. She thinks that the index will go up in a week after the announcement of the government budget, but she does not have a feel for the magnitude of the increase. Clearly, a vanilla call option is not going to be helpful in strictly reflecting the direction of a market movement. Binary options—also known as bet, digital, or all-or-nothing options—are instruments that allow the buyer to target the directional movement of the market. More precisely, if an investor has a view that the market will not be trading below a certain level in a week and wants to receive a prespecified dollar amount if she is right, she could buy a binary option that will help monetize her view. The following sequence of events helps to better illustrate the nature of the product:

Time 0 wk: Three-month LIBOR is currently trading at 3.5 percent. Despite the steepness of the yield curve on the short end, the investor feels that given the current economic environment, this three-month LIBOR will never exceed 4.5 percent over the next two weeks. To monetize her view, she pays a premium to buy a binary option that pays out U.S.$1 million if LIBOR trades below 4.5 percent at the end of two weeks. If the view turns out to be wrong, she gets no payoff from the option.

Time 2 wk: *Case 1.* Three-month LIBOR is now trading at 3.8 percent. The option finishes in-the-money. The investor gets a net payoff of \$1 million $- P^*_{2\,wks,\,P}$, where $P^*_{2\,wks,\,P}$ represents the bet-option premium future valued to two weeks.

TABLE 2–5
Payoffs of the European-Style Binary Option

Type of Binary Option	*Payoff at Expiry Time* T	
C_E $(X, B, 0, T, S_0)$	$-P^*_{T, C}$	if $S_T < X$
	$B - P^*_{T, C}$	if $S_T \geq X$
P_E $(X, B, 0, T, S_0)$	$-P^*_{T, P}$	if $S_T > X$
	$B - P^*_{T, P}$	if $S_T \leq X$

where $C_E(X, B, 0, T, S_0)$ and $P_E(X, B, 0, T, S_0)$ represent the European-style binary call and put options respectively when S_0 represents the current value of the index, strike value is X, B represents the dollar payoff the buyer of the option receives if she is right, the current time is *0*, and the option maturity is T; $P^*_{T, C}$ and $P^*_{T, P}$ represent the binary call and put option premiums respectively that are future valued to time T.

N.B.: Regardless of how much the option finishes in-the-money, the investor's payoff is a constant amount of $1 million $P^*_{2\ wks,\ P}$.

Case 2. Three-month LIBOR is now trading at 4.8 percent. The option finishes out-of-the-money and the investor loses the premium.

The payoffs of a binary option can be more generally written, as detailed in Table 2–5.

Because the binary option has a payoff that is inherently a bet, it is easy to value this product. Furthermore, it is intuitively reasonable to expect the premium of such an option to be equal to the present value of the product of the bet payoff and probability that the option would finish in-the-money. Figure 2–4 shows the difference between the premiums of a binary call option for a varying B. As shown in the figure, it is intuitively reasonable to expect the option premiums to increase when the bet payoff increases.

Unlike the pricing, the hedging of this product is not easy. In practice, the sale of a binary option is usually hedged by buying call options at a lower strike rate and selling the same amount of call options at a higher strike rate. It is important to note that because of the discontinuous nature of the payoff, the above-mentioned static hedge strategy does not perfectly replicate the payoff profile of a binary option. As such, these hedge amounts should be rebalanced as required during the life of the option.

FIGURE 2–4
European-Style Binary Option Premium for Varying B

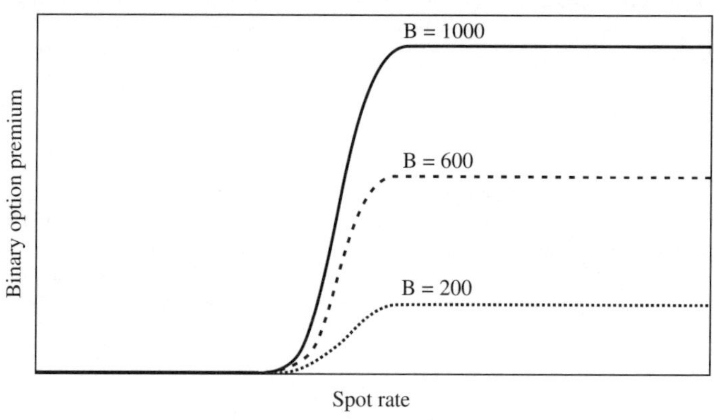

Binary options have also been effectively used in note structures. For example, an investor who thinks that the three-month LIBOR at the end of six months will be trading above 4.25 percent can purchase a six-month note that pays off a coupon of 6.5 percent if he is right and no coupon if he is wrong. An alternative structure that protects the investor against a last-minute spike in LIBOR is a payoff that is a fraction of a coupon of 5 percent, where this fraction represents the proportion of the business days in the six-month period during which the three-month LIBOR exceeds 4.25 percent. See Ravindran (1993) and Das (1995) for examples of such structures.

Investors can also use the notion of a bet on spread options. To illustrate this, suppose that the difference between the current 10- and 2-year U.S. Treasury bond yields is about 100 basis points and the investor feels almost certain that, based on the current market conditions, this difference in yields will widen further in a month. He does not have a good feel for how much the widening is going to be and, as such, is only interested in betting that the spread between the 10- and 2-year U.S. Treasury bond yields in a month will surpass the 100 basis point mark. To monetize his views, he can buy a binary spread-option, which will pay him $1 million if his view is right and nothing if he is wrong. The notion of betting on a yield-curve spread can easily be extended to entertain the possibility of betting on the yield-curve differential across different environments.

Binary options also lend themselves naturally to liability management in the form of contingent-premium or pay-later options, which are essentially insurance products that allow the buyer to pay only for the option if the option finishes in-the-money. More precisely, suppose that the current three-month LIBOR is 4.5 percent and a liability manager wants to protect herself against the rise in interest rates by purchasing a one-year interest-rate cap that is struck 150 basis points out-of-the-money (or 6.0 percent) on the three-month LIBOR. Since the cost of this purchase turns out to be expensive due to a steeply upward sloping yield curve, the liability manager is reluctant to pay the premium. Furthermore, she has a view that the three LIBOR resets over the next year will never be greater than the 6 percent level when the caplets expire. To monetize her view and protect herself against increasing interest rates, she could buy a one-year pay-later contingent-premium cap that is struck at 6.0 percent. In purchasing such a cap, she does not have to pay any premium up front for the cap. In the event her view is right and each of the caplets finishes out-of-the-money, she would walk away without losing a cent. On the other hand, if her view turns out to be wrong on any LIBOR reset, she would have to pay a prespecified premium for the appropriate caplet she ends up using. It is important to note that in purchasing such an option, the manager ends up paying the premium for the protection even if the option finishes in-the-money by a fraction of a basis point.

Chooser Options

It is common for someone with a view about the impact of a major event (e.g., election results, outbreak of a war, etc.) on a financial market to buy an option (e.g., a vanilla call-option) that will help monetize the view. Come the event date, it is also common for the same person to realize that the view had been totally wrong and wish that a vanilla put-option was purchased instead. For such a person, an option that gives the opportunity to choose between a vanilla call-option and a vanilla put-option on the event date would serve as a useful and valuable instrument. The chooser option, also known as the pay-now/choose-later option, is an option that allows the buyer to choose between a vanilla call-option and a vanilla put-option at a prespecified time in the future. More precisely, the investor pays an up-front premium to make a choice between a call and a put option, both of which, are struck at the same level and expire on the same day. The following sequence of events better illustrates the mechanics involved with the purchase of a chooser option:

Time 0 mo: The Canadian dollar is currently trading at Can$1.32/U.S.$1.00, and the federal election is in three months. An investor who has no view about the impact of election results wants the ability to buy an instrument that will enable him to make a choice between a call and a put option at the end of three months. The investor pays a premium to buy a European-style chooser option (i.e., an option to choose three months from now between a European call and a European put option on U.S. dollars with both the options being struck at Can$1.32/U.S.$1.00 and expiring three months after the choice date).

Case 1: A European call option is chosen at time 3 months.

Time 3 mo: Election results have been announced and currency is now trading at Can$1.35/U.S.$1.00 (i.e., the U.S. dollar is now stronger). The call option is now in-the-money and the put option is out-of-the-money. Since the call option is more valuable than the put option, the investor chooses the call option on the U.S. dollar.

Time 6 mo: *Case 1a*. The dollar is now trading at Can$1.34/U.S.$1.00 The option finishes in-the-money, and the payoff to the investor is $(1.34 - 1.32 - P^*_{6\,mo,\,S})$ Can/U.S., where $P^*_{6\,mo,\,S}$ represents the premium of the chooser option future valued to six months.

Case 1b. Currency is now trading at Can$1.29/U.S.$1.00. The option finishes out-of-the-money, and the investor has lost his option premium.

Case 2: A European put option is chosen at time 3 months.

Time 3 mo: Election results have been announced and the currency is now trading at Can$1.30/U.S.$1.00 (i.e., the U.S. dollar is now weaker). The put option is now in-the-money and the call option is out-of-the-money. Since the put option is more valuable than the call option, the investor chooses the put option on the U.S. dollar.

Time 6 mo: *Case 2a*. The dollar is now trading at Can$1.29/U.S.$1.00. The option finishes in-the-money, and the payoff to the in-

TABLE 2–6
Payoffs of the European-Style Chooser Option

Type of Chooser Option	*Payoff at Choice Time t*	*Payoff at Expiry Time*
Simple	max $[C_E(X_1, t, T, S_t), P_E(X, t, T, S_t)]$	If call chosen at time t: max $[-P^*_{T,S}, S_T - X - P^*_{T,S}]$ If put chosen at time t: max $[-P^*_{T,S}, X - S_T - P^*_{T,S}]$
Complex	max $[C_E(X_1, t, T_1, S_t), P_E(X_2, t, T_2, S_t)]$	If call chosen at time t: max $[-P^*_{T1,C}, S_{T1} - X_1 - P^*_{T1,C}]$ If put chosen at time t: max $[-P^*_{T2,C}, X_2 - S_{T2} - P^*_{T2,C}]$

where $C_E(X_1, t, T_1, S_t)$ and $P_E(X_2, t, T_2, S_t)$ represent the European-style vanilla call and put option premiums respectively when the strike rates are X_1 and X_2 respectively, the current (choice) time is t, the option maturity times are T_1 and T_2 respectively, and the current spot rate is S_t; $P^*_{T,S}$ represents the simple chooser option premium that is future valued to time T, $P^*_{T1,C}$ and $P^*_{T2,C}$ represent the complex chooser option premiums that are future valued to times T_1 and T_2 respectively.

vestor is (1.32 − 1.29 − $P^*_{6\,mo,S}$ Can/U.S., where $P^*_{6\,mo,S}$ represents the premium of the chooser option future valued to six months.

Case 2b. Currency is now trading at Can$1.34/U.S.$1.00. The option finishes out-of-the-money, and the investor has lost his option premium.

It is important to first note from the above example that the investor, upon choosing the call option at the end of the three-month period, could have alternatively sold the chosen option in the market instead of holding it for another three months. Second, the type of chooser option mentioned in the above example is known as a simple chooser option. The investor could have alternatively bought a complex chooser option that would have allowed him a choice between a European call option with strike X_1 and time to maturity T_1 and a European put option with strike X_2 and time to maturity T_2. Table 2–6 details the payoffs of both the simple and complex chooser options.

Third, if the choice date in the above example of a simple chooser option was set to six months, which in our example is the maturity date of the option, the investor would have effectively bought himself a straddle (i.e., a call and a put both struck at Can$1.32/U.S.$1.00 and expiring

FIGURE 2–5
***Simple Chooser Option Premiums for Varying* t**

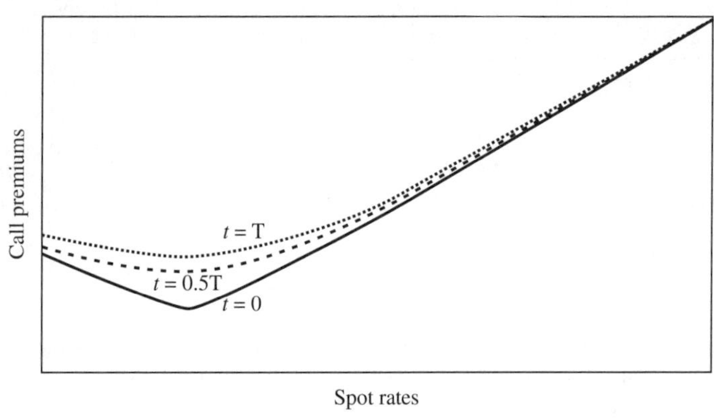

in six months). Because of the ability to choose at the end of six months, the investor will always get a positive payoff. Thus, the closer the choice date to the option maturity, the more expensive the chooser option will be. Figure 2–5 shows the effect of varying the choice time *t* for a simple chooser option. The reason for this increase in premium is that there is less uncertainty about the chosen option finishing in-the-money.

Fourth, although the above example illustrated the choosing between a European-style call and put option, we could have just as well offered the investor a choice between an American-style call and put option. Furthermore, the added twist of offering the investor the ability to make a choice at any moment from the inception of the contract till the final choice time *t* has no value. This is because market information increases as time decays and as such, it is always beneficial for the investor to delay his decision of choice.

A chooser option is usually bought by someone who does not want to be affected by the uncertainty toward the run-up to a major event (e.g., elections, a referendum, war). Buyers who want to avoid paying for the volatility caused by the event and are uncertain about the direction of the market should buy a chooser option with the choice date being set about one day after the event. Furthermore, when buying a chooser option, the buyer should also be careful about the short-end volatility spiking up, which in turn would cause a straddle to be cheaper than a chooser option. This is due to the fact that as the event date draws closer and the outcome of the event becomes more uncertain (or equally split), the volatility of the market to the event date increases. Furthermore, since the outcome of the event will be realized on the event date, the volatility of the market out to a day past the event date becomes lesser, hence making a straddle cheaper.

The pricing of the chooser options, both simple and complex, has been given in Rubinstein (1991). These exotic options can be hedged using either the underlying asset or other appropriate vanilla options.

Compound Options

A manufacturer is bidding for a contract to manufacture a certain set of goods. If he is awarded the contract (e.g., a month after the bid was submitted), he is required to manufacture the goods at the bidded price. He also runs the risk of being exposed to the rising cost of the materials used in the manufacturing process, if he waits until the date of award to purchase the raw materials. To hedge himself, he needs a call option on the price of the materials that is struck at the level of his tendered bid, only if he is awarded the contract. Due to the hedging difficulties arising from the nonmarket risk, it is usually difficult for an investment house to sell an option that is contingent on the buyer's being awarded a contract. As such, the manufacturer's best alternative would be to buy an option that would allow him to receive a call option at the award date for an extra premium. This option—also known as a compound option, option-on-option, or a split-payment option—is a derivative that allows the buyer to pay an initial up-front premium for an option that he may need later. The buyer then pays an additional premium only if he decides that he needs this option. The mechanics associated with a compound-option transaction are best illustrated with the following example:

Time 0 mo: The Canadian dollar is currently trading at Can$1.34/U.S.$1.00. The client bids on a contract based on today's exchange rate and will only know the outcome of the bidding one month from now. If the outcome is successful, he would be faced with a currency exposure six months after the results of the bidding. He is afraid that if the U.S. dollar strengthens seven months from now, he is bound to lose money on the contract, which he tendered using an exchange rate of Can$1.34/U.S.$1.00. Thus, he needs a protection against a rising U.S. dollar in seven months only if he is awarded the contract. His needs will be fulfilled if he had a call option on the U.S. dollar that has a strike rate of Can$1.34/U.S.$1.00, a life of six months, and conditionally starts one month from now. To do this, he could purchase a call option (so that he can receive his second call option by paying an additional premium of Can$0.050/ U.S.$1.00, which would be less than the amount that is prescribed by the market if the first call option goes in-the-money) on the call option.

More precisely, he would pay a small initial premium today to buy a call option with a life of one month, which exercises into another call option (with strike rate Can$1.34/U.S.$1.00 and a life of six months) upon the payment of an additional premium of Can$0.050/U.S.$1.00 that is prespecified at the inception of the contract. Since there is a possibility of him not being awarded the contract, he obviously would not mind paying a smaller initial premium and a higher second premium upon winning the contract.

Case 1: The client is awarded the contract.

Time 1 mo: The contract is now awarded to the client. He needs a call option on the U.S. dollar with a life of six months and a strike of Can$1.34/U.S.$1.00. He compares the second premium of Can$0.050/U.S.$1.00 that was prespecified at the inception of the contract to the premium required to buy the call option from the market. If the size of his second additional premium is smaller, he exercises the compound option. However, if it is cheaper for him to buy this option from the market, he does not exercise his compound option and forgoes the initial premium paid at the inception of the contract.

Time 7 mo: (assuming that the compound option (or first call option) is exercised)

Case 1a. Currency is now trading at Can$1.32/U.S.$1.00. The call option acquired by the client is out-of-the-money, and as such he loses both his premiums.

Case 1b. The U.S. dollar is stronger and the exchange rate is now at a level of Can$1.35/U.S.$1.00. The call option

FIGURE 2–6
Effect of X_t on the Premium of a Call-on-Call Option

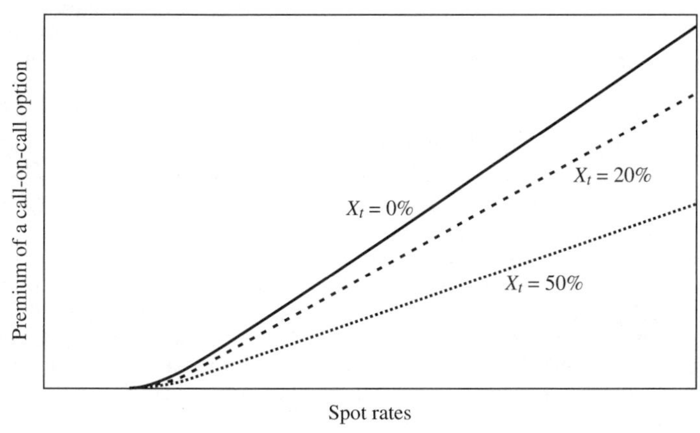

finishes in-the-money, and the payoff to the client is $(1.35 - 1.34 - P^*_{7\ mo,\ CP})$ Can/U.S., where $P^*_{7\ mo,\ CP}$ represents the sum of the two premiums that are future valued to a time of seven months.

Case 2: The client is not awarded the contract.

Time 1 mo: He does not receive the contract. Since he has no use for the call option, he does not exercise the compound option and forgoes his initial premium.

One should first note from the above example that the lower the initial compulsory payment, the higher the second optional payment and vice versa. Furthermore, when there is no second optional payment, it would be intuitively reasonable to expect the initial compulsory payment of a call-on-call option to be equal to the premium of a structurally similar vanilla call option with life of seven months. Under this circumstance, it is also intuitively reasonable to expect a structurally similar put-on-call option would be worthless. Figure 2–6 illustrates the effect of varying the second optional premium on the initial compulsory premium for a call-on-call option.

The curve $X_t = 0\%$ represents the premium (or the first compulsory payment) of a call-on-call option when there is no second installment. As discussed above, this curve also represents the European-style vanilla call option premium. The curves $X_t = 20\%$ ($X_t = 50\%$) represent the

TABLE 2–7
Payoffs of the European-Style Compound Option

Type of Compound Option	*Payoff at Time* t	*Payoff at Expiry Time* T *If Compound Option Is Exercised at Time* t
$C_EC_E(X_t,X_T,0,t,T,S_0)$	$\max[-P^*_{t,CC},C_{E,t}-X_t-P^*_{t,CC}]$	$\max[-P^*_{T,CC},S_T-X_T-P^*_{T,CC}]$
$P_EC_E(X_t,X_T,0,t,T,S_0)$	$\max[-P^*_{t,PC},X_t-C_{E,t}-P^*_{t,PC}]$	$\max[-P^*_{T,PC},S_T,-X_T-P^*_{T,PC}]$
$C_EP_E(X_t,X_T,0,t,T,S_0)$	$\max[-P^*_{t,CP},P_{E,t}-X_t-P^*_{t,CP}]$	$\max[-P^*_{T,CP},X_T,-S_T-P^*_{T,CP}]$
$P_EP_E(X_t,X_T,0,t,T,S_0)$	$\max[-P^*_{t,PP},X_t-P_{E,t}-P^*_{t,PP}]$	$\max[-P^*_{T,PP},X_T,-S_T-P^*_{T,PP}]$

where $C_EC_E(X_t,X_T,0,t,T,S_0)$, $P_EC_E(X_t,X_T,0,t,T,S_0)$, $C_EP_E(X_t,X_T,0,t,T,S_0)$, and $P_EP_E(X_t,X_T,0,t,T,S_0)$ represent the European-style call-on-call, put-on-call, call-on-put, and put-on-put options respectively when X_t is the strike rate (i.e., second additional premium) at time t, X_T is the strike rate at time T, 0 is the current time, t is the time that the first option expires, T is the time that the second option expires, and S_0 is the current exchange rate; $C_{E,t}$ and $P_{E,t}$ represent the European call and the put option premiums respectively when the current time is t, option maturity time is T, the strike rate of the option is X_T, and the current spot rate is S_t; $P^*_{t,CC}$, $P^*_{t,PC}$, $P^*_{t,CP}$, and $P^*_{t,PP}$ represent the initial premiums of the call-on-call, put-on-call, call-on-put, and put-on-put respectively that are future valued to time t and $P^*_{T,CC}$, $P^*_{T,PC}$, $P^*_{T,CP}$, and $P^*_{T,PP}$ represent the sum of the initial and the second additional premiums (X_t) of these respective options that are future valued to time T.

premiums or the first compulsory payments of a call-on-call option when 20% (50%) of the vanilla call option premium has been paid as a second installment. As illustrated in Figure 2–6, the higher this percentage, the lower the first compulsory premium.

Second, even if the client does not get awarded the contract, it may still be optimal for him to exercise his compound option and sell off the underlying call option as long as the second additional premium is lower than the premium obtained by selling the call option in the market. Although the above example illustrates the use of a European-style call-on-call option, one can find the justification for the use of put-on-call options, call-on-put options, and put-on-put options. The payoffs corresponding to these various compound options are given in Table 2–7.

Although compound options can be priced using the binomial method, Geske (1979) and Rubinstein (1991) have provided analytical expressions for the pricing of European-style compound options. The concept of a compound option can easily be adapted to embed either a vanilla option exercising into any exotic option or any exotic option exercising into a vanilla option, depending on the type of risk the client is trying to manage. Furthermore, the philosophy of paying the option premium in two installments, with the first being compulsory and the second being optional, can be extended to paying of the premium in n (where $n \geq 2$) installments, with the first being compulsory and the remaining $n - 1$ being optional.

Extrema Options

A Canadian investor observes that the TSE 35 and TSE 100 indices are currently trading at 220 and 250 points, respectively. Based on both current and historical levels, the investor feels that the Canadian equity market should rally enough over the next week so that the maximum of the TSE 35 index and (0.88 * TSE 100 index) should easily exceed a level of 225 in a week, where $0.88 = \frac{220}{250}$. The instrument that would help him monetize his view is called an extrema option. An extrema option, also known as a rainbow or maxima\minima option, is a derivative that allows the buyer to pay an initial up-front premium for a call option that provides a payoff that is the maximum of zero and the difference between the maximum of the two underlying variables and the strike rate. The mechanics associated with an extrema-option transaction are best illustrated with the following example:

Time 0 wk: The TSE 35 and TSE 100 indices are currently trading at 220 and 250 points, respectively. The investor pays a premium for a maxima call-option that is struck at a level of 225 and expires in a week. If his view is right, ignoring the premium of the option paid, he would receive a payoff of the difference between the maximum of the TSE 35 index and (0.88 * TSE 100 index) one week from now and a strike level of 225.

Time 1 wk: *Case 1.* The TSE 35 and the TSE 100 indices are currently trading at 223 and 260, respectively. The maximum of the TSE 35 and (0.88 * TSE 100) is max [223, (0.88 * 260)] = max [223,228.8] = 228.8. The option finishes in-the-money and the payoff to the buyer is (228.8 − 225) − $P^*_{1wk, CMa}$, where $P^*_{1wk, CMa}$ represents the premium of the extrema option future valued to one week.

TABLE 2–8
Payoffs of the European-Style Extrema Option

Type of Extrema Option	*Payoff at Expiry Time* T
$C_{E,\,Ma}(X,0,T,S_{10},S_{20},a,b)$	$-P^*_{T,\,CMa}$ max $[aS_{1T},bS_{2T}]-X-P^*_{T,\,CMa}$
$P_{E,\,Ma}(X,0,T,S_{10},S_{20},a,b)$	$-P^*_{T,\,PMa}$ $X-$max $[aS_{1T},bS_{2T}]-P^*_{T,\,PMa}$
$C_{E,\,Mi}(X,0,T,S_{10},S_{20},a,b)$	$-P^*_{T,\,CMi}$ min $[aS_{1T},bS_{2T}]-X-P^*_{T,\,CMi}$
$P_{E,\,Mi}(X,0,T,S_{10},S_{20},a,b)$	$-P^*_{T,\,PMi}$ $X-$min $[aS_{IT},bS_{2T}]-P^*_{T,\,PMi}$

where $C_{E,\,Ma}(X,0,T,S_{10},S_{20},a,b)$, $P_{E,\,Ma}(X,0,T,S_{10},S_{20},a,b)$, $C_{E,\,Mi}(X,0,T,S_{10},S_{20},\,a,b)$, and $P_{E,\,Mi}(X,0,T,S_{10},S_{20},a,b)$ represent the European-style call-maxima, put-maxima, call-minima, and put-minima options respectively when the strike rate is X, the current time is 0, the option maturity time is T, the current spot rates are S_{10} and S_{20} and their corresponding nonnegative multiples are a and b respectively; $P^*_{T,\,CMa}$, $P^*_{T,\,PMa}$, $P^*_{T,\,CMi}$, and $P^*_{T,\,PMi}$ represent the call-maxima, put-maxima, call-minima and put-minima option premiums respectively that are future valued to time T.

Case 2. The TSE 35 and TSE 100 indices are currently trading at 223 and 250 points, respectively. The maximum of the TSE 35 and (0.88 * TSE 100) is max [223, (0.88 * 250)] = max [223,220] = 223. The option finishes out-of-the-money, and the buyer has lost his premium.

The payoffs relating to an extrema option can be more generally written as in Table 2–8.

Although these options can be priced using the binomial method that has been illustrated in Rubinstein (1991), analytical expressions for valuing the above payoffs when $a = b = 1$ have been provided by Stulz (1982). Like the basket, product, and spread options, the correlation between asset S_{1T} and asset S_{2T} is an important input to the price of an extrema option. When X in the payoffs in Table 2–8 is set to zero, the call-maxima option, for example, simplifies to a function of the exchange options. More precisely, when X is zero, the purchase of a call-maxima option is equivalent to the purchase of an option that allows b times asset 2 to be exchanged for a times asset 1 at expiry time T and the purchase of b times asset 2. Furthermore, purchasing a call-minima option is equivalent to purchasing b times asset 2 and selling an option that allows the buyer to exchange a times asset 1 for b times asset 2 at time T. Both the maxima and minima put options will be worthless when X is zero by virtue of the fact that an asset price cannot be negative. The section on spread options discusses the relationship between an exchange option and a spread option.

Although, the above discussion was based on two underlying variables, nothing prohibits us from offering an extrema option on a basket of n indices, where $n \geq 2$. See Boyle and Tse (1990) for a detailed discussion on the pricing of an extrema option on n assets. The philosophy of buying or selling derivatives on the best or the worst of n assets is apparent in certain exchange-traded derivative contracts. In selling a bond futures contract in either the Montreal or the Chicago exchange, the seller must typically deliver the cheapest of a basket of 25 bonds. Furthermore, although not very liquid, options on these cheapest-to-deliver contracts or extrema options on a basket of 25 bonds do trade in the exchanges.

Extrema structures can also be embedded into binary quanto options in the structuring of notes. A Canadian investor, for example, could buy a one-month note that pays off a coupon that is a fraction of 5 percent, where this fraction represents the proportion of business days in the six-month period during which the maximum of three-month BA and (1.15 * three-month LIBOR) exceeds a level of 4 percent, where all the transactions are carried out in Canadian funds. Such a note can be similarly structured to pay out in U.S. funds.

Forward-Start Options

Forward-start options are options that are paid for today but start at some prespecified time in the future. The simplest forms of forward-start options that exist in abundance in the capital markets are caps and floors. In these simplest forms, the caplets and floorlets that make up a cap and floor, respectively, start at prespecified times in the future, with the strike rates being prespecified at the inception of the contract. Variations on the simplest form of forward-start options have more recently developed in the interest-rate market in the form of periodic caps and floors and in the equity and currency markets in the form of cliquet or ratchet options. Instead of buying vanilla caps (where the strike rate of each caplet is prespecified and may be different from one another), which could prove expensive during a period of rapidly rising interest rates or a steeply upward sloping yield-curve environment, liability managers could buy periodic caps where the strike rate of each caplet is set at a certain spread above the previous LIBOR setting. The following example better illustrates the mechanics behind the transaction of a periodic cap:

Time 0 mo: The client pays a premium to buy a one-year periodic cap where there are three caplets expiring at the three-month, six-month, and nine-month time periods. The strike rate of each caplet will be set equal to the sum of the previous three-month LIBOR setting and 50 basis points. The current three-month LIBOR is 3.5 percent. The strike rate of the first caplet expiring in three months is (3.5 percent + 50 basis points) = 4 percent.

Time 3 mo: LIBOR is 3.75 percent. The first caplet finishes out-of-the-money and the strike rate for the next caplet is set at (3.75 percent + 50 basis points) = 4.25 percent. The second caplet commences and matures in three months' time.

Time 6 mo: LIBOR is currently at 4.3 percent. The second caplet finishes in-the-money by five basis points and the strike rate for the third caplet is set at (4.3 percent + 50 basis points) = 4.8 percent. The third caplet commences and expires in three months.

Time 9 mo: LIBOR is at 4 percent. The third caplet finishes out-of-the-money.

Forward-start options can also be used by investors to bet on reset LIBOR values. Suppose, for example, that the current yield-curve environment is such that the 3 x 6 FRA (forward rate agreement) rate is higher than the 6 x 9 FRA rate, and an investor feels that this inversion in the yield curve is only temporary. To monetize her view, she could buy a forward-start call option on the three-month LIBOR starting three months from now. The strike rate on this option is the three-month LIBOR in three months' time, following which the vanilla option on the three-month LIBOR expires another three months later. Due to the current inversion in this part of the yield curve, the cost of this option would be minimal. It is important to note that the naive strategy of buying and selling the appropriate FRAs has a large downside if the view turns out to be wrong. See for example Ravindran (1995a).

The payoffs for a generic forward-start option can be generally written as in Table 2–9, and the pricing expressions for these options when X (also called an offset in the context of a spread option) is zero and $t = t_1$ are given in Hull (1993).

TABLE 2–9
Payoffs of the European-Style Forward-Start Option

Type of Forward Start Option	*Payoff at Expiry Time* T
$C_E(X,0,T,S_0,t,t_1)$	$-P^*_{T,C}$ if $S_T - S_t < X$ $S_T - S_t - X - P^*_{T,C}$ if $S_T - S_t \geq X$
$P_E(X,0,T,S_0,t,t_1)$	$-P^*_{T,P}$ if $S_T - S_t > X$ $X - (S_T - S_t) - P^*_{T,P}$ if $S_T - S_t \leq X$

where $C_E(X,0,T,S_0,t,t_1)$ and $P_E(X,0,T,S_0,t,t_1)$ represent the European-style forward-start call and put options respectively when the strike value is X, the current time is 0, option starts at time t_1, the option maturity is T, floating strike is set at time t and the current value of the index is S_0; $P^*_{T,C}$ and $-P^*_{T,P}$ are the premiums of the call and put options respectively that are future valued to time T.

Hull shows that the premium of a forward-start option is proportional to the premium of a vanilla European-style at-the-money option with life $T - t$. Furthermore, if the underlying asset does not pay any dividend, he shows that the purchase of the forward-start option is equivalent to the purchase of a vanilla European-style at-the-money option with life $T - t$. These results can be extended to show that as long as $X = 0$, these valuation formulae hold true even if $t \neq t_1$. To intuit this, consider the case where the underlying asset does not pay any dividend, $t_1 = 0$ and the option premium is paid today. In this instance, the buyer has effectively bought an option that expires at time T and allows the strike price to be set at time t. Since the value of this option is solely based on the difference in prices of the same asset at times T and t, this option has no value until the strike price is set. Thus, the effective life of the option is $T - t$. As long as the asset does not pay any dividend, this is equivalent to the buyer purchasing an option today with a life of $T - t$.

Since a forward-start option is indeed a vanilla European-style option once the floating-strike component has been set, risk management on a forward-start option is identical to that of a vanilla option, only after the floating strike is set. Prior to the fixing of the floating strike, we can still delta hedge a forward-start option due to the fact that we can many times implicitly calculate the correlation coefficient between S_T and S_t.

As long as $t_1 < t$, a forward-start option described above can also be thought of as a spread option starting at time t_1. In the example on the

3×6 and the 6×9 FRAs that was given earlier, as long as the forward-start option commences before the three-month period, this option can also be viewed as a spread option with the two variables being the three-month LIBOR six months from now and the three-month LIBOR three months from now. Unlike a typical spread option where the correlation coefficient can only be historically calculated, the autocorrelation can usually be implicitly calculated due to the fact that we are actually monitoring a single variable at two different points in time rather than two variables at the same time. This phenomenon is similar in philosophy to the discussion earlier in this chapter where the arithmetic average-rate option was compared to a basket option.

Despite the fact that the forward-start option starts out at a future time, it is important to note that the value of a forward-start option will be exactly the same as that of a structurally similar vanilla option expiring at time T, as long as the floating component of the strike rate is absent from the option's payoff. To intuit this, observe that when the floating-strike component is absent, the payoff of a forward-start option is only dependent on the exchange rate at option maturity. Since this is exactly the same as that of a structurally similar vanilla option, an investor should not favor one structure over the other. Thus, we can expect both the option premiums to be the same. Furthermore, when X is 0, the purchase of a forward-start call option is equivalent to the purchase of a maxima call-option with $a = 1$, $b = 1$, $S_{1T} = S_T$, and $S_{2T} = X = S_t$. See the discussion on extrema options.

Lookback Options

A U.S. manufacturer receives his raw materials from Canada. Upon the receipt of his bills, he has until the end of the month to settle his accounts. He knows the total currency risk he is exposed to at the end of every month and wants to protect himself against a weakening U.S. dollar. As such, he wants to buy a one-month put option on the U.S. dollar and at the same time be able to lock in a better rate if the Canadian dollar strengthens during the life of the option. Since he has no view on the market, to address his concerns he would need to buy a European-style lookback put option on the U.S. dollar. A lookback option is a derivative that allows the buyer to pay an initial up-front premium for an option that provides maximum protection. The mechanics associated with a lookback option transaction are best illustrated with the following example:

Time 0 mo: The Canadian dollar is currently trading at Can$1.34/U.S.$1.00. A manufacturer who is faced with a currency exposure in a month is worried about the U.S. dollar weakening. At the same time, he wants to lock in the highest possible level the Canadian dollar may strengthen to during this one-month period. As such, he wants to pay an up-front premium for a European-style lookback put option on the U.S. dollar that pays off in one month an amount that is the maximum of zero and the difference between the spot rate on the option maturity date and the lowest value the U.S. dollar reaches during the life of the option (inclusive of the spot rates at both the inception of the contract and the maturity of the option). The spot rates are observed at noon on each business day.

Time 1 mo: *Case 1.* The Canadian dollar is trading at Can$1.32/U.S.$1.00. The weakest value attained by the U.S. dollar during the one-month sampling period is at the maturity date of the option. The option therefore expires worthless and the manufacturer has lost his premium paid out at the inception of the contract.

Case 2. The Canadian dollar is trading at Can$1.33/U.S.$1.00. The lowest value attained by the U.S. dollar during the sampling period was a level of Can$1.28/U.S.$1.00. The option finishes in-the-money and the payoff to the manufacturer is $(1.33 - 1.28 - P^*_{1mo,\,PLo})$ Can/U.S., where $P^*_{1mo,\,PLo}$ represents the premium of the lookback option future valued to one month.

It is first important to note from the above example that the lookback option is not really an option. This follows from the observation that the sampling period, which contains the exchange rates encountered during the life of the option, also includes as its points the spot rate at the option maturity date, and as such, one cannot do any worse than the spot rate at the option maturity date.

Second, we could have created an option that paid the buyer at the option maturity date a maximum of zero and the difference between a prespecified strike rate and the lowest exchange rate realized during the

FIGURE 2–7
European-Style Lookback Call Option Premiums

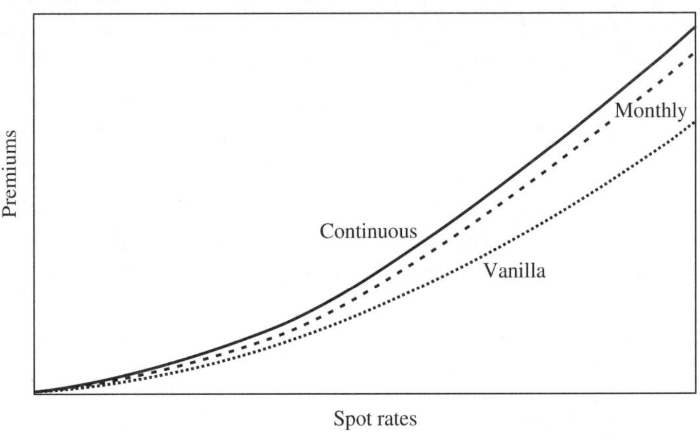

life of the option. Since it is possible for this difference in payoff to be negative, we will call these options modified lookback options. Third, due to the high level of insurance provided, one can expect a lookback option to be costly. More precisely, the cost of a lookback option is directly proportional to the frequency of sampling. Thus, the greater the frequency of sampling (or larger the sampling period), the more expensive the option. Figure 2–7 shows the difference in premiums between a modified lookback call option with continuous sampling frequency, a modified lookback call-option with discrete sampling frequency, and a vanilla call-option when the strikes and the times to maturity of the options are identical.

Furthermore, if the manufacturer has a strong view that the Canadian dollar over the last three of the four weeks is never going to get any stronger than the exchange rate at inception, he could use this view to lower the cost by purchasing a partial lookback option, where the sampling period for the lookback feature commences in a week's time and ends on the option maturity date. The payoffs for the various European-style lookback options can be more generally written as detailed in Table 2–10.

Although both the European and American-style lookback options can be priced using the binomial method regardless of the sampling

TABLE 2–10
Payoffs of the European-Style Lookback Option

Type of Lookback Option	*Payoff at Expiry Time* T
$C_{E,\,F}(0,T,S_0,t_1,\ldots,t_n)$	$-P^*_{T,\,CLo}$ if $S_T < \min S_{t_i}$ $S_T - \min S_{t_i} - P^*_{T,\,CLo}$ if $S_T \geq \min S_{t_i}$
$P_{E,\,F}(0,T,S_0,t_1,\ldots,t_n)$	$-P^*_{T,\,PLo}$ if $S_T > \max S_{t_i}$ $\max S_{t_i} - S_T - P^*_{T,\,PLo}$ if $S_T \leq \max S_{t_i}$
$C_{E,\,M}(X,0,T,S_0,t_1,\ldots,t_n)$	$-P^*_{T,\,CMLo}$ if $X > \max S_{t_i}$ $\max S_{t_i} - X - P^*_{T,\,CMLo}$ if $X \leq \max S_{t_i}$
$P_{E,\,M}(X,0,T,S_0,t_1,\ldots,t_n)$	$-P^*_{T,\,PMLo}$ if $X < \min S_{t_i}$ $X - \min S_{t_i} - P^*_{T,\,PMLo}$ if $X \geq \min S_{t_i}$

where $C_{E,\,F}(0,T,S_0,t_1,\ldots,t_n)$, $P_{E,\,F}(0,T,S_0,t_1,\ldots,t_n)$, $C_{E,\,M}(X,0,T,S_0,t_1,\ldots,t_n)$, and $P_{E,\,M}(X,0,T,S_0,t_1,\ldots,t_n)$ represent the European-style lookback call, lookback put, modified lookback call and, modified lookback put options respectively when the current time is *0*, option maturity is T, current spot rate is S_0, strike rate of the modified lookback option is X and the sampled times are t_i (where $i = 1,\ldots,n$; $t_0 \leq 0$ and $t_n = T$); $P^*_{T,\,CLo}$, $P^*_{T,\,PLo}$, $P^*_{T,\,CMLo}$, and $P^*_{T,\,PMLo}$ represent the premiums of the lookback call, lookback put, modified lookback call, and modified lookback put options respectively that are future valued to time T, $\min S_{t_i}$ represents the smallest value of all the spot rates sampled and $\max S_{t_i}$ represents the largest value of all the spot rates sampled. For the partial lookback options and the modified partial lookback options, the payoffs are essentially the same as above, with the size of the sampling points being reduced.

frequency, Goldman, Sosin, and Gatto (1979) have provided closed-form solutions to price European-style full lookback options on non-dividend-paying stocks when the assumption of a continuous time sampling period is used. These assumptions have been used by Garman (1987) and by Conze and Viswanathan (1991) to value European-style full lookback options on dividend-paying stocks and European-style modified lookback options on non-dividend-paying stocks, respectively. Lookback options can easily be hedged by using either the notion of delta hedging or by replicating the payoffs using European-style vanilla options.

The concept of a lookback strategy can also be embedded into a swap and used effectively by a liability manager. Suppose for example that based on the current yield curve, the three-year swap rate starting six months from now is 6.5 percent, which is higher than the current three-year spot swap rate of 4.73 percent. A client who wants to get into a three-year swap rate can receive the six-month LIBOR and pay a fixed rate of 4.73 percent. If she thinks that the realized three-year swap rate in six months is going to be lesser than 4.73 percent, she could get into a swap whereby she receives a floating rate of the six-month LIBOR plus some spread on each coupon date and pays a fixed rate on the swap that will be the maximum of the current three-year swap rate and the three-year swap rate in six months' time.

Mid-Atlantic Options

A European-style vanilla option is an option that can be exercised only at the maturity date of the option, and an American-style vanilla option is an option that can be exercised at any time during the life of the option. An option that is an intermediary between these two options is called the Mid-Atlantic option. The Mid-Atlantic option—also called the quasi-American-style option, the limited exercise option, or the Bermudan option—is an option that can be exercised only at discrete points during the life of the option. Thus, at the inception of the contract, in addition to specifying the usual parameters of a vanilla European-style option, the buyer of a Mid-Atlantic option must also specify the times of exercise.

Mid-Atlantic options lend themselves very naturally as hedge instruments in the interest-rate market. The following example better illustrates the mechanics underlying the use of this option:

Time 0 yr: An investor owns a large amount of semiannual 8-percent-coupon callable bonds that were issued by a corporate at \$100. The issued bond has a five-year life and can be recalled by the issuer for \$102 at any one of the coupon dates during the last year of the bond. More precisely, the bond can be recalled by the issuer on the eighth or ninth coupon date at \$102. To hedge against this recall, the investor pays an up-front premium to buy a Mid-Atlantic option on a synthetic bond with an 8-percent semiannual coupon that matures on the same day as the callable bond for \$102.

Case 1: Bond is called at the end of 4 years.

Time 4 yr: The bond is trading at \$105 and the issuer pays the investor the coupon payment of \$4 and recalls the bond at \$102. The investor then pays \$102 to exercise the Mid-Atlantic option into a one-year synthetic bond with a semiannual coupon of 8 percent.

Case 2: Bond is called at the end of 4½ years.

Time 4 yr: The bond is trading at \$99.50. The investor receives the coupon payment of \$4. The issuer does not recall the bond and hence the investor does not exercise the option.

Time 4½ yr: The bond is trading at \$103. The issuer pays the investor the coupon payment of \$4 and recalls the bond for \$102. The investor exercises the Mid-Atlantic option into a six-month synthetic bond with a semiannual coupon of 8 percent by paying \$102.

Case 3: Bond is not called.

Time 4 yr: The bond is trading at \$99.50. A coupon of \$4 is paid to the investor. The issuer does not recall the bond, and hence the investor does not exercise the option.

Time 4½ yr: The bond is trading at \$101. The issuer does not recall the bond. The investor gets a coupon of \$4 and does not exercise the option.

Time 5 yr: The bond matures at par. In addition to the face value, the investor also receives the \$4 coupon payment. The investor has lost the premium paid for the Mid-Atlantic option.

It is important to note that although the above example illustrates a scenario where the issuer recalls the bonds only when they are in-the-money, due to accounting or tax reasons, it is not uncommon for the issued bonds to be recalled even when they are out-of-the-money. Since the number of exercise points in a Mid-Atlantic option can never exceed that of an American-style option and never be lesser than that of a European-style option, it is intuitively reasonable to expect the premium of a Mid-Atlantic option to be no lesser than that of a European option and no greater than that of an American option. Like the American-style options, Mid-Atlantic options can easily be priced using the binomial method, and the concept of discretizing the times of exercise can easily be implemented into the other types of exotic options in any asset class. The hedging of a Mid-Atlantic option is no different from that of any vanilla option and the payoffs of a Mid-Atlantic option can be more succinctly written, as shown in Table 2–11.

Nonlinear-Payoff Options

A vanilla option has a linear payoff if the derivative finishes in-the-money. More precisely, if S_T and X represent the exchange rates at the

TABLE 2–11
Payoffs of the Mid-Atlantic Option

Type Of Option	*Payoff at Time* t	*Payoff at Expiry Time* T
$C_{MA}(X,0,T,S_0)$	$\max[S_t - X - P^*_{t,C}, C_{MA,t} - P^*_{t,C}]$	$\max[-P^*_{T,C}, S_T - X - P^*_{T,C}]$
$P_{MA}(X,0,T,S_0)$	$\max[X - S_t - P^*_{t,P}, P_{MA,t} - P^*_{t,P}]$	$\max[-P^*_{T,P}, X - S_T - P^*_{T,P}]$

where $C_{MA}(X,0,T,S_0)$ and $P_{MA}(X,0,T,S_0)$ represent the Mid-Atlantic call and put options respectively when X is the strike rate, the current time is *0*, the life of the option is T, the current spot rate is S_0, and t is one of the discrete exercise times $0 \leq t_0, t_1, \ldots, t_n \leq T$; $P^*_{t,C}$ and $P^*_{t,P}$ represent the call and put option premiums respectively that are future valued to time t; $C_{MA,t}$ and $P_{MA,t}$ represent the values of the Mid-Atlantic call and put options respectively at time t when the strike rate is X, the current time is t, the option expiry time is T, and the current spot rate is S_t.

maturity of the option and the strike rate, respectively, neglecting the cost of the option premium paid at the inception of the contract, a European-style vanilla call option would have a payoff of $S_T - X$ if the option goes in-the-money and zero otherwise. The in-the-money payoff in this instance is a linear function of the exchange rate at maturity. By the same token, a European-style nonlinear-payoff option has an in-the-money payoff that is a nonlinear function of the exchange rate at maturity. Examples of these in-the-money payoffs at the maturity date, which are illustrated in Figure 2–8, are $e^{S_T} - X$, $S_T^2 - X$, $S_T^{0.5} - X$.

Nonlinear-payoff options that have payoffs where S_T appears as a base rather than a power (e.g., $S_T^2 - X$ and $S_T^{0.5} - X$) are also called power or turbo options. The following example, although applied to a power option, can easily be modified for any nonlinear-payoff option.

Time 0 wks: The Canadian dollar is currently trading at Can\$1.30/U.S.\$1.00. The investor feels that in one week, the Canadian dollar is going to be much weaker. Because of the certainty in his view, he wants a payoff function at the expiry date to be $S_T^2 - 1.31^2$ if the option finishes in-the-money (i.e., if the U.S. dollar strengthens pass the Can\$1.31 mark). He pays a premium to buy the power option that is struck at Can\$1.31²/U.S.\$1.00 and has a life of one week.

Time 1 wk: *Case 1.* Currency is now trading at Can\$1.30/U.S.\$1.00. The option finishes out-of-the-money, and the investor loses his option premium.

FIGURE 2–8
Nonlinear Call-Payoffs

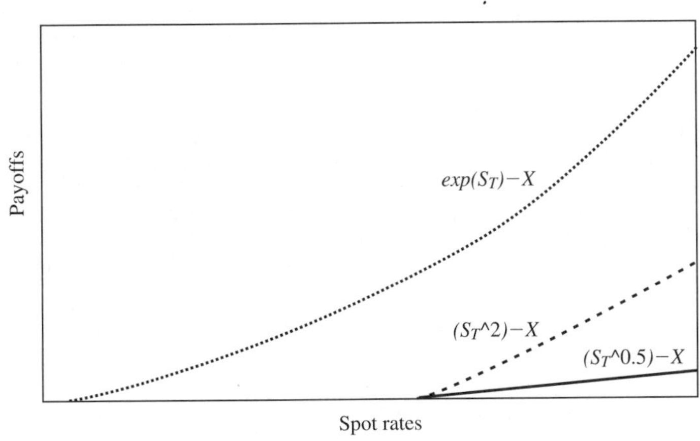

Case 2. Currency is now trading at Can$1.34/U.S.$1.00. The option finishes in-the-money and the payoff to the client is $(1.34^2 - 1.31^2 - P^*_{1wk,\,C})$ Can/U.S., where $P^*_{1wk,\,C}$ represents the premium of the power option future valued to time of one week.

It is first important to note that, neglecting the premiums paid out for the options at the inception of the contract, if the investor had bought a vanilla call-option instead, the payoff to the client would have been $(1.34 - 1.31)$ Can/U.S., which is approximately 40 percent of the payoff value obtained from the purchase of the power option. The payoff to the investor can be further leveraged by increasing the index (or the power) of S_T in the above example from 2 to 4. Second, due to the high leveraging effect in the payoff function, we can expect the premium of the power option to be higher than that of a vanilla option. Letting $f(S_T)$ represent any nonlinear function of S_T and X be the strike rate of the option, the payoff to the investor can be more generally written as detailed in Table 2–12.

As always, the binomial method can easily be used to price both European and American-style nonlinear-payoff options. Although a nonlinear-payoff option can be hedged using the concept of delta hedging, due to the amount of leveraging involved, hedging the sale of a nonlinear-payoff option can be quite expensive because of the high

TABLE 2–12
Payoffs of the European-Style Nonlinear-Payoff Option

Type of Nonlinear-Payoff Option	*Payoff at Expiry Time* T
$C_E(X,0,T,S_0)$	$-P^*_{T,C}$ if $f(S_T) < X$ $f(S_T)-X-P^*_{T,C}$ if $f(S_T) \geq X$
$P_E(X,0,T,S_0)$	$-P^*_{T,P}$ if $f(S_T) > X$ $X-f(S_T)-P^*_{T,P}$ if $f(S_T) \leq X$

where $C_E(X,0,T,S_0)$ and $P_E(X,0,T,S_0)$ represent the European call and put nonlinear payoff options when the strike rate is X, the current time is 0, the option maturity time is T, the current spot rate is S_0; $P^*_{T,C}$ and $P^*_{T,P}$ represent the call- and the put-option premiums that are future valued to time T.

gamma feature in the option. This hedging cost can be reduced by alternatively hedging a nonlinear-payoff option using a sequence of vanilla options of varying notional amounts that are struck at varying levels.

Nonlinear-payoff options can also be easily used for liability or risk management. More precisely, a client could have a nonlinear risk profile for the various interest-rate and foreign-exchange levels due to their total borrowing costs and exchange-rate risks. A perfect hedge for the client would be to buy a nonlinear-payoff option that replicates his nonlinear risk-profile.

Product Options

A Canadian investor observes the current values of the S&P 100 and TSE 100 indices to be 350 and 280, respectively. Based on the historical numbers, the investor notices that the current spread between these yields is relatively small as compared to the historical values of this difference, which she feels will widen in a week. To monetize her view, she wants to buy an instrument that allows her to achieve her objective without being exposed to the currency risk. More precisely, she wants her payoff to be strictly the product of the notional amount of the contract and the difference in the indices if she is right. The instrument that she actually needs is called a quanto-spread option. To understand a quanto-spread option better, we will have to first discuss a simple quanto option. A quanto option, also known as a guaranteed-exchange-rate option, is a member of the product-option family, which allows the buyer to pay an initial upfront premium in domestic currency for an option that trades in a foreign country and receive the payoff at a guaranteed exchange rate. The mechanics associated with a simple quanto-option transaction are best illustrated by the following example:

Time 0 wk: The current S&P 100 is trading at 350. A Canadian investor has a view that this value will be higher in a week. To monetize her view, she wants to buy an option that will pay her the difference between the S&P 100 index in a week and 350 if she is right. However, she, wants to pay the premium and receive her payoff, if she is in-the-money, in Canadian funds and does not want to be exposed to the currency risk.

Time 1 wk: *Case 1.* The S&P 100 index is trading at a level of 430. The option finishes in-the-money, and the payoff to the buyer in Canadian dollars is [Notional Principal * (430 − 350)] $-P^{*}_{1wk,\ CII}$, where $-P^{*}_{1wk,\ CII}$ represents the premium in Canadian dollars of the quanto option future valued to one week.

Case 2. The S&P 100 index is trading at a level of 345. The option finishes out-of-the-money and the investor has lost the premium paid out at the inception of the contract.

It is important to note in the above example that although the investor did not have to undergo any currency exposure, the investor had implicitly bought an option guaranteeing her an exchange rate of Can$1.00/ U.S.$1.00. Furthermore, it is just as easy to structure an instrument where the investor receives her payoff, if she is in-the-money, at any other guaranteed exchange rate or the exchange rate realized on the option maturity date. The payoffs for the product-options family can be more generally written as in Table 2–13.

Quanto options, which are the category II options shown in Table 2–13, are usually priced like their vanilla counterparts with adjustments made to the drift term. As in the basket, spread, and extrema options, correlation is a necessary input for valuing quanto options. In our example, this will be the correlation between the S&P 100 index and the exchange rate. However, the effect of the correlation in the price of a quanto option is smaller than the contribution of the correlation component to the price of a spread option. Although both European-style and the American-style quanto options can be priced using the binomial method, Reiner (1992) and Wei (1995) have provided analytical

TABLE 2–13

Payoffs of the European-Style Product Option

Type of Product Option	*Payoff at Expiry Time* T
$C_{E,\ I}(X,0,T,S_0,F_0)$	$\max\{-P^*_{T,\ CI},(S_T - X)F_T - P^*_{T,\ CI}]$
$P_{E,\ I}(X,0,T,S_0,F_0)$	$\max[-P^*_{T,\ PI},(X - S_T)F_T - P^*_{T,\ PI}]$
$C_{E,\ II}(X,0,T,S_0,F_{0,F})$	$\max[-P^*_{T,\ CII},(S_T - X)F - P^*_{T,\ CII}]$
$P_{E,\ II}(X,0,T,S_0,F_{0,F})$	$\max[-P^*_{T,\ PII},(X - S_T)F - P^*_{T,\ PII}]$
$C_{E,\ III}(X,0,T,S_0,F_{0,F})$	$\max[-P^*_{T,\ CIII},S_TF - XF_T - P^*_{T,\ CIII}]$
$P_{E,\ III}(X,0,T,S_0,F_{0,F})$	$\max[P^*_{T,\ PIII},XF_T - S_TF - P^*_{T,\ PIII}]$
$C_{E,\ IV}(X,0,T,S_0,F_{0,F})$	$\max[-P^*_{T,\ CIV},S_TF_T - XF - P^*_{T,\ CIV}]$
$P_{E,\ IV}(X,0,T,S_0F_{0,F})$	$\max[-P^*_{T,\ PIV},XF - S_TF_T - P^*_{T,\ PIV}]$
$C_{E,\ V}(X,0,T,S_0,F_0)$	$\max[-P^*_{T,\ CV},(F_T - X)S_T - P^*_{T,\ CV}]$
$P_{E,\ V}(X,0,T,S_0,F_0)$	$\max[-P^*_{T,\ PV},(X - F_T)S_T - P^*_{T,\ PV}]$

where $C_{E,\ I}(X,0,T,S_0,F_0)$, $C_{E,\ II}(X,0,T,S_0,F_{0,F})$, $C_{E,\ III}(X,0,T,S_0,F_{0,F})$, $C_{E,\ IV}(X,0,T,S_0,F_{0,F})$, and $C_{E,\ V}(X,0,T,S_0,F_0)$ represent the European-style category I, II, III, IV, and V call options respectively and $P_{E,\ I}(X,0,T,S_0,F_0)$, $P_{E,\ II}(X,0,T,S_0,F_{0,F})$, $P_{E,\ III}(X,0,T,S_0,F_{0,F})$, $P_{E,\ IV}(X,0,T,S_0,F_{0,F})$, and $P_{E,\ V}(X,0,T,S_0,F_0)$ represent the European-style category I, II, III, IV, and V put options respectively when the strike rate is X, the current time is 0, the option maturity time is T, the current foreign-asset value is S_0, the current (guaranteed) exchange rate expressed as the value of one unit of foreign currency in domestic dollars is F_0 $(_F)$, $P^*_{T,\ Ci}$ *and* $P^*_{T,\ Pi}$ represent the premium of the category i call and put option respectively that is future valued to time T; where $i = 1, 2, \ldots, 5$.

expressions for pricing the payoffs of the product options given in Table 2–13. Depending on the category, the hedging of certain product-options can be quite complicated. Despite this, hedging any product option would imply hedging both the foreign asset and the currency risk. The static hedge parameters for all the categories have been given in Wei (1995).

As mentioned in the introduction, quanto-spread options can easily be used by asset managers to help monetize views on relative movements between two different environments without being exposed to currency risk. Due to the nature of the assets and liabilities in different environments, liability managers can also exploit the cheap borrowing cost in one environment (for example, the United States) to fund the activities in the other environment (for example, Canada) by using a differential swap to swap from a BA to a LIBOR plus some spread without undergoing any currency risk or exchange of principal.

Quanto structures can also be easily embedded into binary options and presented as structured notes. For example, a Canadian investor could buy a six-month note with a coupon that pays a fraction of 5 percent, where this fraction represents the proportion of business days in the six-month period during which the three-month LIBOR exceeds a level of 3.5 percent, where all the transactions are carried out in Canadian funds. One can similarly structure a binary note where the fraction instead depends on the proportion of business days in the life of the note during which the three-month BA exceeds the three-month LIBOR by 50 basis points.

Shout Options

A shout option is a hybrid of a European-style lookback option and American-style vanilla option. To understand how a shout option works, it is useful to first revisit the payoffs of a European-style vanilla option, lookback option, and modified lookback option. A European-style vanilla call-option on a currency gives the buyer of the contract, on the expiry date of the option, an exchange-rate payoff that is the maximum of zero and the difference between the spot exchange-rate at the expiry date and the strike rate. The buyer of a European-style lookback call option has a payoff on the option expiry date that is the greater of zero and the difference between the spot rate at the option maturity date and the lowest exchange rate achieved by the currency during the life of the option. The buyer of a European-style modified lookback call-option has a payoff on the expiry date of the option that is the maximum of zero and the difference between the highest exchange rate achieved by the currency during the life of the option and a predefined strike rate. The payoffs corresponding to the above options are shown in Table 2–14.

Unlike the above options, a shout option gives the buyer a payoff at maturity date that is the maximum of zero and the difference between the spot rate at the maturity date and the minimum of the spot rate at both the maturity date and the time of shout. The nature of this payoff is best illustrated by the following example:

Time 0 wk: The Canadian dollar is currently trading at Can$1.35/U.S.$1.00. Due to an expected currency exposure in one month's time, a client wants to be protected against a weakening U.S. dollar. At the same time, the client wants to be able to lock in the best rate that the Canadian dollar might achieve during the life of the option. The cost incurred in

TABLE 2–14
Payoffs of the European-Style Call Option

Type of European Call-Option	*Payoff at Expiry Time* T
vanilla	$\max[-P^*_{T,\,C}, S_T - X - P^*_{T,\,C}]$
lookback	$\max[-P^*_{T,\,CLo}, S_T - \min S_{t_i} - P^*_{T,\,CLo}]$
modified lookback	$\max[-P^*_{T,\,CMLo}, \max S_{t_i} - X - P^*_{T,\,CMLo}]$

where $P^*_{T,\,C}$, $P^*_{T,\,CLo}$, and $P^*_{T,\,CMLo}$ represent the premiums of the European-style vanilla, lookback, and modified lookback call-options that are future valued to time T; T denotes the expiry time of the option, X denotes the strike rate of the option; S_{t_i} denotes the spot rate at time t_i; where $i = 1, 2, \ldots, n$; $t_0 = 0$, $t_n = T$.

buying a lookback put-option on the U.S. dollar is quite high. The client feels that because he is good at calling the markets, he is not prepared to pay for an option that guarantees him a maximum payoff. However, he would not mind paying a lesser premium for a European-style shout put option on the U.S. dollar that matures in a month, with which he could possibly achieve the same payoff as the lookback option.

Time 1 wk: Currency is now trading at Can\$1.30/U.S.\$1.00. This has been the weakest U.S. level in the past week. The option holder feels that it is very unlikely that the U.S. dollar will weaken any further and as such calls up the seller of the option to "shout" at the current level of Can\$1.30/U.S.\$1.00.

Time 1 mo: *Case 1.* The Canadian dollar is now trading at Can\$1.34/U.S.\$1.00. Since the min [1.34,1.30] Can/U.S. = 1.30 Can/U.S., the option finishes in-the-money and the payoff to the buyer of the option is the $(1.34 - 1.30 - P^*_{1mo,\,CSh})$ Can/U.S., where $P^*_{1mo,\,CSh}$ represents the premium of the option future valued to time of one month, while 1.34 and 1.30 represent the spot rate at maturity and the shout rate, respectively.

Case 2. Currency is now trading at Can\$1.28/U.S.\$1.00. Since the min [1.28,1.30] Can/U.S. = Can\$1.28/U.S.\$1.00, the option finishes out-of-the-money and the client loses his option premium.

FIGURE 2–9
European-Style Call-Option Premiums

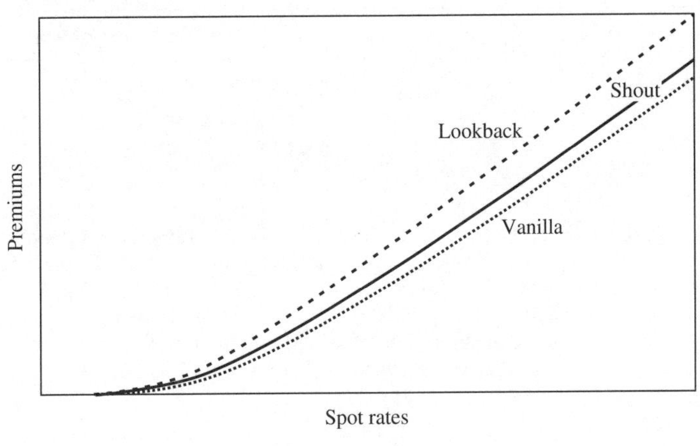

From the example above, it should first be noted that in illustrating the payoffs at option maturity (i.e., one month) it was assumed that there was an opportunity for the owner of the option to shout. Ignoring the option premium paid at time 0, if the buyer had shouted at a level that was the strongest level of the Canadian dollar during the life of the option, the payoff to the buyer would be similar to that of a lookback option. On the other hand, if the shout had been made at a level that turns out to be equal to or lesser than the spot rate at maturity, the payoff would be equal to zero. Because the shout level can either be greater than or lesser than the spot rate at maturity, it readily follows that the premium of a shout option should be no larger than that of a lookback option.

Second, like the lookback option, the shout option is not really an option because of the nonnegative nature of its payoff. By prespecifying a strike rate, however, the nonnegativity is removed and the modified shout option behaves like an option, where the premium of a modified shout option will be no lesser than the premium of a vanilla option that is struck at the same level and no greater than the premium of a modified lookback option that is also struck at the same level. Figure 2–9 illustrates the difference in premiums between a European-style vanilla call-option and the European-style modified versions of a lookback and shout call-options when the strike rates and option maturity times are identical.

TABLE 2–15

Payoffs of the European-Style Shout Option

Type of Shout Option	*Payoff at Expiry Time* T
$C_{E,F}(0,T,S_0)$	$\max[-P^*_{T,CSh}, S_T-\min[S^*,S_T]-P^*_{T,CSh}]$
$P_{E,F}(0,T,S_0)$	$\max[-P^*_{T,PSh}, \max[S^*,S_T]-S_T-P^*_{T,PSh}]$
$C_{E,M}(X,0,T,S_0)$	$\max[-P^*_{T,CMSh}, \max[S^*,S_T]-X-P^*_{T,CMSh}]$
$P_{E,M}(X,0,T,S_0)$	$\max[-P^*_{T,PMSh}, X-\min[S^*,S_T]-P^*_{T,PMSh}]$

where S^* represents the exchange rate at which the buyer of the option shouted; $P^*_{T,CSh}$, $P^*_{T,PSh}$, $P^*_{T,CMSh}$, and $P^*_{T,PMSh}$ represent the premiums of a call, put, modified call, and modified put shout options that are future valued to time T; $C_{E,F}(0,T,S_0)$, $P_{E,F}(0,T,S_0)$, $C_{E,M}(X,0,T,S_0)$, and $P_{E,M}(X,0,T,S_0)$ represent the European-style call shout, put shout, modified call shout, and modified put shout options respectively when X is the strike rate of the option, 0 is the current time, T is the time of option maturity, and S_0 is the current spot rate.

The payoffs of the shout options can be more generally written as shown in Table 2–15.

Although the buyer of a modified shout option can theoretically shout at any level that the exchange rate realizes during the life of the option, it is rational for the buyer to consider shouting only if the intrinsic value of the option is greater than zero. More precisely, it is rational for the buyer to shout at any time during the life of the option if the expected value of the option obtained by shouting is greater than the expected value of the option that can be obtained without shouting. It is crucial to note that this is analogous to the exercising of a vanilla American-style option. Although there is no notion of intrinsic value when dealing with a regular shout option, the buyer of such an option would again shout only at any given time if the expected value due to shouting at that time is greater than what he would get by not shouting. The shout option can be most easily valued using the binomial method and incorporating this rational behavior of shouting. See Thomas (1993) for the use of a binomial method to value a shout option.

Unlike the lookback option, which tends to be expensive, the shout option is cheaper and has the ability to give the buyer (typically an asset manager who is paid for his or her market-calling abilities) the same payoff if the market is called correctly. This was illustrated in

Figure 2–9. Thus, a shout option serves as a useful and inexpensive yield-enhancement tool with a limited downside for someone who is good at predicting market movements. Because of its value, the shout option can also be used effectively for liability management by managers who are good at predicting market movements. For example, a liability manager could pay a fixed rate on a five-year swap and receive a six-month LIBOR. If his view over the next two months is that the five-year swap rate cannot get any higher, he could embed a shout option in his trade and end up with the following transaction.

The liability manager pays a fixed rate on a five-year swap with the fixed rate being determined at the end of two months by setting it to the max [five-year swap rate at time of shout, five-year swap rate at the end of two months] if his counterparty decides to shout. If no shout has been made, the counterparty receives a fixed rate given by the five-year swap rate at the end of two months. In return, he receives a floating rate of (six-month LIBOR + spread) on every reset date.

Other variations of the uses of the shout options for liability management are also possible.

Spread Options

Spread options are options that can be used to monetize a view on the relative movement between any two indices in the same economy. Suppose that a fund manager feels that the current yield differential of 100 basis points between the ten-year government bond and the two-year government bond is too narrow based on historical data and that this difference in yield will widen in a month. To monetize her view, as her first strategy, she could purchase the underlying bonds by going long and short the appropriate notional amount of the bonds. With this strategy, if she is wrong in a month's time, she has the potential for large losses when liquidating the position. Thus, the downside of replicating the spread using the underlying bonds can be costly and sometimes disastrous. See Ravindran (1995a) for a detailed discussion.

An alternative way to monetize her view would be to buy a spread option that pays at the end of one month the difference between the ten-year bond yield, the two-year bond yield, and an offset of 100 basis points if her view is right, and nothing if her view is wrong. More precisely, her payoff at the end of one month could be written as the max [0, ten-year yield − two-year yield − 0.01]. Clearly, if the market view was wrong, the only downside of this strategy is the loss of the premium that was paid at the inception of the contract.

The spread option can also be used to bet on the movement of the swap spreads (i.e., swap rate − bond yield). Suppose, for example, that an investor feels that based on current market conditions, the current three-year swap spread (i.e., the difference between the three-year swap rate and the three-year on-the-run bond yield) is 28 basis points and she thinks this will narrow in two months' time by at least 5 basis points. She could easily monetize her view by purchasing a spread option on the three-year swap spread with an offset of 23 basis points that expires in two months. At the maturity of the option, the investor gets a payoff that is the max [0.0023 − (three-year swap rate − three-year bond yield)]. The following sequence of events help illustrate this example better.

Time 0 mo: The current swap-spread is 28 basis points. The investor feels that in two months, the swap spread will narrow by at least 5 basis points. She pays a premium for a spread option on a $100 million notional amount with an offset of 23 basis points that allows her to monetize this view. Thus, for every basis point the option finishes in-the-money, the investor gets paid $10,000.

Time 2 mo: *Case 1.* The current swap-spread is 18 basis points. The option finishes in-the-money and the payoff to the buyer of the option is $100 million * (0.0023 − 0.0018) − $P^*_{2mo,\,CSp}$, where $P^*_{2mo,\,CSp}$ represents the premium of the spread option future valued to two months.

Case 2. The current swap-spread is 35 basis points. The option finishes out-of-the money. Hence, the investor loses her premium.

It is important to note that although the above two examples illustrate the use of European-style spread options, we can just as well structure an American-style spread option where the buyer of the option is allowed to exercise at any time during the life of the option. Like the above two examples, a spread option can easily be created to monetize a leveraged view on any part of the same yield curve. Table 2–16 shows a generalized payoff structure for a spread option.

The payoff function shown in Table 2–16 could be written more generally as max [0,(a^*Yield$_1$) + (b^*Yield$_2$) + c], where a, b and c are any three real numbers and Yield$_1$ and Yield$_2$ represent the values of the two

TABLE 2–16
Payoffs of the European-Style Spread Option

Type of Spread Option	*Payoff at Expiry Time* T
$C_E(a,b,c,0,T,S_{10},S_{20})$	$-P^*_{T,\,CSp}$ *if* $aS_{1T}+bS_{2T} < c$ $aS_{1T}+bS_{2T}-c-P^*_{T,\,CSp}$ *if* $aS_{1T}+bS_{2T} \geq c$
$P_E(a,b,c,0,T,S_{10},S_{20})$	$-P^*_{T,\,PSp}$ *if* $aS_{1T}+bS_{2T} > c$ $c-aS_{1T}-bS_{2T}-P^*_{T,\,PSp}$ *if* $aS_{1T}+bS_{2T} \leq c$

where $C_E(a,b,c,0,T,S_{10},S_{20})$ and $P_E(a,b,c,0,T,S_{10},S_{20})$ represent the European call and put spread-options respectively when the current time is *0*, the option maturity time is *T*, *a* and *b* are any two real numbers, *c* is a positive real number, and the current spot rates are S_{10} and S_{20}; $P^*_{T,\,CSp}$ and $P^*_{T,\,PSp}$ represent the premiums of the call and put spread-options that are future valued to time *T*.

underlying variables describing the option. These variables can represent the two different swap rates or bond yields or one of each on the same yield-curve environment.

Although closed-form solutions do exist, due to Margrabe (1978), when *c* (called the offset in the spread option) is zero and the two underlying assets are non-dividend-paying stocks, the spread option has to be generally evaluated numerically. (See Ravindran [1993] for an intuitive approach to spread-option pricing.) In addition to the volatilities of both the variables, the correlation between these variables is also an extremely important input into the price. Unlike volatilities, which can easily be traded, there is no market for correlation trading. Thus, the only means of getting a good estimate for the correlation number would be to use the historical data. Hence, correlation estimation is very crucial to the pricing of a spread option. Like a vanilla option, the spread option can also be hedged using the delta-hedging technique on each of the variables.

As mentioned earlier, when the offset *c* is zero, the spread option, also known as an exchange option, was first valued by Margrabe (1978). The pricing formulae of Margrabe can be extended to encompass dividend paying assets. This is given in Hull (1993). It is important to note that both Magrabe's and Hull's results do not contain the risk-free rate parameter. An intuitive explanation for this is given in the discussion portion of Gerber and Shiu (1994) by Kolkiewicz and Ravindran (1994).

Sudden Birth/Death Options

When valuing any option, a fundamental input to the Black-Scholes equation is the life of the option, which has traditionally been assumed to be a known constant that is prespecified at the inception of the contract. An option that violates this assumption by allowing the maturity date to be a random variable is called a sudden birth/death option. Although the class of sudden birth/death options may at the first glance appear to be somewhat impractical, on careful examination it can be seen that variations on the sudden birth/death theme have been and will continue to be widely used. An example of a sudden-death option that has been and still is quite popular in the insurance industry is the guaranteed minimum death benefit (GMDB). Succinctly put, a GMDB is essentially a principal guaranteed note that is linked to some index (e.g.,TSE 35, S&P 500) and has an upside participation. The fundamental distinction between this note and any other structured note is the fact that a GMDB expires only at the time of the purchaser's death. The interested reader is referred to Bernard (1993), Gootzeit et al. (1994), Mitchell (1994), Mueller (1992), and Ravindran and Edelist (1995) for in-depth discussions on valuing GMDBs and variations on GMDBs.

Another variation of the sudden birth/death option that is widely used in the financial markets is the barrier option. Although vanilla options serve as good disaster insurance, prevailing market conditions sometimes make such insurance costly. In these circumstances, the premium can be effectively reduced by using barrier options. A barrier option, alternatively known as a trigger or a knock-in/knock-out option, is an option that serves as a conditional insurance that may suddenly come into effect (or cease to exist) upon the occurrence of an event. Although the investor pays a premium for such an instrument at the inception of the contract, the option would come into existence (or cease to exist) only if a prespecified barrier or level is triggered during the life of the option. The following example better illustrates the use of a barrier option in practice:

Time 0 mo: The Canadian dollar is currently trading at Can$1.33/U.S.$1.00. Because of expected currency exposure in one month, the client is worried about the U.S. dollar weakening below the Can$1.31/U.S.$1.00 level. Buying a one-month put option on the U.S. dollar with a strike rate of Can$1.31/U.S.$1.00 would be an ideal solution. Current market conditions, however, make this insurance costly. To overcome the cost, the put option can be purchased with an added feature that if the exchange rate during the life of the option exceeds a Can$1.36/U.S.$1.00 barrier, the put option would cease to exist. Presumably, if the U.S. dollar can strengthen to a level of Can$1.36/U.S.$1.00, it is unlikely to weaken below a level of Can$1.31/U.S.$1.00 by the time the option expires. This type of option, also called the up-and-out option (where the term "up" refers to the fact that the current spot level must transverse up toward the barrier, and the term "out" refers to the option being extinguished upon hitting the barrier), has a smaller premium than the vanilla option.

N.B.: The further the barrier is from the current exchange-rate level, the more expensive the up-and-out option. This is due to the fact that the probability of the option extinguishing diminishes as the level of the barrier is raised.

Case 1: Barrier Is Not Breached During the One-Month Period.
Because the exchange rate has not exceeded or gone beyond the 1.36 barrier level, the put option is still alive. Thus,

Time 1 mo: *Case 1a.* Currency is now trading at a level of Can$1.32/U.S.$1.00. The option finishes out-of-the-money and the client has lost the premium paid at the inception of the contract.

Case 1b. U.S. dollar has now weakened to a level of Can$1.29/U.S.$1.00. The option finishes in-the-money and the payoff to the client is $(1.31 - 1.29 - P^*_{1mo,\,PO})$ Can/U.S., where $P^*_{1mo,\,PO}$ is the premium of the option future valued to one month.

Case 2: Barrier Is Breached During the One-Month Period.
Because the U.S. dollar has strengthened past Can$1.36/U.S.$1.00 (i.e., breached the barrier of 1.36) at some time during the one-month period, the put option gets extinguished and the client loses the premium.

Unlike a GMDB, which has a completely random time of expiry, the knock-out option that was discussed above has a random time of expiry for only one month. Thus, if the option does not get extinguished during the one-month period, it will be forced to mature at the end of the one-month time period. Although the above example illustrates the use of an up-and-out put option, it is not difficult to construct practical examples

TABLE 2–17
Payoffs of the European-Style Barrier Option

Type of Barrier Option	*Payoff at Expiry Time* T *if Barrier Is Breached*	*Payoff at Expiry Time* T *if Barrier Is Not Breached*
$C_{E,\,In}(X,H,0,T,S_0)$	$\max[-P^*_{T,\,CI}, S_T-X-P^*_{T,\,CI}]$	$-P^*_{T,\,CI}$
$C_{E,\,Out}(X,H,0,T,S_0)$	$-P^*_{T,\,CO}$	$\max[-P^*_{T,\,CO}, S_T-X-P^*_{T,\,CO}]$
$P_{E,\,In}(X,H,0,T,S_0)$	$\max[-P^*_{T,\,PI}, X-S_T-P^*_{T,\,PI}]$	$-P^*_{T,\,PI}$
$P_{E,\,Out}(X,H,0,T,S_0)$	$-P^*_{T,\,PO}$	$\max[-P^*_{T,\,PO}, X-S_T-P^*_{T,\,PO}]$

where $C_{E,\,In}(X,H,0,T,S_0)$, $C_{E,\,Out}(X,H,0,T,S_0)$, $P_{E,\,In}(X,H,0,T,S_0)$, and $P_{E,\,Out}(X,H,0,T,S_0)$ represent the European-style in-call, out-call, in-put, and out-put options respectively when the strike rate is X, the barrier level is H, the current time is *0*, the life of the option is T and the current spot rate is S_0; $P^*_{T,\,CI}$, $P^*_{T,\,CO}$, $P^*_{T,\,PI}$, and $P^*_{T,\,PO}$ represent the in-call, out-call, in-put, and out-put option premiums respectively that are future valued to time T; the terms "in" and "out" describe the coming alive and the dying respectively of an option upon breaching the barrier.

where the up-and-in, down-and-out, and down-and-in call and put options can be used effectively. The payoffs of all these barrier options can be written as detailed in Table 2–17.

It is important to note that each of the above four payoffs can be decomposed further into the up and down options depending on whether $S_0 < H$. Assuming a continuous trading market, the pricing formulae for the barrier options corresponding to the above payoffs have been given by Rubinstein and Reiner (1991). If a barrier option is bought on an underlying index that is trading in an illiquid market, the exact times of monitoring the breaching of the barrier by the index must be specified in the contract in advance. Furthermore, when the monitoring of the index is done at discrete times, no analytical expressions exist for the pricing of the barrier options and, as such, the prices can only be evaluated numerically. It can, however, be shown that the cost of a continuously monitored knock-out barrier option cannot be greater than the cost of a discretely monitored knock-out barrier option. The converse is true for the knock-in barrier options.

Although the barrier options are usually hedged using the classic delta-hedging methodology, the effect of gamma is very eminent in these options. To overcome this, a static hedging strategy that is philosophically motivated by the ability to replicate the payoff profile of a barrier option could be used. It should be noted that with the payoff structures

FIGURE 2–10
In, Out, and Vanilla Option-Premiums

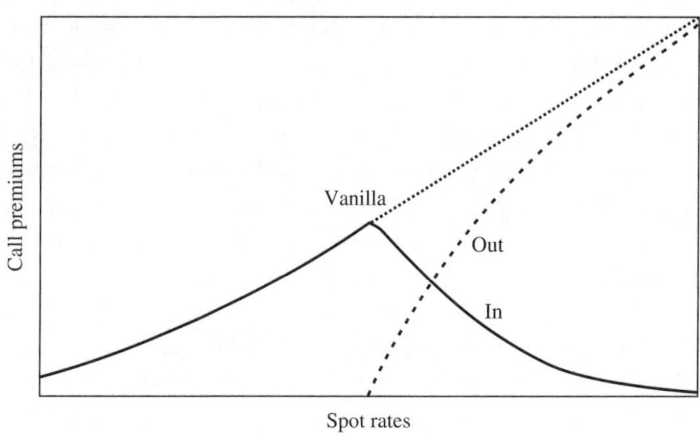

given in Table 2–17, going long a vanilla call-option is equivalent to going long an up-and-in and an up-and-out call option if $S_0 < H$ or going long a down-and-in and a down-and-out call option if $S_0 > H$ regardless of the barrier level, where we have implicitly assumed that all the options are struck at the same level and have the same time to maturity. Hence, we can conclude that the premium of any barrier option can never be greater than that of a corresponding vanilla option. Figure 2–10 illustrates this fact for a structurally similar vanilla call-option, an up-and-in call option, and an up-and-out call option.

An alternative solution that addresses the client's concerns about high option-premiums is an option with a knock-out feature set only on the expiry date. More precisely, instead of monitoring the breaching of the barrier during the life of the option, one can monitor this breaching on the option expiry date itself. Unlike the example discussed above, if we set a barrier level of Can$1.36/U.S.$1.00 at the expiry date, there is no cheapening effect from the use of a barrier. To have a cheapening effect, we have to set the barrier to a level that is less than Can$1.31/U.S.$1.00, which is the strike rate of the option. We could, for example, set a barrier of Can$1.10/U.S.$1.00 at the expiry date such that if the exchange rate at the end of one month is above Can$1.31/U.S.$1.00 or less than Can$1.10/U.S.$1.00, the option expires worthless and the client loses his premium. In the range Can$1.10/U.S.$1.00 Cad/U.S. to Can$1.31/U.S.$1.00, in addition to losing the premium, the client's payoff will be the difference between the strike rate and the exchange rate at maturity. It is important to note that this type of one-point barrier strategy amounts to the client giving up some of the upside due to the view that in the event the U.S. dollar weakens below Can$1.31/U.S.$1.00 in a month, it will never weaken below the Can$1.10/U.S.$1.00 level. It is important to note that this strategy is different from simply buying and selling vanilla European-style put options on the U.S. dollar at strike levels 1.31 and 1.10, respectively. One can similarly create an example where the client buys a vanilla call-option and gives away part of the upside.

One-point barrier options are also seen in the issues of the convertible/callable bonds and stock warrants where the issuer is forced to call (or convert) the bond (or warrant) if the price of the asset underlying the issue trades beyond/below a prespecified level on a certain date, which may not necessarily be the warrant maturity date. Single-barrier and dual-barrier options can also be very effectively used by technical analysis traders to monetize their market views.

CONCLUSION

To methodologically understand the dynamics, the uses, and the explosion of exotic options, it is important to first identify the basic blocks of the exotic options. Due to the fact that a cutting-edge product can quickly become outdated, it makes more sense to understand philosophically these basic ingredients of exotic options rather than trying to cover all the products on the market. By presenting a building-block approach to exotic options in this chapter, we have provided the ammunition to do just that. Any individual can use these building blocks as a platform to better understand and decompose complex option structures. With minor modifications, this platform can also be effectively used to understand complex derivative structures that are currently available in the marketplace. It is our hope that the building-block approach will remove the mystery and fear of nontraditional derivatives, resulting in more participants in both the over-the-counter and exchange-traded markets.

REFERENCES

Bernard, G. A. (1993), *A Direct Approach to Pricing Death Benefit Guarantees in Variable Annuity Products.* Product Development News (June), Society of Actuaries.

Boyle, P. P., and Y. K. Tse (1990), "An Algorithm for Computing Values of Options on the Maximum or Minimum of Several Assets," *Journal Of Financial And Quantitative Analysis*, 25, 2, 215–227.

Conze, A., and R. Viswanathan (1991), "Path Dependent Options: The Case of Lookback Options," *Journal Of Finance,* XXVI, 1111–1127.

Das, S. (1995), "Range Floaters," *Handbook Of Derivative Instruments,* 2d ed. (Chicago: Probus Publishing).

Garman, M. (1989), "Recollection in Tranquility," *Risk,* (March).

Geske, R. (1979), "The Valuation of Compound Options," *Journal of Financial Economics,* 7, 63–81.

Goldman, M. B., H. B. Sosin, and M. A. Gatto (1979), "Path Dependent Options: Buy at the Low, Sell at the High," *Journal of Finance,* XXXIV, 5, 1111–1127.

Gootzeit, A., D. Knowling, P. Schuster, and S. Sonlin (1994), "Guaranteed Minimum Death Benefit Provisions—How Much Variable Annuity Risk Do We Want?" *Product Development News,* (June). Society of Actuaries.

Hull, J. (1993), "Options, Futures, and Other Derivative Securities," 2d ed. (Englewood Cliffs, NJ: Prentice Hall).

Huynh, C. B. (1994), "Back to Baskets," *Risk,* (May), 59–61.

Kemna, A.G.Z., and A.C.F. Vorst (1990), "A Pricing Method for Options Based on Average Asset Values," *The Journal Of Banking And Finance,* 14, 113–129.

Kolkiewicz, A., and K. Ravindran (1995), *Option Pricing by Esscher Transforms by Gerber, H. U., and Shiu, E.S.W.* Transactions of the Society of Actuaries. Discussion. To appear.

Levy, E. (1992), "Pricing European Average Rate Currency Options," *Journal of International Money and Finance,* 11, 474–491.

Margrabe, W. (1978), "The Value of an Option to Exchange One Asset for Another," *Journal Of Finance,* XXXIII, 1, 177–186.

Mitchell, G. T., "Variable Annuity Minimum Death Benefits—A Monte Carlo Pricing Approach," *Product Development News* (February), Society of Actuaries.

Mueller, H. (1992), "Update on Variable Products," *Product Development News* (July), Society Of Actuaries.

Ravindran, K. (1993), "Option Pricing: An Offspring of the Secretary Problem?" *Mathematicae Japonica,* 38, 905–912.

Ravindran, K. (1993), "Low-Fat Spreads," *Risk* (October).

Ravindran, K. (1993), "LIBOR Binary Notes," *Derivatives Week* (December 6).

Ravindran, K., and A. W. Edelist (1995), "Deriving Benefits from Death," *Handbook Of Derivative Instruments,* 2d ed. (Chicago: Probus Publishing).

Ravindran, K. (1995a), "Effectively Riding the Yield Curve," *Journal of Derivatives Use, Trading and Regulation,* 1, 2. To appear.

Ravindran, K. (1995b), "Effectively Hedging a Currency Exposure," *Journal of Derivatives Use, Trading and Regulation,* 1, 3. 93-103.

Reiner, E. (1992), "Quanto Mechanics," *Risk* (March).

Rubinstein, M. (1991), "Options for the Undecided," *Risk* (April).

Rubinstein, M. (1991), "Somewhere over the Rainbow," *Risk* (November).

Rubinstein, M. (1991), "Double Trouble," *Risk* (December–January), 73.

Rubinstein, M., and E. Reiner (1991), "Breaking Down the Barriers," *Risk* (September).

Stulz, R. (1982), "Options on the Minimum or Maximum of Two Risky Assets, Analysis and Applications," *Journal Of Financial Economics*, 10, 161–185.

Thomas, B. (1993), "Something to Shout About," *Risk* (May), 56–58.

Wei, J. (1995), "Valuing Derivatives Linked to Foreign Assets," *Handbook Of Derivative Instruments,* 2d ed. (Chicago: Probus Publishing). To appear.

Chapter Three

When to Use Exotic Derivatives*

David C. Shimko
Vice President
J.P. Morgan, Inc.

INTRODUCTION: EXOTIC DERIVATIVES OR CUSTOMIZED RISK MANAGEMENT?

The unfortunate term "exotic" once described exotic derivatives well. Wall Street researchers and finance academics seemed to invent new products in continuous time. Products like knock-out caps and lookback swaptions captured the imagination of Wall Street firms and their clients, and often provided the best solution to risk-management problems. Some clients were eager to experiment with these new instruments. Traders were fascinated by the business possibilities for exotics and plagued by mathematical and hedging difficulties. It seemed that as soon as one set of instruments had been understood and implemented, a newer and more exotic set would arrive fast on its heels.

Derivatives markets have since changed. Some market participants fear the potential losses from derivatives that they don't understand and exotics that they can't fathom. They have retreated from some derivatives, rightly arguing that "exotics for the sake of being exotic" is an

*The views expressed in this chapter are the express views of the author, and do not necessarily correspond to the views of J.P. Morgan, Inc., or any of its subsidiaries. Cases discussed in this chapter have been dramatically simplified in order to be instructive, and do not reflect any judgment on the actions of derivatives managers, derivatives marketers, or regulators. Finally, the examples used do not necessarily reflect any actual transactions completed, and any connection of the situations herein to actual client situations is completely unwarranted.

indulgence of the past, not to be tolerated in the future. Exotic "toys" were fun when they were new, but now they can be seen as a diversion whose time has passed.

It is unfortunate that many have come to this conclusion. In this chapter, we argue that opponents of the use of exotic instruments may not completely understand the exotics context. Of course, some users have abused exotics, but many more have used exotics properly. Exotic derivative products serve two extremely important purposes. First, exotics help those with naturally complex risk exposures convert their exposures into something more simple and manageable. Second, exotics help those who need to create precise exposures to create those exposures more efficiently. In our understanding, the term "exotic" might better be replaced with the word "custom."

Clearly, the term "custom" suggests that custom derivative products are not intended for all participants in derivatives markets. Many find their risk-management needs adequately served by exchange-traded futures and option markets. The exchanges are wholesale markets where standardized short-term risk-management instruments trade. Wholesale markets are best for price-sensitive consumers who are willing to settle for products (futures and options) that may not fit their exposures exactly. The retail over-the-counter market addresses consumers' needs specifically. When a dealer sells an OTC product to a client and hedges its exposure on the exchange, it is in fact converting a wholesale exposure into a retail exposure. The dealer adds value if it provides a service to the client that (1) the client values and (2) is not available in the wholesale market. When the product is customized or exotic, at least (2) is satisfied. It can also be the case that the client is receiving exactly the exposure it desires either to offset a complex exposure it already holds or to create a new and precisely tailored exposure that fits its views perfectly. Under these conditions, (1) is satisfied as well, and the transaction adds value for both the customer and the dealer.

In this chapter, we explain several cases where the customization of a risk exposure suggests the use of an exotic derivative product. This is not an exhaustive set of cases, merely a set of examples to help derivatives professionals structure better products, and for others to understand the process by which custom transactions are tailored. But before we discuss the question of when to use derivatives, it may be prudent to first cover a number of cases when users should not enter exotic derivative positions.

WHEN *NOT TO USE EXOTIC DERIVATIVES: A CHECK LIST*

Do not use exotic derivatives (or any derivative) until

- You can understand and explain the risks of the instrument to others responsible for the transaction.
- Your understanding of the risks extends beyond deltas and gammas (which show instrument sensitivity for small changes in the underlying instrument) to the full range of possible market events.
- You convince yourself that the exotic derivative in the context of your portfolio moves you closer to your exposure goal, whether your goal is to be perfectly hedged or precisely exposed.
- You have fully considered tax treatment and accounting for the exotic transaction.
- You perform simulations to determine how much you could lose in the transaction.
- You have made provisions for the possibility of losses.
- You prepare beforehand for the range of possible outcomes and responses.
- When possible, you consider incorporating your optimal trading response into the derivative instrument.[1]
- You verify that the extra benefits exceed the costs of establishing and monitoring an exotic position.

This is a partial list of personal responsibilities in using exotic derivatives. The Group of 30 study goes further in establishing reporting guidelines, systems guidelines, and other issues. The Group of 30 study is strongly recommended for all participants in derivatives markets.[2]

Derivatives can be highly levered, and can cause damage if misused. Derivatives are like electricity—they perform an extremely valuable role when applied to the right purposes, but if they are applied incorrectly or in the wrong circumstances, the results can be shocking.

---

[1]For example, if you know you will reverse the position when the primary instrument reaches a predetermined level, structure the custom instrument to knock out (cease protection) at that level, rather than allowing the transaction to take place at an unsuitable price. Of course, the other side of the coin is to make sure your coverage does not knock out when you want it to continue.

[2]The full name of the G-30 study is *Derivatives: Practices and Principles,* published by the Group of Thirty, Washington, DC, July 1993.

Keeping the potential dangers in mind, we may now feel safe to explore and understand the conditions under which exotic derivative transactions are not only appropriate, but recommended.

WHEN TO USE EXOTIC DERIVATIVES: PROGRESSIVE CASE STUDY #A1

The Gold Producer

In this case study, we show how a gold producer might consider selling production forward (forward/futures contracts), selling call options on gold, selling knock-in call options, and purchasing credit derivatives in an attempt to get the best possible hedge for a gold mine.

Assumptions

We-R-Golden (WRG), a hypothetical gold producer, operates a gold mine in the Arizona desert. The marginal extraction cost for gold is $325 per ounce on this site, and the mine is expected to produce 100,000 ounces of gold per year for the next five years. There are no costs or risks other than those presented. The spot price of gold (i.e., the price of an ounce of physical gold) is $375 per ounce. For simplicity, we assume the forward prices of gold are also $375 at all maturities.[3]

Question

Assuming WRG wants the best possible hedge, how can it best achieve that hedge? The best possible hedge is defined to be one that minimizes the total variability of WRG's cash flows.

Answer #1

Conventional wisdom would have it that WRG should hedge by selling its gold production forward for the next five years. By locking in a price today for its known output, the gold producer can minimize variability

[3]This assumption is not realistic; forward gold prices at the time of this writing are 5.5 percent per year higher than spot prices.

FIGURE 3–1
WRG Fixed/Floating Swap Deal

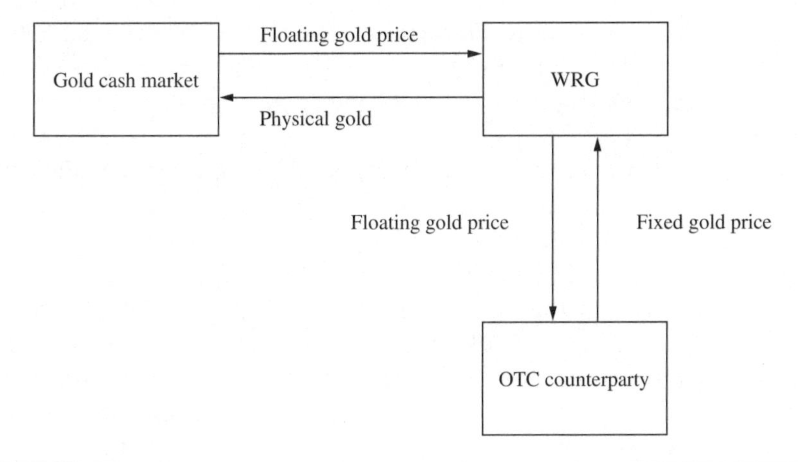

in its cash flows and accomplish the perfect hedge (of course we assumed that costs were known, and there was no risk of mining less than 100,000 ounces per year).

The well-known fixed/floating swap diagram in Figure 3–1 shows that although WRG is receiving floating gold payments, it passes these payments through to the OTC counterparty. The net impact of the swap is that WRG receives a fixed precontracted price for the delivery of physical gold.

Discussion

Answer #1 does not in fact provide the perfect hedge. For example, suppose that gold prices fall. The counterparty to the gold company may prefer to default on its contractual obligations rather than pay the contracted (and apparently inflated) price for gold. (This problem is similar to purchasing insurance and finding that the insurance company declares bankruptcy before your claim is processed.)

A second problem relates to the operating strategy of the gold producer. Suppose, for example, that gold prices fall to $300. If the producer can stop producing, it may find it in its best interest to close the mine, at least temporarily. Since we assumed there are no other costs in this example, we conclude that the producer will close the mine when prices are below $325, and open the mine when prices are above $325. While our simplifying assumption abstracts somewhat from the true complexity of this problem, the setup suggests an important derivatives structuring problem: tailoring operating flexibility (or options) to financial options.

Of course, instead of tailoring the derivatives transaction, the producer could continue to maintain its short positions at high prices, stop producing, and enjoy the profits on the financial side of its hedge transaction. If it closes the mine when gold is below $325, it continues to get cash payments from the swap counterparty of at least $50 per ounce without incurring the costs of operating the mine. In addition, the producer has not lost the gold in the ground, but has merely pushed the production schedule forward to a time when it may be profitable to mine again. But equally important, if gold prices never rise above $325, the producer will have made the correct decision not to incur the gold-extraction costs.

Answer #2

These complications lead us to a second possible answer that takes into account the operating risk of the gold mine. In particular, if we assume the mine is open when the price of gold exceeds $325, and closed when the price is less than $325, in each period, the cash flow without hedging is

Max(Gold price − marginal cost, 0)

In other words, in every decision period, the gold producer can choose whether or nor to produce. If it decides to produce, its profit is guaranteed positive at (Gold − 325) per ounce. If it decides not to produce, its profitability is zero. Therefore, the producer does not really own gold, but a series of interconnected call options on gold. Its best hedge is to sell what it owns forward, which in this case is call options.

A better hedge, then, would be one that sells call options forward, at a volume of 100,000 ounces per year. Therefore, in years when the producer produces nothing, it receives the forward call-premium, and when it produces, it also receives the agreed-upon call premium. The intrinsic value of the option represents the price levels attainable by selling production forward, and the time value of the options represents the extra optionality the producer has been able to capture. In other words, when the producer sells call options, it converts physical mining optionality into cash. Of course, this eliminates the windfall gains it might have experienced with Answer #1. Yet, it has succeeded in reducing cash flow volatility, and this is a better hedge.

Discussion

Clearly, Answer #2 solves some of the optionality problem, but not all of it. If production is deferred, the gold may eventually be mined if prices are high enough to support it. Therefore, while production is hedged out to five years, the operating life of the mine will be longer than five years if some production is deferred as a result of low prices.

Answer #3

A better hedge than Answer #2 would be an extendable option sale, where the producer has the option of extending the terms of its option sales to cover its actual production schedule, even if after five years. However, instead of the option being exercised optimally by the producer, the option should be structured so as to trigger the extension each time the gold price dips below $325 per ounce. In the world of exotic derivatives, this instrument is a knock-in call option. That is, when the gold price is less than $325, two things happen:

- The option on that year's production expires worthless.
- A new option is sold by the producer under the original terms, but in the year following the termination of the contract.

This binary structure is complicated by the fact that it is path-dependent. The timing of the reinstated call option depends on the number of times gold has dipped below $325 per ounce. The more dips, the longer the extension.

Discussion

Answer #3 clearly moves closer to the best hedge. Under this structure, the producer receives a fixed revenue per period, but does not know for how many periods it will receive the revenue. Unfortunately, the single problem that remains is credit risk, or risk that the producer's OTC counterparty will fail to honor (or be unable to honor) the terms of the contract. This is particularly problematic since the counterparty theoretically has the greatest incentive to default when prices drop. This is precisely when the producer needs the most protection.

Without covering too much detail, suffice to say that progressive commercial and investment banks have already solved this problem by creating credit derivatives that guarantee counterparty performance in a swap transaction.

Finally, one could say that all of the proposed structures, even in their totality, cannot capture the full nature of the gold-mining business or its embedded optionality. For example, the corporation has a default option on the debt, a limited-liability option granted by the government, and many other options that we have assumed away for analytical convenience. Is there in fact a perfect hedge for the gold producer?

Answer #4

The answer is yes. The best possible hedge that protects the producer against all fluctuations in gold prices, operating policy, credit risk, default options, and limited-liability options is the following exotic-derivative strategy:

- Sell the mine.

This apparently simple financial transaction is in fact one of the most exotic derivatives structures imaginable. The best pricing experts on Wall Street would shudder to value an option of such complexity and to understand the exact contribution each of the hundreds of interlinking parts makes to value.

Answer #4 highlights a key hedging observation that can be seen in the sequence of answers offered. The best hedge is to sell what you have. Answer #1 sold gold, but a gold mine is more valuable than gold. In fact, the gold miner owns options on gold, which we proposed selling forward in Answer #2. Recognition of the exact nature of the physical optionality forced us to construct an exotic knock-in option structure to hedge the gold-mining risk in Answer #3. Yet, the exotic-derivatives transaction is closer to the physical market transaction of selling the mine than the simple forward gold sale. Subtlety in risk analysis often requires the design of structures deemed by casual observers to be exotic when in fact they are carefully tailored to corporate risks.

WHEN TO USE EXOTIC DERIVATIVES: PROGRESSIVE CASE STUDY #A2

The Refinery

In this case study, we show how a petroleum refiner might consider selling crack-spreads forward, selling call options on crack spreads, selling "better-of" call options on baskets, and selling synthetic storage options. In every case, the exotic instrument is designed to offset ordinary refining exposures.

Assumptions

A refinery transforms crude oil into gasoline, heating oil, and other products. Production amounts to 1 million barrels per month, and the refinery can optimize its production slate to maximize market value net of production costs. For example, other things being equal, as the price of gasoline rises relative to other fuel products, the refiner will switch to producing more gasoline. The refinery also has unused storage facilities, which could be opened in the future at a known cost. The refinery is somewhat cash-starved, and would like to use any strategy it can to add cash flow to the bottom line, including speculative position taking.

Question:

What is the best hedging strategy for the refinery?

Answer #1

Conventional wisdom would have it that for a refiner to hedge, it should sell the "crack spread" forward. The crack spread is the difference in value between a basket of refined products and crude oil. Therefore, selling the spread forward implies that the refiner should short the products and long the crude. Since the crude purchases take place before the product sales, the maturities of the long crude positions and the short product positions do not match exactly.

Discussion

This is a perfect hedging strategy for a refinery that is committed to production of a fixed product slate at a particular point in time. Unfortunately, it does not take account of the refiner's optionality in at least two ways. First, the refiner has the right to stop producing if the crack spread becomes too low. Second, the refiner has the ability to change product slates in response to changes in the relative value of the products.

Proponents of Answer #1 will generally agree that the refiner retains its production optionality even when it sells forward. For example, should the crack spread fall to very low values (so as to make it worthwhile to stop producing), the producer would find it in its interest to purchase the crack spread (buy products, sell crude) in order to meet any delivery obligations. In the absence of delivery obligations, the contracts could be offset to generate a profit immediately, or be untouched, allowing the producer to collect more revenue from shutting down than from operating.

For example, suppose the crack spread was sold forward at $3.00 per barrel, and the refiner ceases production if the crack spread falls to $1.50, the marginal production cost. By selling forward, the refiner locks in a constant net revenue of $3.00 − $1.50 = $1.50. If the crack spread falls to $1.00, the producer stops producing and earns $3.00 − $1.00 = $2.00 on its production. This is good for the producer in the sense that it has a higher net revenue whenever it stops producing, but in effect it has not hedged as well as it might have. It could have converted this contingent profitability to cash flows up front, which according to the assumptions is desperately needed. Therefore, Answer #1 is not the best hedging strategy for the refiner.

Answer #2

The refiner should sell call options on the crack spread, with a strike price equal to the marginal cost of production. In so doing, the refiner sells what it owns, namely the *right* to produce, which it will exercise when the crack spread exceeds the marginal cost of production. Because call options have time value in addition to their intrinsic value, the producer will earn more money up front by effectively capitalizing its production option.

Discussion

Answer #2 is better than #1 because it explicitly considers the value of the refiner's option to shut down, and brings it early cash flow, which it needs. However, suppose that relative product-prices make it profitable for the producer to switch refining slates. It can only benefit by doing so, since it always has the option of producing the current slate—it will only change its slate if it can do better. This is another form of optionality, which Answer #2 has not captured.

Answer #3

Answer #3 is the same as Answer #2, but the underlying crack-spread should be defined as the maximum crack-spread attainable within the feasible product slates. The payoff to the refiner's option is then effectively:

$$\text{Max}(\text{Slate 1} - \text{MC1}, \text{Slate2} - \text{MC2}, \ldots, 0)$$

where there are several different possible slates, each of which may have a different marginal cost (MC) of production. Slate 1 might be 70 percent gasoline and 30 percent heating oil, and Slate 2 might be 60 percent gasoline and 40 percent heating oil, for example.

Discussion

Answer #3 seems to capture most of the stated optionality, and as you can see, the structure might be considered quite exotic—a call option on the maximum difference between slate values and their respective marginal costs. But it does not address the issue of the unused storage facility, which we tackle in Answer #4.

Background information on storage: Storage is currently uneconomical, but it may be economical sometime in the future. The desirability of storing fuel increases as the slope of the forward curve increases. For example, if the October price of crude oil is $17.50, and the November price of crude oil is $18.00, and storage costs $0.25 per barrel per month (assuming no in-out charges), many market participants would like to use the storage between October and November.

Answer #4

Sell the storage forward in exchange for prepayments today to finance the improvements to the storage facility.

Discussion

This strategy is desirable in the sense that it generates cash for the refiner, which will be used for capital improvements and perhaps other investments. The problem with this strategy is that potential buyers of the storage will recognize that they may never use the storage, and will discount the price they will pay accordingly. A true economic loss results if the storage is improved and then never used.

Answer #5

Sell a call option on future storage, with the strike price equal to the cost of improvements plus cost of running the facility. The timing of exercise of the option must allow for the improvements to be made before storage is used.

Discussion

Answer #5 is preferable for the buyer of the option, since it provides the opportunity for storage when it is most valuable. From an economic perspective, the storage facility is built only when it has an economic value. The structure of the option was chosen to best mimic the real physical storage option the refiner owns.

SUMMARY OF CUSTOM DERIVATIVE STRATEGY: (A) COMPLEX TO SIMPLE EXPOSURE

Progressive studies A1 and A2 had several elements in common. In particular, each example begins with a complex exposure that is part of the natural course of doing business for a gold miner and a fuel refiner. The "options" that the producer holds are not seen as exotic; they simply arise as a result of optimal management of the assets of the companies. Indeed, much of microeconomic theory concentrates on value-maximizing strategies for firms—the choice of production levels, the choice of optimal investments, and the choice of operating leverage. The simple call option can also be likened to a value-maximizing strategy. Its value at maturity is

$$\mathrm{Max}(S - X, 0)$$

the maximum of the stock minus the strike or zero. The call option is exercised according to a simple value-maximizing strategy, but the operations of firms are clearly more complex. By tailoring exotic options to the actual physical optionality (i.e., profit-maximizing behavior) of firms, firms can better hedge their risks by having the opportunity to sell some of their options synthetically. This allows them to retain the upside for the things they cannot sell—managerial skill in controlling the costs of production and marketing.

The steps for hedging a complex exposure are the following:

- Construct a profile of the company starting from nothing.
- Determine the formula for net cash flow as accurately as possible, considering the firm's optimal behavior.
- Replicate the net-cash-flow formula as closely as possible, using the prices of traded instruments or other indices that may be used for hedging purposes.
- Restate the replication in terms of forward positions, option positions, and customized option positions. (This replication can be thought of as a synthetic version of the firm.)
- Sell the synthetic replicating package.

The resulting exposure does not depend in any way on market factors, except to the extent that the perfect customized hedge may not be attainable.

WHEN TO USE EXOTIC DERIVATIVES: PROGRESSIVE CASE STUDY #B1

In this section, we show that investors with precise views are better off using customized derivative instruments that correspond to their views rather than plain-vanilla products. We concentrate on the case of an investor who thinks a commodity firm (Nickelco) is an attractive investment, but finds the nickel exposure unappealing.

Assumptions

An investor wants to invest in Nickelco, but is worried that nickel prices will fall. Suppose, for example, that the management team can increase share prices by $1.00, but a drop in nickel prices will cause Nickelco shares to drop by $3.00. The shareholder, in spite of being right about management, will lose $2.00 by investing, and therefore decides not to invest.

Question

What can be done to help this investor structure her investment correctly?

Answer #1

The investor should determine the beta of Nickelco's shares with nickel futures contracts, and go short the appropriate number of futures contracts to offset the risk in Nickelco's equity. Then, if nickel prices drop, losses on the stock are covered by gains on the short nickel position.

Discussion

To a first approximation, this strategy works well as long as the holding period is less than the futures maturity. If the holding period is longer, some rolling of futures positions may be required, introducing possibly undesired elements of nickel curve risks. However, the major risk is the assumption that an increase and decrease in the nickel price have an equal and opposite effect on the equity. Nickelco has a combination of real options (as in the previous examples) and also financial options (like the option to default on debt). Futures hedging may cause the problem of hedging an asymmetric exposure with one that is symmetric, leading to more volatility than might be desired by the investor.

Answer #2

Answer #2 is the same as Answer #1, but the investor should trade in and out of the futures contract as the nickel price changes. For example, if the nickel price drops, reduce the size of the short-nickel-futures position by going long. If the nickel price rises, increase the short position. In so doing, one creates a dynamic hedge of the nickel exposure in the equity.

Discussion

Dynamic hedging may be better than static (fixed) hedging, but it introduces at least two risks. First, transaction costs and bid/offer eat away at returns. Second, by not rebalancing continuously, the hedge may fail to track appropriately, particularly in a market like nickel, which is known for gapping price movements (i.e., nonsmooth transitions from one price level to another). However, the dynamic strategy avoids the explicit payment of option premium, which is discussed in the next answer.

Answer #3

In Answer #1, we calculated a beta of the futures with respect to the equity in order to determine an appropriate hedge ratio. If the beta on the upside is different from the beta on the downside, perhaps one could construct a hedging instrument that had this characteristic as well. One example of such an instrument is a call option; the beta on the upside is higher than the beta on the downside. Therefore, repeat Answer #1, but instead of using futures to find the beta and hedge, use one or more call options instead. The optimal hedge portfolio may then be a portfolio of call options (some long and some short), which mimic the optionality in the equity.

Discussion

Answer #3 goes a long way in capturing the asymmetric and/or nonlinear impact of nickel prices on Nickelco's equity. Furthermore, the "exotic" equity hedge in this case is nothing more than a portfolio of plain-vanilla call options. Risks of the strategy include (1) not covering other risks (like risks of the general stock market), and (2) not fully capturing the nonlinearity in the equity exposure. (For simplicity, we will ignore the S&P exposure.)

Answer #4

Determine the exact relationship between beta and the nickel price; i.e., measure the function $\beta(P)$ beta, as a function of price. Construct a customized instrument where the beta of the payoff changes in exactly the same way. Since the hedge is essentially a short position of β(P) units of the futures price (P), effectively, the variable beta can be interpreted as a variable volume swap—the volume, instead of being constant, varies when the price varies.

Discussion

This is like Answer #2, and probably better, if the customization costs are not too high. In effect, the dynamic trading strategy is completed with a derivative that does it automatically. This avoids the need to constantly rebalance and run the risks of high transaction costs and tracking error.

Summary

In each one of these answers, the investor is seeking a leveraged play that reflects his or her view, and eliminates risks to which the investor desires no exposure. Every time one of the ancillary risks is eliminated (assuming it is eliminated at a fair price), the investor enjoys the same expected dollar return with much lower risk. An investor with many such hedged investments diversifies across the sources of information and opinion, and creates a portfolio (like a hedge fund) that is largely uncorrelated with market forces. The market force in this case was nickel price, but it could just as well be equity risk, interest-rate risk, foreign-exchange risk, or one of many others.

The overall maxim is, when investing because you believe you have superior information, isolate the performance of the investment to be responsive to the specific source of information. Anything else is inefficient.

WHEN TO USE EXOTIC DERIVATIVES: CONSTRUCTIVE CASE STUDY #B2

Traders often make decisions based on their views of market prices and volatilities. In this section, we take that idea one step further, and show how traders can speculate on *probability*, e.g., the probability that oil prices will go above $20 per barrel in 6 months. Every probability view corresponds to a derivatives strategy and vice versa. A more detailed version of the summary presented here can be found in "Optimal Probability Trading Strategies," which appeared in *Risk* magazine, September 1994.

In this case, an exotic instrument may be the result of a carefully chosen strategy that corresponds to a simple view on the probability distribution of futures prices. In other words, the exotic instrument expresses the investor's views perfectly.

The market prices of options describe a probability distribution for (risk-neutral) returns of the underlying assets.[4] For example, the Black-Scholes model effectively assumes that the distribution of the underlying asset value is lognormal, that is, roughly a symmetric bell-shaped curve, but slightly positively skewed. Other models imply other distributions—indeed, every pricing model corresponds to a probability distribution and vice versa.[5]

Suppose a trader has a proprietary view of the shape of the probability distribution that differs from the market's view. This is represented graphically by Figure 3–2.

In the preceding example, the proprietary trading view is that the market has underestimated both the average level of prices and the volatility. Of course, the proprietary view may reflect any combination of views: the market is going up or down, the volatility is going up or down; indeed, the entire shape of the probability distribution may be different from the market prediction.

How does this observation translate into strategy? The trader recognizes that his estimate of the probability of falling in any range to the left of (*) is less than the market probability. He thinks the market has overpriced probability in this range, and therefore he should sell the *probability* that the underlying level will fall below (*). Similarly, he should buy probability in the range to the right of (*).

In fact, under the assumption of quadratic utility (used before by Markowitz in building modern portfolio theory), it is possible to determine the derivative that best takes advantage of this probability view. The derivative is expressed as a payout function at maturity—the investor wants a high payout in ranges where he assigns higher probability

---

[4]The actual distribution of future prices is indeterminate, but the risk-neutral distribution, used to price derivative instruments, can be determined.

[5]The implied probability-distribution can be constructed in several ways. One method was published by the author in *Risk* magazine, April 1993, under the title "Bounds of Probability."

FIGURE 3–2
Market and Proprietary Probability-Views

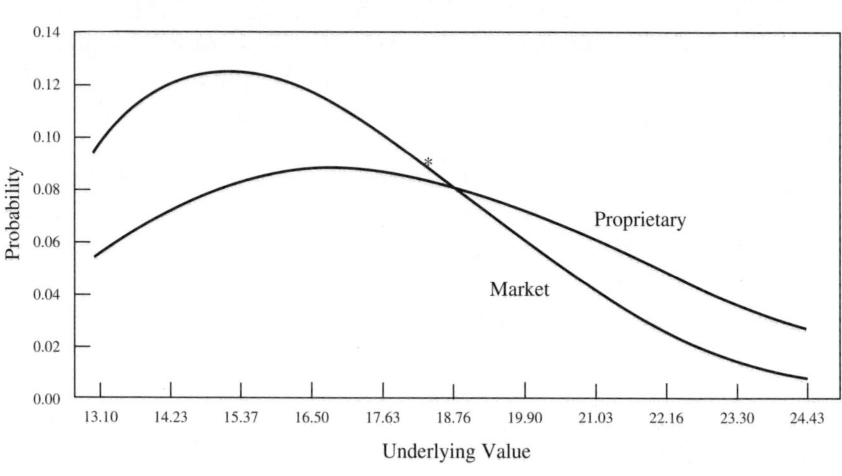

(than the market), and a low payout in ranges where he assigns lower probability than the market. In addition, the derivative instrument can be chosen so that the cost of the derivative is zero.[6]

The optimal derivative to create is one that has a terminal payout equal to the optimal-payout diagram in Table 3–1.

The strategy calls for higher derivative payouts wherever the investor places higher probability than the market; these are scaled by market probabilities, and scaled by risk aversion. (More risk-averse investors with the same view will take the same position, but in smaller size.) For example, using the proprietary distribution shown in Figure 3–2, the optimal speculative strategy is shown in Figure 3–3.

The optimal strategy in this case looks something like a call option, which benefits if either the mean of the distribution (the forward price) rises, or volatility rises; this was the original view. However, the diagram also shows that the optimal-payout function is smoother than the "kinky" piecewise linear call-payoff.

---

[6]This is not a necessary assumption, and it does not change the results except by scaling the derivative payout.

TABLE 3–1

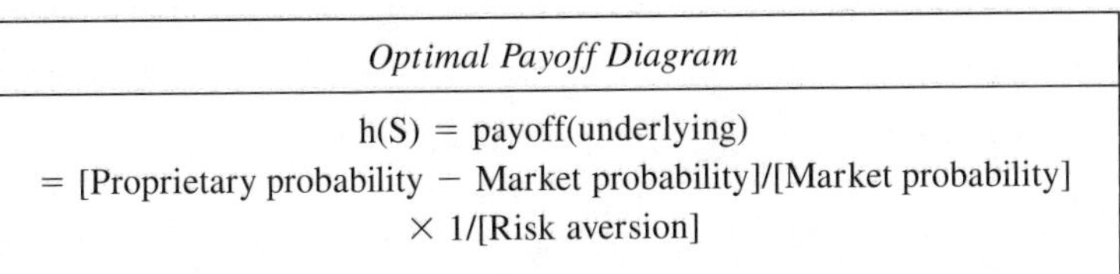

Optimal Payoff Diagram

h(S) = payoff(underlying)
= [Proprietary probability − Market probability]/[Market probability]
× 1/[Risk aversion]

FIGURE 3–3
Optimal Trading Strategy: Higher Volatility & Underlying

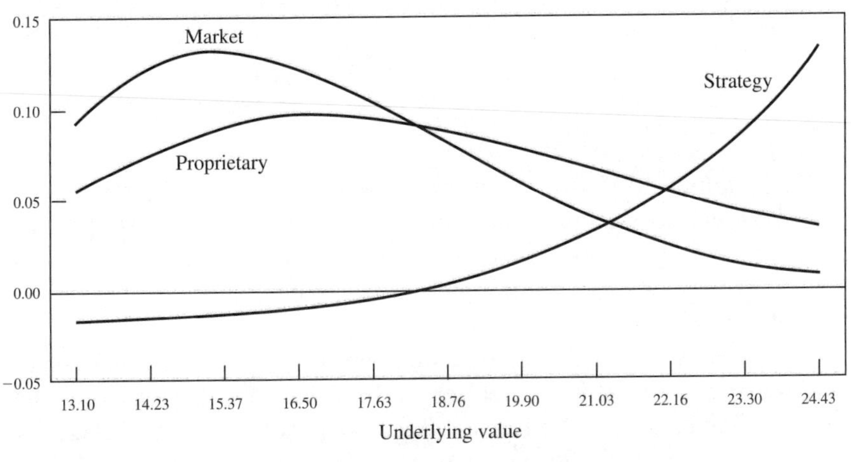

Recall that the proprietary view forecasts both higher underlying values and higher volatility. In this case, the optimal strategy is approximated by a call option, but would be better approximated by a custom product that pays a combination of the forward and the forward squared. If the proprietary view does not express a difference in volatility opinion, but only a higher forward price, the pattern shown in Figure 3–4 is observed.[7]

[7]In the case of lognormal distributions, shifts in mean and volatility are related. For this reason, the proprietary distribution has slightly higher volatility if it has a higher mean.

FIGURE 3–4
Optimal Trading Strategy: Higher Underlying

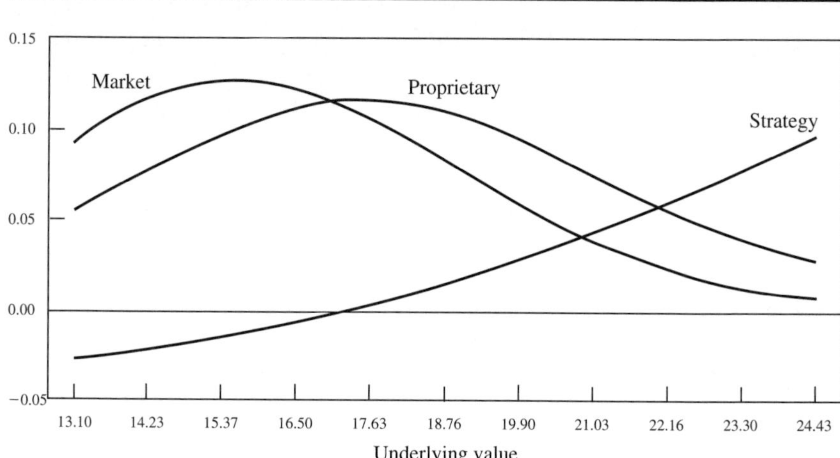

The recommended strategy in this case is closer to a linear strategy than the previous example. This calls for a strategy that is best approximated by a long forward position. Another simple case obtains when only the volatility view is different, but the trader thinks the forward is correctly priced (see Figure 3–5).

The strategy calls for a strangle of some sort, not a surprising result. Yet, the trader would be better served by a security that pays out the square of the change in the forward price. Why is this the case? A strangle may become volatility-insensitive if the forward moves too far. A quadratic security retains its volatility exposure regardless of the level of the underlying.

WHEN ARE SIMPLE OPTION STRATEGIES OPTIMAL?

We showed in the previous section that the optimal speculative strategy in general requires a custom derivative product. In some cases, the custom product can be satisfactorily approximated by positions in standard forward and option contracts. In this section, we show what proprietary distribution assumptions lead to investment in simple option strategies.

FIGURE 3–5
Optimal Trading Strategy: Higher Volatility

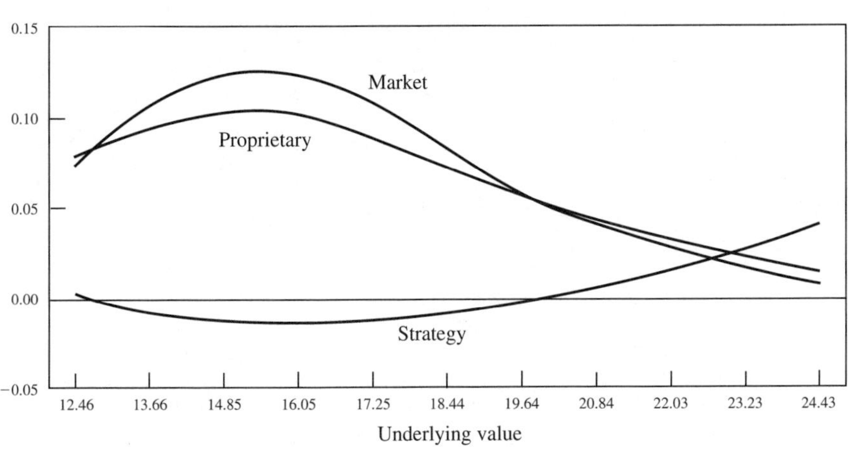

First, we ask the question, "What proprietary-distribution belief causes an investor to buy a call option?" Since we have a formula linking the optimal payout diagram to the proprietary distribution, it is a simple matter to reverse the equation and ask what proprietary distribution generates a call-option payout. Figure 3–6 shows exactly the distributional assumption required.

Using our optimization technique, the belief that causes investors to buy call options corresponds to the proprietary distribution shown in Figure 3–6. The probability distribution is approximated by averaging the current market distribution with a second distribution having a higher mean. The combined distribution also has higher variance.

This "reversal" strategy can be used to determine what probability view is implied by every possible derivative instrument (in this case, the instruments whose values only depend on terminal payouts).

WHEN TO USE EXOTIC DERIVATIVES: CONSTRUCTIVE CASE STUDY #B3

In the last section, we showed how investors might choose terminal derivative payouts to correspond to their view of terminal probability distributions. In this section, we briefly show how that logic

FIGURE 3–6
Optimal Trading Strategy: Long Call Option

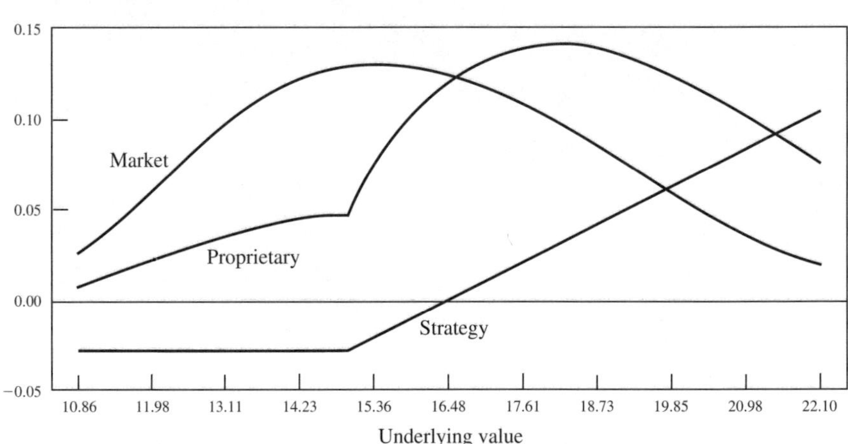

might be extended to the choice of optimal path-dependent derivative instruments.

A path-dependent derivative instrument is one whose payouts depend somehow on the path prices take over the course of time. Some examples of path-dependent instruments are shown in Table 3–2. There are an infinite variety of possible path-dependent derivative instruments; Table 3–2 represents merely a sampling.

The question is, When would anyone choose to use a path-dependent instrument over a plain-vanilla derivative instrument? There are many possible answers. One example is that in the commodity markets, averaging options better reflect the risks that producers have, and help prevent adverse impacts of manipulative squeezes that may last for a few days, but not for an entire month. In this section, we concentrate on *one* reason for choosing a path-dependent instrument, namely the probability view the investor has about the relative likelihood of prices following any given path.

We use the technology in the last section to convert each strategy into an implied-probability view. We begin with a very simple tree for a security whose price starts at $10, and always has a 50 percent probability of rising or falling by $1.00. The tree is shown in Figure 3–7, with the terminal probabilities.

TABLE 3–2

Instrument	*Payout*
Averaging (Asian) option	Underlying instrument is the average price over a time period instead of the value at a single moment
Lookback option	Many types; for example, a call option where the underlying is the maximum value of the underlying over a prespecified time period
Down-and-in option	For example, a call option that is activated only if the price first falls through a lower barrier before rising
Continuous binary	A payment is triggered if the underlying reaches a prespecified level during a prespecified time period

FIGURE 3–7

				14	6.25%
			13		
		12		12	25.00%
	11		11		
10		10		10	37.50%
	9		9		
		8		8	25.00%
			7		
				6	6.25%

The averaging option has a payout of Maximum(Average price − 10, 0), like a call option, but the underlying is the average price over the life of the instrument. In this case, inverting the path probabilities, we find that the paths can be assigned different relative weights as shown in Figures 3–8 and 3–9 (the circles show relative probability weights along paths that are more positively weighted than the market).

This analysis implies that an investor who chooses this type of averaging option places relatively higher probability than the market on the

FIGURE 3–8
Relative Probabilities for Call Option on the Average, Strike 10

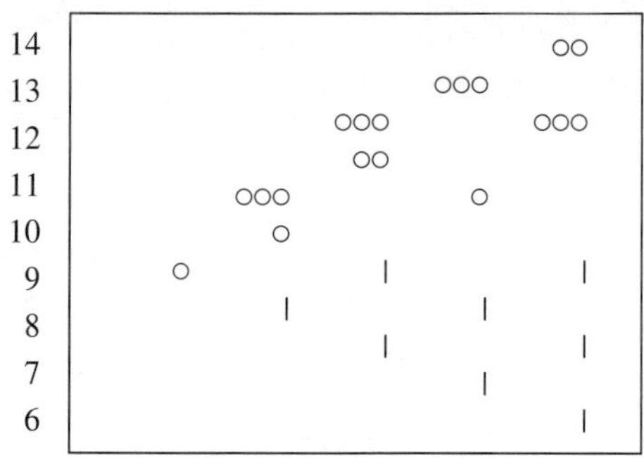

FIGURE 3–9
Relative Probabilities for Ordinary European Call Option, Strike 10

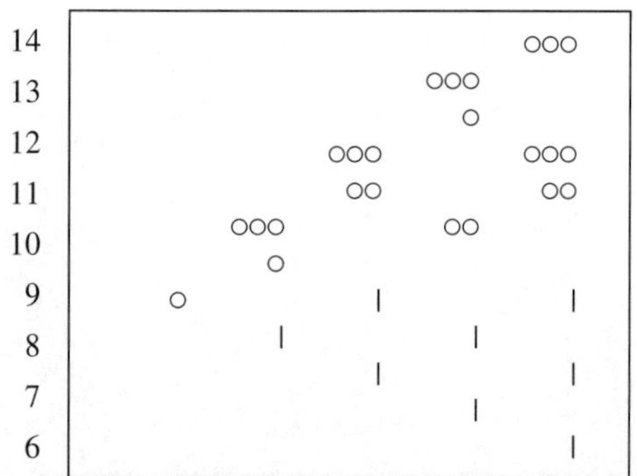

path with the fastest appreciation. At first, this may seem counterintuitive—if you think the market is going to take off, why not just buy the ordinary call option? On further consideration, one may find that a better way to leverage that view is to use this type of averaging option. The averaging option is much cheaper, and the relative change in the average if the security follows the high path increases the value of the averaging option more in percentage terms.

FIGURE 3–10
Relative Probabilities for Double Lookback; max − min

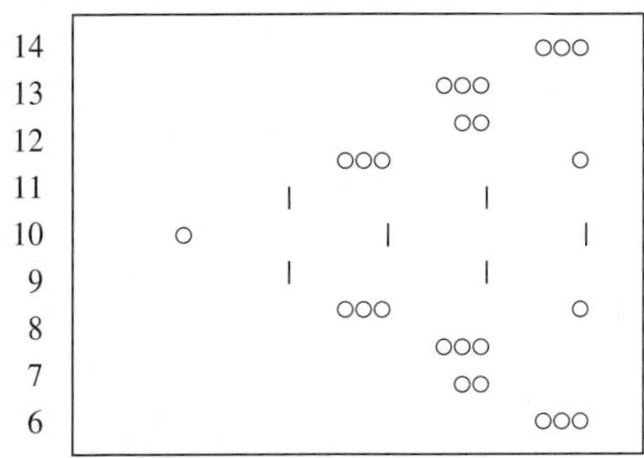

We now examine a double lookback option, where the payoff is the maximum value observed over the life of the instrument minus the minimum value. The relative probabilities are shown in Figure 3–10.

The double lookback stresses extreme movements relative to central movements.

A final example, the down-and-in call option, is triggered if the underlying hits $8, and if triggered, pays off exactly like a call option with a strike also set at $8. However, if the $8 level is never reached, the option never pays off. The relative probability diagram for the down and in call option is shown in Figure 3–11.

Clearly, in this diagram, there is only one path that pays off, and this path clearly receives the lion's share of the probability weight.

SUMMARY OF CUSTOM DERIVATIVE STRATEGY: (B) SIMPLE TO COMPLEX EXPOSURE

In this section, we have shown that apparently exotic instruments can arise from precise (and often simple) views about the probability distribution of future prices, or the path of future prices. In each case, the exotic instrument is customized to meet the particular needs of investors. What makes these examples different from the corporate examples is that in most cases, except the Nickelco case, the investor starts with a

FIGURE 3–11

Relative Probabilities for Down-and-In, Triggered and Struck at $8

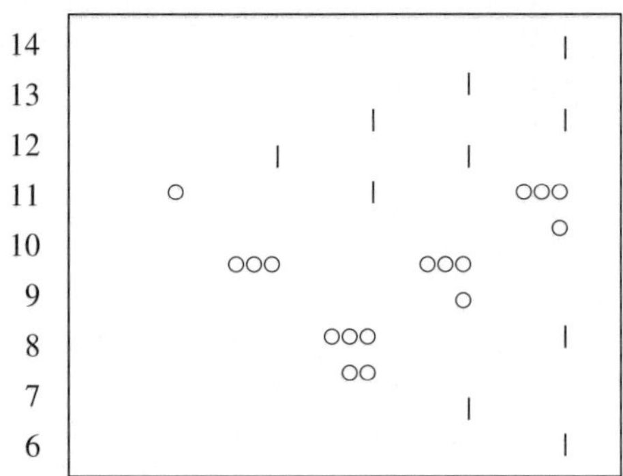

simple profile (i.e., no exposure) and works up to a complex exposure based on his or her views. In the corporate cases, the companies started with inherently complex exposures, and reduced those exposures to simple risk profiles using customized derivative instruments.

The Nickelco case is different in the sense that when the investor attempts to establish a simple exposure to Nickelco's growth and management, she is forced to buy the stock and hedge out the inherently complex exposure she inherits with the stock, but does not desire to retain. Note that the equity risks can be very different than the cash-flow risks.[8] The Nickelco example also shows that exotic derivatives can be used to incorporate trading strategies into an instrument and thereby avoid execution and tracking risks.

CONCLUSION

This chapter, admittedly, is a bit more forward-looking than representative of current practice. Fear of derivatives (or more precisely, fear of misusing derivatives) has kept many corporations away from all deriva-

[8]For example, if a company can perfectly hedge its cash flows to guarantee a flat income stream in the future, it will trade like a perpetual constant-coupon bond, with fluctuations in value based on changes in interest rates. Similarly, a stable value instrument (say, a mutual fund) must by necessity have income that varies in direct proportion to short-term interest rates.

tives, and especially customized derivatives. The word "structured" (as in "structured product") has often come to mean "booby-trapped." The fear is justified in the short run, but not defensible in the long run. As we have shown in this chapter, derivative instruments can do a great deal to enhance risk management and ultimately contribute to shareholder value for corporations. For investors, derivatives provide the opportunity to fine-tune exposures to those on which the investor takes a view. Corporations who don't learn to use derivatives properly run the risk of falling behind their competitors in an important element of their business. Investors who don't learn to use derivatives will continue to see volatility around their short-term performance figures, even if on average, their views tend to materialize. The extra volatility adds noise to performance measurement and, in an environment of limited capital, needlessly soaks up capital-at-risk.

Before using a derivative instrument, corporations and investors should assure themselves that they have passed the preliminary tests listed above and the more comprehensive tests of the G-30 study and recommendations.

As to the question, "When should one use exotic derivatives?" the answer is the same as any other decision the corporation or investor makes. Use exotic derivatives when they add more value than they cost. If there are several mutually exclusive derivative transactions, choose the one that adds the most value subject to the constraints placed upon that choice.

P A R T

II

PRODUCTS AND APPLICATIONS

Chapter Four

Compound Options and Chooser Options

Izzy Nelken
President
Super Computing Consulting

INTRODUCTION

A "chooser" is an option that is neither a call nor a put. On a specific date, the investor chooses between receiving a call or receiving a put. If both the call and the put have the same expiry dates and the same strikes, this is known as a "simple chooser," otherwise it becomes a "complex chooser." A "compound" is an option whose underlying is itself an option. It is known as an option on an option. Thus there is a call on a call, a call on a put, a put on a call, and a put on a put.

Unlike other exotics whose pricing formulas consist of closed-form solutions, both complex choosers and compound options require the use of numerical techniques. In [6] and [7] Rubinstein shows how to price these, using methods that rely on finding a solution to a nonlinear equation.

There are several methods of solving a nonlinear equation. Most of these methods (e.g., Newton-Raphson) rely on an initial guess. It is well-known that there are cases where these methods diverge and fail to find a solution or, alternatively, converge very slowly. In a typical application we need to compute prices for portfolios of many options and repeat this computation over many possible scenarios. Thus there is a major requirement for quick, stable algorithms.

Quadrature methods are more robust; they converge to the correct answer, and there may be an advantage to using them whenever possible.

Following this logic, we have applied quadrature techniques to complex choosers and compound options (Nelken [5]). Later on, we were asked to price a Bankers Trust installment warrant. It turned out that the installment warrant was a European-style compound on an American-style underlying option. The Rubinstein paper solved for the problem of a European compound option on a European underlying option. It was unclear how to extend it to solve for a European on an American. The quadrature method, on the other hand, was readily extendible to that case. The results of this analysis were presented in an interview with *Risk* magazine, (see reference [2]).

In what follows, we cast the option-pricing problem in terms of an integral, the analytic solution of which is the Black-Scholes equation. We then discuss chooser options and compound options, and explain how the quadrature methodology is applied. The Bankers Trust installment warrant is also discussed. Finally, we discuss some quick and robust numerical quadrature techniques.

A EUROPEAN OPTION

Consider a European style call option that on expiry will pay out

$$\max(S_t - K, 0)$$

where K is the strike price and S_t is the spot price of the underlying at expiry, which is assumed to be t years from now.

Let the continuous-compounding interest rate be r. The price of a call option can be written as

$$C = e^{-rt}E[\max(S_t - K, 0)]$$

where $E(A)$ is the expected value of A.

Utilizing integral notation we can write

$$E[A] = \int A\, p(A)\, dA$$

That is, the expected value of A is the integral of the product of the value of A times the probability of reaching that value, $p(A)$. The integral is computed over all possible values of A.

Standard option pricing theory postulates that the spot price of the underlying follows a lognormal random walk. We assume that the spot price today is S_0, the volatility of the spot price of the underlying is σ, the dividend rate is q. We let z be a random variable, which is normally distributed with a mean of zero and a standard deviation of 1. Then,

$$S_t = S_0\, e^{\mu t + \sigma z \sqrt{t}}$$

where

$$\mu = r - q - \sigma^2/2$$

Putting this together, we obtain

$$C = e^{-rt} \int_{-\infty}^{\infty} [\max(S_0 e^{\mu t + \sigma z \sqrt{t}} - K, 0) n(z)] dz$$

Here $n(z)$ is the standard normal distribution function

$$n(z) = 1/\sqrt{2\pi}\, e^{-z^2/2}$$

However, the integrand is zero for values of z that are smaller than

$$g = (\ln (K/S_0) - \mu t)/(\sigma \sqrt{t})$$

Therefore, we can rewrite the integral as

$$C = e^{-rt} \int_{g}^{\infty} [(S_0 e^{\mu t + \sigma z \sqrt{t}} - K) n(z)] dz$$

Applying some integral calculus, we can obtain the closed-form analytical solution of this integral, which is equivalent to the Black-Scholes pricing formula

$$C = e^{-qt} S_0 N(x) - e^{-rt} K N(x - \sigma \sqrt{t})$$

with

$$x = [\ln (S_0/K) + rt - qt]/[\sigma \sqrt{t}] + \sigma \sqrt{t}/2$$

The Black-Scholes formula for a European put can be derived in a similar manner.

A CHOOSER OPTION

A chooser is an option that is neither a call nor a put. At a certain date, known as the "choice date," the holder of the chooser may trade it in for either a call or a put. We distinguish between two types of chooser options:

1. A simple chooser, in which the call and the put have the same strike prices and the same expiry dates.
2. A complex chooser, in which the call and the put have different strike prices and/or different expiry dates.

Of course, we assume that on the choice date, the holder will always choose to receive the more expensive option. Typically, if the spot price of the underlying on the choice date is low, the holder will choose to receive the put option. If, on the other hand, the price of the underlying is high, the holder will choose the call option.

Thus on the choice date, the value of the chooser is the maximum of the value of the call and the value of the put:

$$\max[C(S_t, K_C, T_C - t), P(S_t, K_P, T_P - t]$$

The notations K_C, T_C, K_P, and T_P denote the strike price of the call, the time to expiry of the call, the strike of the put, and the time to expiry of the put; t is the time until the choice date; and S_t is the price of the underlying on the choice date. In a simple chooser, $K_C = K_P$ and $T_C = T_P$.

We use $C(S, K, T)$ and $P(S, K, T)$ to denote the prices of a call option and a put option when the underlying is priced at S, the strike is K, and there are T years to expiry. These may be computed using the standard Black-Scholes methodology [1]. The risk-free rate and the volatility, which also have an impact on option prices, have been omitted from this notation for clarity.

It is instructive to compare a simple chooser with a conventional straddle. The straddle consists of being long a call and a put struck at the same strike price and with the same expiry date. If the choice date of the chooser is the same as the expiry date (and so $t = T$), then either the call or the put will be in-the-money. The investor who has the chooser will choose the option that is in-the-money. Thus, in this case, being long a chooser is equivalent to being long a straddle.

$$\textit{chooser} = \textit{put} + \textit{call}$$

Now, consider the other extreme in which $t = 0$, and the investor must immediately choose between a put and a call. Obviously, the investor will choose the more expensive of the two. Thus, if $t = 0$, the price of the chooser is equal to the higher priced option.

chooser = max(put, call)

These observations make sense. The further away the choice date is, the more information the investor has and the higher the probability of ending in the money. Therefore, the further away the choice date is, the more expensive the chooser becomes. It ranges in price between the above two extremes. At the low end is *max(put,call)* and at the high end is *put+call.*

It is well-known that simple choosers have a closed-form solution. For complex choosers, however, a numerical method must be used.

A COMPOUND OPTION

This type of option is an option on an option. That is to say, an option whose underlying itself is also an option. Thus we have the compound option and the underlying option. The underlying option is itself a derivative of some underlying equity, commodity, currency, interest rate, or index.

We differentiate between four types of compound options: a call on a call, a call on a put, a put on a call, and a put on a put. For a compound, we must consider two expiry dates: the expiry of the compound option and the expiry of the underlying option. The time to expiry of the compound option is denoted by t, and the time to expiry of the underlying option is denoted by T. Obviously, $t \leq T$. We also have to consider the exercise styles of these options. It is usual to assume that the compound option is European. An investor would not want to exercise the compound option before the beginning of the underlying option. However, when you've exercised the compound option, you receive the underlying option, which may be either European or American. In the case of a European-style underlying option, you may exercise it only at time T. If the underlying is American, you may exercise it any time before T (but of course after t, when it started).

When a compound call option is exercised, its holder pays the strike and receives the underlying option. Likewise, when a compound put is exercised, the holder must deliver the underlying option and, in return, receive the strike as a payout. For example, we write the payout of a call on a call

$$\max[C(S_t, K1, T - t) - K2, 0]$$

where S_t is the spot price of the underlying on the day the compound option expires, $K1$ is the strike price of the underlying option and $K2$ is the strike price of a compound option. The expression $T - t$ signifies the time left to the life of the underlying option when the compound option expires. $C(S_t, K1, T - t)$ is therefore the price of the underlying call option on the expiry date of the compound option, assuming that the spot price of the underlying instrument is S_t.

The original work on call on a call was done by Geske [3] and was later generalized by Rubinstein [7] to cover all four cases.

NONLINEAR EQUATIONS

Rubinstein presented pricing methods for complex choosers and compound options which rely on the solution of nonlinear equations. These are usually solved using iterative methods, which can be divided into two categories:

1. *Bracketing methods.* In these methods, a linear segment that is known to contain the solution is manipulated. At each iteration, the segment becomes smaller and smaller. After enough iterations, the root of the nonlinear equation is localized to the desired accuracy. The *bisection method* divides the interval at which the solution is found. At each iteration, the interval is divided in two. Although bisection is robust, it only gains one bit of information at every iteration and is therefore quite slow. The *false position* method usually converges faster but in certain cases it results in stagnation.
2. *Root finders.* Given a guess of the root of the equation, these methods constantly improve on the guess. The *Newton-Raphson* method generally has a quadratic order of convergence but, depending on the guess and on the first derivative of the function, it may not converge at all. Similar comments apply to *Regula-Falsi* or the *Secant method.*

All methods that solve nonlinear equations are iterative in nature. Almost all rely on an initial guess, and their behavior is highly dependent on that guess. Further, there are cases in which each of these methods diverges or converges very slowly.

INTEGRATION

Numerical quadrature is known to be robust. There are many numerical packages that are simple to use and produce a result quite quickly. Some advantages of using quadrature techniques are:

- Since they are more robust, they are more likely to give a meaningful solution. In a typical application, traders evaluate a portfolio with many hundreds of options. This portfolio may be evaluated many times under different scenarios. A major requirement is therefore to use robust, accurate algorithms that are also quick.
- For compound options, the quadrature method lends itself to generalizations. It was easy to extend the methodology to cover the case of European compound options on American underlying options (see below).

Consider a complex chooser. Using the same logic we've applied to European options, we may write its value as:

$$V = e^{-rt}\int_{-\infty}^{\infty} \max[C(S_0 e^{\mu t + \sigma z\sqrt{t}}, K_C,$$
$$T_C - t), P(S_0 e^{\mu t + \sigma z\sqrt{t}}, K_P, T_P - t)]n(z)dz$$

Where the terms in the above formula have been defined above.

We can also write a similar expression for the value of a compound option. For example, we write the expression for a call on a call:

$$O = e^{-rt}\int_{-\infty}^{\infty} \max[C(S_0 e^{\mu t + \sigma z\sqrt{t}}, K1, T - t) - K2, 0]n(z)dz$$

In theory, the range of integration on both of these integrals is from minus infinity to plus infinity. To implement a numerical quadrature application, though, we need a finite range of integration. Fortunately, if the absolute value of z is very large, $n(z)$ is very small and the contribution to the integral is negligible. Therefore, we only need to integrate between $-M$ and M for a suitably large value of M. The precise value of M can be determined by the desired accuracy and speed of the algorithm. By integrating from $-M$ to M, we are, in effect, cutting the "tails of the distribution" from $n(z)$, which is a normally distributed random variable. If M is large enough, the resulting loss in accuracy will be acceptable. Usually, setting $M = 6$ results in an approximation that is accurate to four decimal places, since we are computing everything within six standard deviations from the mean.

NUMERICAL QUADRATURE

In principle, many quadrature techniques may be used to numerically evaluate the integrals above. Perhaps the simplest numerical integration method is the left end point quadrature. To evaluate

$$I = \int_a^b f(x)dx$$

choose a large enough n and set $h = (b - a)/n$. Then use the approximation

$$I \approx h \sum_{i=0}^{n-1} f(a + ih)$$

Other well-known methods are the trapezoidal method and Simpson's rule. The main drawback of these methods is that the step size, h, is fixed in advance. If the integrand $f(x)$ changes rapidly, to get accurate results, h must be small. On the other hand, if $f(x)$ is a constant, h can be made much larger with no loss of accuracy. Of course, a small h implies a large n which, in turn, means many function evaluations and a slow algorithm. For example, the left-hand quadrature rule requires n function evaluations at equally spaced points. The functions that we are integrating are smooth in some areas and erratic in other areas. If the absolute value z is very large, the integrand becomes very small. We do not need to waste function evaluations in those areas. On the other hand, consider the chooser. At the point where the *max( )* function changes behavior from a call to a put, the function may not be so smooth and we may need to spend more function evaluations there.

Some of the most commonly used quadrature methods are based on an adaptive control strategy coupled with a local quadrature module. The adaptive control strategy works as follows: It divides the integration region into two subregions. Then, the integral is approximated at these two subregions and the error is also evaluated. If the error in a subinterval is small enough, the approximation is accepted. Otherwise, we divide the region in two and continue in the same manner. To approximate an integral and evaluate the error, we can use the same local quadrature module twice with two different step sizes, a fine quadrature and a coarse one. We can use the coarse integration as the approximation to the integral. The difference between the coarse and the fine approximations can be the computed error estimate. Alternatively, use the fine quadrature as the approximation to the integral and a computation involving both approximations can be used to estimate the error. The advantage of the adaptive approaches is that they reduce the number of function evaluations in areas where the integrand does not change much but use a sufficiently large number of evaluations where the integrand swings wildly.

Q1DA

An adaptive routine is Q1DA by Kahaner, Moler, and Nash [4], which is based on the Gauss Kronrod local-quadrature module. This routine has been found to be extremely reliable and very efficient. We briefly describe the ideas behind it.

The quadrature routine is used to evaluate the integral

$$I = \int_a^b f(x)dx$$

to a predetermined accuracy tolerance ϵ. The two main parts are the local quadrature module (LQM) and the adaptive control strategy. The LQM computes an approximation to the integral, R, and an approximation to the error, E, such that

$$|I - R| \leq E$$

The LQM in Q1DA uses the Gauss Kronrod rules known as (G_7, K_{15}) to compute R and E. The advantage of the Gaussian rules is their high polynomial degree. Kronrod added to them an effective error estimate. So given an integration region and an integrand, the LQM uses G_7, which is a 7-point rule, to compute the coarse approximation and K_{15}, a 15-point rule, to compute the finer approximation. Both of these are given by rules of the type

$$I \approx \sum_{i=1}^{n} w_i f(x_i)$$

where the w_i's are the weights and the x_i's are the node points (or knots). The LQM evaluates the function at the knots, multiplies the results by the appropriate weights, and sums these products. The LQM uses K_{15} as R and

$$(200\,|G_7 - K_{15}|\,)^{1.5}$$

as E, the estimate to the error.

The adaptive control strategy evaluates the integral by dividing it into two parts $I = I_1 + I_2$, where

$$I_1 = \int_a^{(a+b)/2} f(x)dx$$

and

$$I_2 = \int_{(a+b)/2}^{b} f(x)dx$$

Using the LQM, Q1DA evaluates I_1 and I_2 and obtains the approximations R_2 and R_2 and the error estimates E_1 and E_2. There are several possibilities:

- If $E_1 + E_2 \leq \epsilon$ we accept the approximations and output the result $R = R_1 + R_2$.
- Otherwise, $E_1 + E_2 > \epsilon$ and the approximation is not within our error bound. In this case, we consider the region with the larger error, subdivide that region, and continue. For example, suppose $E_1 > E_2$ we will reconsider the integral I_1 and compute an approximation to it with a new error bound of $\epsilon - E_2$. This will be done by dividing it into two subregions and continuing as before.
- In the case where $E_1 > \epsilon$ and $E_2 > \epsilon$, we separately consider both regions. Each region is further divided into appropriate subregions and we continue as before.

In areas where the function is smooth, the error estimates will be small, the approximations will be accepted, and only a few function evaluations will be performed. The adaptive control strategy will divide and continue to divide areas in which there are large swings in the function until the desired accuracy has been reached. In this manner, more function evaluations are done in the areas where the function is swinging and fewer evaluations in areas where the function is close to a constant.

TABLE 4–1
A Compound Option Priced on January 1, 1995

Date	*Chooser*	*Compound*
February 1, 1995	\$5.18538	\$3.85616
March 1, 1995	\$5.58273	\$4.11055
April 1, 1995	\$5.93480	\$4.39400
May 1, 1995	\$6.21549	\$4.65685
June 1, 1995	\$6.45841	\$4.91745
July 1, 1995	\$6.65484	\$5.16204
August 1, 1995	\$6.82061	\$5.41063

NUMERICAL EXAMPLES

Consider a complex chooser being priced on January 1, 1995. (See Table 4–1.) Let the spot price of the underlying be \$100, the risk-free rate 6 percent, the dividend rate 3 percent, and the volatility 20 percent. The call has a strike price of \$110 and an expiry of December 1, 1995. The put has a strike of \$90 and an expiry of November 1, 1995. The choice date is in the left column of the table, and the price of the chooser is in the middle column. Note that as the choice date is pushed into the future, the price of the chooser increases.

We also consider a compound option being priced on January 1, 1995. It is a compound call option on an underlying call option. The spot price of the underlying asset, the risk-free rate, and the volatility are as above. Let the strike of the underlying option be \$100 and the strike of the compound call option be \$5. The left column represents the expiry date of the compound option. The right column is its price. Again, we see that the price of the compound increases as its expiry date is pushed into the future. This is a common feature of options and agrees with our intuition.

Let us reconsider the chooser. Change the expiry dates of both the call and the put to December 1, 1996, and both of their strike prices to \$100. This new structure is a regular chooser. If the choice date is January 1, 1995, the price is \$8.70632. If the choice date is moved to December 1, 1995, the price is \$14.77809. Even though closed-form solutions for regular choosers exist, we obtain these prices using the quadrature method outlined above. We also consider a regular European call option with a strike price of $100 and an expiry date of December 1, 1995. It is priced at $8.70829. A put option with the same expiry date and the same strike is priced at $6.07177.

All of this agrees with our intuition. If the choice date is equal to the pricing date, then the investor must choose today. The investor will choose the more expensive of the call and the put, and therefore the price of the chooser should be the maximal price of the call and the put. Note that the European call is priced at $8.70829 and the chooser at $8.70632. The small difference is due to the round-off errors in the quadrature method. If the choice date is equal to the expiry date, the chooser becomes a straddle and its price should be equal to the sum of the call and the put. Indeed, the chooser is priced at $14.77809 and the straddle at $14.78006. Again, there are small differences due to round-off errors.

INSTALLMENT WARRANTS

On April 14, 1994, Bankers Trust Canada issued installment put warrants on the TSE-35 index. These warrants have the following structure: The investor was required to pay $2.50 on the purchase date. One year later, on April 14, 1995, the investor may chose to invest another $2.50 and receive an American put option on the TSE-35 (which is a major Canadian stock exchange index). Alternatively, the investor may also chose not to pay the $2.50 and let the option expire worthless. (In this section, all funds are quoted in Canadian dollars.) A total of 2.8 million warrants were sold. In addition, the same issuer has come out with call and put warrants on the S&P 500 index with similar characteristics.

It is easy to explain the popularity of these issues with retail investors. Rather than purchasing a regular warrant outright and paying the full premium, investors only needed to pay half of the premium up front. An additional option is included in this structure, as they can choose what to do after an entire year—pay the extra $2.50 and receive a put option or decline the additional payment and let the option expire worthless. An extra incentive is the high leverage that these options have. If a $5.00 warrant increases in price by $0.50, it represents a 10 percent return. However, if the $2.50 warrant increases by the same $0.50, the return is 20 percent.

How does one value such a compound option?

The existing papers on compound options by Geske [3] and Rubinstein [7] have assumed that both the compound option and the underlying option have European expiries. That is, the underlying option can only be exercised at maturity. Under this assumption, Rubinstein developed a pricing method that relies on the Newton-Raphson method to iteratively solve a nonlinear equation.

Unfortunately, iterative methods of this type may sometimes diverge and fail to arrive at a solution. When pricing portfolios of options we need stable numerical algorithms that are guaranteed to converge. In addition, the Bankers Trust structure is a European option whose underlying is an American option. That is to say, the investor may only pay the $2.50 on April 14, 1995. However, after that is done, the investor receives the underlying American put option, which may be exercised at any time up to its expiration. It was not clear how to extend Rubinstein's model to cover this case.

Our quadrature approach, which is described above, is easily extendible to the case of a European compound option on an American underlying option. All one has to do is replace the Black-Scholes computation in the integrand with an appropriate American put option evaluator.

The expression for the Banker's Trust warrant becomes

$$O = e^{-rt}\int_{-\infty}^{\infty} \max[P(S_0 e^{\mu t + \sigma z\sqrt{t}}, K1, T - t) - K2, 0]n(z)dz$$

where $P(S, K, T)$ is the price of an American put option with a strike price of K and a time to expiry of T, assuming that the underlying spot price is S.

At the time, we used the above techniquc to compute that the approximate fair value of the Bankers Trust warrant was $2.14, which implies that $0.36 has been tacked on to the price.

REFERENCES

1. Black, F., and M. Scholes, "The Pricing of Options and Corporate Liabilities," *Journal of Economics* (May 1973).
2. Falloon, W., "Canadian Compounds," *Risk* magazine (July 1994).
3. Geske, R., "The Valuation of Compound Options," *Journal of Financial Economics* (March 1979).

4. Kahaner, D., C. Moler, and S. Nash, *Numerical Methods and Software,* Prentice Hall Series in Computational Mathematics, 1989.
5. Nelken, I., "Square Deals," *Risk* magazine (April 1993).
6. Rubinstein, M., "Options for the Undecided," *Risk* magazine (April 1991).
7. Rubinstein, M., "Double Trouble," *Risk* Magazine (December 1991–January 1992).

Chapter Five

Two-Color Rainbow Options

J. P. Hunziker

P. Koch-Medina

Winterthur Insurance Group

INTRODUCTION

In general, an investor is involved in various markets at the same time. The desire to manage the resulting combined risk leads us to consider *multiasset options* (MAOs), i.e., options on more than one asset. We shall concentrate on options on two assets, which are sometimes called *two-color rainbow* options. The price processes for the first and second assets will be denoted by $S_1(t)$ and $S_2(t)$, respectively. By abuse of language we shall sometimes refer to the *i*-th asset as the asset S_i. We are thus confronted with a situation where there are two sources of price risk. In general, a European call option with S_1 and S_2 as underlying and maturity T will have a payoff of the type

$$\max\{0, F(S_1(T), S_2(T)) - K\}$$

where K is the strike price of the option and F is a given function of the two asset prices. Of course the payoff of the corresponding put option will be

$$\max\{0, K - F(S_1(T), S_2(T))\}$$

The simplest case is where $K = 0$ and $F(x_1, x_2) := x_2 - x_1$. This option may be interpreted either as the option to exchange one unit of asset S_1 for one unit of asset S_2 or, alternatively, as an option on the outperformance of the second over the first asset. This type of option has been treated elsewhere in this book and shall be briefly revisited here.

More generally, K will be a nonnegative number and F will typically denote one of the following operations:

- Maximum (best of): $F(x_1, x_2) := \max\{x_1, x_2\}$
- Minimum (worst-of): $F(x_1, x_2) := \min\{x_1, x_2\}$
- Sum (basket): $F(x_1, x_2) := x_1 + x_2$
- Product (quanto): $F(x_1, x_2) := x_1 \cdot x_2$

We shall look at each of these option types, giving formulas for their valuation and hinting at possible applications. We start by recalling the relevant stochastic model for dealing with two risky assets and by sketching the basic philosophy for valuing options depending simultaneously on both of them. In particular we derive the corresponding partial differential equation of Black-Scholes type. We continue by giving an overview of the different option types covering the payoff structure, valuation, and applications. We divide this overview into two separate sections. The first of these covers best-of/worst-of and basket options, while the second one is devoted to payoffs involving products. This distinction seems justified, since products appear naturally in the context of foreign equity investments with domestic reference currency. Here, one of the assets is the foreign equity and the other the exchange rate. Scattered throughout the sections, short historical and bibliographical notes are included.

One of the basic insights in financial engineering is that it is not necessary to develop price formulas for every conceivable payoff. The payoffs of a great variety of options can be expressed as a linear combination of the payoffs of basic building blocks. So one of the main tasks is to recognize which are the elementary building blocks. We have emphasized this point by providing formulas not for all the options discussed here but only for a few basic ones. For the other options, we have indicated how to replicate them from the basic ones. We have stuck to this principle with two exceptions. The first is that we treat Margrabe's formula for spreads and then Stulz's formula for calls on the worst of two assets, although, strictly speaking, the latter would suffice to derive the former. We have done this to underscore the simplicity of Margrabe's setting. In his formula, only univariate cumulative normal distributions appear, while in Stulz's, setting the bivariate versions are needed. The second exception concerns the foreign-currency context. There the basic options are: Flexible FX-rate calls on foreign stock, calls on the currency translated foreign stock, fixed FX-rate calls on foreign stock, and equity-linked FX-rate floors. The price of an equity-linked FX-rate floor, what we call a beach option, is just the sum of the prices of an equity-linked FX-rate call and an equity-linked FX-rate forward for which we derive explicit formulas. The reason for stating an explicit version of the price of a beach option is that we just like it.

The hedging of MAOs is in theory not any different from the hedging of single-asset options. For single-asset options there is already one troublesome point: volatility. Since this is not a traded parameter, hedging a position against volatility risk is a tricky business. For MAOs, one is exposed to more than one volatility parameter. Even worse, a new troublemaker appears on the set: correlation. This parameter is extremely difficult to estimate, let alone to hedge.

TWO PRICING STRATEGIES

The standard risk-adjusted approach to valuing European options on one asset is summarized in the following prescription: Look for a probability space (Ω, Σ, P) and a stochastic process on it describing the evolution in time of the price of the underlying asset, given the known initial state of the world (actual price). Incorporate risk-aversion in the model by exchanging the objective probability measure P for the *risk-adjusted probability measure* Q (under Q the discounted price process is a martingale). This furnishes you with the risk-adjusted distribution of the price of the underlying, and consequently with that of the payoff function, at any future time. Prices of contingent claims whose value depend on this underlying can now be computed: Calculate or estimate the expected value of the payoff function at the time of exercise T with respect to Q and discount it subsequently using the risk-free interest rate.

Another popular approach is to use Ito's formula to obtain a differential equation that must be satisfied by the value of the option $v(t, S)$, where $t \in [0, T]$ is the time the valuation is undertaken and $S \in (0, \infty)$ is the price of the underlying asset at time t. This differential equation is a backward parabolic equation, and its solution is *uniquely* determined after specifying a *terminal value,* i.e., the payoff of the option at maturity, and appropriate *boundary conditions,* i.e., the values $v(t, 0)$ and

$\lim_{S\to\infty}$ v(t, S) for t[0, T]. For each option we may deduce terminal values and boundary conditions characterizing that particular option type. Hence, solving the differential equations with these terminal and boundary data will yield the price function v(t, S).

Each of the strategies we just sketched also works for two (or, in fact, more than two) assets. We shall now describe them.

The Basic Mathematical Model

The two assets will have a stochastic price processes $S_1(t)$ and $S_2(t)$. We admit the possibility that the two assets pay continuous dividends with *dividend yield* q_i. We shall assume that both asset prices are driven by geometric Brownian motions, i.e.,

$$dS_1(t) = (\mu_1 - q_1)S_1(t)dt + \sigma_1 S_1(t)dB_1(t)$$

and

$$dS_2(t) = (\mu_2 - q_2)S_2(t)dt + \sigma_2 S_2(t)dB_2(t)$$

where μ_1 and σ_1 denote the *expected rate of return* and *volatility* of S_i, respectively. These parameters are assumed to be constant. Moreover, since investors are *risk-averse,* we must have that $\mu_i > r$, where r is the *risk-free interest rate.* Here $B_1(t)$ and $B_2(t)$ are two standard Brownian motions on the same probability space (Ω, Σ, P), which may or may not be independent. We assume that $S_1(t)$ and $S_2(t)$ are *jointly log-normally distributed,* i.e., the joint distribution function of $e^{S_1(t)}$ and $e^{S_2(t)}$ is given by

$$f_t(x_1, x_2) = \frac{1}{2\cdot\pi\cdot\sigma_1\cdot\sigma_2\cdot t\cdot\sqrt{1-\rho^2}}\cdot e^{-\frac{1}{2}\cdot\Phi_t(x_1, x_2)}$$

where

$$\Phi_t(x_1, x_2) := \frac{1}{1-\rho^2}\cdot\left[\left(\frac{x_1-\mu_1\cdot t}{\sigma_1\cdot\sqrt{t}}\right)^2 - 2\cdot\rho\cdot\frac{x_1-\mu_1\cdot t}{\sigma_1\cdot\sqrt{t}}\cdot\frac{x_2-\mu_2\cdot t}{\sigma_2\cdot\sqrt{t}} + \left(\frac{x_2-\mu_2\cdot t}{\sigma_2\cdot\sqrt{t}}\right)^2\right]$$

and the *instantaneous correlation coefficient* ρ between $e^{S_1(t)}$ and $e^{S_2(t)}$, which we assume to be constant in time and therefore is a number lying between -1 and 1. This coefficient reflects the degree of dependence $(\rho \neq 0)$ or independence $(\rho = 0)$ of the two Brownian motions.

The Risk-Adjusted Probability

Recall that under the objective probability P, the expected value of $S_1(t)$ is given by $e^{(\mu_i - q_i)\cdot t} \cdot S_i(0)$, which is the expected return on the stock less dividends paid up to time t. Hence,

$$S_i(0) < e^{-(r - q_i)\cdot t} \cdot E_P[S_i(t)]$$

holds true (of course $E_P[\cdot]$ denotes the expectation operator with respect to the measure P). This reflects the *risk-aversion* of investors: For a risky asset, they will pay less than the discounted expected value of the return (including dividends) of that investment, since they want to be remunerated for taking extra risk. It can be shown that a new probability measure Q on (Ω, Σ) can be defined such that under this new measure the price process $S_i(t)$ is still a geometric Brownian motion, albeit with drift parameter $r - q_i$ and volatility parameter σ_i:

$$dS_i(t) = (r - q_i)S_i(t)dt + \sigma_i S_i(t)dB_i(t) \quad i = 1, 2$$

which is the *risk-adjusted formulation* we shall adhere to. Strictly speaking, the Brownian motions appearing in the above equations are different from the original ones, but since the latter will not be referred to in the sequel, we may use the same symbols to denote them without fear of confusion. The risk-adjusted formulation implies that

$$S_i(0) = e^{-(r - q_i)\cdot t} \cdot E_Q[S_i(t)]$$

holds. In other words, we have incorporated the risk-aversion of the investor in our model by assigning a greater weight to unfavorable events and less weight to favorable ones. This does not alter the external reality of the world—it is just a means of saying how the investor expects to be compensated for taking risks stemming from $S_i(t)$. The probability measure Q is usually called the *joint risk-adjusted probability* for S_1 and S_2. Its existence is a consequence of a deep theorem in the theory of stochastic calculus called Girsanov's theorem.

The Partial Differential Equation

We now review the differential equation approach. If we want to imitate the strategy used for derivative instruments involving just one asset, it is clear that one now needs a two-dimensional Ito formula in order to obtain the corresponding partial differential equation of Black-Scholes type.

The two-dimensional Ito formula. Suppose $v(t, x_1, x_2)$ denotes a sufficiently smooth function. We think of $v(t, x_1, x_2)$ as the value at time t of a derivative security depending on our two assets provided $S_1(t) = x_1$ and $S_2(t) = x_2$. We do not as yet specify which particular type of derivative we are dealing with. Set

$$V(t) := v(t, S_1(t), S_2(t)).$$

The needed two-dimensional version of Ito's formula states that the process V(t) is governed by the following stochastic differential equation:

$$dV(t) = \Psi(t, S_1(t), S_2(t)) \cdot dt + \delta_1(t, S_1(t), S_2(t)) \cdot dS_1(t) + \delta_2(t, S_1(t), S_2(t)) \cdot dS_2(t) \qquad \text{(IF)}$$

where we have set

$$\Psi(t, x_1, x_2) := \partial_t v(t, x_1, x_2) + \frac{1}{2} \cdot \sum_{i=1}^{2} \sigma_i^2 \cdot x_i^2 \cdot \partial_{x_i}^2 v(t, x_1, x_2) + \rho \cdot \sigma_1 \cdot \sigma_2 \cdot x_1 \cdot x_2 \cdot \partial_{x_1} \partial_{x_2} v(t, x_1, x_2)$$

and

$$\delta_i(t, x_1, x_2) := \partial_{x_i} v(t, x_1, x_2).$$

The above formula is called the *two-dimensional Ito formula*. (By the way, an excellent reference for Brownian motion, stochastic calculus, "and all that" is the book by Karatzas and Shreve [1991]).

The replicating portfolio and the PDE. For notational convenience we set

$$\Delta_i(t) := \delta_i(t, S_1(t), S_2(t))$$

for i = 1,2. Consider now a *dynamic portfolio* consisting at time t of $\Delta_1(t)$ units of S_1, $\Delta_2(t)$ units of S_2, and

$$\Delta_0(t) := [V(t) - \Delta_1(t) \cdot S_1(t) - \Delta_2(t) \cdot S_2(t)] \cdot e^{-r \cdot t}$$

units of the risk-free asset. If we denote by R(t) the value of this portfolio at time t, we immediately see that

$$R(t) = \Delta_0(t) \cdot e^{r \cdot t} + \Delta_1(t) \cdot S_1(t) + \Delta_2(t) \cdot S_2(t) = V(t)$$

so that this portfolio in fact *replicates* at each time the value of our derivative security. Moreover, we have

$$dR(t) = \Delta_0(t)e^{r \cdot t} \cdot rdt + \Delta_1(t)dS_1(t) + \Delta_2(t)dS_2(t).$$

The first term comprises the gains due to holdings in the risk-free asset. The second and third terms the gains from the holdings in S_1 and S_2, respectively. Therefore, we have a *self-financing portfolio,* i.e., the dynamic portfolio may be financed with an amount of money equal to its initial value.

Since $R(t) = V(t)$, it follows that $dR(t) = dV(t)$. Using the expression we have derived for $dR(t)$ and $dV(t)$, we see that the terms involving $dS_1(t)$ and $dS_2(t)$ cancel out, leaving us with

$$\Delta_0(t) \cdot r \cdot e^{r \cdot t} \cdot dt = \Psi(t, S_1(t), S_2(t))dt.$$

After substituting the defining expressions for $\Delta_0(\cdot)$ and $\Psi(\cdot, \cdot, \cdot)$ in this last equation we conclude that

$$\begin{aligned} 0 = \partial_t v + \frac{1}{2} \cdot [\sigma_1^2 \cdot x_1^2 \cdot \partial_{x_1}^2 v + \sigma_2^2 \cdot x_2^2 \cdot \partial_{x_2}^2 v] \\ + \rho \cdot \sigma_1 \cdot \sigma_2 \cdot x_1 \cdot x_2 \cdot \partial_{x_1} \partial_{x_2} v \qquad \text{(PDE1)} \\ + (r - q_1) \cdot x_1 \cdot \partial_{x_1} v + (r - q_2) \cdot x_2 \cdot \partial_{x_2} v - r \cdot v \end{aligned}$$

must hold. What we have found is a *partial differential equation,* which must be satisfied by the value v of any derivative security depending on S_1 and S_2. Solutions of this equation are functions of the variables $t \in [0, T]$, $x_1 \in [0, \infty)$ and $x_2 \in [0, \infty)$ and are *uniquely determined* if we prescribe a *terminal value* and *boundary conditions.* To prescribe the terminal value means specifying a function $v_T(x_1, x_2)$ and requiring that the solution satisfy

$$v(T, x_1, x_2) := v_T(x_1, x_2).$$

The prescription of boundary conditions entails choosing functions v_{bc1} (t, x_2) and v_{bc2} (t, x_1) requiring that

$$v(t, 0, x_2) = v_{bc1}(t, x_2)$$

and

$$v(t, x_1, 0) = v_{bc2}(t, x_1)$$

are both satisfied by the solution. We shall show for each of the basic option types how to specify the right terminal and boundary conditions.

Hedging

The above approach to deriving the partial differential equation shows clearly how the option writer should hedge his liability against adverse movements of the underlying assets once he is in possession of a valuation formula: He just has to compute the derivatives of the price formula with respect to S_1 and S_2, determine the values of $\Delta_0(t)$, $\Delta_1(t)$, as well as $\Delta_2(t)$, and invest in the different assets in the indicated proportions.

The Black-Scholes Function

It will be convenient to introduce the following function for easy reference

$$C(\tau, S(t), K, r, \sigma, q) := S(t) \cdot e^{-q \cdot \tau} \cdot N_1(d_1) - K \cdot e^{-r \cdot \tau} \cdot N_1(d_1 - \sigma\sqrt{t})$$

where $N_1(\cdot)$ denotes the cumulative standard normal distribution function and

$$d_1 := \frac{\ln\left[\dfrac{S(t) \cdot e^{-q \cdot \tau}}{K \cdot e^{-r \cdot \tau}}\right] + \dfrac{1}{2} \cdot \sigma^2 \cdot \tau}{\sigma \cdot \sqrt{\tau}}.$$

Of course, this is just the standard *Black-Scholes function,* which can be used to determine the value of a European call option on an asset paying a continuous dividend at the rate q if the time to maturity is τ ($\tau := T - t$, where t is actual time and T is the maturity of the option), the spot price is S(t), the strike price is K, the risk-free rate is r, and the return on S is lognormally distributed, i.e., $\ln\left[\dfrac{S(T)}{S(t)}\right]$ is normally distributed with mean $\left(r - q - \dfrac{\sigma^2}{2}\right) \cdot \tau$ and standard deviation $\sigma \cdot \sqrt{\tau}$.

THE RED BOOK OF MAOs I: SINGLE CURRENCY

In this section we consider in more detail the various types of two-color rainbow options, with the exception of those involving products of the

FIGURE 5–1
Payoff Regions for a Spread Option

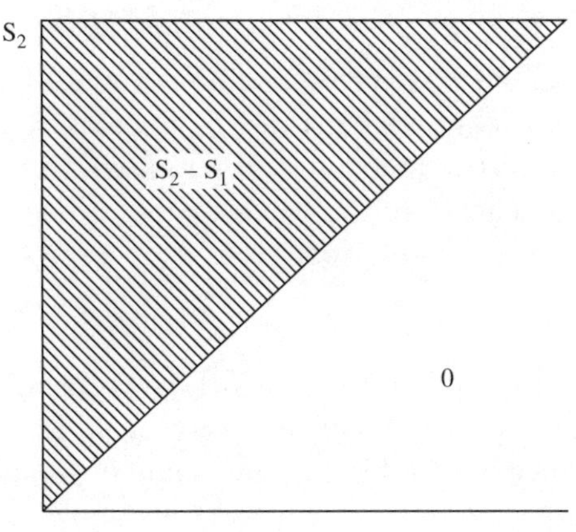

two asset prices. This type arises more naturally in the context of foreign-currency assets, which are the subject of the next section. All options considered here will be European and have maturity T.

Margrabe's Formula for Spread Options

In 1978, William Margrabe published a paper on the price of an option to *exchange one* asset *for the other,* i.e., an option with payoff

$$\max\{0, S_2(T) - S_1(T)\}.$$

These options are also called *spread* or *outperformance* options. (See Figure 5–1.)

A typical instance where spread options offer an attractive investment opportunity is when the investor has a particular view on the relative performancc of two assets. For example, a German investor might expect the DAX to perform well relative to some German bond index. A cost-efficient strategy to take profit—should this view turn out to be right—is to buy an option on the spread between the DAX and the bond index. Note that this strategy is based on anticipating *relative* moves. The investor may expect both the DAX and the bond index to do poorly (well) but the former less (more) so than the latter.

Terminal and boundary conditions. The terminal condition is always the payoff at maturity. Hence we prescribe

$$v(T, x_1, x_2) = \max\{0, x_2 - x_1\}.$$

In order to derive the boundary conditions, note that if $S_2(0) = 0$ then our model for $S_2(t)$ implies that $S_2(T)$ remains equal to 0 for all times t. Hence the payoff at maturity will be $\max\{0, S_2(t) - S_1(T)\} = \max\{0, S_1(T)\} = 0$. Therefore the value of the option will also be 0. This means that we have to prescribe

$$v(t, x_1, 0) = 0.$$

On the other hand if $S_1(0) = 0$ then $S_1(t) = 0$ for all times. Therefore the payoff at maturity will be $\max\{0, S_2(T) - S_1(T)\} = \max\{0, -S_2(T)\} = S_2(T)$. In this case the value of the option at time t will be obviously equal to $e^{-q_2 \cdot (T-t)} \cdot S_2(t)$. It follows that the second boundary condition to be prescribed is

$$v(t, 0, x_2) = e^{-q_2 \cdot (T-t)} \cdot x_2.$$

Having prescribed terminal and boundary conditions, we can determine the correct value of the option by solving (PDE1) subject to these conditions.

The formula. By solving (PDE1) subject to the proper terminal and boundary conditions, Margrabe obtained the following formula:

$$\begin{aligned} v(t, S_1, S_2) &= S_2 \cdot e^{-q_2 \cdot (T-t)} \cdot N(d_1) - S_1 \cdot e^{-q_1 \cdot (T-t)} \cdot N(d_2) \\ &= C(T - t, S_2, S_1, q_1, \sigma, q_2). \end{aligned}$$

Here C is the Black-Scholes function introduced above. The parameters d_1 and d_2 are given by

$$d_1 := \frac{\ln\left[\dfrac{S_2 \times e^{-q_2 \cdot (T-t)}}{S_1 \times e^{-q_1 \cdot (T-t)}}\right] + \dfrac{\sigma^2 \cdot (T-t)}{2}}{\sigma \cdot \sqrt{T-t}}$$

and

$$d_2 := d_1 - \sigma \cdot \sqrt{T-t}$$

where

$$\sigma^2 := \sigma_1^2 - 2 \cdot \rho \cdot \sigma_1 \cdot \sigma_2 + \sigma_2^2.$$

That this is a solution to (PDE1) additionally satisfying the right terminal and boundary conditions can be readily verified by direct computation.

An alternative approach. We would just like to mention that the appearance of the Black-Scholes function in Margrabe's formula is more than a mere coincidence. Assume that no dividends are paid. Choose $S_1(t)$ as a new accounting unit, i.e., as a new *numeraire,* and write the payoff as

$$S_1(T) \cdot \max\left\{0, \frac{S_2(T)}{S_1(T)} - 1\right\}$$

This looks like a traditional call on S_2, written in terms of the new numeraire, with strike 1. Noting that in this world, with $S_1(t)$ as numeraire, the risk-free rate would be zero, one obtains Margrabe's formula from the Black-Scholes function. This elegant approach was suggested to Margrabe by Ross. The article by Geman, El Karoui, and Rochet shows how fruitful it is to consider things from the change of numeraire point of view.

Options on the best and worst of two assets. From Margrabe's formula we immediately obtain pricing formulas for options on the *best of two assets,* i.e., options with payoff

$$\max\{S_1(T), S_2(T)\}$$

and options with payoff

$$\min\{S_1(T), S_2(T)\}$$

which are options on the *worst of two assets* (see Figures 5–2 and 5–3). To see this, note that the following identities hold:

$$\max\{S_1(T), S_2(T)\} = S_1(T) + \max\{0, S_2(T) - S_1(T)\}$$

and

$$\min\{S_1(T), S_2(T)\} = S_2(T) - \max\{0, S_2(T) - S_1(T)\}.$$

This implies that holding an option on the best of two assets is equivalent to holding an option on the spread between S_2 and S_1 and being long one unit of the first asset. Analogously, holding an option on the worst of two assets is the same as being long one unit of the second asset

FIGURES 5–2 and 5–3
Payoff Regions for Best-of and Worst-of Options

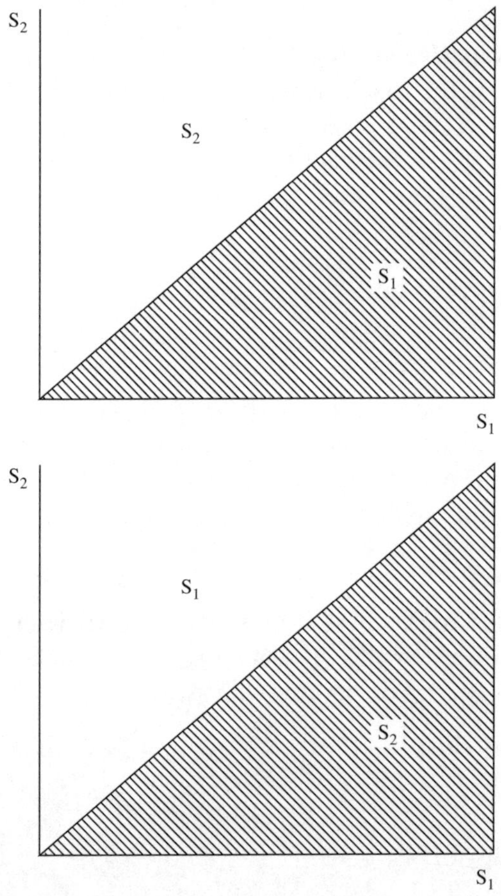

and writing an option on the spread between S_2 and S_1. We remark that these options are also known as *alternative* options.

An investor who has no definite view on which of two assets will perform better than the other might want to buy an option on the better performer. In contrast to the present situation, the spread-option investor has to take a view on which asset will perform better.

An observation on options of American type. Assume we have an American-type option on the spread between S_2 and S_1 and that $q_1 = q_2 = 0$ holds, so that no dividends are paid. Thus, this option can be exercised at any time before maturity to obtain

$$\max\{0, S_2(t) - S_1(t)\}.$$

Obviously, since we have more freedom of choice, the value of this option is greater than or equal to the corresponding European one. On the other hand we have

$$\max\{0, S_2(T) - S_1(T)\} \geq S_2(T) - S_1(T).$$

This implies that the value of the European option at any time t must be greater than the amount we have to invest at time t to get $S_2(T) - S_1(T)$ at maturity. Since no dividends are paid, this amount is obviously equal to $S_2(t) - S_1(t)$, which is what one would obtain when exercising the American option at that time. It follows that early exercise of the American option would never be advisable. Therefore, the rational value of American and European spreads is the same whenever dividend yields are zero. From the above observations and the identities shown above, it is immediately clear that the American and European versions of options on the worst or the best of two nondividend-paying assets do not differ in value.

Notes. Spread options and the equivalent alternative options were first treated in Margrabe (1978) by solving the corresponding partial differential equation. Rubinstein (1991a) derived Margrabe's formula using a binary-tree method.

Stulz's Formula for Calls and Puts on the Worst or Best of Two Assets

Stulz's 1982 paper provides an analysis of calls and puts on the worst of two assets (see Figures 5–4 and 5–5). The payoff at maturity for a call on the worst of two assets is given by

$$\max\{0, \min\{S_1(T), S_2(T)\} - K\},$$

where K is the strike price. The corresponding put has payoff

$$\max\{0, K - \min\{S_1(T), S_2(T)\}\}.$$

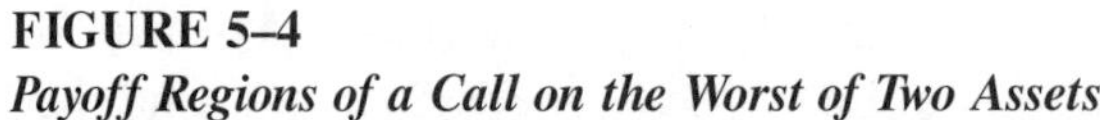

FIGURE 5–4
Payoff Regions of a Call on the Worst of Two Assets

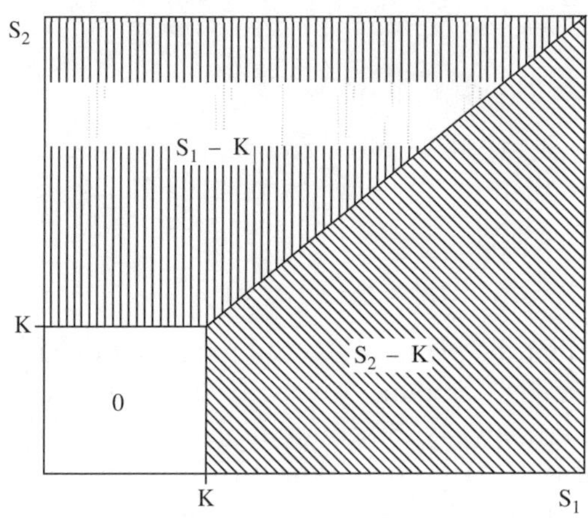

A possible application is the following. Assume a portfolio manager has two negatively correlated assets and expects a movement but does not know which of the assets will go up or down. She seeks protection for possible resulting losses. Since the effect of negative correlation is that if one of the assets goes down the other one will go up, the portfolio manager will only need to buy a put on the worst of the two assets.

Terminal and boundary conditions. As always, the terminal condition is just the payoff at maturity, i.e.,

$$v(T, x_1, x_2) = \max\{0, \min\{x_1, x_2\} - K\}.$$

For the boundary conditions we again use the fact that in our model if the spot price of an asset is zero, it remains zero for all times. If $S_1(t) = 0$ then the payoff at maturity will be

$$\max\{0, \min\{0, S_2(T)\} - K\} = 0,$$

so that the option will be worthless, i.e., we must prescribe

$$v(t, 0, x_2) = 0.$$

FIGURE 5–5
Payoff Regions of a Put on the Worst of Two Assets

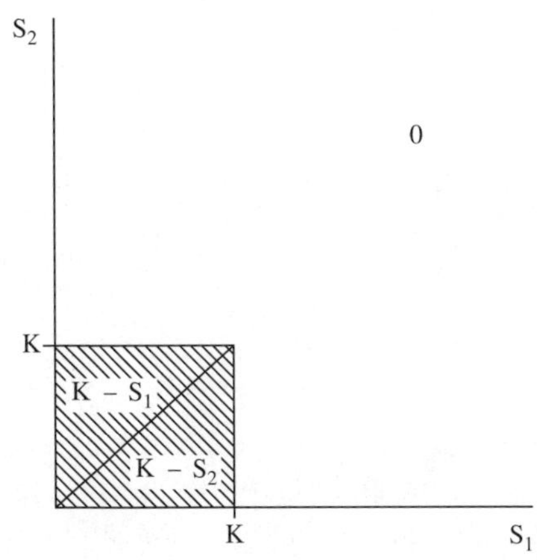

Analogously we can argue that we must have

$$v(t, x_1, 0) = 0.$$

The formula for a call on the worst of two assets. In case of nondividend-paying assets, i.e., $q_1 = q_2 = 0$, Stulz's formula for a call on the worst of two assets reads

$$\begin{aligned} v(t, S_1, S_2) = {} & S_1 \cdot N_2(d_1(S_1, \sigma_1), d_2(S_1, S_2), d_3(\sigma_1, \sigma_2)) \\ & + S_2 \cdot N_2(d_1(S_2, \sigma_2), d_2(S_2, S_1), d_3(\sigma_2, \sigma_1)) \\ & - K \cdot e^{-r \cdot (T - t)} \cdot N_2(d_1(S_1, \sigma_1) \\ & - \sigma_1 \cdot \sqrt{T - t}, d_1(S_2, \sigma_2) - \sigma_2 \cdot \sqrt{T - t}, \rho). \end{aligned}$$

Here $N_2(\cdot, \cdot, \cdot)$ denotes the bivariate cumulative standard normal distribution function. Furthermore, the different parameters appearing in the formula are defined as follows:

$$d_1(S_i, \sigma_i) := \frac{\ln\left[\dfrac{S_i}{K \cdot e^{-r \cdot (T - t)}}\right] + \dfrac{1}{2} \cdot \sigma_i^2 \cdot (T - t)}{\sigma_i \cdot \sqrt{T - t}}$$

for $i = 1, 2$,

$$d_2(S_i, S_j) := \frac{\ln\left[\dfrac{S_j}{S_i}\right] - \dfrac{1}{2} \cdot \sigma^2 \cdot (T - t)}{\sigma \cdot \sqrt{T - t}},$$

for i, j = 1, 2 and

$$d_3(\sigma_i, \sigma_j) := \frac{\rho \cdot \sigma_j - \sigma_i}{\sigma},$$

where

$$\sigma := \sqrt{\sigma_1^2 - 2 \cdot \rho \cdot \sigma_1 \cdot \sigma_2 + \sigma_2^2}.$$

The validity of this formula may be proved by substituting it in the partial differential equation and verifying the prescribed terminal and boundary conditions. Of course, this formula can be readily modified to cover the case of dividend-paying assets. By well-known arguments this can be accomplished by substituting $S_i(t)$ by $e^{-(T-t) \cdot q_i} S_i(t)$ in Stulz's formula.

Put-call parity relationships. It is very easy to establish a relationship between calls and puts on the minimum of two assets. Evidently, the identity

$$\max\{0, K - \min\{S_1(T), S_2(T)\}\} =$$
$$K + \max\{0, \min\{S_1(T), S_2(T)\} - K\} - \min\{S_1(T), S_2(T)\}$$

implies that holding a put on the worst of two assets is the same as holding a call on the worst of the two assets and a cash position K and shorting a plain option on the worst of the two assets. Recall that the value of the option on the worst of two assets was treated above.

Options on the worst of two assets and cash. An option on the *worst of two assets and cash* has the payoff

$$\min\{S_1(T), S_2(T), K\},$$

where K is a given amount of cash (see Figure 5–6). From the identity

$$\min\{S_1(T), S_2(T), K\} = K - \max\{0, K - \min\{S_1(T), S_2(T)\}\}$$

FIGURE 5–6

Payoff Regions for an Option on the Worst of Two Assets and Cash

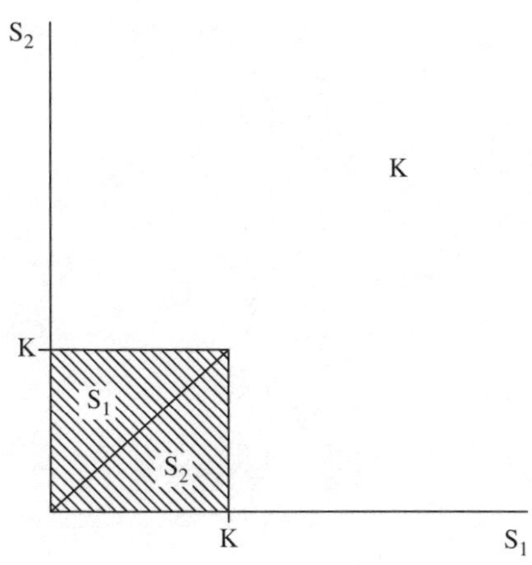

we can infer that an option on the worst of two assets and cash is the same thing as holding a cash position K and writing a put on the worst of the two assets with strike K. Therefore all elements needed for the valuation have already been made available.

Calls and puts on the best of two assets. A European *call on the best of two assets* with strike K has the payoff

$$\max\{0, \max\{S_1(T), S_2(T)\} - K\}.$$

From the identity

$$\begin{aligned}\max\{0, \max\{S_1(T), S_2(T)\} - K\} &= \max\{0, S_1(T) - K\} \\ &+ \max\{0, S_2(T) - K\} \\ &- \max\{0, \min\{S_1(T), S_2(T)\} - K\}\end{aligned}$$

we conclude that holding a call on the best of two assets is equivalent to holding standard calls on both assets with strike price K and shorting a call on the worst of two assets also with strike price K. Hence, this option can be replicated with known ones and its pricing and handling offer no difficulties.

FIGURE 5–7
Payoff Regions of an Option on the Best of Two Assets and Cash

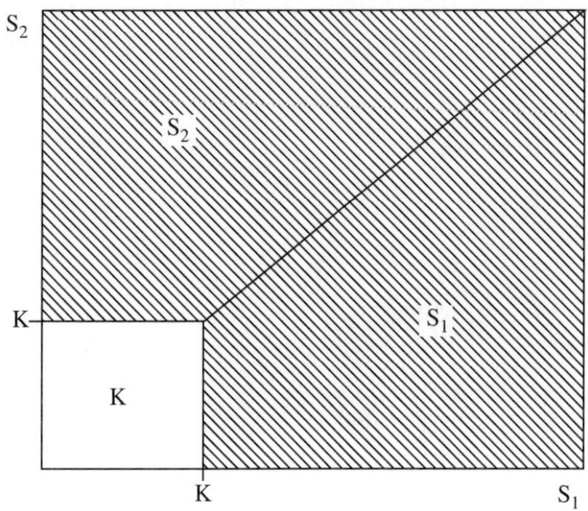

A European *put on the best of two assets* with strike K has the payoff

$$\max\{0, K - \max\{S_1(T), S_2(T)\}\}.$$

Again we can replicate this payoff with options we already know by using the identity

$$\max\{0, K - \max\{S_1(T), S_2(T)\}\} = K - \max\{S_1(T), S_2(T)\} + \max\{0, \max\{S_1(T), S_2(T)\} - K\}$$

which gives us a *put-call parity* relationship for puts and calls on the best of two assets.

Options on the best of two assets and cash. An option on the *best of two assets and cash* (see Figure 5–7) has the payoff

$$\max\{S_1(T), S_2(T), K\}.$$

As expected, this option can be replicated by investing K in cash and holding a call on the best of the two assets with strike K. This immediately follows from the identity

$$\max\{S_1(T), S_2(T), K\} = K + \max\{0, \max\{S_1(T), S_2(T),\} - K\}.$$

This option could be used by a portfolio manager who knows that at some particular time in the future he wants to buy the better of two stocks for his portfolio but does not yet know exactly which of both will turn out to be the best. Again in the case of negative correlation between the assets, this would be an attractive opportunity when he expects a movement but has no view on the direction.

A warning on options of American type. We saw that for spread options or plain options on the best or worst of two non-dividend-paying assets (which correspond to the options of this section with $q_1 = q_2 = 0$ and $K = 0$), the European and American versions have identical valuation formulas. In contrast in the present context for the case $K > 0$, this is no longer true! For instance, in the case of a put on the best of two assets this can be seen from the fact that if one of the asset prices is zero, we just have the Black-Scholes situation for a put on a single asset for which we know that the American and European versions have different prices.

Notes. The results of this section were first published in Stulz (1982). There the formulas were obtained by solving the partial differential equation. Rubinstein (1991b) obtained the same results by evaluating the risk-adjusted expectation of the payoff directly. Extensions to more than one asset can be found in Johnson (1987).

Basket Options

Basket options are becoming increasingly popular. Their payoff has the form

$$\max\{0, w_1 \cdot S_1(T) + w_2 \cdot S_2(T) - K\}$$

where the weights w_1 and w_2 are positive numbers (see Figure 5–8). Hence we are dealing with a call *option on a portfolio* consisting of w_1 units of the first asset and w_2 units of the second. For this type of option no closed-form solution is known at present. Therefore, numerical techniques are instrumental in calculating their value.

Basket options can be used, for example, as a means of simultaneously hedging exposure to two assets (e.g., two foreign currencies). In this case, a portfolio manager will be primarily interested in the performance of her portfolio as a whole and not of the individual assets.

FIGURE 5–8
Payoff Regions of a Basket Option

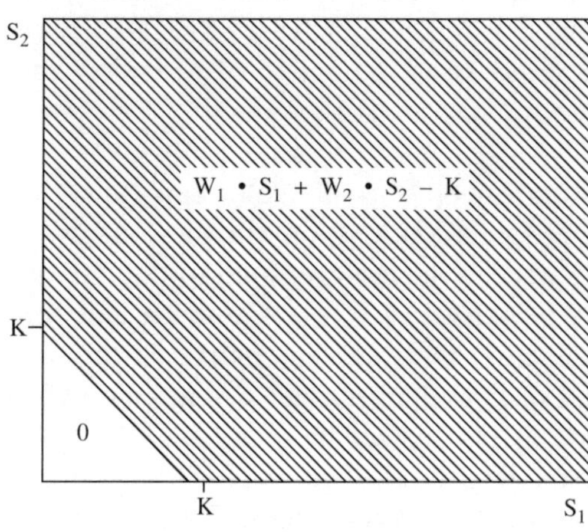

The terminal and boundary conditions. The terminal value is given by

$$v(T, x_1, x_2) = \max\{0, w_1 \cdot x_1 + w_2 \cdot x_2 - K\}.$$

For the boundary conditions, we proceed as usual and note that if $S_1(t) = 0$ holds, then the payoff at maturity will be

$$\max\{0, w_2 \cdot S_2(T) - K\} = w_2 \cdot \max\left\{0, S_2(T) - \frac{K}{w_2}\right\}.$$

This is w_2 times the payoff of a standard European call on the second asset with strike $\frac{K}{w_2}$ so that the first boundary condition to be prescribed is

$$v(t, 0, x_2) = w_2 \cdot C\left(T - t, x_2, \frac{K}{w_2}, r, \sigma_2, q_2\right)$$

where C is the Black-Scholes function defined above. Analogously, we can argue that for the other boundary condition

$$v(t, x_1, 0) = w_1 \cdot C\left(T - t, x_1, \frac{K}{w_1}, r, \sigma_1, q_1\right)$$

must hold.

Notes. As already mentioned, no closed-form solutions for basket options are known at present. The basic difficulty is that the sum of lognormal variables is no longer lognormal so that the usual techniques break down in this case. The same kind of situation can be found when valuing options on an index that is just the weighted sum of various assets. There one resolves the dilemma by bluntly assuming that the index itself follows a geometric Brownian motion, which looks more like a strategy of last resort than a genuine solution. Options on the arithmetic average of an asset price are another kind of derivative for which this difficulty arises. There, using quite advanced methods, a true solution has been found by Geman and Yor (1994), so there might yet be hope for baskets.

One can calculate prices of basket options by numerically solving the partial differential equation subject to the appropriate terminal and boundary conditions. For options on one asset, this approach has been described in detail in Wilmot, Dewynne, and Howison (1994). But similar methods also apply for the multidimensional case. Rubinstein (1991b) offers a numerical approach for computing the expectation of the payoff directly. Analytical approximations for the price of basket options can be found in Huynh (1994). However, no precise error estimates are given so that the reliability of these approximations is not quite clear.

THE RED BOOK OF MAOs II: TWO CURRENCIES

In this section we deal with MAOs involving products. They arise quite naturally in the framework of investors having domestic reference currency and stock in some foreign currency. In this case the two assets would be the foreign stock and the exchange rate. We shall deal with different possible protections the investor may want to seek. Some of the cases considered here will not be genuine multiasset options—the dependence on the exchange rate being almost trivial. But we include them here for completeness.

The Mathematical Model

We choose our notation to make as clear as possible the dependency on the particular currency. The risk-free rate in *foreign currency* will be denoted by r_f and the one in *domestic currency* by r_d. The asset will be an asset in foreign currency and its price process $S_f(t)$ will follow a geometric Brownian motion given by

$$dS_f(t) = (r_f - q_f)S_f(t)dt + \sigma_f S_f(t)dB_f(t).$$

The (constant) parameters q_f and σ_f are dividend yield and volatility, respectively. Moreover, B_f is a standard Brownian motion.

Denote by $X_{f\to d}(t)$ the rate at which the investor can exchange one unit of foreign currency into domestic currency at time t. We shall assume that $X_{f\to d}(t)$ is a geometric Brownian motion governed by

$$dX_{f\to d}(t) = (r_d - r_f)X_{f\to d}(t)dt + \sigma_{f\to d}X_{f\to d}(t)dB_{f\to d}(t)$$

where $\sigma_{f\to d}$ is the volatility of the exchange rate and $B_{f\to d}$ is a standard Brownian motion. Again all parameters are assumed constant in time. Observe that we have adopted a representation of $S_f(t)$ and $X_{f\to d}(t)$ with respect to the joint risk-adjusted probability measure Q. Furthermore, the exponentials $e^{S_f(t)}$ and $e^{X_{f\to d}(t)}$ are assumed to be jointly normally distributed with constant correlation coefficient ρ.

The Stochastics of the Derivative's Price

In the context of a derivative security denominated in domestic currency but with a foreign asset as underlying, we have three instruments with which to hedge: domestic and foreign risk-free bonds and the foreign asset. The exchange rate enters naturally into the picture, since our reference currency is the domestic one and we have to convert everything into it.

As usual we denote by v(t, x, s) the value of the derivative security at time t when the exchange rate $X_{f\to d}(t)$ is equal to x and the foreign stock price $S_f(t)$ equals s. An application of the multidimensional Ito formula shows that the process followed by $V(t){:} = v(t, X_{f\to d}(t), S_f(t))$ is governed by a stochastic differential equation given by

$$\begin{aligned} dV(t) = \Bigg[& \partial_t v(t, x, s) + \frac{1}{2}\cdot \sigma_{f\to d}\cdot X_{f\to d}(t)\cdot \partial_x^2 v(t, x, s) \\ & + \frac{1}{2}\cdot \sigma_f \cdot S_f(t)\cdot \partial_s^2 v(t, x, s) \\ & + \rho\cdot \sigma_{f\to d}\,\sigma_f\cdot X_{f\to d}(t)\cdot S_f(t)\cdot \partial_x\partial_s v(t, x, s) \Bigg] dt \\ & + \partial_x v(t, x, s)dX_{f\to d}(t) + \partial_s v(t, x, s)dS_f(t). \end{aligned} \tag{VE}$$

The Replicating Portfolio and the PDE

We now consider a dynamic portfolio consisting of $\Delta_0(t)$ units of the domestic risk-free bond, $\Delta_1(t)$ units of the foreign risk-free bond, and $\Delta_2(t)$ units of the foreign asset, where we have set:

$$\Delta_2(t) := \frac{\partial_s v(t, X_{f \to d}(t), S_f(t))}{X_{f \to d}(t)},$$

$$D_1(t) := e^{-r_f \cdot t} \cdot \left[\partial_x v(t, X_{f \to d}(t), S_f(t)) - \frac{\partial_s v(t, X_{f \to d}(t), S_f(t))}{X_{f \to d}(t)} \right],$$

and, finally,

$$\begin{aligned} \Delta_0(t) :&= e^{r_d \cdot t} \cdot [v(t, X_{f \to d}(t), S_f(t)) - \Delta_1(t) \cdot X_{f \to d}(t) \cdot e^{r_f \cdot t} \\ &\quad - \Delta_2(t) \cdot X_{f \to d}(t) \cdot S_f(t)] \\ &= e^{r_d \cdot t} \cdot [v(t, X_{f \to d}(t), S_f(t)) - X_{f \to d}(t) \cdot \partial_x v(t, X_{f \to d}(t) \cdot S_f(t)]. \end{aligned}$$

Denote the value of this portfolio by R(t). It is given by

$$\begin{aligned} R(t) &= \Delta_0(t) \cdot e^{r_d \cdot t} + \Delta_1(t) \cdot X_{f \to d}(t) \cdot e^{r_f \cdot t} + \Delta_2(t) \cdot X_{f \to d}(t) \cdot S_f(t) \\ &= v(t, X_{f \to d}(t), S_f(t)). \end{aligned}$$

It follows that this dynamic portfolio replicates at any time the value of the derivative security. Moreover, the change in value of this portfolio is described by

$$\begin{aligned} dR(t) = \Delta_0(t) \cdot e^{r_d \cdot t} \cdot r_d dt + \Delta_1(t) d(X_{f \to d}(t) \cdot e^{r_f \cdot t}) \\ + \Delta_2(t) d(X_{f \to d}(t) \cdot S_f(t)). \end{aligned}$$

Using the product rule for stochastic differentials we find that

$$\begin{aligned} dR(t) = [&\Delta_0(t) \cdot e^{r_d \cdot t} \cdot r_d + \Delta_1(t) \cdot e^{r_f \cdot t} \cdot r_f \cdot X_{f \to d}(t) \\ &+ \Delta_2(t) \cdot \rho \cdot \sigma_{f \to d} \cdot \sigma_f \cdot X_{f \to d}(t) \cdot S_f(t)] dt \\ &+ [\Delta_1(t) \cdot e^{r_f \cdot t} + \Delta_2(t) \cdot S_f(t)] dX_{f \to d}(t) + \Delta_2(t) \cdot X_{f \to d}(t) dS_f(t). \end{aligned}$$

Again, this is a self-financing portfolio. From $V(t) = R(t)$ it follows that $dV(t) = dR(t)$ holds. Utilizing equation (VE) for dV(t) and the above expression for dR(t), we see that in the equation $dV(t) = dR(t)$, the stochastic terms—i.e., the terms in $dX_{f \to d}(t)$ and $dS_f(t)$ cancel out, leaving us with the partial differential equation for v.

FIGURE 5–9
Payoff Region for Flexo Option

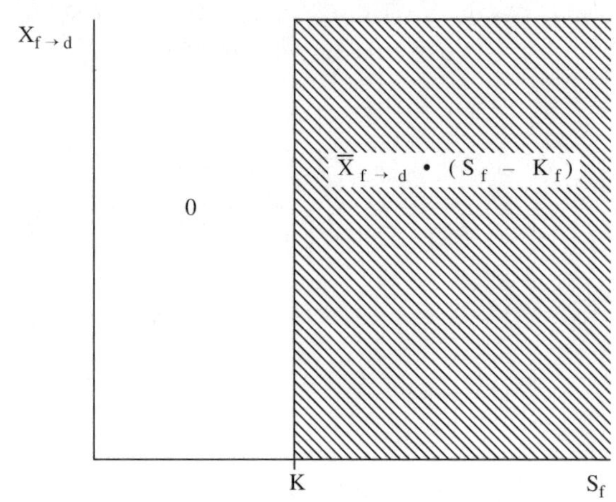

$$\begin{aligned} 0 = \partial_t v &+ \frac{1}{2} \cdot [\sigma_{f\to d}^2 \cdot x^2 \cdot \partial_x^2 v + \sigma_f^2 \cdot s^2 \cdot \partial_s^2 v] \\ &+ \rho \cdot \sigma_{f\to d} \cdot \sigma_f \cdot x \cdot s \cdot \partial_x v \cdot \partial_s v \\ &+ (r_d - r_f) \cdot x \cdot \partial_x v \\ &+ (r_f - q_f - \rho \cdot \sigma_{f\to d} \cdot \sigma_f) \cdot s \cdot \partial_s v + r_d \cdot v. \end{aligned} \tag{PDE2}$$

Hence, the formula for the price of any derivative on S_f denominated in domestic currency is the unique solution of (PDE2) subject to the right terminal and boundary conditions.

Flexo Options

Consider an investor who is buying a European call with strike K_f on the foreign asset and taking the full currency-risk exposure. The payoff of this instrument (see Figure 5–9), which not surprisingly is also known as a *flexible-rate call,* or *flexo,* is given by

$$X_{f\to d}(T) \cdot \max\{0, S_f(T) - K_f\}.$$

The investor might be someone who sees great potential in the foreign stock and thinks that the exchange rate will remain stable or that the domestic currency will appreciate against the foreign currency.

Terminal and boundary conditions. The right terminal condition for a flexo is

$$v(T, x, s) = x \cdot \max\{0, s - K_f\}.$$

To establish the right boundary conditions, we do the usual analysis. We note that the payoff of the flexible-rate option is equal to 0 if at any time either the exchange rate or the stock price are equal to 0. Therefore, we have to prescribe

$$v(t, 0, s) = v(t, x, 0) = 0.$$

The formula for a flexo. The above equation can be solved by purely economical arguments. Assume that an investor wants to invest in an instrument denominated in foreign currency whose price follows a process S(t) and paying dividends at a rate q. If he is indifferent to currency risk, he will just buy the instrument, hold it until maturity, and convert it into domestic currency at the exchange rate prevailing at maturity, i.e., the payoff will be

$$X_{f \to d}(T) \cdot S(T).$$

Since the investor is taking the full foreign-exchange risk himself, the price of this instrument will be

$$X_{f \to d}(0) \cdot e^{-q \cdot (T - t)} \cdot S(0).$$

This is rather obvious but useful. By the above argument, the price of the flexible-rate call option is given by

$$\begin{aligned} v(t, S_f, X_{f \to d}) &= X_{f \to d} \cdot C(T - t, S_f, K_f, r_f, \sigma_f, q_f) \\ &= C(T - t, X_{f \to d} \cdot S_f, X_{f \to d} \cdot K_f, r_f, \sigma_f, q_f) \end{aligned}$$

where C is the Black-Scholes function defined above.

Compo Options

Another situation arises when the investor wants the following payoff at maturity

$$\max\{0, X_{f \to d}(T) \cdot S_f(T) - K_d\}.$$

Note that we have a domestic strike price K_d. Such an option is sometimes called a *compo.* (See Figure 5–10.) These options offer simultaneous protection both on the assets risk and the currency risk and they

FIGURE 5–10
Payoff Regions of a Compo Option

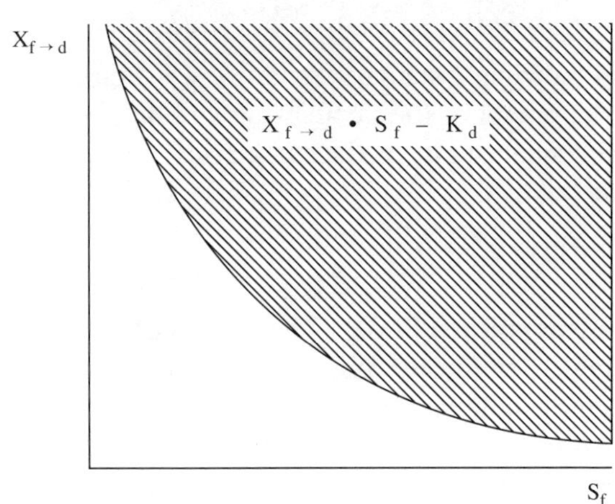

will be favored by a prudent investor looking for opportunities in foreign markets.

Terminal and boundary conditions. For the compo option we impose the following terminal condition:

$$v(T, x, s) = \max\{0, x \cdot s - K_d\}.$$

Also in this case, if either $x = 0$ or $s = 0$ holds, the payoff will be equal to 0. Therefore, the right boundary conditions to prescribe are again:

$$v(t, 0, s) = v(t, x, 0) = 0.$$

The formula for a compo. Instead of solving (PDE2) directly, we deduce the price of a compo by applying Margrabe's formula. We may trivially rewrite the payoff as

$$\begin{aligned}&\max\{0, X_{f \to d}(T) \cdot S_f(T) - K_d\}\\ &= X_{f \to d}(T) \cdot \max\{0, S_f(T) - X_{d \to f}(T) \cdot K_d\}.\end{aligned}$$

Here, $X_{d\to f}(t) := \dfrac{1}{X_{f\to d}(t)}$, $t \geq 0$, is the rate at which domestic currency is translated into foreign currency. Arguing as in the case of a flexo, we see that the price of a compo is the price of the instrument with (foreign) payoff

$$\max\{0, S_f(T) - X_{d\to f}(T) \cdot K_d\}$$

converted at the prevailing exchange rate. The structure of this payoff is the same as that of an outperformance option. Hence to price it, we just need to know the stochastic differential equation governing $(X_{d\to f}(t))_{t\geq 0}$. Obviously the risk-adjusted representation of the rate to exchange domestic for foreign currency is

$$dX_{d\to f}(t) = (r_f - r_d) \cdot X_{d\to f}(t)dt + \sigma_{f\to d} \cdot X_{d\to f}(t) \cdot dB_{d\to f}(t)$$

where $(B_{d\to f}(t))_{t\geq 0}$ is a standard Brownian motion. Observe that the volatility of $X_{d\to f}(t)$ is the same as the one of $X_{f\to d}(t)$ and that the correlation between $X_{d\to f}(t)$ and $S_f(t)$ is $-\rho$. From Margrabe's formula we now immediately obtain

$$\begin{aligned} v(t, S_f, X_{f\to d}) &= X_{f\to d} \cdot C(T - t, S_f, X_{d\to f} \cdot K_d, r_d, \sigma, q_f). \\ &= C(T - t, X_{f\to d} \cdot S_f, K_d, r_d, \sigma, q_f) \end{aligned}$$

where we have set $\sigma := \sqrt{\sigma_f^2 + 2 \cdot \rho \cdot \sigma_f \sigma_{f\to d} + \sigma_{f\to d}^2}$. Note that the plus sign in the term involving the correlation comes from the correlation between $X_{d\to f}(t)$ and $S_f(t)$ being $-\rho$.

Quanto Options

Another kind of protection is offered by a *quanto* call option. Here the investor wants a call option on the foreign asset but seeks to neutralize the currency risk by fixing the exchange rate at which the proceeds of the call option are converted into domestic currency. A quanto's payoff (see Figure 5–11) is given by

$$\overline{X}_{f\to d} \cdot \max\{0, S_f(T) - K_f\}.$$

Observe that this involves a foreign-exchange forward but on the unknown amount $\{0, S_f(T) - K_f\}$. This explains the name *quantity adjusted option* (quanto).

FIGURE 5–11
Payoff Regions for a Quanto Call

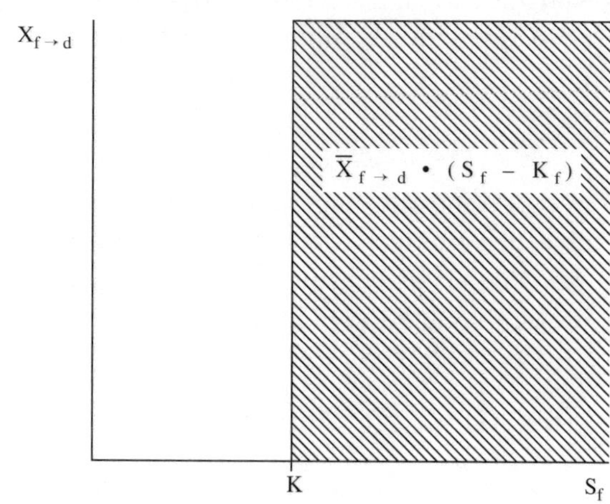

The reduced differential equation. The analysis of a quanto option can be simplified by making a few easy observations first. Since the payoff at maturity is totally independent from the level of the exchange rate at any time, the value of the option *cannot* depend on $X_{f\to d}(t)$. This means that the derivatives of v(t, x, s) with respect to x have to vanish. Therefore, (PDE2) simplifies to a differential equation involving only the time variable t and the foreign stock price variable s:

$$\partial_t v + \frac{1}{2} \cdot \sigma_f^2 \cdot s^2 \cdot \partial_s^2 v + (r_d - q_d) \cdot s \cdot \partial_s v + r_d \cdot v = 0 \qquad \text{(PDE3)}$$

where we have set $q_d := r_d - r_f + q_f + \rho \cdot \sigma_{f\to d} \cdot \sigma_f$.

This equation for the function v(t, s) has to be solved subject to the terminal condition

$$v(T, x) := \overline{X}_{f\to d} \cdot \max\{0, s - K_f\}$$

and the boundary conditions

$$v(t, 0) = 0 \qquad \text{and} \qquad v(t, s) \approx s \qquad \text{as } s \to \infty.$$

The formula for quantos. Now, (PDE3) with the corresponding terminal and boundary conditions displays exactly the same structure as the partial differential equation for a standard European call, which is solved by the Black-Scholes function discussed above. By uniqueness of the solutions, we conclude that

$$
\begin{aligned}
v(t, S_f) &= \overline{X}_{f \to d} \cdot C(T - t, S_f, K_f, r_d, \sigma_f, q_d) \\
&= C(T - t, \overline{X}_{f \to d} \cdot S_f, \overline{X}_{f \to d} \cdot K_f, r_d, \sigma_f, q_d)
\end{aligned}
$$

The equity-linked FX-forward. The *equity-linked FX-forward* has payoff

$$\overline{X}_{f \to d} \cdot S_f(T).$$

Note that it corresponds to the payoff of the quanto with strike $K_f = 0$. Hence its price is given by taking the limit in the above formula as K_f tends to 0. This is a straightforward computation and gives

$$\overline{X}_{f \to d} \cdot S_f(t) \cdot e^{-q_d \cdot (T - t)}.$$

Recall that $q_d := r_d - r_f + q_f + \rho \cdot \sigma_{f \to d} \cdot \sigma_f$. We shall use this fact in the next section.

Beach Options

In the quanto option setting, the investor is hedging her currency risk away by fixing the exchange rate. Hence she will not be able to profit from an appreciation of the domestic against the foreign currency. If she wants to take advantage of favorable movements in the exchange rate, she would rather buy a *beach option* (best equity-adjusted currency hedge). These options have the following payoff

$$S_f \cdot \max\{\overline{X}_{f \to d}, X_{f \to d}\},$$

where $\overline{X}_{f \to d}$ is the floor for the exchange rate level based on the variable amount $S_f(T)$. (See Figure 5–12.) Hence the investor is taking the full asset price risk but is hedged against adverse exchange-rate movements.

Decomposing the beach option. This option can be decomposed into two parts

FIGURE 5–12
Payoff Regions for a Beach Option

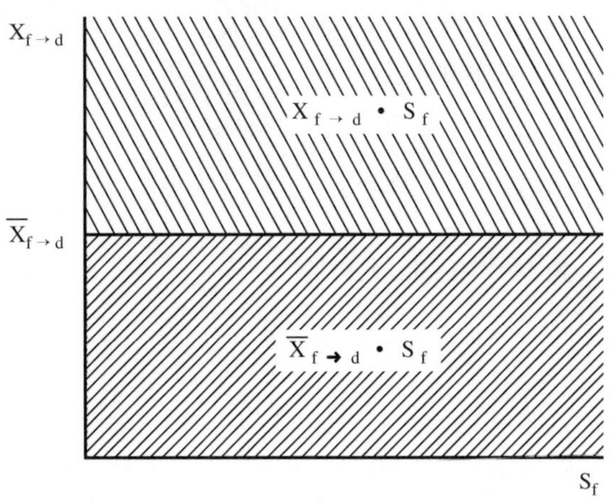

$$S_f(T) \cdot \max\{\overline{X}_{f\to d}, X_{f\to d}(T)\}$$
$$= S_f(T) \cdot \overline{X}_{f\to d}(T) + S_f(T) \cdot \max\{0, X_{f\to d}(T) - \overline{X}_{f\to d}\}.$$

This is like holding an equity-linked FX-forward and an FX-call with strike $\overline{X}_{f\to d}$ on the unknown amount $S_f(T)$. Hence the real challenge is now to value this *equity-linked FX-call* with payoff

$$S_f(T) \cdot \max\{0, X_{f\to d}(T) - \overline{X}_{f\to d}\}.$$

Terminal and boundary conditions for the equity-linked FX-call. The terminal condition is given by the payoff at maturity, i.e.,

$$v(T, x, s) = s \cdot \max\{0, x - \overline{X}_{f\to d}\}.$$

If either $x = 0$ or $s = 0$, the payoff is equal to 0. Hence the boundary conditions are

$$v(t, 0, s) = v(t, x, 0) = 0.$$

The formula for the equity-linked FX-call. The boundary conditions are the same as for the flexible-rate call. Moreover, the terminal conditions of the present option are almost the same as the terminal conditions of the flexible-rate option. The only difference is that x and s must be interchanged! Therefore, by the uniqueness of solutions, we conclude that the value of the equity-linked FX-call is given by

$$\begin{aligned} v(t, \overline{X}_{f \to d}, S_f) &= S_f \cdot C(T - t, X_{f \to d}, \overline{X}_{f \to d}, q_d, \sigma_{f \to d}, q_f) \\ &= C(T - t, X_{f \to d} \cdot S_f, \overline{X}_{f \to d} \cdot S_f, q_d, \sigma_{f \to d}, q_f). \end{aligned}$$

The formula for the beach option. Combining the formula for the equity-linked FX-forward and the equity-linked FX-call, we obtain the formula for the beach option

$$\begin{aligned} v(t, \overline{X}_{f \to d}, S_f) &= \overline{X}_{f \to d} \cdot S_f \cdot e^{-q_d \cdot (T - t)} \\ &\quad + S_f \cdot C(T - t, X_{f \to d}, \overline{X}_{f \to d}, q_d, \sigma_{f \to d}, q_f) \\ &= \overline{X}_{f \to d} \cdot S_f \cdot e^{-q_d \cdot (T - t)} \\ &\quad + C(T - t, X_{f \to d}, S_f, \overline{X}_{f \to d}, S_f, q_d, \sigma_{f \to d}, q_f). \end{aligned}$$

Notes. Standard references for domestic-currency-denominated options on a foreign asset are the articles by Derman, Karasinski, and Wecker (1990); Reiner (1991); and Dravid, Richardson, and Sun (1993).

REFERENCES

1. Derman, Emanuel, *Valuing and Hedging Outperformance Options,* Quantitative Strategies, Research Notes, Goldman Sachs, (1992).
2. Derman, Emanuel, Piotr Karasinski, and Jeffrey S. Wecker, *Understanding Guaranteed Exchange-Rate Contracts in Foreign Stock Investments,* International Equity Strategies, Goldman Sachs, (1990).
3. Dravid, Ajay, Mathew Richardson, and Tong-sheng Sun, "Pricing Foreign Index Contingent Claims: An Application to Nikkei Index Warrants, *The Journal of Derivatives* (1993).
4. Geman, Helyette, Nicole El Karoui, and Jean-Charles Rochet, "Changes of Numeraire, Changes of Probability Measure and Option Pricing," to appear in *The Journal of Applied Probability.*
5. Geman, Helyette, and Marc Yor, "Bessel Processes, Asian Options, and Perpetuities," *Mathematical Finance,* Vol. 3, No. 4 (1993).
6. Huyhn, Chi Ban, "Back to Baskets," *Risk,* Vol. 7, No. 5 (1994).

7. Johnson, Herbert, "Options on the Maximum or the Minimum of Several Assets," *Journal of Financial and Quantitative Analysis,* Vol. 22, No. 3 (1987).
8. Karatzas, Ioannis, and Steven E. Shreve, *Brownian Motion and Stochastic Calculus,* 2d ed., (New York: Springer, 1991).
9. Margrabe, William, "The Value of an Option to Exchange One Asset for Another," *The Journal of Finance,* Vol. 33, No. 1 (1988).
10. Reiner, Eric, "Quanto Mechanics," *Risk,* Vol. 5, No. 3 (1992).
11. Rubinstein, Marc, "One for Another," *Risk,* Vol. 4, No. 7 (1991a).
12. Rubinstein, Marc, "Somewhere over the Rainbow," Vol. 4, No. 10 (1991b).
13. Stulz, Rene, "Options on the Minimum or the Maximum of Two Risky Assets," *Journal of Financial Economics,* Vol. 10 (1982).
14. Wilmot, Paul, Jeff Dewynne, and Sam Howison, *Option Pricing: Mathematical Models and Computation,* Oxford Financial Press (1994).

Chapter Six

Averaging Options*

Ton C. F. Vorst
Department of Finance
Erasmus University, Rotterdam

INTRODUCTION

Since the mid-1980s the average-rate, or Asian, option has become one of the most popular exotic option products that is mainly traded in the over-the-counter (OTC) market. Already by the end of the 1970s, average-rate options were part of so-called commodity-linked bonds. One of the first commodity-linked bonds was the Mexican Petrobond, issued in 1977 and featuring redemption at 25-day-interval averages. In May 1985 the Dutch company Oranje Nassau issued bonds with a maturity of eight years in local currency; the redemption value was defined as the maximum of the average price of 10.5 barrels of Brent Blend oil over the last year of the contract and the face value of the bond. The average was based on monthly prices and when the bonds were issued, the value of the amount of oil was equal to the face value. Hence, these were at-the-money options. By adding this feature to the contract, the company could set the coupon rate at 1 percent below the prevailing market rate. The company had two reasons for using an average-rate option in the contract. First, its profits were correlated with the oil price, and for high oil prices it would be no problem to pay the higher redemption value out of their profits. For low oil prices the options would expire worthless. However, profits would only be large enough if the oil price was high during a substantial part of the final year and not only at the maturity

*The author is grateful to Terry Cheuk for his excellent computational assistance.

date. The average-rate option would end in-the-money only in the first case. This is still the main reason for the use of average-rate options. The second reason at that time was that the company feared oil price manipulation near the maturity date of the bonds.

Other examples of commodity-linked bonds were the Delaware gold-indexed bond, based on an average gold price over 10 trading days; Petrolewis oil-indexed notes, based on three-month averages; and BT Gold Notes Limited notes, based on monthly averages. Only later on, trading in stand-alone products started. In January 1988 AB Svensk Exportkredit, a Swedish export corporation, issued average-exchange-rate options on the yen and the deutsche mark against the dollar, where the average was taken over the first fixings over all trading days during a year. This contract traded at the Luxembourg Exchange. However, trading of stand-alone products started earlier in the OTC market. Also, trading takes place mostly over-the-counter today, since the options are structured to suit the specific needs of the end users. Average-rate options can be based on stock indexes, interest rates, foreign currencies, and commodities and by their very nature they are cash-settled. It is said that the name "Asian options" was coined by employees of Bankers Trust, which sold these options to Japanese firms that wanted to hedge their foreign-currency exposure. These firms used these options because their annual reports are also based on average exchange rates over the year.

In the remainder of this chapter we first present some examples where Asian options are suitable hedging instruments and we compare Asian options with their European counterparts. Then we compare some valuation methods for average-rate options based on stocks, stock indexes, currencies, and commodities. Next, we discuss the hedge parameters and some other specific issues and we focus on interest-rate-based average-rate options. Finally, there will be a concluding section.

HEDGING WITH ASIAN OPTIONS

One of the best-known applications of average-rate options occurs in the foreign-exchange markets. Let us assume that Widgets Unlimited, a U.S.-based firm, receives monthly cash flows in deutsche marks of approximately DM 1 million. The firm fears a depreciation of the mark against the dollar and wants to hedge its cash flows over the next calendar year. However, the firm wants to keep its upside potential when the mark appreciates. If it wants to use options, there are three alternatives. First, it can buy 12 put options with a notional value of DM 1 million each, one for each month within the year. These options differ only with respect to their maturity. Second, it can buy a put based on DM 12 million, that expires at the end of the year. Third, it can buy an Asian put option with a nominal value of DM 12 million, based on monthly averages of the exchange rate and with expiration at the end of the year. The payoff of the Asian put option at maturity is the difference between the strike price and the average exchange rate as long as the difference is positive. The first two alternatives are more expensive than the average-rate option. For example, using at-the-money options, where the exchange rate for one DM is $0.70, interest rates in both countries are equal to 6 percent, and the volatility of the exchange rate is 15 percent, the three alternatives cost, respectively, $340,000 $473,000, and $290,000, at the start of the year. The second alternative is more expensive than the first, since it can be seen as 12 identical options on a face value of DM 1 million. Each of the options can be compared with one of the twelve options in the first alternative and each is more expensive because it has a longer maturity. The first alternative is more expensive than the third, the Asian option, since it protects the holder each month against unfavorable exchange rates. The Asian option only gives protection against the average. The first alternative will always generate a higher payoff than the average-rate option. In most cases, firms might consider the first alternative as overprotective and choose the Asian option because it gives enough protection and it is much cheaper. There is another disadvantage in using the second alternative. If one exchanges the deutsche-mark cash flows by the end of each month into dollars, the DM 12 million puts might not give protection when the exchange rate is low during the year, but is suddenly high by the end of the year. The cash flows in dollars are low, while the puts expire out-of-the-money. One way to overcome this problem is to exchange only at the end of the year, in which case one could invest the marks in a riskless account until the end of the year. If a firm needs the cash flows for its daily operations, one might have to borrow in dollars at the same time. It is clear that there will be a spread between the two rates, which are costs for the firm.

Table 6–1 shows the payoffs of the earlier specified options and the underlying cash flows of the different alternatives for several exchange-rate scenarios over the year. For the second alternative, we consider both

TABLE 6–1
The Different Hedging Alternatives

Scenario	*1*	*2*	*3*	*4*	*5*	*6*
			Exchange rates			
January	.70	.70	.70	.70	.68	.72
February	.71	.69	.68	.72	.66	.74
March	.72	.68	.66	.74	.64	.76
April	.72	.68	.64	.76	.62	.78
May	.73	.67	.62	.78	.62	.78
June	.74	.66	.62	.78	.66	.74
July	.71	.69	.60	.80	.67	.73
August	.69	.71	.60	.80	.68	.72
September	.68	.72	.60	.80	.69	.71
October	.66	.74	.62	.78	.70	.70
November	.67	.73	.62	.78	.71	.69
December	.67	.73	.62	.78	.71	.69
Average exchange rate	.70	.70	.63	.77	.67	.73
			Total cash flows in million US $			
Without puts	8.40	8.40	7.58	9.22	8.04	8.76
12 monthly puts	8.53	8.53	8.40	9.22	8.42	8.78
12 million put immediate exchange	8.76	8.40	8.54	9.22	8.04	8.88
12 million put year-end exchange	8.40	8.76	8.40	9.36	8.52	8.40
Asian options	8.40	8.40	8.40	9.22	8.40	8.76

the case where the exchange takes place at the end of the month and the case where it takes place at year-end. In the latter case, we do not consider the influence of borrowing and lending. This omission is justified, since the interest rates in both countries are assumed to be equal. From Table 6–1 we see that the Asian option always guarantees a total cash flow of at least $8.4 million. The 12 monthly puts always give higher cash flows, but the option is more expensive, as we have explained earlier. The single year-end put is even more expensive and does not guarantee a minimum cash flow if the marks are exchanged immediately, as scenario three indicates. With year-end exchange the payoffs are always higher, but next to the higher option price there is also the spread between borrowing and lending rates that has to be paid. For a spread of 2 percent this amounts to \$84,000. Another alternative to the single put would be to buy American puts for the same amount. Each month puts with DM 1 million notional value could be exercised early, when necessary. This would generate payoffs that exceed the payoffs of the 12 monthly puts. However, the American options would be even more expensive than the most expensive alternative previously mentioned.

There are numerous other possible applications of Asian options. Firms that have a stream of liabilities in foreign currencies might buy Asian calls. As in the example of Oranje Nassau, firms might write options if their profits depend on some commodity or exchange rate. In this way, they cash the option premium, giving up a large upside potential profit. Also in the commodities markets there are numerous applications. The contract, among others, has been used by Brazilian coffee farmers to hedge against a low coffee price. They needed protection against a persistent price decline instead of a single low price.

VALUATION OF ASIAN OPTIONS

In this section we focus on average-rate options where the underlying instrument is a foreign currency. The valuation formulas can be extended straightforwardly to options on stocks, stock indexes, or commodities. If one is working with averages of interest rates, the formulas should not be applied. We assume that the options are European in the sense that they cannot be exercised early. To our knowledge most traded contracts are indeed European. As with most exotic options, Asian options can be priced in the familiar Black-Scholes framework. This means that the value of the option is the discounted expectation of the payoff at maturity. The expcctation has to be taken in a risk-neutral world. For an Asian call on a foreign currency this amounts to

$$C = e^{-r(T_n - t)}E\left[Max\left(\frac{1}{n}\sum_{i=1}^{n} S(T_i) - X, 0\right)\right] \tag{1}$$

where the expectation is taken under the assumption that the exchange-rate process is described by the following risk-neutral stochastic process:

$$dS = (r - r_f)Sdt + \sigma SdW_t \tag{2}$$

In these formulas X is the exercise price, $T_1, \ldots, T_n$ are the dates over which the average is taken, $S(T_1), \ldots, S(T_n)$ are the exchange rates at these dates, r_f is the riskless interest rate in the foreign currency, while r is the domestic riskless rate. The payoff of the option takes place at date T_n. Actual time is t and we assume for the moment that $t \prec T_1$. Hence, the valuation of the option amounts to evaluating the expectation in (1). From (2) it follows that all $S(T_i)$ have lognormal distributions, i.e., $\ln S(T_i)$ has a normal distribution. However, the sum $\sum S(T_i)$ of lognormally distributed variables no longer has a known distribution. This is the reason why there are no analytic formulas, such as the Black-Scholes formulas, for average-rate options.

Monte Carlo Simulation

There are two ways to derive explicit option prices from equations (1) and (2). First, through Monte Carlo simulation based on equation (2), one can generate averages of the underlying currency values and calculate the discounted average payoff of the Asian option. Monte Carlo simulation is never exact, and one always has to take the standard deviation of the estimate into account. Kemna and Vorst (1990) describe this methodology in the first published paper[1] on average-rate options. They also show that there are several so-called variance reduction techniques to improve the accuracy of the Monte Carlo simulated values. In Tables 6–2 and 6–3 values for two kinds of average-rate options are given under the heading MC. Table 6–2 gives values for a weekly averaging option and Table 6–3 for a monthly averaging option. The averaging period is six months in both cases. Option values are given for several strike prices, volatilities, and domestic interest rates. The spot price of the foreign currency is 2 and the foreign interest-rate is 8 percent. Also, standard deviations of the Monte Carlo simulated values are given in the next columns. Especially for low volatilities, as is usually the case for foreign currencies, the standard deviations are small, indicating a high accuracy of the values. In the remaining columns we provide average-rate option values, as calculated by approximation

[1]Bergman wrote a paper on average-rate options in 1981. However, to our knowledge this paper was never published. Furthermore, it only considers zero strike price options, which can be valued in a trivial way because they are essentially forward contracts.

TABLE 6–2
Weekly Average-Exchange-Rate Call Option Values for 10,000 Units of Foreign Currency

σ	r	K	MC	Std Err	Vorst	Levy	TW	RS
0.1	0.06	1.9	925.01	0.21	925.94	925.84	925.11	925.09
		2.0	295.13	0.20	295.34	295.18	295.24	295.16
		2.1	50.05	0.16	49.61	49.53	50.18	50.12
	0.10	1.9	1098.89	0.24	1099.59	1099.86	1099.20	1099.17
		2.0	401.66	0.24	401.54	402.13	401.90	401.83
		2.1	82.04	0.23	80.93	81.32	81.98	81.89
0.2	0.06	1.9	1188.60	0.88	1190.54	1191.39	1188.49	1188.75
		2.0	641.62	0.87	641.53	642.49	642.16	641.95
		2.1	302.25	0.85	299.76	300.56	302.67	302.13
	0.10	1.9	1324.95	0.96	1326.32	1328.30	1325.11	1325.44
		2.0	743.07	0.97	742.29	744.74	743.73	743.64
		2.1	365.24	0.96	362.03	364.24	365.88	365.38
0.5	0.06	1.9	2184.18	6.28	2140.51	2164.55	2141.32	2148.95
		2.0	1679.69	6.25	1666.44	1691.11	1683.10	1681.10
		2.1	1298.18	6.24	1277.41	1301.53	1306.72	1297.47
	0.10	1.9	2244.52	6.61	2234.54	2261.57	2235.21	2245.04
		2.0	1766.02	6.59	1750.99	1779.13	1767.79	1767.85
		2.1	1374.20	6.60	1351.16	1379.04	1381.27	1373.54

Note: $T_1 - t = 1/24$, $T_i - T_{i-1} = 1/52$, $n = 27$, $S(t) = 2$, $r_f = 0.08$.

MC is Monte Carlo method. Std Err is the standard error for Monte Carlo values. TW is the Turnbull-Wakeman method, and RS stands for Rogers and Shi.

formulas to be discussed below. Monte Carlo simulation is very time-consuming.

Vorst's Approximation

The second way to derive Asian option prices is through approximations. Several authors have proposed approximations. Vorst (1992) proposes an approximation based on the geometric average of the

TABLE 6–3
Monthly Average-Exchange-Rate Call Option Values for 10,000 Units of Foreign Currency

σ	r	K	MC	Std Err	Vorst	Levy	TW	RS
0.1	0.06	1.9	920.15	0.24	921.53	921.41	920.47	919.98
		2.0	287.38	0.23	287.82	287.59	287.68	286.82
		2.1	46.43	0.20	45.92	45.81	46.64	46.20
	0.10	1.9	1095.44	0.28	1096.38	1096.69	1095.86	1095.50
		2.0	394.16	0.29	394.15	394.87	394.56	393.74
		2.1	76.93	0.26	76.11	76.57	77.42	76.84
0.2	0.06	1.9	1173.62	1.04	1177.50	1178.38	1174.61	1173.60
		2.0	625.67	1.04	626.34	627.33	626.91	625.15
		2.1	288.51	1.01	286.82	287.63	290.39	288.49
	0.10	1.9	1311.65	1.14	1314.41	1316.72	1312.60	1311.77
		2.0	727.72	1.16	727.34	730.21	728.91	727.33
		2.1	351.27	1.15	348.34	250.94	353.09	351.16
0.5	0.06	1.9	2107.00	7.49	2103.17	2130.23	2099.96	2106.47
		2.0	1642.95	7.51	1627.36	1655.19	1644.57	1638.81
		2.1	1262.91	7.47	1238.59	1265.77	1272.31	1257.41
	0.10	1.9	2204.18	7.90	2198.23	2229.12	2194.85	2204.24
		2.0	1729.76	7.93	1712.53	1744.77	1729.84	1726.77
		2.1	1340.39	7.92	1312.49	1344.44	1347.15	1334.20

Note: $T_1 - t = 1/24$, $T_2 - T_{i-1} = 1/52$, $n = 27$, $S(t) = 2$, $r_f = 0.08$.

MC is Monte Carlo method. Std Err is the standard error for Monte Carlo values. TW is the Turnbull-Wakeman method, and RS stands for Rogers and Shi.

underlying exchange rates. Assume that the final payoff of the Asian call would be

$$Max\left(\prod_{i=1}^{n} S(T_i)^{1/n} - X, 0\right) \tag{3}$$

instead of

$$Max\left(\frac{1}{n}\sum_{i=1}^{n} S(T_i) - X, 0\right) \tag{4}$$

This is called a geometric average-rate option. The value C^G of this option would be

$$C^G = e^{-r(T_n - t)} E\max\left(\prod_{i=1}^{n} S(T_i)^{1/n} - X, 0\right) \tag{5}$$

where the expectation is once again taken under the process specified by (2). However, the product of the lognormally distributed variables $S(T_i)$ is itself lognormally distributed, since the logarithm of a product is equal to the sum of the logarithms. Hence (5) can be explicitly calculated, and we find a Black-Scholes formula for the geometric average-rate option

$$C^G = e^{-r(T_N - t)}\{e^{M + V/2}N(d) - XN(d - \sqrt{V})\} \tag{6}$$

$$d = \frac{M - \ln(X) + V}{\sqrt{V}} \tag{7}$$

and where M and V are, respectively, the mean and variance of $\ln \prod_{i=1}^{n} S(T_i)^{1/n}$. M and V are explicitly given by the following formulas:

$$M = \ln(S(t)) + \frac{1}{n}\sum_{i=1}^{n} (r - r_f - \sigma^2/2)(T_i - t) \tag{8}$$

$$V = \frac{\sigma^2}{n^2}\sum_{i=1}^{n}\sum_{j=1}^{n} \min(T_i - t, T_j - t) \tag{9}$$

In (6) and (7) we easily recognize a Black-Scholes type formula. However, this is only the value of a geometric average-rate option. The value of a normal average is always larger than the value of a geometric average, and hence (6) and (7) only give a lower bound for the Asian call. Vorst (1992) proposes to approximate the Asian call value by formulas (6) and (7), but where the exercise price X is replaced by the downward adjusted exercise price X' with

$$X' = X - \left[E\left(\frac{1}{n}\sum_{i=1}^{n} S(T_i)\right) - E\left(\prod_{i=1}^{n} S(T_i)^{1/n}\right)\right] \tag{10}$$

In this way the higher expected value of the standard average compared with the geometric average is taken into account. There are explicit formulas for the expectations in (10) given by

$$E\left(\frac{1}{n}\sum_{i=1}^{n} S(T_i)\right) = S(t)\sum_{i=1}^{n} e^{(r-r_f)(T_i-t)}/n \tag{11}$$

and

$$E\left(\prod_{i=1}^{n} S(T_i)^{1/n}\right) = e^{M+V/2} \tag{12}$$

Also, the variance reduction techniques of Vorst and Kemna (1990), mentioned earlier, are based on the comparison with geometric average-rate options. Under the heading "Vorst" in Tables 6–2 and 6–3, values of average-rate options based on this method are given. If we compare these values with the Monte Carlo values, the differences are small.[2] Certainly for low volatilities the differences are less than 1 percent.

Figure 6–1 shows the value of the Italian average-exchange-rate option as a function of the underlying exchange rate and time to maturity.

If the averaging points T_i are regularly spaced over time, Vorst (1992) gives more comprehensive formulas for expressions (8) and (9). This method is much faster than the Monte Carlo simulation.

Levy's Approximation

Levy (1992) also gives an approximation formula. As explained earlier, $lnA(T) = \ln\left(\frac{1}{n}\sum_{i=1}^{n} S(T_i)\right)$ is not normally distributed. However, Levy cites some evidence that the distribution of $lnA(T)$ might be very well approximated by a normal distribution. This is the crucial observation in deriving his formula. Assume that $lnA(T)$ is normally distributed with mean α and variance ν^2. From the moment-generating function of $lnA(T)$, it then follows that

$$E(A(T)^k) = e^{k\alpha + k^2\nu^2/2} \tag{13}$$

For $k = 1$ and 2, we find two equations in the unknowns α and ν^2, which can be explicitly solved as

$$\alpha = 2lnE(A(T)) - lnE(A(T)^2)/2 \tag{14}$$

[2]Different valuation methods are also compared in Levy and Turnbull (1992). However, they use another parameter set and do not consider the Rogers and Shi method.

FIGURE 6–1
Value of Average-Exchange-Rate Options

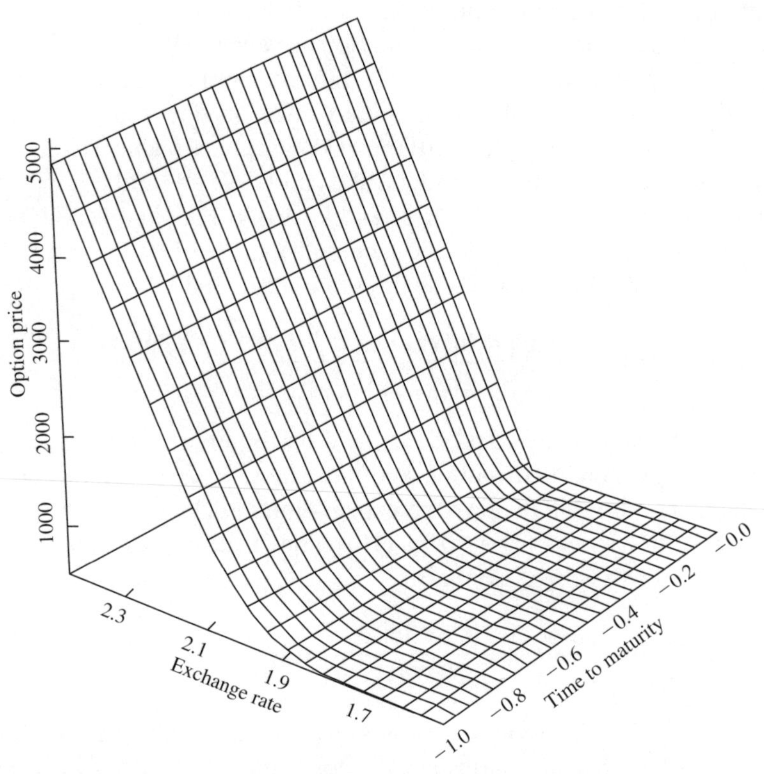

$r = r_f = 0.06$, $\sigma = 0.10$, $X = 2$, monthly average, $T = 0.5$.

$$\nu^2 = lnE(A(T)^2) - 2lnE(A(T)) \tag{15}$$

Levy's approximation is given by formulas (6) and (7), where $M = \alpha$ as given in (14) and $V = \nu^2$ as given in (15). An explicit expression for $E(A(T))$ in (14) and (15) is given by (11), while Levy also gives an explicit expression for $E(A(T)^2)$. Values for the Levy approximation are given in Tables 6–2 and 6–3. The accuracy of Levy's approximation is roughly the same as Vorst's approximation if we use the MC-values as a reference point. Levy's method is slightly better for out-of-the money options and slightly worse for in-the-money options.

The Turnbull and Wakeman Approximation

In Levy's method, the true distribution of $A(T)$ is approximated by a lognormal distribution, which was such that the mean and variance of $A(T)$ and the approximating distribution are equal. Of course, this leaves the possibility of differences in the higher moments between the two distributions. They might, for example, differ in skewness and kurtosis. For higher volatilities, these differences might be sizeable and should be taken into account. Turnbull and Wakeman (1991) describe a method to adjust for differences in skewness and kurtosis. They use an Edgeworth series expansion to compare the true distribution of $A(T)$ with the lognormal distribution LN that has the same mean and variance as $A(T)$:

$$A(T)(x) = \ln(x) + \frac{C_2}{2!}\frac{d^2\ln(x)}{dx^2} - \frac{C_3}{3!}\frac{d^3\ln(x)}{dx^3} + \frac{C_4}{4!}\frac{d^4\ln(x)}{dx^4} + e(x) \tag{16}$$

The constants C_2, C_3 and C_4 depend on the higher moments of $A(T)$ and the lognormal distribution and are explicitly given in Turnbull and Wakeman. With this relation the expectation in (1) can be approximated explicitly if we set $e(x) = 0$ in (16). The resulting formula is Levy's formula plus the correction term

$$\frac{C_2}{2!}\ln(X) - \frac{C_3}{3!}\frac{d\ln(X)}{dx} + \frac{C_4}{4!}\frac{d^2\ln(X)}{dx^2} \tag{17}$$

Values for call options are also given for this method in Tables 6–2 and 6–3. We observe that especially for high volatilities we get an improvement over the previous two methods. Also the Turnbull and Wakeman method is much faster than the Monte-Carlo simulation, but it is more complicated to implement than the aforementioned methods.

The Rogers and Shi Approximation

All approximation methods described above are in some sense connected with a kind of Black-Scholes formula. Rogers and Shi (1995) give two methods to value Asian options that are not based on Black-Scholes. The fundamental step in the theory of option pricing is the derivation of the two-dimensional Black-Scholes partial differential equation. For European options this partial differential equation (PDE) with variables $S(t)$ and t can be solved explicitly, resulting in the Black-Scholes formula.

For American options there are no explicit formulas, and the PDE has to be solved numerically. In most cases the Cox, Ross, Rubinstein (1979) binomial tree is used to value American options. This method can be seen as a way to numerically solve the PDE. Also for Asian options, a PDE can be determined. The partial differential equation depends not only on $S(t)$ and t, but also on $B(t)$, the average build-up until time t (see the next section); thus, a three-dimensional PDE results. It is well-known that three-dimensional PDEs are much harder to solve. The first method of Rogers and Shi reformulates the Asian option problem into a two-dimensional PDE by observing that the Asian option value is equal to the underlying currency value multiplied by a function that depends only on time t and one other variable.[3] The resulting two-dimensional PDE can be easily solved. The second method of Rogers and Shi (1995) is quite different. Denote $Y = A(T) - X$ and $Y^+ = Max(Y, 0)$. Then equation (1) amounts to calculating $E(Y^+)$. For every random variable Z one has

$$E(Y^+) = E(E(Y^+|Z)) \geq E(E(Y|Z)^+), \tag{18}$$

where $E(Y^+|Z)$ denotes a conditional expectation.

In this way we find a lower bound for $E(Y^+)$. Rogers and Shi specify Z such that the lower bound can be numerically calculated and is very tight. Hence, it gives a good approximation. They consider the continuous average-rate option with $A(T) = \int_0^t S(t)dt$. We have adjusted their method for the discrete average-rate options that have been discussed in this chapter. We also assume that the averaging points are equally spaced and denote $\Delta t = T_i - T_{i-1}$. Define the random variable

$$Z = \int_0^T W_\tau d\tau \tag{19}$$

with W_τ the Brownian motion of equation (2) and $T = T_n + \frac{1}{2}\Delta t$. It follows from the properties of the Brownian motion that Z has a zero mean

[3]A similar kind of trick has been used by Cheuk and Vorst (1994) to price lookback options in a discrete time model.

normal distribution with variance v equal to $(T')^3/3$. Using (18), the lower bound is

$$E(E(Y|Z)^+) = \int_{-\infty}^{\infty} \left(\frac{1}{n} \sum_{i=1}^{n} E(S(T_i)|Z) - K \right)^+ f(Z)dz \tag{20}$$

with $f(Z)$ the density function of Z. The factors $E(S(T_i)|Z)$ can be calculated explicitly, since $E(W_{T_i}|Z) = m_{T_i}Z$ with $m_{T_i} = 3T_i(2T - T_i)/2T^3$.

It follows that:

$$E(E(Y|Z)^+) =$$

$$\int_{-\infty}^{\infty} \left[\frac{S_t}{n} \sum_{t=1}^{n} \exp\left(\sigma m_{T_i} Z - \frac{1}{2}\sigma^2 v m_T^2 + rT_i\right) - K \right]^+ f(Z)dZ \tag{21}$$

If we multiply the right-hand side of (21) with the discount factor of equation (1), we have a lower bound for the Asian call. The integral in the right-hand side of (21) has to be calculated numerically. Since $f(Z)$ is a normal density function, excellent software can be used to evaluate the integral. Since the numerical value is not exact, we can no longer say that our numerical outcome is a lower bound. This heavily depends on the accuracy of the integration procedure. If the lower bound is very tight, the probability is higher that rounding errors will shift the outcome above the value of the option.

Tables 6–2 and 6–3 indicate Asian-call-option values based on this second method of Rogers and Shi. The values are surprisingly close to the Monte Carlo simulated values.

Other Valuation Methods

Several other authors have proposed methods to value Asian options. Ruttiens (1990) takes the value of a geometric average-rate option, as given by equation (6), as an approximation of the Asian option value. Earlier in this chapter, we explained that this gives only a lower bound, which in most cases is not very tight. Carverhill and Chewlow (1990) approximate the density function of $A(T)$ by convoluting the density functions of the individual $S(T_i)$. They use fast Fourier transforms to do the convolution and then integrate the payoff function against the convoluted density function. This method is clearly very time-consuming, especially if there are many points over which the average is taken.

Geman and Yor (1993) as well as Rogers and Shi concentrate on continuous Asian options. They make use of the theory of Bessel processes to find explicit formulas involving complex integrals for the values of continuous Asian options. To calculate prices, one has to evaluate these integrals numerically. A few more alternative methods are described in Levy and Turnbull (1992).

MORE ON ASIAN VALUATION

In the previous section we discussed several alternative valuation methods for average-rate options. In this section we focus on some specific issues, such as the accuracy of the approximations compared with the uncertainty about the future volatility of the underlying asset, the number of days in the average, valuation of the Asian options in the averaging period, put-call parity, the hedge ratios, floating-strike Asian options, and finally interest-rate Asian options.

Accuracy of Approximations

To assess the accuracy of the approximation formulas, one can calculate the estimation error in the volatility of the underlying asset that would result in the same valuation error as the approximation formula gives. Vorst (1992) has done this for his approximation method. In Table 6–4 the errors in volatilities are given for weekly and monthly averaging options. The first line of Table 6–4 indicates that the approximation value, 1011.93, and the Monte Carlo value, 1011.15, are different for the weekly averaged call with strike price 1.9 and volatility 0.10. However, if the value 0.0996 is inserted in the approximation formula, the call price is reduced to 1011.15, the Monte Carlo value for a volatility of 0.10. All other numbers in the implied volatility column of Table 6–4 have the same interpretation. We see that small mistakes in the estimation of the volatility already result in the same magnitude of mistakes as the approximation formula. Given that we observe in the option markets phenomena like smile patterns in implied volatilities, where differences in volatility are much larger for different options, one can conclude that the accuracy of all the methods that we described clearly is sufficient for them to be used in practice.

TABLE 6–4
Implied Volatilities for the Monte Carlo Simulated (MC) in the Approximation Formula ($\tilde{C}$)

Averaging frequency	*Volatility*	*Exercise price*	*Approximation*	*Monte Carlo value*	*Implied volatility*
weekly	0.10	1.9	1011.93	1011.15	0.0996
weekly	0.10	2.0	345.96	345.95	0.1000
weekly	0.10	2.1	63.74	64.53	0.1004
monthly	0.10	1.9	1008.12	1007.02	0.0993
monthly	0.10	2.0	338.44	338.30	0.1000
monthly	0.10	2.1	59.48	60.11	0.1003
weekly	0.20	1.9	1257.75	1255.95	0.1994
weekly	0.20	2.0	690.86	691.99	0.2001
weekly	0.20	2.1	329.85	332.72	0.2009
monthly	0.20	1.9	1245.25	1242.04	0.1988
monthly	0.20	2.0	675.74	675.61	0.2000
monthly	0.20	2.1	316.51	381.75	0.2008
weekly	0.50	1.9	2187.36	2196.28	0.5028
weekly	0.50	2.0	1708.48	1722.76	0.5043
weekly	0.50	2.1	1314.01	1335.96	0.5066
monthly	0.50	1.9	2150.52	2155.41	0.5016
monthly	0.50	2.0	1669.69	1686.07	0.5050
monthly	0.50	2.1	1275.24	1301.25	0.5080

Note $T_1 - t = 1/24$, $r = r_f = 0.08$, $S(t) = 2$.
The results are taken from Vorst (1992).

The Number of Days in the Average

It is well-known that the value of an average-rate option is always smaller than the value of a comparable standard option. From Tables 6–2 and 6–3 we can infer that if we take more averaging points in the same time period, the option price increases. For example, for $\sigma = 0.1$, $r = 0.06$, and $K = 1.9$ (see first lines of Tables 6–2 and 6–3), the monthly average-rate option has a value of 921.53, while the weekly average-rate option has a value of 925.94. This kind of result also holds for other parameter values. This seems to contradict the fact that averaging leads to a lower option value. To understand this phenomenon, we

TABLE 6–5
Influence of Starting Date

n	$C\left(\frac{1}{2}, 1\right)$	$\tilde{C}\left(\frac{1}{n}, 1\right)$
2	581.77	581.77
4	591.44	503.78
8	596.22	464.46
20	599.07	440.72
100	600.85	428.01

$r = r_f = 0.08$, $S = 2$, $K = 2$, $\sigma = 0.1$
n is the number of observations in the average
$\tilde{C}(1/2, 1)$ starts averaging after 1/2 year
$\tilde{C}(1/n, 1)$ starts averaging after 1/n years

have to split the effect of averaging into two parts. First, due to the averaging of prices of the underlying asset, earlier dates are taken into account and these typically have a lower volatility. Second, if we keep the first day in the averaging fixed, with more observations in the averaging, these first dates get a lower weight and hence influence less the variance reduction. We can illustrate these remarks by means of Table 6–5. In the second column, we give Asian call values where the averaging period starts at 0.5 year and has the first observation at that point, and ends after one year. In the third column, the averaging also ends after one year but the averaging starts after 1/n year, where n is the number of observations in the average. We see from the first column of Table 6–5 that the option value increases if we fix the starting date and increase the number of averaging points. In the second column we see that the option value decreases, owing to the fact that the first observation moves forward to actual time. The last effect is stronger and hence, in general, averaging leads to a decrease of the option value.

Extension to Points in the Averaging Interval

In the previous section, we considered the value of average-rate options where the averaging period has not yet started. In this section, we will show how the more general case, where actual time t lies between T_1 and T_n, can be reduced to the previous case.

Assume that $T_m \leq t < T_{m+1}$ for some $1 \leq m < n$. Hence, at time t the values of $S(T_1), \ldots, S(T_m)$ are known. Consider

$$B(t) = \frac{1}{m}\sum_{i=1}^{m} S(T_i) \tag{22}$$

and

$$D(t, T) = \frac{1}{n-m}\sum_{i=m+1}^{n} S(T_i) \tag{23}$$

$B(t)$ is the average of the first m exchange rates and is known at time t, while $D(t, T)$ is the unknown average over the periods to come. It is evident that:

$$A(T) = \frac{m}{n}B(t) + \frac{n-m}{n}D(t, T) \tag{24}$$

Hence,

$$Max(A(T) - X, 0) =$$
$$\frac{n-m}{n}Max\left\{D(t, T) - \frac{n}{n-m}\left(X - \frac{m}{n}B(t)\right), 0\right\} \tag{25}$$

Since none of the values that form the average $D(t, T)$ are known, we can view the right-hand side, except for the $(n - m)/n$ factor, as the payoff of an average-exchange-rate option, where the averaging still has to start, with exercise price equal to X''

$$X'' = \frac{n}{n-m}\left(X - \frac{m}{n}B(t)\right) \tag{26}$$

We can approximate the value of this option by using the method of the previous section, and then multiply by $(n - m)/n$ and the discount factor to find the value for the average-rate option in this more general case.

This method only works as long as $X'' > 0$. Otherwise, we would have an option with a negative exercise price. However, if $X'' \leq 0$, it follows that $A(T) > X$ with probability one and the call option value is

$$\begin{aligned} C &= e^{-r(T-t)}E[\max(A(T) - X, 0)] = e^{-r(T-t)}\{EA(T) - X\} \\ &= e^{-r(T-t)}\left\{\frac{m}{n}B(t) + \frac{n-m}{n}E[D(t, T)] - X\right\} \end{aligned} \tag{27}$$

where $E[D(t, T)]$ is the expectation of an arithmetic average, which can be calculated the same way as we calculated $EA(T)$. Earlier in this chapter, we remarked that Asian options are always cheaper than their European counterparts. This of course only holds before the averaging period starts. If at some time t during the averaging period, $B(t)$ is close to or larger than X and $S(t)$ is low, then the European option will be out-of-the money, while the Asian option will end up in-the-money with a high probability. In that case the Asian option is more expensive than the European option.

Put-Call Parity for Asian Options

Until now, we only gave approximation methods for Asian call options. All of these methods can be easily extended to value Asian put options. However, there also exists a put-call parity relationship between the European versions of Asian calls and puts. At maturity, the following relation holds

$$Max[X - A(T), 0] + A(T) = Max[A(T) - X, 0] + X \tag{28}$$

The first term of the left-hand side is the payoff of the Asian put at maturity. The claim $A(T)$ can be replicated by the following strategy. For each i = 1, . . . , n, buy at time t, $e^{-r(T_n - t)}e^{(r - r_f)(T_i - t)}/n$ units of the foreign currency and lend this money at the foreign riskless rate until time t_i. At that date, exchange the foreign currency plus accrued interest into domestic currency and lend again against the domestic rate. The value at time T_n is equal to $S(T_i)/n$. This strategy, which is self-financing, replicates the payoff $A(T)$. Its initial cost is

$$e^{-r(T_n - t)}S(t) \sum_{i=1}^{n} e^{(r - r_f)(T_i - t)}/n \tag{29}$$

Hence, put-call parity for Asian options reads as follows

$$P + e^{-r(T_n - t)}S(t)\left[\sum_{i=1}^{n} e^{(r - r_f)(T_i - t)}/n\right] = C + e^{-r(T_n - t)}X \tag{30}$$

The put-call parity can be used to derive approximations for Asian put values from the approximations for Asian calls. For the methods of Vorst and Kemna; Vorst, Levy, and Turnbull; and Wakeman, the Asian put values derived through this put-call parity are equal to the values derived from extending the similar methods for calls. This result does not necessarily hold for the approximation of Rogers and Shi, since that heavily depends on the accuracy of the numerical integration.

Hedge Ratios

Option traders, whether they trade on an exchange or over-the-counter, are interested not only in the valuation of options, but also in comprehensive methods for determining the hedge ratios. One might argue that good approximations for the option value suffice, since one can always use numerical differentiation to determine the hedge ratios. Pelsser and Vorst (1994) show that numerical differentiation might give disastrous results even for very good approximations. Hence, one should be very careful in applying numerical differentiation procedures. For the Monte Carlo simulation method, the hedge ratio can be determined numerically if one uses the following procedure: Generate paths starting at $S(t)$ and calculate the Asian call value $C(S(t))$. Use the same set of paths again but multiply all exchange rates with $(S(t) + \epsilon)/S(t)$. Calculate the Asian call value $C(S(t) + \epsilon)$ and approximate the hedge ratio Δ by

$$\Delta = \frac{C(S(t) + \epsilon) - C(S(t))}{\epsilon}. \tag{31}$$

It is important that the same set of paths up to a factor is used in both calculations. This reduces the standard deviation in the calculation of the hedge ratio.

Vorst (1992) gives explicit formulas for the hedge ratio based on his approximation formula. These are just straightforward calculations that result in complicated formulas that can easily be evaluated on a computer. He compares the hedge ratios with the Monte Carlo simulated hedge ratios and concludes that the differences are very small. Also, for the approximation of Levy, explicit formulas for the hedge ratio can be given in the same way as is done in Vorst (1992). The comparison with the Monte Carlo simulated hedge ratios will also give only small differences in this method. Not only the delta, $\Delta = \delta C/\delta S$, is important for traders but also gamma and the other derivatives with respect to time, underlying volatility, and interest rates. For the Vorst and Levy methods, one can calculate these derivatives explicitly. For the Monte

Carlo simulation one can use numerical differentiation as long as one uses essentially the same randomly generated numbers to generate future exchange rates.

Floating-Strike and Flexible Asian Options

Bouaziz, Briys, and Crouhy (1994) discuss the so-called floating-strike Asian options where the payoff at maturity of a call option is equal to

$$Max[S(T_n) - \frac{1}{n}\sum_{i=1}^{n} S(T_i), 0] \tag{32}$$

Hence, for these kinds of options there is no fixed strike price, but the option value depends on the value of the underlying at maturity and the average exchange rate.

Using the familiar replicating strategy technique, it follows that the value of the floating-strike Asian call option is equal to

$$e^{-r(T_n - t)}E\left[Max[S(T_n) - \frac{1}{n}\sum_{i=1}^{n} S(T_i), 0] \right], \tag{33}$$

where the expectation is again taken in the risk-neutral economy specified by equation (2). Also in this case an analytic expression is not possible, since the distribution of the average $A(T)$ is not known. Furthermore, this distribution has to be combined with the lognormal distribution of $S(T_n)$. Bouaziz, Briys, and Crouhy (1994) approximate the expression (33) by using a first-order approximation of the exponential function. Their method can also be applied to the standard Asian options that have been described in this chapter. Furthermore, they can also give an upper bound for the estimation error. An upper bound is also given by Rogers and Shi (1995) and is implicit in the method of Vorst, since it gives lower and upper bounds on the Asian option values. This implies an upper bound on the estimation error. Values of the floating-strike Asian options can also be approximated by extensions of the methods for standard Asian options by Levy, Turnbull, and Wakeman; and Rogers and Shi. The method of Vorst is based on an adjustment of the fixed strike price and hence cannot be straightforwardly applied in the floating-strike case.

Another variant of the Asian option is the so-called flexible Asian option. For these options the observations that count for the average do not all get the same weight. These options can be used, for example, by Widgets Unlimited (discussed above), which knows that its cash flows in deutsche marks are larger for some months than in other months. The firm might give the months with more cash flow a higher weight in the average. Zhang (1995) describes a valuation method for Asian options based on an arithmetic average. All of the valuation methods described in the preceding section can easily be extended to flexible Asian options.

Interest-Rate Asian Options

Up to now we have described valuation models for Asian options, where the underlying variable is a stock, stock index, future, foreign currency, or commodity. However, a large part of the over-the-counter market in exotic options is based on fixed-income instruments, which depend on interest rates. For Asian options, one can distinguish two categories of averages: averages based on bond prices and averages based on interest rates such as LIBOR or forward rates. In the first category one might use the valuation methods discussed in the preceding section, as long as standard options on these bonds are also valued using the Black-Scholes formula, for example, for short-maturity options on long-term bonds.

If the standard options cannot be valued by the Black-Scholes formula, one mostly uses a term structure approach such as those of Ho and Lee (1986); Hull and White (1990); Heath, Jarrow, and Morton (1992); or Black and Karasinski (1991) to value standard options. As yet, there are no publications on the valuation of Asian options in this context, as far as we know. A possible approach would be the method that Hull and White (1994) described. They value path-dependent options on stocks, foreign currencies, and the like by using a binomial tree in which each point in the tree is subdivided according to the value of the variable that describes the path-dependency. For Asian options, this state variable would be the average up to that point in the tree. In order to reduce the number of states in each point of the tree, values of the state variable that are close to each other are considered the same. This keeps the method manageable. The method of Hull and White (1994) can also be applied to Asian interest-rate options if one uses a tree structure linked to one of the aforementioned term structure models to value standard interest-rate options. For Asian options one has to subdivide all the points in the term-structure tree according to the average up to that point. This method can be applied for both categories of interest-rate

Asian options. One should not subdivide each point in too many states because that will make the method computationally intractable.

Sometimes simpler models are used to value standard options. For example, Hull (1993, Section 5.5) describes such a model to value interest-rate caps, where a kind of Black-Scholes formula results with interest rates and forward rates instead of underlying asset and exercise prices. It is assumed that the interest rates follow a lognormal process in this case. This method can be extended easily to average-rate options, through the methods used in the preceding section. Although in some cases this method might be used for an overall fixed-income portfolio management, it might not work, since it cannot value all fixed-income instruments. In that case one has to stick to the term-structure models.

Finally, one can always use Monte Carlo simulation to value Asian options, as long as one simulates the properly risk-adjusted economy. It goes without saying that Monte Carlo simulation is more time-consuming.

CONCLUSIONS

In this chapter we discussed average-rate, or Asian, options. Asian options are usually classified as exotic options. However, among the exotic options they are one of the best applicable options. There are many situations in which a firm or fund would be better off using average-rate options rather than standard options. Hence, the valuation of these options is of utmost importance. In the familiar Black-Scholes world, analytic formulas for the values of Asian options cannot be given, since the distribution of the sum of lognormal distributions cannot be described analytically. In this chapter, several alternative methods to value Asian options are given and compared. Certainly in terms of implied volatilities, all approximations are very accurate and can certainly be used in practice. Furthermore, all the Greeks—such as delta, gamma, rho—can be easily calculated if one uses Vorst's approximation method. These Greeks allow a portfolio manager and/or market maker to consider the Asian options as an integral part of his or her options portfolio. There is no need to run a specific book for the Asian options.

We have discussed several specific issues such as the number of observations in the average and the sometimes counterintuitive results if the number of observations is increased but the first observation is fixed.

We have tried to give an overall account of the theory on Asian options. Users of these options will be able to derive values of their contracts by the methods described in this chapter.

REFERENCES

Bergman, Y. (1981). *Pricing Path-Dependent European Options.* Working paper, University of California, Berkeley, CA.

Black, F., and P. Karasinski (1991). "Bond and Option Pricing when Short Rates are Lognormal," *Financial Analysts Journal*, July–August, 52–59.

Bouaziz, L., E. Briys, and M. Crouhy (1994). "The Pricing of Forward Starting Asian Options," *Journal of Banking and Finance* 18, 823–839.

Carverhill, A. P., and L. J. Chewlow (1990). "Valuing Average Rate (Asian) Options," *Risk* 3(4), 25–29.

Cheuk, T., and T. Vorst (1994). *Lookback Options and the Observation Frequency: A Binomial Approach,* Report 9403, Erasmus Center for Financial Research, Rotterdam.

Cox, J., M. Rubinstein, and S. Ross (1979). "Option Pricing: A Simplified Approach," *Journal of Financial Economics* 7, 229–264.

Geman, H., and M. Yor (1993). "Bessel Processes, Asian Options and Perpetuities," *Mathematical Finance* 3, 349–375.

Heath, D., R. Jarrow, and A. Morton (1992). "Bond Pricing and the Term Structure of Interest Rates: A New Methodology," *Econometrica* 60, 77–105.

Ho, T. S. Y., and S. B. Lee (1986). "Term Structure Movements and Pricing Interest Rate Contingent Claims," *Journal of Finance* 41, 1011–1029.

Hull, J., and A. White (1990). "Pricing Interest Rate Derivative Securities," *Review of Financial Studies* 3, 573–592.

Hull, J. (1993). *Options, Futures and Other Derivative Securities,* 2d ed. (Englewood Cliffs, NJ: Prentice Hall).

Hull, J., and A. White (1994). "Efficient Procedures for Valuing European and American Path-Dependent Options," *Journal of Derivatives* 1(1), 21–32.

Kemna, A. G. Z., and A. C. F. Vorst (1990). "A Pricing Method for Options Based on Average Asset Values," *Journal of Banking and Finance* 14, 113–129.

Levy, E. (1992). "The Valuation of Average Rate Currency Options," *Journal of International Money and Finance* 11, 474–491.

Levy, E., and S. M. Turnbull (1992). "Average Intelligence," *Risk* 5(2), 55–59.

Pelsser, A., and T. Vorst (1994). "The Binomial Model and the Greeks," *Journal of Derivatives* 1(3), 45–49.

Rogers, L. C. G., and Z. Shi (1995). "The Value of an Asian Option," to appear in *Journal of Applied Probability.*

Ruttiens, A. (1990). "Classical Replica," *Risk* 3(2), 33–36.

Turnbull, S. M., and L. M. Wakeman (1991). "Quick Algorithm for Pricing European Average Rate Options," *Journal of Financial and Quantitative Analysis* 26, 377–389.

Vorst, T. (1992). Prices and Hedge Ratios of Average Exchange Rate Options, *International Review of Financial Analysis* 1, 179–193.

Zhang, P. G. (1995). "Flexible Arithmetic Asian Options," *Journal of Derivatives* 2(3), 53–63.

Chapter Seven

The Log Contract and Other Power Contracts

Anthony Neuberger
S.G. Warburg Group Research Fellow
Institute of Finance and Accounting, London Business School

INTRODUCTION

Exotic options tend to be complicated, sometimes to an extreme degree. In the *Oxford English Dictionary,* exotic is given the definition: ". . . of or pertaining to, or characteristic of a foreigner, or what is foreign (now *rare*); hence outlandish, barbarous, strange, uncouth (*obs*)" Exotic options have complex payoffs, they are complicated to hedge and they are complicated to price. It may therefore seem somewhat perverse to write about the simplest possible type of option—the log contract—in a book devoted to exotic options.

A log contract is a European-style contingent claim whose value at maturity is equal to the natural logarithm of the price of the underlying asset. As is shown in the following box, it is easy to price. It also has a number of other features that should make it attractive to investors and market intermediaries.

The log contract's only claim to being called an exotic option is that it is a nonlinear function of the underlying asset, and hence can be regarded as an option, and that it is not a standard call or put option, and hence deserves the title "exotic."

To understand the attractions of the log contract it is best to go back a bit and think about why traders and investors want to make use of options at all.

Box 1

Pricing the Log Contract

Denote the price of the underlying asset at time t as S_t. Suppose that the log contract matures at time T. If we make the normal Black-Scholes assumptions of a constant riskless interest rate r and a constant asset price volatility σ, the Black-Scholes partial differential equation specifies that the value of a log contract at time t when the asset price is S must satisfy:

$$\frac{1}{2}\sigma^2 S^2 \frac{\partial^2 L}{\partial S^2} + rS\frac{\partial L}{\partial S} + \frac{\partial L}{\partial t} = rL$$

with the boundary condition that $L(S, T) = \text{Log } S$. The solution is

$$L = \left\{\text{Log } S - \left(\frac{1}{2}\sigma^2 - r\right)(T - t)\right\}e^{-r(T-t)}$$

This can be considerably simplified by working with forward prices, where the forwards mature at the same time as the option. Using a superscript F to denote a forward price, the valuation equation becomes

$$L^F = \text{Log } S^F - \frac{1}{2}\sigma^2(T - t)$$

THE DEMAND FOR OPTIONS— SIXTH CENTURY B.C.

Gastineau (1979) records one of the earliest examples of the use of options as appearing in Aristotle's *Politics,* where Thales the Milesian learns, through his skill at long-range weather forecasting, that the next olive harvest will be very large. Thales is a philosopher, and lives in poverty. Presumably he has limited ability to borrow. But he would probably not wish to borrow a lot of money even if someone were prepared to lend it to him. Losing a lot of money is very painful if you have little enough to start with. In economists' jargon, he probably had strongly decreasing relative risk aversion. He wants to reduce his exposure to risk as he gets poorer.

He faces the problem faced by any investor with a view on future developments: how to exploit it efficiently. In particular he needs a strategy that reflects his attitude to risk, and that is efficient—so he will make money if his view is correct and will be protected from losses caused by events on which he has no particular views.

A more foolish man than Thales might have tried to short olive oil futures in the belief that a glut of olives would force the price of olive oil down. But the price of olives is affected by many other forces; Thales could be right about the bumper harvest but still lose money if the price of olive oil were to rise because, for example, of its superb quality.

Thales decided to go long olive presses. A bumper harvest requires a lot of olive-press capacity, and the supply of presses in the short term is inelastic. He decided to put down some deposits on olive presses. Presumably, although Aristotle is not explicit on the details, Thales was not committed to using the presses and paying the full fee; rather, at harvest time, he could either pay the balance of the rental that was still outstanding (an amount agreed in advance) or he could abandon his deposit and walk away without further liability to the press owners. In other words, he bought a call option on the presses.

It is worth considering whether and why the call option strategy was better than buying presses outright. If Thales was certain that his information was good, and he was constrained by limited capital, then options make sense. They provide enormous leverage. Futures too, had they existed, would provide leverage but they have a major drawback. While the amount of capital required to establish a futures position may be small, the amount required to maintain it may be very large. If Thales had taken out a large olive press futures position, he could have been absolutely right about the bumper harvest and yet have been bankrupted by margin calls if olive-press prices had declined before rising again.

If Thales were not certain about his information, then options may be attractive because of the nature of the payoff if he is wrong. If Thales is wrong, he will lose the option premium. Had he tried to get the same degree of exposure using forwards, the losses if he is wrong are more uncertain—if prices plummet, the potential loss is huge. There are no free lunches in markets that are reasonably efficient. The option payoff must be attractive because he is more inclined to take a large chance of a substantial loss than a small chance of a much larger loss. In effect, the attraction of the option strategy is that it incorporates insurance.

The features, then, that make an option attractive relative to an outright claim are

- The investor's limited access to capital
- Particular risk preferences, which make it attractive to vary one's risk exposure according to one's wealth level.

THE DEMAND FOR OPTIONS—TWENTIETH CENTURY A.D.

How far are the considerations that led Thales to use options more than two millennia ago still relevant to the twentieth-century investor? The story told about Thales could well suit a retail investor today. But it appears to suit an institutional investor less well. Most institutional investors (apart possibly from some hedge funds) have relatively limited gearing. They do not need options to get leverage.

They also tend to have many pieces of mediocre information, rather than just one piece of very good information. They have no reason to bet their capital (as Thales did) on one or two positions. Rather, they place a large number of relatively small bets. There is no point in insuring lots of small risks. Diversification of risks across many different positions provides adequate insurance without the need for options.

Furthermore, with very liquid capital markets and many more sources of information, investors think in terms of dynamic strategies, adjusting their portfolios, taking profits and closing out losses all the time in the light of prevailing prices and the investor's latest assessment of future prospects. The behavior of a call option if held to maturity is less relevant to them than its behavior over a shorter horizon.

WHY DO INSTITUTIONAL INVESTORS USE OPTIONS TODAY?

But even investors who have no great need for leverage or insurance may still be interested in options and other claims with nonlinear payoffs. The reasons can be divided into two categories: the attractions of an option as a stand-alone instrument and the attractions of the option as part of a portfolio.

Examples of the former include an investor who has a view about the likely path of prices that is more elaborate than a belief that prices will simply go up or down. The investor may believe that prices will stay within a given range, or that they will go through some critical level and then move decisively in one direction. A tailored option versus a dynamic trading strategy may provide a more efficient means of backing that view.

Other examples of the stand-alone use of options include the investor who has to beat or match some benchmark where underperformance and overperformance are not treated symmetrically. The investor may therefore wish to buy a kind of insurance policy to mitigate the downside risks.

The log contract has no obvious role here. Where it has a part to play is in modifying the characteristics of a portfolio. One of the central advances of modern investment theory has been the understanding of the importance of analyzing performance at a portfolio level. A major attraction of an option is that it enables the investor to get exposure or to hedge exposure to volatility, and to get the benefits of a dynamic trading strategy in a way that would not be possible otherwise. The argument for the log contract versus a conventional option is that it gives this exposure in a far more controlled and predictable way.

GREEKS IN THE TWENTIETH CENTURY

An option can be replicated, more or less, by a dynamic trading strategy. Someone buying an option is buying a dynamic trading strategy. The investor is buying the option rather than employing the strategy because the option writer has lower costs or is better able to take implementation risks. Replication strategies may fail to work as intended because of the behavior of volatility or because of discontinuities in prices.

In buying a call option the investor is buying exposure to the underlying asset. He is buying an exposure that is not constant but that increases as the asset price rises, and declines as it falls. He is buying an exposure to volatility—the more volatile the asset becomes, the more valuable the call option.

In other words, when a modern institutional investor buys an option, he is buying an exposure to all the Greek letters beloved of options fans:

- The *delta,* or exposure to the underlying, which he could get by buying the spot asset;
- The *gamma,* or change in delta with asset price, which he could get through an active trading strategy in the underlying asset; and

FIGURE 7–1

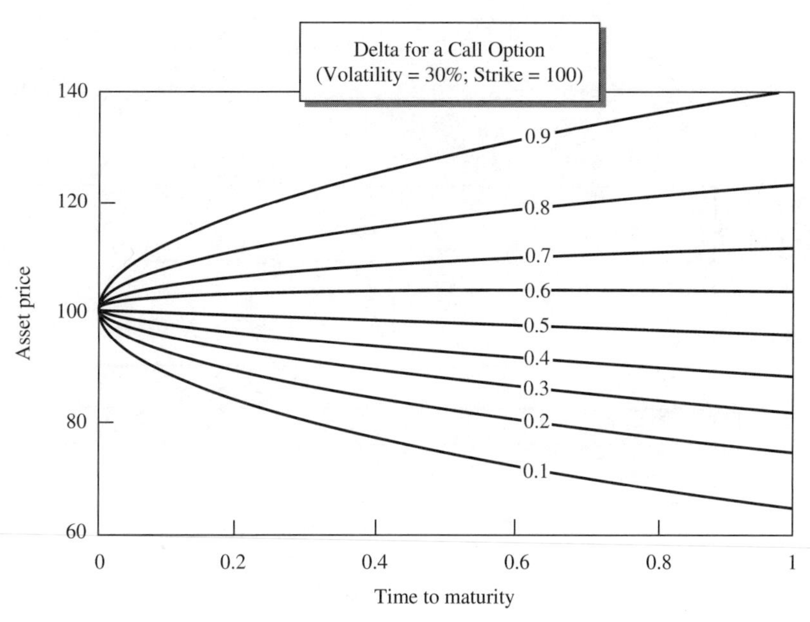

- The *lambda* (sometimes called *vega*), or exposure to volatility, which he can get only through nonlinear contingent claims such as options.

If you are buying a derivative instrument for its Greek letters, then you want an option whose exposure to the Greeks is simple. The log contract has this property. Calls and puts do not.

PROBLEMS WITH CALL OPTIONS

When looked at as a collection of Greek letters, the common call option looks rather peculiar. Figure 7–1 shows the delta of a call option. The delta varies not only with the level of the asset price—that is after all what one expects with an option—it also varies according to the time to maturity. The pattern is quite attractive, but it is not clear why someone would want to achieve an exposure with this rather

FIGURE 7–2

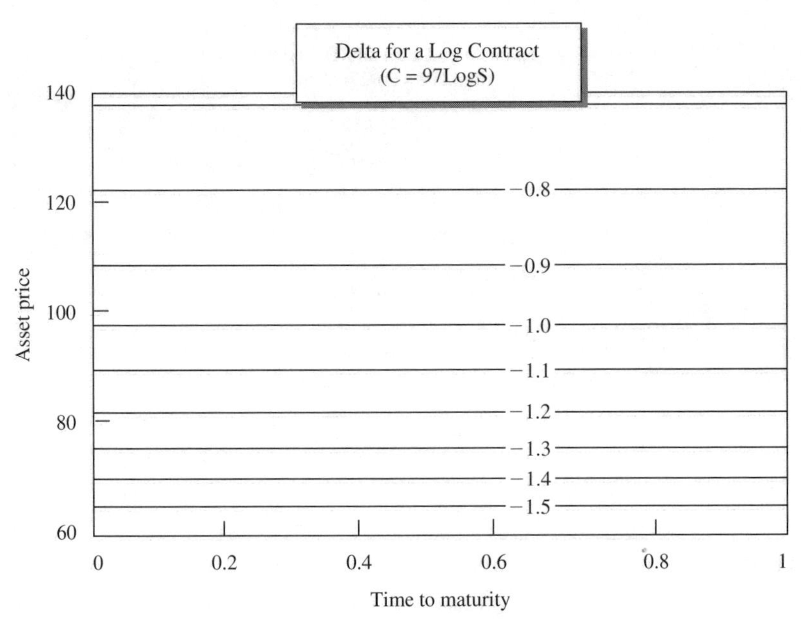

complex form. By contrast Figure 7–2 shows a similar graph for the log contract. It is less beautiful, but it can at least be characterized in a fairly simple way—the dynamic strategy is a stable strategy that depends only on the level of the asset price, and not on the time to maturity.

Similarly, Figures 7–3 and 7–4 show gamma contours for the two options. If you buy an at-the-money call option, and the option remains at-the-money, the gamma will rise, and indeed go to infinity as the option approaches maturity. On the other hand, if the option moves away from the money, the gamma will go to zero. An investor buying a call for its gamma is buying a highly unpredictable quantity. By contrast, the gamma of a log contract remains rather stable, as shown by Figure 7–4.

Another way of looking at the same issue is to recognize that options are attractive precisely because they are unlike forward contracts. The exposure of a forward contract to the underlying is constant; the exposure of an option varies. Most calls are bought and written reasonably

FIGURE 7–3

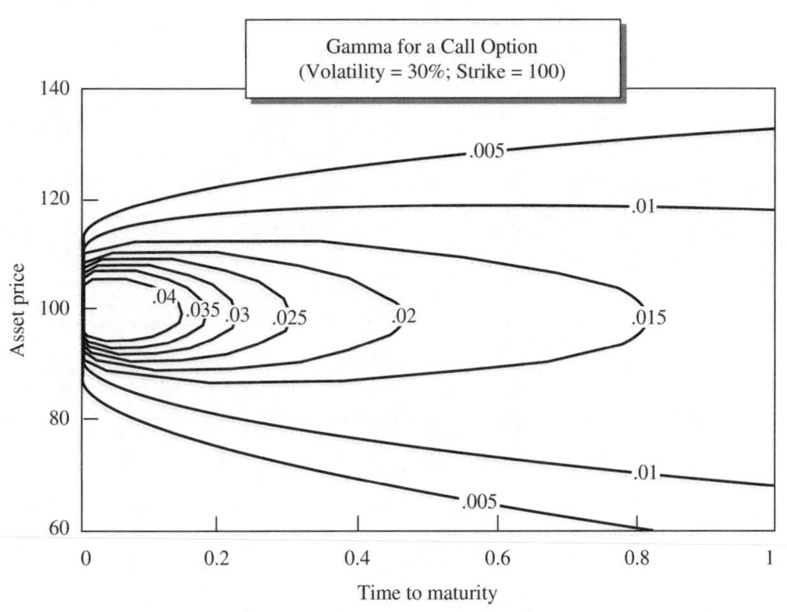

close to the money. At issue their delta is quite variable, depending on what happens to the underlying asset price. As time progresses, however, the underlying price will probably either rise sufficiently to force the option deep into the money, or drop leaving the option well out-of-the-money. It loses its optionlike characteristics. This has the added disadvantage that it becomes an unattractive derivative asset, which may therefore be expected to trade at a wide spread.

By contrast, the log contract never loses its optionlike character. The gamma remains relatively stable. If the investor is buying options for their effect on the gamma and the lambda of her portfolio, the log contract is far more suitable than the conventional call option.

The fact that the gamma never goes very low means that the log contract always retains its convexity. The fact that it never rises very high is also advantageous: A high gamma means that the hedge ratio is very sensitive to the asset price. That means that the replication strategy becomes both costly (high turnover) and risky (the hedge is unbalanced if

FIGURE 7–4

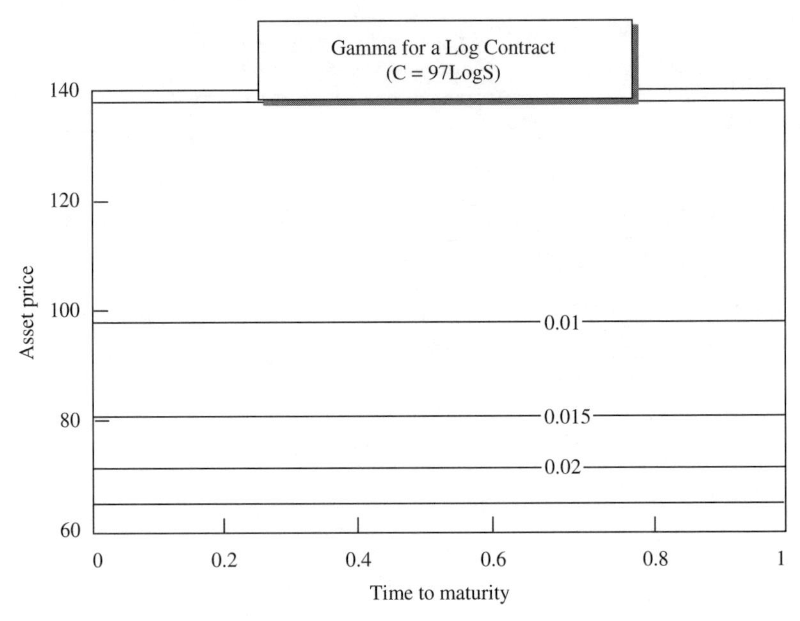

the asset price jumps). The option writer will charge accordingly. That does not matter if the high gamma is a feature that the option buyer actually wants. But if the high gamma is simply a consequence of the way the contract is written, and in particular the kinked payoff for a call, then the buyer is paying for a service she neither wants nor needs.

For an investor who is interested in buying or selling options to gain exposure to the Greek letters, the log contract provides a far more suitable instrument than the conventional call or put option.

HEDGING THE LOG CONTRACT

One key feature of the log contract is the simplicity of its delta or hedge ratio—the delta is simply the reciprocal of the forward price of the asset. So, for example, suppose that the forward price of the asset is \$1.00, then the investor trying to replicate a log contract should go long one forward contract. If the next period the forward price has gone to $1.10, then the investor should reduce the hedge to 1/1.10 or 0.9091 forward contracts.

Note that the hedge ratio is independent of the forecast level of volatility. This is in contrast to a call option where the hedge ratio is a complex function of asset price, time to maturity, and future volatility. If you misestimate future volatility in replicating a call option, you will not be properly hedged against changes in the asset price. Thus the hedge error in hedging a call option will depend not only on the actual volatility over the life of the option, but also on when the volatility occurred, the level of the asset price at the time, and also on the hedger's forecast of volatility over time.

In the case of a log contract, Box 2 shows that the hedge error depends almost entirely on the difference between the implied volatility of the option at the time it was written and the volatility that actually occurred over the life of the option. This result is quite robust. In

Box 2

Hedging the Log Contract

Suppose an investor has written a log contract at time 0 and wants to delta-hedge her position using forward contracts on the underlying asset. The delta or hedge ratio is given, in the normal way, by

$$\frac{\partial L^F}{\partial S^F} = \frac{1}{S^F}$$

Now consider a strategy of delta-hedging, rebalancing each day. Since everything is being done in forward markets, all cash flows occur at maturity. The investor will receive L_0^F for writing the log contract; she will pay Log S_T at maturity. Denote the return on the futures contract over day t by x_t, so $x_t = S_{t+1}^F/S_t^F$. Then the investor will make $x_t - 1$ on her hedge on day t. Her net position will be

$$\text{Net} = L_0^F - \text{Log } S_T^F + \sum_{t-0}^{T-1} (x_t - 1)$$

Box 2 ***Hedging the Log Contract*** **(continued)**

But we have already seen that

$$L_0^F = \text{Log } S_0^F - \frac{1}{2}\hat{\sigma}^2 T$$

where the hat over the sigma shows that this is the implied volatility. So the net position of the investor at maturity can be written as

$$\text{Net} = \sum_{t=0}^{T-1} (x_t - 1 - \text{Log } x_t) - \frac{1}{2}\hat{\sigma}^2 T$$

Now the actual volatility σ over the period 0 to T can be measured by taking the sum of squared log returns

$$\sigma \equiv \sqrt{\sum_{t=0}^{T-1} y_t^2/T} \quad \text{where } y_t \equiv \text{Log } x_t$$

so the investor's delta-hedged log contract will have a payoff equal to

$$\text{Net} = \sum_{t-0}^{T-1} \left(\frac{1}{6}y_t^3 + \frac{1}{24}y_t^4 + \cdots\right) + \frac{1}{2}(\sigma^2 - \hat{\sigma}^2)\,T$$

The first term, the summation, is generally negligible relative to the second, which simply reflects the difference between the actual volatility and the volatility implied in the option price. To see this, suppose we rebalance daily on an asset that has an annual volatility of say 30 percent. The daily volatility will be around 2 percent, so each day will add around 2×10^{-4} to the second term (always positive), but only around $\pm 1.3 \times 10^{-6}$ (as likely to be positive as negative) to the first term. For evidence of the insignificance of the first term in practice see Neuberger (1994).

particular, it holds even if the asset price does not conform with the Black-Scholes assumptions of a geometric Brownian diffusion, but instead has jumps, autocorrelation in returns, and returns that are not distributed lognormally.

The log contract is much easier to hedge than a conventional option. This is attractive to the option buyer who does not need to pay the option writer a large premium for handling or taking the risk of the asset price behaving in a way that conflicts with the assumptions of the pricing model.

PURE BETS ON VOLATILITY

For many investors, the decision on whether to buy or sell an option is based heavily on the implied volatility. If the volatility implied in the price of an option is significantly below the volatility that they believe will occur in future, the investors will buy; conversely, if forecast volatility is lower than implied, they will sell. In effect they are using options to trade volatility. But a delta-hedged option is an imperfect volatility-play. Even if actual volatility turns out to be lower than the implied volatility, an investor can write an option, delta-hedge it, and still lose money. For example, the volatility may be quite high when the option is close to the money and low only when the option is far away from the money.

The log contract provides a much easier and more reliable way of betting on volatility. It also allows the investor considerable flexibility in his definition of volatility. If the investor can forecast the volatility of daily returns, he can rebalance his hedge daily and ensure a payoff that depends on the volatility of daily returns. If the investor forecasts the volatility of minute-by-minute returns, then the hedge can be rebalanced every minute.

But the log contract is useful not only for an investor who wants a pure volatility play; it is also useful for anyone who wants to hedge a portfolio of options. An investor or trader holding a portfolio of long and short positions in options and other derivatives will wish to measure and manage the risk exposure of the portfolio. One of the main risk-measures is the portfolio's lambda or vega—the portfolio's exposure to volatility changes. The log contract offers a straightforward means of managing lambda exposure, since the lambda of a log contract (unlike that of a call option) does not vary rapidly.

GENERALIZING THE LOG CONTRACT

The log contract is not the only type of contract where the optionlike nature remains reasonably stable over time whatever happens to the asset price. The same is true of power contracts—that is, options where the payoff is a power of the underlying asset price. They too are simple to price; their deltas, gammas, and lambdas barely change with time to maturity.

What is special about the log contract is that its delta or hedge ratio does not depend at all on the assumed volatility. This means that it is the only instrument where the value of the delta-hedged portfolio at maturity depends only on the difference between the actual volatility and the implied volatility at the time the contract was written. This property does not assume Brownian motion for the asset price. This means that the log contract is uniquely well designed to give the investor exposure to volatility, substantially uncontaminated by exposure to other factors such as jumps, variations in volatility over time, and changes in the level of the asset price.

CONCLUSIONS

The log contract is in many ways much simpler than a traditional call or put option. It does not have sharp corners (like an at-the-money call close to maturity) that make it hard to hedge. Its concavity remains regardless of the asset price, so it does not lose its optionlike features. It is easy to delta-hedge. When delta-hedged, it is a pure volatility play, unlike a delta-hedged call option.

There will always be a demand for tailor-made options with specific features designed to respond to particular views about the market or to meet performance measurement, accounting, or regulatory concerns. But there is also a need for simple option-products that enable investors to trade views on future volatility. In the past this role has largely been filled by trading at-the-money call options. But call options do not stay at-the-money. Perhaps in the future, log contracts could take over that role, since they always remain at-the-money.

REFERENCES

Gastineau, G. L., *The Options Manual,* 3d ed. (New York: McGraw-Hill, 1979).

Neuberger, A. J., "The Log Contract," *Journal of Portfolio Management* (Winter 1994), pp. 74–80.

Chapter Eight

Barrier Options*

Eric Berger
Berger Financial Research, Ltd.
in association with Bloomberg Financial Markets

INTRODUCTION

Barrier options have become increasingly popular in recent years. In this chapter we define a variety of barrier options, discuss the advantages they provide to the buyer as well as to the writer, and consider the problems of valuation. Particular issues considered include: (1) the difference between continuous monitoring and discrete monitoring of the barrier condition; (2) double barrier options; (3) partial barrier options; and (4) numerical problems associated with some valuation techniques. Although most barrier options are customized and trade over-the-counter (OTC), there are some exchange-traded barrier options and listed securities with embedded barrier options. We describe a few examples. We show how the embedded calls in a convertible bond can be approximately described as barrier options. Some of the valuation sections involve a fair amount of mathematics. In cases where detailed derivations of formulas are provided, these are generally to be found in the appendix to this chapter. The appendix also includes the statement of Girsanov's Theorem and carefully shows its use in deriving the valuation formula for standard barrier options. This is instructive, since Girsanov's

The author thanks David Klein for helpful discussions and for his careful reading of an earlier version.

Theorem plays a fundamental role in modern financial theory, yet is difficult to get a feel for. Readers who wish to pursue topics only briefly touched on here should consult the relatively extensive list of references at the end of this chapter.

WHAT ARE BARRIER OPTIONS?

Terms

As with any option, a barrier option is a contract that specifies a payoff to the investor, based on the price (level) of some underlying asset (index). Unlike standard options, there is a critical price for the underlying, called the *barrier,* which is specified at the time the option contract is initiated. Should the price of the underlying *breach* (i.e., cross) this barrier before option expiration, then the option may either be extinguished immediately or may be replaced by a standard option.

Figure 8–1 displays a series of daily prices. An investor in an up-and-out barrier option with barrier level set at $112.50 would see the option get knocked out after 60 days.

More precisely, let S_t be the price (level) of the asset (index) at time t, let $S = S_{t_0}$ be the initial value of S_t and let H be the barrier. The *monitoring frequency* specifies how often S_t is checked to see if the barrier has been breached. For example, S_t may be checked once a day at closing, or it may be monitored continuously.

Going back to Figure 8–1, suppose the barrier is set at $110.00 instead of $112.50. Then if the monitoring frequency is not continuous, the slight breaching of the barrier at the 50-day point might not trigger the knock-out condition.

A *knock-out option* is a barrier option that is automatically terminated if the (monitored) value of S_t breaches the barrier before option expiration. If this happens, a *rebate* R is paid (we allow R to be 0 or greater than 0). The rebate is assumed to be paid at the time that the barrier is breached. If $S < H$, then the barrier may be breached only if the index moves up to the barrier. In such a case, the knock-out option is also called an *up-and-out option.* Conversely, for $S > H$, we would have a *down-and-out option.*

A *knock-in option* is a contract that causes a plain-vanilla option to come into existence automatically if the (monitored) value of the index breaches the barrier before the contract's expiration. If this does not hap-

FIGURE 8–1
Time Series of Daily Asset Prices—Barrier at \$112.50

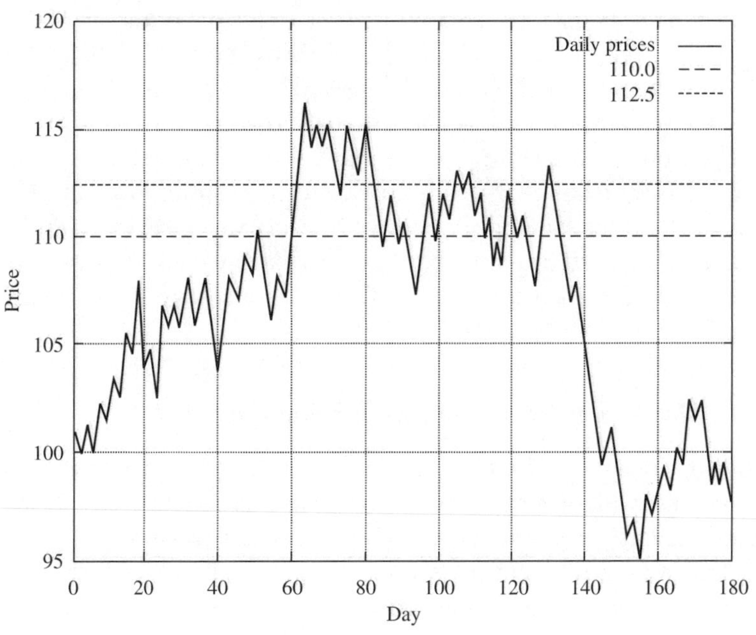

pen, a *rebate* R is paid (we allow R to be 0 or greater than 0). The rebate is assumed to be paid at the option expiration. If $S < H$, then the barrier may bc breached only if the index moves up to the barrier. In such a case, the knock-in is also called an *up-and-in option*. Conversely, for $S > H$, we would have a *down-and-in option*.

A *European* barrier option is one in which the holder can exercise only at the option's expiration (if at all). An *American* barrier option is a knock-out barrier option in which the holder can exercise at any time, provided that the option has not expired. Finally, a *Bermuda* or *Mid-Atlantic* barrier option is a knock-out barrier option in which the holder can exercise only at a set of specific, discrete times. The *Bermuda* exercise feature is between that of a European option and an American option, hence the name. Note that there is some disagreement as to whether the terms *European, American,* and *Bermudan* should apply to the investor's exercise alternatives or to the frequency with which the barrier is monitored. The terminology we use here is consistent with [31], whereas [37] apply these adjectives to the monitoring frequency.

One of the more complex barrier options is the *partial barrier option,* in which the barrier is monitored for only part of the option's lifetime. The special case of this, in which there is an initial delay before the barrier is monitored, is called a *forward start barrier option.*

A *double barrier* option is one with two barriers; for example, a double knock-out option (DKO) would have a simultaneous down-and-out and up-and-out feature ($H^- < S < H^+$). Such an option would terminate the moment either the upper or lower barrier was breached. This is not the same as a portfolio with both an up-and-out and a down-and-out option, since for such a portfolio if one barrier were to be breached, only one of the options would be extinguished.

Motivation for Using Barrier Options

Barrier options provide the investor more flexibility in tailoring the portfolio returns while lowering the cost of option premiums. These options provide attractive conditions for the option writer as well.

To understand this, consider the case of a modestly bullish investor who wants to use options to increase upside exposure, but at a low premium cost. Using standard (or, in the jargon, *plain-vanilla*) options to meet this view, the investor might well put on a bullish vertical spread, going long a call option struck at K_1 and short a call option struck at K_2, where $K_1 < K_2$. This is a reasonable trade, but it has two unattractive properties: first, the investor must transact in two different options, increasing the transaction costs; second, the investor knows ahead of time that the strategy is to unwind both legs simultaneously, but it may be difficult, or at least expensive, to do this in practice. On the other hand, consider the use of an up-and-out call. This option, with a suitable rebate R, would also provide upside exposure, with the transaction costs of only a single option, and with a known, costless "unwinding" if the barrier is hit.

From the option writer's point of view, selling the up-and-out call has one clear advantage over taking the reverse side of the bullish vertical spread discussed above—namely, the writer is not exposed to unlimited liability. For investors with the bearish view this position could be attractive, since they can specify the size of their loss in case they are wrong.

These same considerations apply to the case of double barrier options. For example, an investor in a double up-and-out/down-and-out call option would be able to lower the premium relative to a straight up-and-out option by permitting the up-and-out option to knock out also if a lower barrier is reached. This is comparable to the motivation of the plain-vanilla option buyer who purchases a down-and-out instead, in order to lower the premium.

Example. An investor holds the view that over the next six months a particular market index will rise from its current level of 100, possibly attaining a level as high as 110. He is uncertain as to how soon this will take place, and doubts that the index will rise much beyond 110. His intention is to use options to capture this trade idea, and to liquidate his position should the index rise to 110. Assuming the index has a 20 percent volatility and that the six-month interest rate is at 5 percent, he considers two option trades. The first is the purchase of a standard 6-month American call option struck at 100, which is selling for \$6.87.[1] Alternatively he considers a 6-month up-and-out barrier call option, with a barrier at 110 and a rebate of 10, for a premium of \$5.61, or 18.5 percent less than the standard option. Among the advantages of the barrier option are that it involves less up-front cost and it does not require vigilant monitoring by the investor to match his personal unwinding criterion. Of course, the 18.5 percent discount in price to the standard option indicates less value. For example, if the index breaches the 110 barrier after three months, the knock-out option holder receives \$10, whereas the standard option would have a value of about \$12.00. Changing the rebate payment from \$10 to \$12 would bring the cost of the barrier option to \$6.66.

Motivation against Using Barrier Options

Barrier options have become quite popular, especially in the currency markets. At the time of this writing (April-May 1995), investor George Soros had made several public appearances stating that knock-out options were adding volatility to the currency markets and, furthermore,

---

[1]The option could be American or European. It makes no difference in the valuation, since the assumption of no dividends guarantees that early exercise will never be optimal.

exacerbating the dollar's decline versus the yen.[2] Japanese exporters had hedged their exposure to the JY/USD exchange rate via knock-out puts (the right to sell USD for JY, knocked out if the exchange rate falls below 95 JY/USD), and had collectively purchased options involving tens of billions of dollars. When the exchange rate fell below the knock-out level, the exporters had to limit their exposure, either by putting on new hedges or selling their dollars, the latter method adding pressure to the already weak currency. The exporters had been collectively caught assuming that the yen would trade in a limited range, well away from the 95 barrier. Soros's opinion was that for a large event (such as the loss of an aggregate hedge in the tens of billions of dollars) to be triggered by a relatively arbitrary event, such as the breaching of an arbitrary barrier level on some knock-out options, was dangerous and should be restricted. While it is appealing to try to limit events that cause spurious "crises" (or gaps) in the markets, it seems difficult to imagine how one could create any enforceable mechanism that would have this effect. And of course there is the irony that Soros's investment company, the Quantum Fund, had earned in excess of $1 billion when it exploited the fact that the Bank of England was required to try to keep sterling in a certain range, and could not sustain this effort against the speculators. Finally, the discontinuity on hitting the barrier can be mitigated by an appropriate choice of rebate.

Path Independence and Path Dependence

A security is *path-independent* if its value at a given point in time depends on the so-called state-of-the-world at that time, and not on how the world evolved to that state. For example, the premium of a European option depends on the price and the return volatility of the underlying at a given point in time, but is independent of the actual price history that transpired prior to that time. Barrier options are dependent on price history for determining if a barrier has been hit or not. For an out-option, this type of dependence is theoretically no different from the path-dependence inherent in the early exercise of an American option. A (nonlinear) barrier exists for an American option, defined at each time t by the critical price S_t^* at which the investor should exercise. In practice, this barrier is subjective to the extent that the investor needs to

[2] See [29], [22]

specify volatility before the "American" barrier can be identified. Also, the *rational* investor would exercise, but is not required to do so, whereas the breaching of the barrier triggers a contractual provision in a knock-out or knock-in option.

Financial engineers are concerned with yet another type of path dependence—whether and how backward recursion can be used for pricing.[3] This is of interest because *backward recursion* is flexible and efficient when compared to Monte Carlo simulation methods. In order to use backward recursion one requires that the security (contingent claim) being priced be path-independent (in a weak sense). Fortunately, barrier options are path-independent in this sense. For a solid treatment of these types of methods in the case of the underlying price process being lognormal, see [31]. For the case of interest-rate barrier options, the underlying process (rates or prices) may well not be lognormal, and may or may not be path-independent. In these cases, other types of numerical methods may be required.

A CONTINUOUSLY MONITORED BARRIER

In this section we derive and present the valuation formulas for all the standard barrier options, under the assumption of continuous monitoring of the barrier condition. Some examples are also presented.

Notation

The following list collects the various definitions and notations in one place for easy reference:

- r the continuously compounded risk-free rate.
- q the continuously compounded dividend rate on the asset (index).
- S_t the (unrestricted) process for the underlying price (index). (We assume that S_t follows a risk-neutral lognormal process of $dS_t/S_t = (r - q)\,dt + \sigma dW_t$, $\sigma > 0$.)
- S_t^* the restricted process for the underlying index. $S_t^* = H$ if $S_u = H$ for some $t_0 < u \leq t$. S_t^* is said to have an *absorbing barrier* at H.

[3]Backward recursion refers to valuation methods such as a Cox-Ross-Rubinstein binary tree.

S	$[\equiv S_{t0}]$ the value of the underlying (index) at time $t = t_0$.
T	the option expiration time (so $T - t_0$ is time to expiration).
Z_t	$[\equiv \log(S_t/S)]$ the continuously compounded return process for S_t^*. $S_t^* = Se^{Z_t}$.
μ	$\left[= r - q - \frac{\sigma^2}{2}\right]$ the risk-neutral drift for Z_t, $dZ_t = [\mu dt + \sigma dW_t]$.
Z_t^*	$[\equiv \log(S_t^*/S)]$ the continuously compounded return process for S_t^*. Therefore $S_t^* = Se^{Z_t^*}$.
$F(z, t)$	$[\equiv \text{Prob}(Z_{t_0+t} \le z)]$ the risk-neutral distribution function for Z_t.
$f(z, t)$	$[\equiv \partial/\partial z \quad F(z, t)]$ the risk-neutral density function for Z_t.
H	the barrier.
b	$[\equiv \log(H/S)]$ the barrier as seen by the return process Z_t.
K	the strike.
k	$[\equiv \log(K/S)]$ the strike as seen by the return process Z_t.
R	the rebate.
$G(z, t)$	the risk-neutral distribution function for crossing the boundary and returning. For $S < H$ and $z < b$, $G(z,t) = \text{Prob}(Z_{t_0+t} \le z \text{ and } \sup_{0 \le u \le t} Z_{t_0+u} > b)]$. For $S > H$ and $z > b$, $G(z,t) = \text{Prob}(Z_{t_0+t} \le z \text{ and } \inf_{0 \le u \le t} Z_{t_0+u} < b)]$
$g(z, t)$	$[\equiv \partial/\partial z\, G(z, t)]$ the risk-neutral density function for crossing the barrier and returning. This density is useful for knock-ins and in computing the density for Z_T^*.
$p(z, t)$	the risk-neutral density function for Z_T^*.
τ, τ_b	the random variable giving the first-passage time to the barrier. Explicitly, if the process S_t follows the path ω, then (if $S < H$) $\tau(\omega) = \sup_{t_0 \le t} \{t - t_0 \mid S_t(\omega) < H\} = \sup_{t_0 \le t} \{t - t_0 \mid Z_t(\omega) < b\}$
$h(\tau)$, $h(\tau; b)$	the density function for τ, the first-passage time for Z_t breaching the barrier b (equivalently for S_t breaching the barrier H).
$n(x)$	$[\equiv e^{-x^2/2}/\sqrt{2\pi}]$ the density of the standard normal distribution.
$N(x)$	$[\equiv \int_{-\infty}^{x} n(s)ds]$ the cumulative distribution function for $n(x)$.

FIGURE 8–2
Density Functions f(z), g(z), p(z) for $\mu = 0.03$, $t = 0.5$, $\sigma = 20\%$, $S = 100$, $H = 110$.

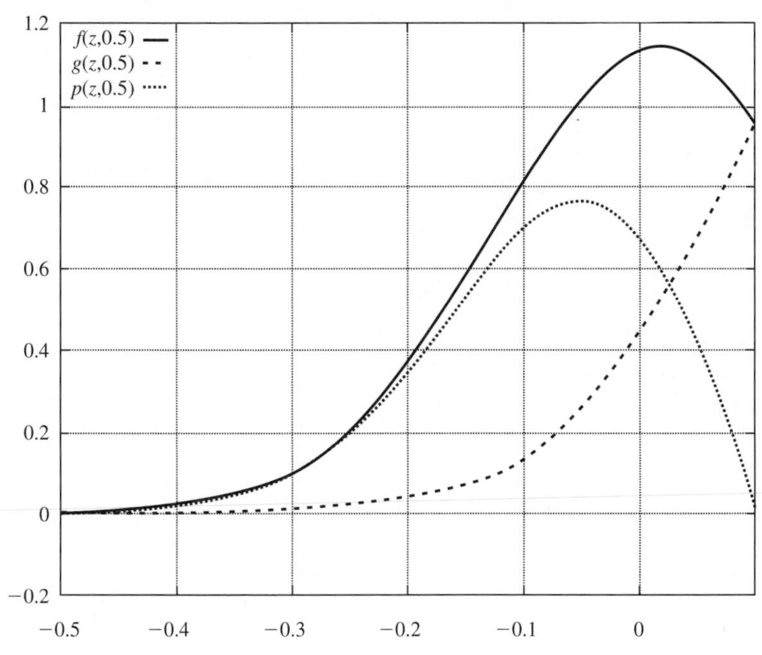

$\phi(\alpha, \beta, \gamma)$ $\equiv \alpha/\sqrt{\gamma} + \beta\sqrt{\gamma} = (\alpha + \beta\gamma)/\sqrt{\gamma}$ a convenient shorthand.

η $\equiv +1(-1)$ if the barrier is approached from below (above). ($\eta = sgn(b)$).

ψ $\equiv 1$ (resp. -1) for a call(put).

Valuation Formulas

Proposition 1 (Density Functions). Under the assumptions and notations of the preceding section, the following density formulas hold:

$$\text{a) } f(z, t) = \frac{1}{\sigma\sqrt{t}}\, n\left(\frac{z - \mu t}{\sigma\sqrt{t}}\right)$$

FIGURE 8–3
Density Function $h(\tau)$ When $\mu = 0.03$, $\sigma = 20\%$, S = 100, and H = 110

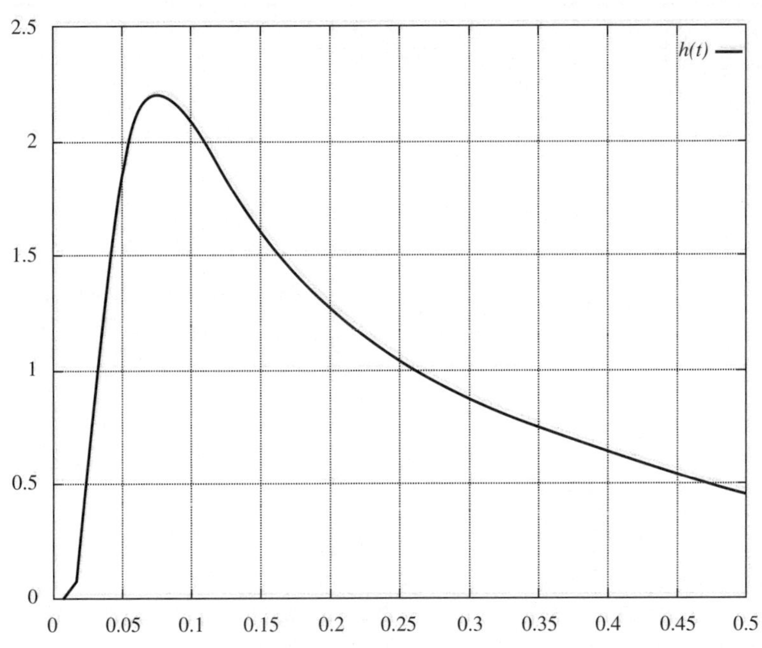

b) $g(z, t) = \dfrac{e^{2\mu b/\sigma^2}}{\sigma\sqrt{t}}\, n\left(\dfrac{z - 2b - \mu t}{\sigma\sqrt{t}}\right)$

c) $p(z, t) = f(z, t) - g(z, t)$

d) $h(\tau) = \dfrac{|b|}{\sigma\sqrt{\tau^3}}\, n\left(\dfrac{b - \mu\tau}{\sigma\sqrt{\tau}}\right)$

For the proof, see the appendix to this chapter.

Figure 8–2 shows density functions $f(z, t)$, $g(z, t)$, and $p(z, t)$ when $\mu = 0.03$, $t = 0.5$, $\sigma = 20\%$, $S = 100$, and $H = 110$. Common range of definition is $(-\infty, b)$, where $b = \log(110/100) = 0.09531$.

Figure 8–3 shows density function $h(\tau)$ when $\mu = 0.03$, $\sigma = 20\%$, $S = 100$, and $H = 110$.

Proposition 2 (Rebate Expected Present Value). Under the assumptions and notations of the preceding section, the expected present value of the rebate R is, for $t = T - t_0$:

FIGURE 8–4
Rebate Expected Present Value as a Function of the Underlying Price

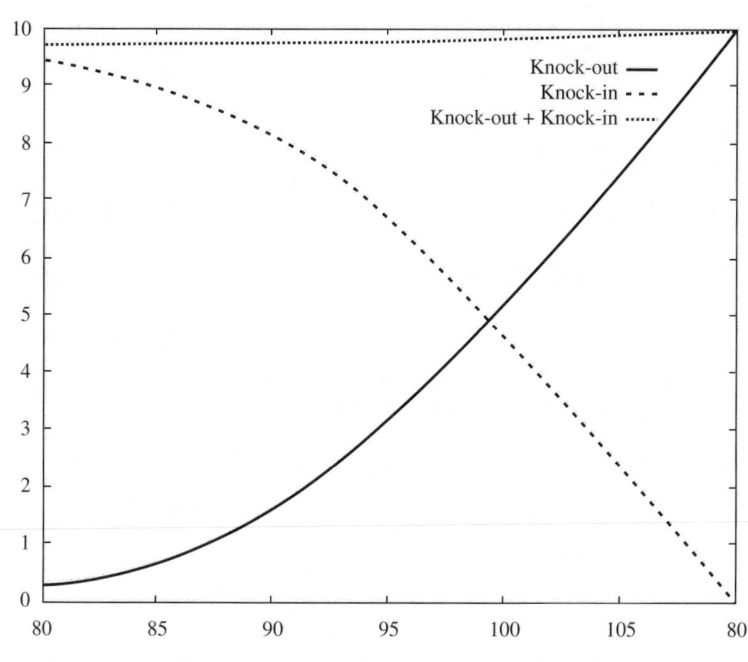

a) $\text{Rebate}_{\text{PV}}^{\text{KO}}(R) \equiv$ expected present value of knock-out rebate

$$= R\left[\left(\frac{H}{S}\right)^{A+B} N\left(\frac{-\eta b - \eta B\sigma^2 t}{\sigma\sqrt{t}}\right) + \left(\frac{H}{S}\right)^{A-B} N\left(\frac{-\eta b + \eta B\sigma^2 t}{\sigma\sqrt{t}}\right)\right]$$

where $A = \mu/\sigma^2$ and $B = \sqrt{\mu^2 + 2\sigma^2 r}/\sigma^2$.

b) $\text{Rebate}_{\text{PV}}^{\text{KI}}(R) \equiv$ expected present value of knock-in rebate

$$= Re^{-rt}\left\{N\left(\frac{\eta(b - \mu t)}{\sigma\sqrt{t}}\right) - e^{2\mu b/\sigma^2} N\left(\frac{-\eta(b + \mu t)}{\sigma\sqrt{t}}\right)\right\}$$

For the proof, see the appendix to this chapter.

Figure 8–4 shows expected rebate present value as a function of the underlying price. Parameters are $H = 110$, $t = 0.5$, $\mu = 0.05$, $\sigma = 20\%$, Rebate $= \$10$.

Exercise. Why is the sum of the rebates, as shown in Figure 8–4, less than \$10, and why is it sloped as it is?

The (nondiscounted) payoff of a knock-out option for which the barrier has not been breached is given by the following expression, where

$\psi = 1(-1)$ for a call(put), and where the appropriate values of α, β are specified in the following proposition:

$$\int_\alpha^\beta \psi \cdot (Se^z - K) \cdot p(z) \cdot dz$$

$$= \int_\alpha^\beta \psi \cdot (Se^z - K) \cdot (f(z) - g(z)) \cdot dz$$

$$= \psi S \left(\int_\alpha^\beta e^z f(z) dz - \int_\alpha^\beta e^z g(z) dz \right) - \psi K \left(\int_\alpha^\beta f(z) dz - \int_\alpha^\beta g(z) dz \right)$$

$$\equiv \psi S\,(J_1 - J_2) - \psi K\,(J_3 - J_4)$$

where J_1, J_2, J_3, J_4 are computed below.

Proposition 3 (Knock-Out Premium). The premium of a European knock-out option with rebate R is given by

$$KO_E(R) \equiv KO_E(H, R; S, K, t_0, T, r, q, \sigma)$$
$$= e^{-rt}[\psi S(J_1 - J_2) - \psi K(J_3 - J_4)] + \mathrm{Rebate}_{\mathrm{PV}}^{\mathrm{KO}}(R)$$

where $t \equiv T - t_0$ and

$$J_1 \equiv e^{(\mu + \sigma^2/2)t} \left[N\!\left(\frac{\beta - (\mu + \sigma^2)t}{\sigma\sqrt{t}}\right) - N\!\left(\frac{\alpha - (\mu + \sigma^2)t}{\sigma\sqrt{t}}\right) \right]$$

$$J_2 \equiv e^{2b} e^{2\mu b/\sigma^2} e^{(\mu + \sigma^2/2)t} \left[N\!\left(\frac{\beta - 2b - (\mu + \sigma^2)t}{\sigma\sqrt{t}}\right) - N\!\left(\frac{\alpha - 2b - (\mu + \sigma^2)t}{\sigma\sqrt{t}}\right) \right]$$

$$J_3 \equiv \left[N\!\left(\frac{\beta - \mu t}{\sigma\sqrt{t}}\right) - N\!\left(\frac{\alpha - \mu t}{\sigma\sqrt{t}}\right) \right]$$

$$J_4 \equiv e^{2\mu b/\sigma^2} \left[N\!\left(\frac{\beta - 2b - \mu t}{\sigma\sqrt{t}}\right) - N\!\left(\frac{\alpha - 2b - \mu t}{\sigma\sqrt{t}}\right) \right]$$

and where α, β are determined by Table 8–1.

For the proof, see the appendix to this chapter.

Example. Continuing with the example described in Section II, we derive the premium of a 6-month up-and-out call option, where the underlying index is at 100, the strike is at 100, volatility is 20 percent, the risk-free rate is 5 percent, and the barrier is set at 110, with a rebate payment of 10. We also assume that the index has no dividends associated with it.[4] In the notation of this section we have

[4]If the index was, for example, an exchange rate, or a basket of stocks, then an adjustment would have to be made for dividends, which appears as q in the definition of μ.

TABLE 8–1
Values of and α and β

	Up-and-Out		*Down-and-Out*	
	$K > H$	$K < H$	$K > H$	$K < H$
call	not needed	$\alpha = k, \beta = b$	$\alpha = k, \beta = \infty$	$\alpha = b, \beta = \infty$
put	$\alpha = -\infty, \beta = b$	$\alpha = -\infty, \beta = k$	$\alpha - b, \beta = k$	not needed

N.B. Only the rebate component has value for those cases labeled "not needed."

$$S = 100, K = 100, H = 110, r = 0.05 \text{ (continuous compounding)}$$
$$\sigma = 0.20, t_0 = 0, T = 0.5, q = 0, \eta = 1, R = 10$$
$$\Rightarrow \mu = r - q - \sigma^2/2 = 0.03, b = \log(110/100) = 0.0953101798$$

From Proposition 2 we have

$$A = \mu/\sigma^2 = 0.75,$$
$$B = \sqrt{\mu^2 + 2\sigma^2 r}/\sigma^2 = \sqrt{0.0009 + 2 * 0.04 * 0.05}/0.04 = 1.75$$
$$\left(\frac{H}{S}\right)^{A+B} = 1.1^{2.5} = 1.2690587$$
$$\left(\frac{H}{S}\right)^{A-B} = 1.1^{-1} = 0.9090909$$

$$\text{Rebate}_{\text{PV}}^{\text{KO}}(R) = R * \left[\left(1.2690587 * N\left(\frac{-0.0953101798 - 1.75*0.04*0.5}{0.2*\sqrt{0.5}}\right)\right)\right.$$
$$\left. + \left(0.9090909 * N\left(\frac{-0.0953101798 + 1.75*0.04*0.5}{0.2*\sqrt{0.5}}\right)\right)\right]$$
$$= 10 * [1.2690587 * N(-0.92143212) + 0.9090909 * N(-0.42645737)]$$
$$= 10 * [1.269057 * 0.178413137 + 0.9090909 * 0.33488811]$$
$$= 5.3086048$$

From Proposition 3 we find that

$$J_1 = e^{0.025}[N(0.42645737) - N(-0.247487)] = 0.2694997$$
$$J_2 = (1.1)^{3.5} \cdot e^{0.025}[N(-0.92143212)) - N(-1.59537686)]$$
$$= 0.1761918$$
$$J_3 = N(0.56787873) - N(-0.10606602) = 0.257175322$$
$$J_4 = (1.1)^{1.5}[N(-0.78001076) - N(-1.4539555)] = 0.1669541895$$

Hence the premium is

$$e^{-.025}100[0.2694997 - 0.1761918 - 0.257175322 +$$
$$0.1669541895] + 5.3086048$$
$$= 0.3011 + 5.309 = 5.61$$

Since a portfolio consisting of one knock-out call (resp. put) option with no rebate and one knock-in call (resp. put) option is equivalent to owning a standard European call (resp. put) option plus the knock-in rebate, we can price knock-in options using standard Black-Scholes formulas and the formulas for knock-out options given by Proposition 3.

Note: (Black-Scholes Premium) The Black-Scholes formula for the premium of a standard European option is given by

$$BS \text{ of standard option} \equiv e^{-rt}\psi\,[Se^{(r-q)t}N(\psi d_1) - KN(\psi d_2)]$$

where $t \equiv T - t_0$, $d_1 = \frac{-k+(\mu+\sigma^2)t}{\sigma\sqrt{t}}$, $d_2 = d_1 - \sigma\sqrt{t}$.

Proposition 5 (Knock-In Premium). The premium of a European knock-in option with rebate R is given by

$$KI_E(R) \equiv KI_E(H,R;\, S,K,t_0,\, T,r,q,\, \sigma)$$
$$= BS - KO_E(0) + \text{Rebate}_{\text{PV}}^{\text{KI}}\,(R).$$

Figure 8–5 shows the component values of a barrier option, as a function of the level of the barrier. The graph is of a 6-month up-and-out call option, where the current value S of the underlying is 100, the strike K is also at 100, and volatility is 20 percent. The rebate is fairly high, at 30, to emphasize the different components. Note that for high barrier-levels, the rebate component goes to zero and the terminal component approaches the value of a standard European option. For low barrier-levels, the knock-out premium is dominated by the rebate component.

FIGURE 8–5

Premium versus Barrier Level for S = 100, t = 0.5, K = 100, σ = 20%, Rebate = 30

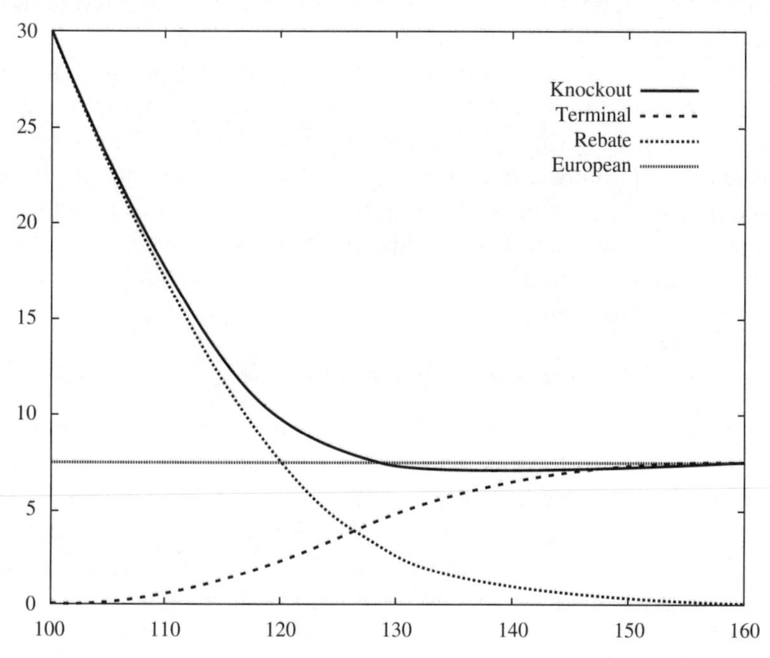

Partial Barrier Options

A generalization of the standard barrier option structure is to provide for the monitoring to take place during only a part of the option's lifetime. For example, consider a one-year partial up-and-out option in which the barrier condition is monitored only for the first 6 months. After the first 6 months, if the barrier has not been breached, the investor is left with a plain-vanilla option. Alternatively, the monitoring period might be for the latter part of the option's life. So, for example, a one-year partial up-and-out option contract might specify that the barrier is monitored only during the last 3 months of the contract. As Heynen and Kat [19] point out, this latter type of option is appropriate for the buyer who is using the barrier option to define an exit strategy.

For a zero rebate, knock-out options gain in value when the period of monitoring is reduced, since there is reduced chance of being knocked out. Similarly, for a zero rebate, partial knock-in options would be less valuable than regular knock-in options, all other things being equal.

Note that in the case when monitoring is deferred, a complication arises: What happens if the barrier has been breached before the monitoring period starts? For example, suppose, as above, the option is a one-year partial up-and-out option with a barrier at 110 and that monitoring is to start 3 months prior to option expiration. Suppose that at the time the monitoring starts the underlying is at 120. Has the option been knocked out? Is there a rebate payment? The option counterparties can decide on a number of possible resolutions to such situations, and several alternatives are considered and valuation formulas derived in [19].

Partial barrier options are also interesting because they can be used as components to synthetically create other types of exotic options.

Special Case: American Capped Call

An American knock-out barrier option is one that gives the investor the right to exercise at any time prior to the termination of the contract. An important special case of such an option is the American capped call. This is an up-and-out (American) call with $H > K$ and rebate $R = H - K$. For such options, Broadie and Detemple [8] have determined explicit analytic formulas for the premium. Their main result is in identifying the optimal exercise boundary, which they determined to be the minimum of the cap level and the optimal exercise boundary of an otherwise similar uncapped call.

DOUBLE BARRIER OPTION VALUATION

We are interested in the valuation of double barrier knock-out options. By this we mean that there are two barriers, H^- and H^+ such that $H^- < S < H^+$. (Equivalently, if $b^- \equiv \log(H^-/S)$ and $b^+ \equiv \log(H^+/S)$ then $b^- < 0 < b^+$.) The option is automatically terminated if the (monitored) value of S_t breaches either of the two barriers before option expiration. A rebate R^- (resp. R^+) is paid at the time the barrier H^- (resp. H^+) is breached. Providing flexibility for different rebate amounts allows the investor to tailor the return to match her requirements. A desirable combination for a double barrier call-option with $K < H^+$ might be to set $R^+ = H^+ - K$ and $R^- = 0$.

With double barrier knock-out options, the positive features of regular knock-out options are present to an even greater extent. The investor who knows ahead of time that she will close out the option position once the underlying price moves outside of a predetermined range can have this take place via the automatic exercise feature of the option. Transaction costs for unwinding are reduced, and the investor is not required to actively monitor the market. We provide explicit formulas for the premium, including the rebate components.

The terminal payoff component of the premium of a double barrier option has been studied by Kunitomo and Ikeda in [25], where they considered the more general case of (exponentially) curved barriers.[5] However, they did not evaluate the rebate components.[6]

Many of the formulas in this section involve infinite series. Kunitomo and Ikeda point out that for typical parameters, these series converge rapidly and can be approximated satisfactorily using only four terms.

Notation

H^+ (H^-)	the upper (lower) barrier.
K	the strike.
S_t	the price process.
Z_t	$\equiv \log(S_t/S)$ the return process.
$b^+(b^-)$	$\equiv \log(H^+/S)$ (resp. $\log(H^-/S)$). (The barrier in the return process.)
k	$\equiv \log(K/S)$. The strike in the return process.
$\Xi(z, T)$	$\equiv \text{Prob}(Z_T < z \text{ and } b^- < \inf_{t_0<t<T} Z_t < \sup_{t_0<t<T} Z_t < b^+)$, for $z \in [-b^-, b^+]$.
$\xi(z, T)$	the (defective) density determined by Ξ. $\Xi(z, T) = \int_{b^-}^{z} \xi(u, T)du$.
τ^+ (τ^-)	the first passage time to the barrier H^+ (H^-) conditional on not first breaching the other barrier. For convenience, we write $\tau^+(\omega) = \infty$ (resp. $\tau^-(\omega) = \infty$) if the barrier H^- (H^+) is breached before H^+ (H^-) has been attained.

[5]Mathematically, the constant barrier and exponential barrier can be treated similarly. We have chosen to focus on constant barriers to retain the similarity with standard barrier options.

[6]See footnote 4 of [25].

$h^+(t)$ the density of τ^+. Note $\int_{t_0}^{t} h^+(s)ds = \text{Prob}(\tau^+ < t \text{ and } \tau^+ < \tau^-)$.

$h^-(t)$ the density of τ^-. Note $\int_{t_0}^{t} h^-(s)ds = \text{Prob}(\tau^- < t \text{ and } \tau^- < \tau^+)$.

A μ/σ^2

B $\sqrt{\mu^2 + 2\sigma^2 r}/\sigma^2$

V $(H^+/H^-)^{2A}$

U $(H^-/S)^{2A}$

$\Theta(x, t)$ $\equiv N\left(\frac{x-\mu t}{\sigma\sqrt{t}}\right)$

$\theta(x, t)$ $-\ \partial/\partial x\ \Theta(x, t) - \frac{1}{\sigma\sqrt{t}}\, x\left(\frac{x-\mu t}{\sigma\sqrt{t}}\right)$

We also define the following operators:

$\mathcal{L}(f, z, w, \alpha, \beta, \gamma, t)$ an operator on an arbitrary function f utilized so that some formulas are clearer, explicitly

$$\equiv \sum_{j=-\infty}^{\infty}\{\alpha^j[f(z - \zeta_j, t) - f(w - \zeta_j, t)] - \beta \cdot \gamma^j \cdot [f(z + \eta_j, t) - f(\mathrm{w} + n_j, t)]\}$$

$$Q(\infty, \beta, \gamma, \epsilon) \quad \equiv \int_0^{T-t_0} e^{-rs} n\left(\tfrac{\alpha}{\sqrt{s}} + \beta\sqrt{s}\right) \cdot \left(\tfrac{\gamma}{\sqrt{s^3}} + \tfrac{\epsilon}{\sqrt{s}}\right) ds$$

Valuation Formulas

Proposition 6 (Double Barrier Density Functions). Together with the notation of the preceding paragraphs and the assumptions and notations of Section III, the following density formulas hold:

$$\xi(z, t) = \sum_{j=-\infty}^{\infty} k_j(z, t)$$

$$\Xi(z, t) = \mathcal{L}(\Theta, z, b^-, V, U, V^{-1}, t)$$

$$h^+(t) \equiv h^+(t; b^+, b^-, \mu, \sigma)$$

$$= n\left(\frac{d_0}{\sqrt{t}} + e_0\sqrt{t}\right)\left(\frac{-d_0}{2\sqrt{t^3}} + \frac{e_0}{2\sqrt{t}}\right)$$

$$+ \sum_{j=1}^{\infty}\sum_{i=1}^{4} c_{i,j}\, n\left(\frac{-d_{i,j}}{\sqrt{t}} + e_i\sqrt{t}\right)\left(\frac{-d_{i,j}}{2\sqrt{t^3}} + \frac{e_i}{2\sqrt{t}}\right)$$

$$h^-(t) \equiv h^-(t; b+, b^-, \mu, \sigma) = h+(t; -b^-, -b^+, -\mu, \sigma)$$

TABLE 8–2

	$c_{i,j}$	$d_{i,j}$	e_i
$i = 1$	$\exp(-\delta[(2j-1)M + P])$	$[(3-4j)M - P]/2$	δ
$i = 2$	$-\exp(-2\delta jM)$	$[(1-4j)M + P]/2$	δ
$i = 3$	$-\exp(2\delta[(2j+1)M - P])$	$[(1-4j)M + P]/2$	$-\delta$
$i = 4$	$\exp(-2\delta jM)$	$-[(1+4j)M + P]/2$	$-\delta$

where the c_{ij}, d_{ij}, e_i are defined in Table 8–2:

$$M = (b^+ - b^-)/\sigma, P = (b^+ - b^-)/\sigma,$$
$$\delta = -\mu/\sigma, d_0 = -(P + M)/2, e_0 = -\delta.$$

For the proof, see the appendix to this chapter.

Lemma 7 (Formula for Q)

$Q(\alpha, \beta, \gamma, \epsilon)$

$$= e^{-\alpha\beta+\infty\beta'}\left[\frac{\gamma}{|\alpha|}\left\{N\left(\frac{-|\alpha|}{\sqrt{t}} - sgn(\alpha)\beta'\sqrt{t}\right) + e^{-2\alpha\beta'}N\left(\frac{-|\alpha|}{\sqrt{t}} + sgn(\alpha)\beta'\sqrt{t}\right)\right\}\right.$$
$$\left. + \frac{sgn(\alpha)\epsilon}{\beta'}\left\{N\left(\frac{|\alpha|}{\sqrt{t}} + sgn(\alpha)\beta'\sqrt{t}\right) + e^{-2\alpha\beta'}N\left(\frac{-|\alpha|}{\sqrt{t}} + sgn(\alpha)\beta'\sqrt{t}\right) - 1\right\}\right]$$

where $t \equiv T - t_0$ and $\beta' \equiv \sqrt{\beta^2 + 2r}$.

Proof. The formula follows by applying identities found in Proposition 13 and in Corollaries 14 and 15 in the appendix.

Proposition 8 (Rebate Present Value). Together with the notation of the preceding paragraphs and the assumptions and notations of the third section of this chapter, the expected present values of the various rebates are:

a) $\text{Rebate}_{\text{PV}}^{\text{DKO}^+}(R^+)$

$\equiv \text{Rebate}_{\text{PV}}^{\text{DKO}^+}(R^+, T, b^+, b^-, \mu, \sigma)$

$\equiv$ Expected present value of rebate due to breaching upper barrier

$$= R^+\left\{Q\left(d_0, e_0, \frac{-d_0}{2}, \frac{e_0}{2}\right) + \sum_{j=1}^{\infty}\sum_{i=1}^{4} c_{i,j}Q\left(d_{i,j}, e_i, \frac{-d_{i,j}}{2}, \frac{e_i}{2}\right)\right\}$$

b) $\text{Rebate}_{\text{PV}}^{\text{DKO}^-}(R^-)$

$$\equiv \text{Rebate}_{\text{PV}}^{\text{DKO}^-}(R^-, T, b^+, b^-, \mu, \sigma)$$

$$\equiv \text{Expected present value of rebate due to breaching lower barrier}$$

$$= \text{Rebate}_{\text{PV}}^{\text{DKO}^+}(R^-, T, -b^-, -b^+, -\mu, \sigma)$$

c) $\text{Rebate}_{\text{PV}}^{\text{DKI}}(R)$

$$\equiv \text{Rebate}_{\text{PV}}^{\text{DKI}}(R, T, b^+, b^-, \mu, \sigma)$$

$$\equiv R\, e^{-rt}\Xi(b^+, t)$$

Proposition 9 (Double Barrier Knock-Out Premium). The premium of a European double barrier knock-out option with rebates R^+ and R^- is given by

$$\begin{aligned} &DKO_E(R^+, R^-) \\ &\equiv DKO_E(H^+, H^-, R^+, R^-; S, K, t_0, T, r, q, \sigma) \\ &= e^{-rt}[\psi e^{(r-q)t} S\mathcal{L}(\Theta, \beta - \sigma^2 t, \alpha - \sigma^2 t, e^{\zeta_1(A+1)}, e^{2b^-(A+1)}, e^{-\zeta_1(A+1)}, t) \\ &\quad -\psi K\mathcal{L}(\Theta, \beta, \alpha, V, U, V^{-1}, t)] \\ &\quad +\text{Rebate}_{\text{PV}}^{\text{DKO}^+}(R^+) + \text{Rebate}_{\text{PV}}^{\text{DKO}^-}(R^-) \end{aligned}$$

where $t \equiv T - t_0$ and where α, β are determined by Table 8–3.

Proposition 10 (Double Knock-In Premium). The premium of a European double barrier knock-in option with rebate R is given by

$$DKI_E(R) = BS - DKO_E(0, 0) + \text{Rebate}_{\text{PV}}^{\text{DKI}}(R)$$

A DISCRETELY MONITORED BARRIER

Until now we have restricted our attention to barrier options where the monitoring is continuous. Other possibilities exist. For example, the capped S&P index options (dubbed *CAPs*) that trade(d) on the CBOE are nominally up-and-out calls (with rebate $R = H - K$), and down-and-out puts (with rebate $R = K - H$). The underlying index is monitored once a day, at the close, to determine whether the barrier has been breached. Using formulas based on continuous monitoring to price discretely monitored barrier options is inaccurate.

TABLE 8–3

	$K > H^+$	$H^+ > K > H^-$	$H^- > K$
call	*n/a*	$\alpha = k, \beta = b^+$	$\alpha = b^-, \beta = b^+$
put	$\alpha = b^-, \beta = b^+$	$\alpha = b^-, \beta = k$	*n/a*

Kat and Verdonk [24] present a compelling analysis showing the importance of the monitoring frequency in barrier option valuation. In addition, they treat other market realities, such as the effect of discrete dividends on the likelihood of breaching a barrier. Their approach is pragmatic, presenting a numerical technique based on an adjusted binomial tree method. Their algorithm appears to give good agreement with the "right answer,"[7] which is defined as the result of a Monte Carlo simulation using 10,000 paths chosen using several variance-reduction techniques. The Monte Carlo technique itself is not an acceptable solution for them, since it takes too much time to calculate.

The Kat-Verdonk proposal is based on a study of the errors found in the standard binomial tree method (i.e., Cox-Ross-Rubinstein method) when it is applied naively to the problem of discretely monitored barrier options.[8] There is a pattern in the errors that is easily identified in graphs, and that stems from the location of the barrier relative to the nodes in the tree. It is possible to determine, as a function of the number of time steps in the tree, when the standard tree will give a price that is too high and when it will give a price that is too low. Their neat solution is to take the average of these two biased prices. The weakness in their article is that it is ad hoc. No hard i.e., precise, error estimates are given, and it is not immediately clear how to combine the handling of discrete dividends with their proposed method.

Another contribution in the study of discrete methods for valuing barrier options is that of Reimer and Sandmann [31]. In their terminology,

[7]They study 130-day options, and consider the following monitoring frequencies: continuous, every day, every second day, and every fifth day.

[8]See also the following section on numerical issues.

a discretely monitored barrier option is called a *local barrier option.*[9] Reimer and Sandmann adopt a rigorous approach and they provide detailed algorithms and formulas for European, American, partial, and local barrier options. Their analysis involves choosing the tree nodes so that the barrier is forced (*knotted* in their terminology) to be one of the nodes. A multinomial formula is produced for valuing discretely monitored barrier options.[10]

For the specific case of capped discretely monitored barrier options, Trippi and Chance [37] produced an approximating formula based on a functional interpolation of a spread position and a continuously monitored barrier option. Recall that a (bullish) vertical call spread position involves being long a call at strike K and short a call at strike L, where $K < L$. These calls are European. The payout of such a vertical spread at option expiration is the same as a continuously monitored up-and-out call with rebate $L - K$ and barrier L, provided that it has not been knocked out. By exploiting the relationship

$$Val(\text{vertical spread}) < Val(\text{discretely mon}) < Val(\text{continuously mon})$$

and the fact that both the left- and right-hand sides can be valued analytically, they perform a regression for the expression

$$Val(\text{discretely mon}) = \alpha \cdot Val(\text{vertical spread}) + (1-\alpha) \cdot Val(\text{continously mon})$$

where $\alpha \equiv \alpha(S/K,T)$. Their finding was $\alpha(S/K,T) = \beta^{T\mu} \cdot (S/K)^{\gamma}$, with $\beta = 1.19$, $\mu = 0.5$, $\gamma = 4.5$.

NUMERICAL ISSUES

Significant valuation errors can result from the naive application of the CRR binomial tree pricing methodology to the case of barrier options. For example, Boyle and Lau [6] report errors as high as 10 percent when pricing a 1-year barrier option using 800 time steps (!). Considering that

---

[9]See Section 6 in [31].

[10]For the mathematically inclined, they exploit the discrete version of some of the density functions presented here in the continuous case. These discrete density functions are attributed to Feller.

using 800 time steps involves 64 times more computational effort than using 100 time steps, a typical number for standard options, the magnitude of this error is enormous.

A discussion of this issue has been partly given in the previous section on discretely monitored barrier options. The work of Reimer and Sandman [31] was mentioned there and is appropriately mentioned here as well. In addition, Boyle and Lau study the nature of the numerical problems and propose an algorithm to improve the stability of the results. Their solution seems not as general as that of Kat and Verdonk, nor as complete as the analysis by Reimer and Sandman. However, an interesting discussion of pricing vulnerable options, which are subject to default by the writer, can be found there.

HEDGING

We do not present a detailed discussion of how one might hedge a position in a barrier option. Rather, we point out some relevant contributions in the literature.

The approach of Bowie and Carr [5] uses a technique called static hedging, as opposed to dynamic trading strategies that synthetically replicate the option. In the static approach, it is permissible to have standard options in the hedging portfolio. As the simplest case, they consider the (valuing and) hedging problem faced by the writer of a down-and-in call, assuming that the strike K is the same as the barrier H, that the rebate is zero, and that interest rates are zero. In this case, a put with strike K and the same expiration as the barrier option is a perfect hedge. This is because if the barrier is hit, put-call parity implies that the put will have the same value as the call that comes into existence, so the writer can buy (or buy back) the call if the barrier is hit. If the barrier is never hit, both the down-and-in call and the put expire worthless. In their generalization of this approach, Bowie and Carr use a generalized put-call symmetry result and introduce the notion of down-and-in bonds. Another effort in this direction is that of Derman, Ergener, and Kani [14] who use a portfolio of options to replicate a barrier option.

Appendix

The main contribution of the Appendix is the explicit use of Girsanov's Theorem in the proof of Proposition 1. Girsanov's Theorem plays a central—if background—role in modern finance theory. It guarantees the existence of a certain measure that can be used to transform difficult problems into analytically tractable ones. Barrier options provide an excellent opportunity to see Girsanov's Theorem at work in detail, since it comes out quite cleanly. In addition, the Appendix contains various formulas, identities, and proofs. The identities are useful tools in manipulating the sorts of expressions that appear throughout the calculations.

Proof of Proposition 1

The argument uses Girsanov's Theorem, which is stated following the proof. Girsanov's theorem is stated both in its general form and with a corollary for the case of Brownian motion with drift, the case that is needed here.

Specifically consider the return process Z_t which satisfies

$$Z_t = \mu(t - t_0) + \sigma W_t,\ W_{t0} = 0. \tag{1}$$

In the following, ϵ will denote a univariate normal random variable with mean 0 and variance 1, i.e., $\epsilon \sim n(0, 1)$.

Proof of a). Setting

$$\begin{aligned} F(z, T) \equiv F(z) &= \text{Prob}\{Z_T \leq Z\} \\ &= \text{Prob}\{\mu(T - t_0) + \sigma\sqrt{T - t_0}\epsilon \leq z\} \\ &= \text{Prob}\left\{\epsilon \leq \frac{(z - \mu(T - t_0))}{\sigma\sqrt{T - t_0}}\right\} \\ &= N\left(\frac{z - \mu(T - t_0)}{\sigma\sqrt{T - t_0}}\right) \end{aligned}$$

$$\Rightarrow f(z) = F'(z) = \frac{1}{\sigma\sqrt{T - t_0}}n\left(\frac{z - \mu(T - t_0)}{\sigma\sqrt{T - t_0}}\right)$$

which completes the assertion of a).

Proof of b). Let P denote the original measure, and let Q denote the measure (as specified by Girsanov's Theorem) under which Z_t has zero drift. Also, introduce the notation that, for any quantity y, we define $\hat{y} \equiv y/\sigma$. We first derive the result for the case where the barrier is approached from below, i.e., $H > S(\equiv b > 0)$.

$$G(z, T) \equiv G(z) = \text{Prob}^P\{Z_T \leq z \text{ and } \sup_{t_0 \leq t \leq T} Z_t > b\}$$

which, using (1)

$$= \text{Prob}^P\{\mu(T - t_0) + \sigma W_T \leq z \text{ and } \sup_{t_0 \leq t \leq T} \mu(t - t_0) + \sigma W_t > b\}$$

$$= \text{Prob}^P\{\tfrac{\mu}{\sigma}(T - t_0) + W_T \leq \tfrac{z}{\sigma} \text{ and } \sup_{t_0 \leq t \leq T} \tfrac{\mu}{\sigma}(t - t_0) + W_t > \tfrac{b}{\sigma}\}$$

which, using indicator functions

$$= E^P[1_{\{\hat{Z}_T \leq \hat{z}\}} \cdot 1_{\{\tau < T\}}]$$

which, by Girsanov's Theorem

$$= E^Q\left[1_{\{\hat{Z}_T \leq \hat{z}\}} \cdot 1_{\{\tau < T\}} \cdot \exp\left(\hat{\mu}\hat{Z}_T - \frac{1}{2}\hat{\mu}^2(T - t_0)\right)\right]$$

Now apply the reflection principle

$$= E^Q\left[1_{\{\hat{Z}_T \geq 2\hat{b} - \hat{z}\}} \cdot \exp\left(\hat{\mu}(2\hat{b} - \hat{Z}_T) - \frac{1}{2}\hat{\mu}^2(T - t_0)\right)\right]$$

$$= \exp(2\hat{\mu}\hat{b})\, E^Q\left[1_{\{\hat{Z}_T \leq \hat{z} - 2\hat{b}\}} \cdot \exp\left(\hat{\mu}\hat{Z}_T - \frac{1}{2}\hat{\mu}^2(T - t_0)\right)\right]$$

$$= \exp(2\hat{\mu}\hat{b}) \int_{-\infty}^{\hat{z} - 2\hat{b}} n(\phi(x, -\hat{\mu}, T - t_0))\phi_x(x, -\hat{\mu}, T - t_0)dx$$

$$= \exp(2\hat{\mu}\hat{b}) \int_{-\infty}^{\phi(\hat{z} - 2\hat{b}, -\hat{\mu}, T - t_0)} n(u)du$$

$$= \exp(2\hat{\mu}\hat{b})\, N(\phi(\hat{z} - 2\,\hat{b}, -\,\hat{\mu}, T - t_0))$$

$$= \exp(2\mu b/\sigma^2)\, N\left(\frac{z - 2B - \mu(T - t_0)}{\sigma\sqrt{T - t_0}}\right)$$

$$\Rightarrow g(z) = G'(z) = \frac{e^{2\mu b/\sigma^2}}{\sigma\sqrt{T - t_0}} n\left(\frac{z - 2b - \mu(T - t_0)}{\sigma\sqrt{T - t_0}}\right)$$

When the barrier is approached from above, a similar derivation produces the same result, beginning from $\text{Prob}^P\{Z_T \geq z \text{ and } \inf_{t_0 \leq t \leq T} Z_t < b\}$. This completes the assertion of b).

Proof of c). This follows by definition.

Proof of d). Again, we start with the case of $H > S \equiv b > 0$. By definition of a destiny function, we have $Prob\{\tau < T\} = E[1_{\{\tau < T\}}] = \int_0^T h(s)ds$, so that

$$
\begin{aligned}
h(T) &= \partial/\partial T\, Prob\{\tau < T\} \\
&= \partial/\partial T\, Prob\{\sup_{t_0 \le u \le T} Z_u > b\} \\
&= \partial/\partial T \left[Prob\{Z_T > b\} + \int_{-\infty}^{b} g(u, T)du \right] \\
&= \partial/\partial T\, [1 - F(b, T) + G(b, T) - G(-\infty, T)] \\
&= \frac{b}{\sigma(T - t_0)^{3/2}} n\left(\frac{b - \mu(T - t_0)}{\sigma\sqrt{T - t_0}}\right)
\end{aligned}
$$

For the case of approaching the barrier from above, we have

$$
\begin{aligned}
h(T) &= \partial/\partial T\, Prob\{\tau < T\} \\
&= \partial/\partial T\, Prob\{\inf_{t_0 \le u \le T} Z_u < b\} \\
&= \partial/\partial T \left[Prob\{Z_T < b\} + \int_{b}^{\infty} g(u, T)du \right] \\
&= \partial/\partial T\, [F(b, T) + G(\infty, T) - G(b, T)] \\
&= \frac{-b}{\sigma(T - t_0)^{3/2}} n\left(\frac{b - \mu(T - t_0)}{\sigma\sqrt{T - t_0}}\right)
\end{aligned}
$$

which completes the assertion of d). Δ

Theorem 11 (Girsanov, 1960).[11] (In one dimension.)

Let $(\Omega,\mathcal{F},F,P)$ denote a probability space Ω with σ-algebra $\mathcal{F}$, filtration $F = (F_t)$ and measure P. Let W_t be a Standard Brownian Motion, and X_t an adapted process, both w.r.t. $(\Omega,\mathcal{F},F,P)$. Suppose also that $E[\exp(\frac{1}{2}\int_0^T X_s^2 ds)] < \infty$. Define

$$\xi(X)_t = \exp\left(\int_0^t X_s dW_s - \frac{1}{2}\int_0^t X_s^2 ds\right)$$

and define a measure Q via

$$Q(A) = E^P[1_A \cdot \xi(X)_T]\ \forall A \in F_T$$

and define the process

[11]See [23] pp. 190 ff. and [15] p. 229.

$$\tilde{W}_t = W_t - \int_0^t X_s ds$$

Then $\tilde{W}_t$ is a Standard Brownian Motion for $(\Omega,\mathcal{F},F,Q)$, restricted to $[0,T]$.

Corollary 12. Given the notation of Girsanov's Theorem above, set $X_s \equiv \alpha$, a constant. Then $W_t = \alpha t + \tilde{W}_t$ appears as Brownian motion with drift for $(\Omega,\mathcal{F},F,Q)$. Furthermore,

$$\xi(X)_t = \exp\left(\alpha W_t - \frac{1}{2}\alpha^2 t\right)$$

so that

$$Prob^Q(A) = E^P\left[1_A \cdot \exp\left(\alpha W_t - \frac{1}{2}\alpha^2 t\right)\right] \forall A \in F_T$$

Proposition 13 (Useful Identities)

$$e^{-\gamma s} n\left(\frac{\alpha}{\sqrt{s}} + \beta\sqrt{s}\right) = e^{-\alpha\beta + \alpha\sqrt{\beta^2 + 2\gamma}} n\left(\frac{\alpha}{\sqrt{s}} + \sqrt{\beta^2 + 2\gamma}\sqrt{s}\right) \quad (2)$$

$$e^z n\left(\frac{z - \alpha - \mu T}{\sigma\sqrt{T}}\right) = e^{\alpha} e^{(\mu + \sigma^2/2)T} n\left(\frac{z - \alpha - \mu T}{\sigma\sqrt{T}} - \sigma\sqrt{T}\right) \quad (3)$$

$$n\left(\frac{\alpha}{\sqrt{s}} - \beta\sqrt{s}\right) = e^{2\alpha\beta} n\left(\frac{\alpha}{\sqrt{s}} + \beta\sqrt{s}\right) \quad (4)$$

Corollary 14

$$\int_0^t \frac{1}{s^{3/2}} n\left(\frac{\alpha}{\sqrt{s}} + \beta\sqrt{s}\right) ds$$

$$= \frac{1}{|\alpha|}\left\{N\left(\frac{-|\alpha|}{\sqrt{t}} - \text{sgn}(\alpha)\beta\sqrt{t}\right) + e^{-2\alpha\beta} N\left(\frac{-|\alpha|}{\sqrt{t}} + \text{sgn}(\alpha)\beta\sqrt{t}\right)\right\}$$

Corollary 15

$$\int_0^t \frac{1}{\sqrt{s}} n\left(\frac{\alpha}{\sqrt{s}} + \beta\sqrt{s}\right) ds$$

$$= \frac{sgn(\alpha)}{\beta}\{N(\frac{|\alpha|}{\sqrt{t}} + sgn(\alpha)\beta\sqrt{t}) + e^{-2\alpha\beta}N(\frac{-|\alpha|}{\sqrt{t}} + sgn(\alpha)\beta\sqrt{t}) - 1\}$$

Proof of Proposition 2

Let $t = T - t_0$.

The expected present value of the knock-out rebate

$$= \int_0^t Re^{-rs}h(s)ds$$

$$= \int_0^t Re^{-rs}\frac{1}{s^{3/2}}\frac{|b|}{\sigma}n\left(\frac{b - \mu s}{\sigma\sqrt{s}}\right)ds$$

$$= \frac{|b|}{\sigma}R\int_0^t e^{-rs}\frac{1}{s^{3/2}}n(\phi(b/\sigma, -\mu/\sigma, s))ds$$

which by Proposition 13

$$= \frac{|b|}{\sigma}Re^{b\mu/\sigma + (b/\sigma^2)\sqrt{\mu 2 + 2\sigma^2 r}}\int_0^t \frac{1}{s^{3/2}}n(\phi(b/\sigma, \sqrt{\mu^2 + 2\sigma^2 r}/\sigma, s))ds$$

which by Corollary 14 gives the desired expression.

The present value of an up-and-in rebate

$$= \int_{-\infty}^b Re^{-rt}p(z)dz$$

$$= \int_{-\infty}^b Re^{-rt}(f(z) - g(z))dz$$

$$= F(b,t) - G(b,t)$$

which is the desired result. For the down-and-in case ($b < 0$), the rebate is the same as the up-and-in case formula, provided that all occurrences of b are replaced by ηb and all occurrences of μ are replaced by $\eta\mu$. $\triangle$

Proof of Proposition 3

In all the following $t = T - t_0$.

$$\int_\alpha^\beta e^z f(z)dz = \int_\alpha^\beta e^z \frac{1}{\sigma\sqrt{t}} n\left(\frac{z-\mu t}{\sigma\sqrt{t}}\right)dz = e^{(\mu+\sigma^2/2)t} \int_\alpha^\beta \frac{1}{\sigma\sqrt{t}} n\left(\frac{z-(\mu+\sigma^2)t}{\sigma\sqrt{t}}\right)dz$$

$$= e^{(\mu+\sigma^2/2)t} \left[N\left(\frac{\beta-(\mu+\sigma^2)t}{\sigma\sqrt{t}}\right) - N\left(\frac{\alpha-(\mu+\sigma^2)t}{\sigma\sqrt{t}}\right)\right] \equiv J_1$$

$$\int_\alpha^\beta e^z g(z)dz = \int_\alpha^\beta e^z \frac{e^{2\mu b/\sigma^2}}{\sigma\sqrt{t}} n\left(\frac{z-2b-\mu t}{\sigma\sqrt{t}}\right)dz$$

$$= e^{2b} e^{2\mu b/\sigma^2} e^{(\mu+\sigma^2/2)t} \int_\alpha^\beta \frac{1}{\sigma\sqrt{t}} n\left(\frac{z-2b-(\mu+\sigma^2)t}{\sigma\sqrt{t}}\right)dz$$

$$= e^{2b} e^{2\mu b/\sigma^2} e^{(\mu+\sigma^2/2)t} \left[N\left(\frac{\beta-2b-(\mu+\sigma^2)t}{\sigma\sqrt{t}}\right) - N\left(\frac{\alpha-2b-(\mu+\sigma^2)t}{\sigma\sqrt{t}}\right)\right] \equiv J_2$$

$$\int_\alpha^\beta f(z)dz = \int_\alpha^\beta \frac{1}{\sigma\sqrt{t}} n\left(\frac{z-\mu t}{\sigma\sqrt{t}}\right)dz = \left[N\left(\frac{\beta-\mu t}{\sigma\sqrt{t}}\right) - N\left(\frac{\alpha-\mu t}{\sigma\sqrt{t}}\right)\right] \equiv J_3$$

$$\int_\alpha^\beta g(z)dz = \int_\alpha^\beta \frac{e^{2\mu b/\sigma^2}}{\sigma\sqrt{t}} n\left(\frac{z-2b-\mu t}{\sigma\sqrt{t}}\right)dz = e^{2\mu b/\sigma^2} \left[N\left(\frac{\beta-2b-\mu t}{\sigma\sqrt{t}}\right) - N\left(\frac{\alpha-2b-\mu t}{\sigma\sqrt{t}}\right)\right] \equiv J_4$$

$\triangle$

Proof of Proposition 6

In all the following $t = T - t_0$. The formula for $\xi(z)$ can be distilled from [25]. The formula for $\Xi(z,t)$ follows by definition of the cumulative distribution of a pdf and integration. We now outline the derivation of $h^+(t)$. From results in [1] it follows that

$$\text{Prob}(\tau^+ < \tau \text{ and } \tau^+ < \tau^-)$$
$$= N\left(\frac{d_0}{\sqrt{t}} + e_0\sqrt{t}\right)$$
$$+ \sum_{j=1}^{\infty} \sum_{i=1}^{4} c_{i,j} N\left(\frac{d_{i,j}}{\sqrt{t}} + e_i\sqrt{t}\right)$$

The rest follows from differentiation. $\triangle$

REFERENCES

[1] T. W. Anderson. "A Modification of the Sequential Probability Ratio Test to Reduce the Sample Size." *Ann. Math. Statist.*, 31:165–197, 1960.

[2] Robert Benson and Nicholas Daniel. *Up, Over and Out,* chapter 26 in [33], 1992. First published in *Risk,* June 1991.

[3] Eric Berger. "A Review of Capped S&P Index Options." *Bloomberg Magazine,* 1, September 1992.

[4] Fischer Black. *The Holes in Black-Scholes,* chapter 5 in [33], 1992. First published in *Risk,* March 1988.

[5] Jonathan Bowie and Peter Carr. "Static Simplicity." *Risk* Magazine, 7, August 1994.

[6] Phelim P. Boyle and Sok Hoon Lau. "Bumping Up Against the Barrier with the Binomial Method." *Journal of Derivatives,* 1(4):6–14, 1994.

[7] Phelim P. Boyle and Stuart M. Turnbull. "Pricing and Hedging of Capped Options." *Journal of Futures Markets,* 9(1):41–54, 1989.

[8] Mark Broadie and Jerome Detemple. "American Capped Call Options on Dividend-Paying Assets." *Review of Financial Studies,* 8(1):161–191, 1995.

[9] Marc Chesney and Rajna Gibson-Asner. "The Investment Policy and the Pricing of Equity in a Levered Firm: A Reexamination of the Contingent Claims Valuation Approach." November 1994. Working Paper.

[10] Neil Chriss and Michael Ong. "Managing the Risk in Digital Options." Working Paper, 1995.

[11] D. R. Cox and H. Miller. *The Theory of Stochastic Processes* (New York: John Wiley, 1965), cf. Chapter 5: "Markov Processes in Continuous Time with Continuous State Space."

[12] J. C. Cox and Mark Rubinstein. *Options Markets* (Englewood Cliffs, NJ: Prentice-Hall, 1985), cf. 408–412.

[13] R. Dattatreya and K. Hotta, eds. *Advanced Interest Rate and Currency Swaps* (Chicago: Probus Publishing, 1994).

[14] Emmanuel Derman, Deniz Ergener, and Iraj Kani. "Forever Hedged." *Risk* Magazine, 7:139–145, September 1994.

[15] Darrell Duffie. *Security Markets: Stochastic Models* (New York: Academic Press, Inc. [Harcourt Brace Jovanovich], 1988).

[16] M. Goldman, Howard Sosin, and M. Gatto. "Path Dependent Options: Buy at the Low, Sell at the High." *Journal of Finance,* 34, December 1979.

[17] Ian Hart and Michael Ross. "Striking Continuity." *Risk* Magazine, 7, June 1994.

[18] R. Heynen and Harry Kat. "Crossing Barriers." *Risk* Magazine, 7, June 1994.

[19] R. Heynen and Harry Kat. "Partial Barrier Options." *Journal of Financial Engineering,* 3(3), 1994.

[20] Mike Hudson. *The Value in Going Out,* chapter 27. First published in *Risk,* March 1991.

[21] John Hull. *Options, Futures, and Other Derivative Securities.* 2d ed. (Englewood Cliffs, NJ: Prentice-Hall, 1993).

[22] "Do Knock-Out Options Need to be Knocked Out?" *The Wall Street Journal*, May 1995.

[23] Ioannis Karatzas and Steven E. Shreve. *Brownian Motion and Stochastic Calculus* (New York: Springer-Verlag, 1991).

[24] Harry Kat and Leen Verdonk. "Tree Surgery." *Risk* Magazine, 8, February 1995.

[25] Naoto Kunitomo and Masayuki Ikeda. "Pricing Options with Curved Boundaries." *Mathematical Finance,* 2(4):272–298, 1992.

[26] J. McConnell and Eduardo Schwartz. "Lyon Taming." *Journal of Finance,* 41:561–577, 1986.

[27] Robert C. Merton. "Theory of Rational Option Pricing." *Bell Journal of Economics and Management,* pp. 141–183, 1973.

[28] J.P. Morgan. *Barrier Options,* 1994. Martin Watts and Hans Tischhauser.

[29] Bloomberg Business Radio, May 1995. Financier George Soros Speaks on Currency and Derivatives.

[30] K. Ravindran. *Exotic Options,* chapter 5. In Dattatreya and Hotta [13], 1994.

[31] Matthias Reimer and Klaus Sandmann. "A Discrete Time Approach for European and American Barrier Options." Working Paper, March 1995.

[32] Don R. Rich. "The Mathematical Foundations of Barrier Option-Pricing Theory." *Advances in Futures and Options Research,* 7:267–311, 1994.

[33] Risk/Finex. *From Black-Scholes to Black Holes*. Risk/Finex, 1992. A collection of articles reprinted from *Risk* Magazine.

[34] Mark Rubinstein. "Pay Now, Choose Later." *Risk* Magazine, 4, February 1991.

[35] Mark Rubinstein and Eric Reiner. "Breaking Down the Barriers." *Risk* Magazine, 4:28–35, September 1991.

[36] Mark Rubinstein and Eric Reiner. "Unscrambling the Binary Code." *Risk* Magazine, 4:75–83, October 1991.

[37] Robert R. Trippi and Don M. Chance. "Quick Valuation of the 'Bermuda' Capped Option." *Journal of Portfolio Management,* 20(1):93–99, 1993.

[38] Paul Wilmott, J. Dewynne, and S. Howison. *Option Pricing: Mathematical Models and Computation*. (Oxford, England: Oxford Financial Press, 1993), cf. Chapter 9: Exotic Options and Chapter 10: Barrier Options.

Chapter Nine

Outperformance Options*

Emanuel Derman
Goldman Sachs & Co.

INTRODUCTION

Outperformance options[1] are especially interesting because of the alternating layers of complexity and simplicity you discover as you probe more deeply into their valuation. This chapter describes a journey through these layers. First we describe the outperformance option's payoff, a simple function of two underlyers. But valuing two-underlyer options seems complicated; each underlyer has to be hedged. It turns out that, if you think about it the right way, a general principle lets you find the correct and simple formula for its value. Even an options novice, who understands only single-underlyer options and the Black-Scholes formula, already knows everything necessary to value it, European- or American-style. We then examine the simple formula for the outperformance option value, and notice a surprising, elegant, and at first puzzling relation among its two hedge ratios. Finally, we explain the origin of this result.

THE PAYOFF

Suppose you are a dollar-based investor with a choice between two stocks, *A* and *B*, with an investment horizon from today out to time *T* from today. Call *A(t)* and *B(t)* the unknown future dollar values at some

*Acknowledgements: I am grateful to Alex Bergier and Barbara Dunn for helpful comments.

[1]William Margrabe, "The Value of an Option to Exchange One Asset for Another," *Journal of Finance* Vol. XXXIII, No. 1 (March 1978), pp. 177–186.

future time t of a one-dollar investment today in stock A and stock B, respectively, so that $A(0) = B(0) = \$1$. A European-style outperformance option on A *vs.* B with time T to expiration and face value of \$1 is a contract whose payoff in dollars at time T is equal to

$$max\,[A(T) - B(T), 0] \qquad (1)$$

If you own just one of these options, you will obtain any positive excess return of A over B at time T. Owning 100 of them is equivalent to owning an outperformance option with a face value of \$100.

An American-style outperformance option allows the holder of the contract to exercise early and receive the payoff shown in Equation (1) at any time t prior to expiration.

Most of this chapter will focus on European-style outperformance options, and we will spell out the simple extension to American-style outperformance options at the end.

THE FINANCIAL PRINCIPLE OF RELATIVITY OF CURRENCY

The outperformance option in Equation (1) is the right to exchange one share of stock B for one share of stock A. The option seems complicated to value because it has exposure to *two underlyers*, and no-arbitrage pricing dictates that you will need to hedge it with two securities.

However, notice that an ordinary call option on stock A with a strike of \$1 has payoff $max\,[A(T) - \$1, 0]$. It is the right to exchange one dollar for one share of stock A. If you can think of one share of stock B in Equation (1) as a sort of monetary unit, such as one dollar, then the outperformance option resembles an ordinary call.

We will show that you can clearly understand outperformance options by thinking of them as call options issued in an imaginary foreign country *(B-Land)* whose currency unit is one share of stock B. In *B-Land*, where all monetary values are denominated in shares of B, the outperformance option is simply a call option on a single stock A with a strike of one *B-share*. The value of the outperformance call in dollars is the value of this call (in *B-shares*), converted to dollars at the current *B-share*/dollar exchange rate. The relevant volatility of the call is the volatility of A in *B-shares*. To hedge the dollar value of the outperformance call, first you must hedge it against changes in the value of A in *B-Land*, and second, against changes in the *B-share*/dollar exchange rate. The procedure is similar to the one that you would follow as a dollar-based investor in a yen-denominated call on the Nikkei index, assuming you wanted to hedge against both changes in the index level and changes in the yen/dollar exchange rate.

This method is sometimes called *the method of change of numeraire.* It's a kind of financial principle of currency relativity, which demands that the relative values of two securities should be independent of the currencies you use to express their value. It has many applications, and using it can remove the apparent complexity of many valuation problems.

NOTATION

We will need a notation that makes explicit the currency in which a security value is being quoted.

T	expiration time
t	any intermediate time between 0 and T
$S_i(t)$	value in currency i at time t of stock S that was worth \$1 at time $t = 0$.
$\sigma(S_i)$	volatility of stock S in currency i
d_s	continuous dividend rate for stock S
$C_i^{AB}(t)$	value in currency i at time t of outperformance option with payoff of Equation (1)
$BS(S, K, r, \sigma, T - t)$	Black-Scholes formula for a stock with price S, strike K, continuous riskless rate r, return volatility σ, time to expiration $T - t$
Δ	the Black-Scholes hedge ratio $\frac{\partial}{\partial S}BS(\ )$

In this notation, Equation (1) says that an outperformance option has the dollar payoff at maturity

$$C_\$^{AB}(T) = max\,[A_\$(T) - B_\$(T), 0] \tag{2}$$

THE OUTPERFORMANCE OPTION'S VALUE IN B-SHARES

Suppose you live in *B-Land*, where the currency is the *B-share*. In this country, the value of one share of stock A in *B-shares* is $A_B(t) \equiv A_\$(t) / B_\$(t)$. The value of one *B-share* in dollars at t = 0 was \$1. The value of one *B-share* in *B-Land* is $B_B(t)$ and is always equal to 1. The riskless interest rate at which you can earn interest on your *B-shares* is B's dividend rate d_B. The outperformance call in Equation (2) has a terminal payoff in *B-shares* given by dividing Equation (2) by $B_\$(T)$:

$$C_B^{AB}(T) = max\,[A_B(T) - 1, 0] \tag{3}$$

This is simply the payoff at time T of an ordinary Black-Scholes European-style option on $A_B(t)$ with strike equal to 1 and volatility $\sigma(A_B)$ equal to the volatility of $A_\$(t)$ measured in *B-shares*. It is well known that

$$\sigma(A_B) = \sqrt{\sigma^2(A_\$) + \sigma^2(B_\$) - 2\rho_{AB}\sigma(A_\$)\sigma(B_\$)} \tag{4}$$

where ρ_{AB} is the correlation between the returns of $A_\$(t)$ and $B_\$(t)$. The value at time t of this European-style call with payoff described by Equation (3) is therefore given by the familiar Black-Scholes formula

$$C_B^{AB}(t) = BS(A_B, 1, d_B, \sigma(A_B), T - t) \tag{5}$$

THE OUTPERFORMANCE OPTION'S VALUE IN DOLLARS

You now know the outperformance option's value in *B-shares*. You can get the value of the outperformance option in dollars at time t by taking its value in *B-shares* at time t, and converting it to dollars by multiplying by the exchange rate $B_\$(t)$, the value of a *B-share* in dollars at time t:

$$C_\$^{AB}(t) = B_\$(t)C_B^{AB}(t) = B_\$(t)BS(A_B, 1, d_B, \sigma(A_B), T - t) \tag{6}$$

HEDGING OUTPERFORMANCE OPTIONS

A long position in the outperformance option $C_B^{AB}(t)$ has exposure to the value of both A- and *B-shares*. The form of Equation (6)—$BS(\ )$ depends only on the value A_B but not on $A_\$$ or $B_\$$ separately—suggests that the natural way to think about hedging is in two steps. First hedge $BS(\ )$, the value of the call in *B-Land*, against changes in the value of A_B. Then hedge this partially hedged position against changes in the dollar value of a *B-share* to achieve a totally hedged position. You can hedge the exposure to changes in $A_B(t)$ by going short Δ shares of A against the call. Delta is the usual Black-Scholes hedge ratio corresponding to Equation (5). It tells you how to hedge the call in *B-Land*. The value of this partially delta-hedged portfolio in *B-shares* is

$$P_B(t) = C_B^{AB}(t) - \Delta A_B(t) \tag{7}$$

The Black-Scholes formula will guarantee that $P_B(t)$ is negative, so if you own the delta-hedged portfolio, you are instantaneously short $(\Delta A_B(t) - C_B^{AB}(t))$ *B-shares*.

Your partially hedged portfolio P_B is long one *B-share*-denominated call on A and short Δ shares of A. Its value in dollars is $P_B(t)B_\$(t)$. You have no exposure to the value of A denominated in *B-shares*. As a dollar investor, though, you are exposed to $B_\$(t)$, the *B-share*/dollar exchange rate. You can eliminate this residual exposure to *B-shares* by buying the *B-shares* you need to cancel the *B-share* exposure of the delta-hedged portfolio in Equation (7)—that is, by buying $(\Delta A_B(t) - C_B^{AB}(t))$ units of *B-shares*, each worth $B_\$(t)$. *You have to hedge the premium against change in the B-share currency as well as the hedge.* Adding these to your portfolio hedges it against the instantaneous changes in value of either underlyer.

The final hedged portfolio, hedged against small moves in both $A_\$$ and $B_\$$, is shown in Table 9–1.

HEDGING AND SCALING

Table 9–1 displays the *A-hedge* plus the *B-hedge* that together remove all exposure of the outperformance option to movements in A and B. Notice that the net position value of the totally hedged portfolio is zero.

There are two ways to interpret this. The first is to conclude that if you want a portfolio to be hedged against changes in all security values, the portfolio must be worth zero.

The second is to notice that the formula for the value of the outperformance option is homogeneous in the value of its underlying securities. You can write its value C in Equation (6) at time t as

$$C(A, B, \ldots, t) = Bf(A/B, \ldots, \mathrm{t}) \tag{8}$$

TABLE 9–1
The Constituents of the Totally Hedged Portfolio

Security	*Hedge Quantity*	*Position Value (dollars)*
Outperformance option	1	$C_B^{AB}(t)B_\$(t)$
A	$\Delta_A = -\Delta$	$-\Delta A_B(t)B_\$(t)$
B	$\Delta_B = \Delta A_B(t) - C_B^{AB}(t)$	$(\Delta A_B(t) - C_B^{AB}(t))B_\$(t)$
	Net position value:	0

or

$$\frac{C(A, B, \ldots, t)}{B} = f(A/B, \ldots, \mathrm{t}) \tag{9}$$

where $f(\ )$ is a dimensionless function, and the . . . denotes other variables—such as volatility, dividend yield, and so on—that are assumed to be independent of the values of *A* and *B*. This scaling or homogeneity means that *B* plays the role of a currency. As a consequence of the functional form of Equation (8), Euler's theorem holds:

$$A\frac{\partial C}{\partial A} + B\frac{\partial C}{\partial B} = C \tag{10}$$

or

$$C + A\Delta_A + B\Delta_B = 0 \tag{11}$$

where $\Delta_A = \dfrac{-\partial}{\partial A} \cdot C$ and $\Delta_B = \dfrac{-\partial}{\partial B} \cdot C$ are the number of shares of *A* and *B* respectively needed to hedge a long position in the outperformance option. In words, Equation (8) implies that the value of the outperformance option, the value of the *A-hedge*, and the value of the *B-hedge* add to zero. This result is true even if the Black-Scholes model is invalid—for example, if stock evolution is non-lognormal. The main prerequisite is that Equation (8) be valid: the outperformance call value must scale, so that its value in units of *B* is a function of *A*/*B* alone. If $f(\ )$ contains other terms that depend on *A* or *B* alone, and not simply on their ratio, Equation (11) will no longer hold.

AMERICAN-STYLE OPTIONS VALUATION

For European-style options, Equation (6) above showed that

$$C_{\$}^{AB}(t) = C_{B}^{AB}(t)B_{\$}(t) = B_{\$}(t)BS(A_B, 1, d_B, \sigma(A_B), T - t)$$

As long as the scaling property of the previous section holds, this general decomposition is still valid, except that the *BS*( ) function must be replaced by the American option value *AM*( ):

$$C_{\$}^{AB}(t) = C_{B}^{AB}(t)B_{\$}(t) = B_{\$}(t)AM(A_B, 1, d_B, \sigma(A_B), T - t) \qquad (12)$$

You can use your favorite American-style valuation model (the binomial method, for example), to determine the value of *AM*( ).

THE REAL WORLD

Despite their elegance, outperformance options are relatively rare instruments. One reason is that the pricing volatility is determined by the correlation ρ_{AB} in Equation (4). Correlations are considered to be less stable than volatilities and are consequently harder to forecast. Market makers often take this into account by adding a larger risk premium to their theoretical prices for outperformance options than they do for standard options, which usually has the effect of making these instruments less attractive in practice than in theory.

Chapter Ten

Volatility-Insensitive Option Structures

Eran Yehudai
Head of Risk Management, Global Derivatives Group

Richard Kleinberg
Director of Global Derivatives
D. E. Shaw & Co.

INTRODUCTION

This chapter does not discuss the theoretical pricing of a specific type of exotic option. Instead, we try to discuss in some detail the use of a class of derivative structures, both ordinary and exotic. The common element to these structures is that, relative to plain calls and puts, they are insensitive to (although not completely independent of) underlying volatility.

We start with a discussion of possible motivations for looking at volatility-insensitive structures, both from the dealer's and from the investor's viewpoint. We then proceed to outline several types of derivative instruments, both plain and exotic.

Before discussing the motivation and structuring of volatility-insensitive derivatives, we should make a few introductory remarks defining and discussing what we mean by "volatility insensitivity." The local measure for volatility sensitivity is vega, defined as the derivative of option price with respect to volatility. Rather than look at vega for a specific volatility level, we use the price variation over a wide volatility range (15 to 60 percent) to quantify volatility sensitivity.

Vega is often correlated with gamma. Each in its own way measures the nonlinear nature of the derivative instrument. The difference between them is that gamma is local in time. It measures the nonlinearity at the current time and price. Vega captures the expected aggregate nonlinearity over the remaining lifetime of the option. The volatility-insensitive structures discussed below tend to have low gamma, and consequently they are easily delta hedgeable. Volatility insensitivity and low gamma only hold initially; both attributes are typically lost as time goes by and the underlying price changes.

MOTIVATION

Why would anybody care to design a derivative structure with the express purpose of making it insensitive to underlying volatility?

Unknown Volatility

Thousands of different stocks trade in the United States alone. Their volatilities range from the low teens to over 100 percent. Figure 10–1 shows the distribution of historic volatilities versus market capitalization of U.S. stocks. Regardless of industry, high-capitalization stocks tend to be less volatile due to both fundamental (diversified sources of income) and technical (more liquid secondary market) reasons. Typically, relatively liquid listed options allow volatility discovery of the most liquid equities. Still, there are many circumstances in which there remain great uncertainty regarding the appropriate volatility.

The most obvious example is a recent IPO. Historic price data simply do not exist. Investors who would like to gain exposure to a recent IPO while enjoying either the leverage or the downside protection that options provide would look for options written on the new stock. A prudent dealer would either decline to price, or would build in to the price a wide margin to allow for the great uncertainty associated with the actual future volatility of the new stock.

Companies emerging from bankruptcies, mergers, or other significant restructurings are in many ways "new" companies. Their price history, while technically available, is of little relevance to their future volatility.

Uncertain Volatility

When relevant price history and listed options are available, volatility can be estimated. Still, significant uncertainty with respect to future volatility persists. Figure 10–2 shows past values of historic three months,

FIGURE 10–1
Distribution of Six-Month Historic Volatility versus Market Capitalization of Listed U.S. Corporations

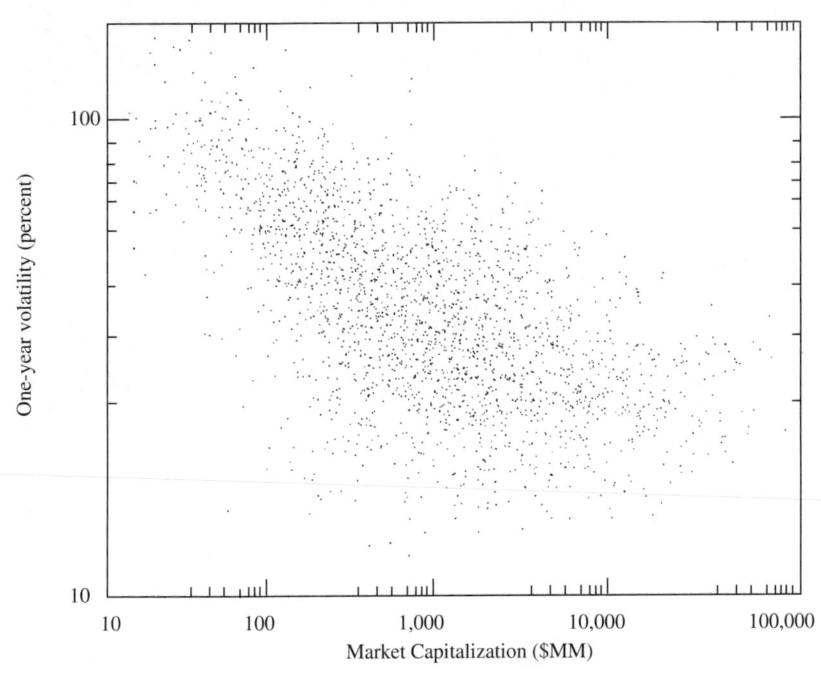

historic one year, and implied volatility of one U.S. stock. A spread on the order of 5 to 10 percent between the various volatility measures makes pinpointing future volatility with high accuracy difficult.

Another example where volatility uncertainty is likely to occur is in pricing derivatives on baskets with a priori unknown composition. When precise pricing is important, even a 5 to 10 percent uncertainty in volatility may be unacceptable.

Affordable Options in High-Volatility Situations

Ordinary options, by virtue of being sensitive to volatility, tend to be very expensive when applied to high-volatility situations. The premium on a one-year option can approach and exceed 50 percent of the

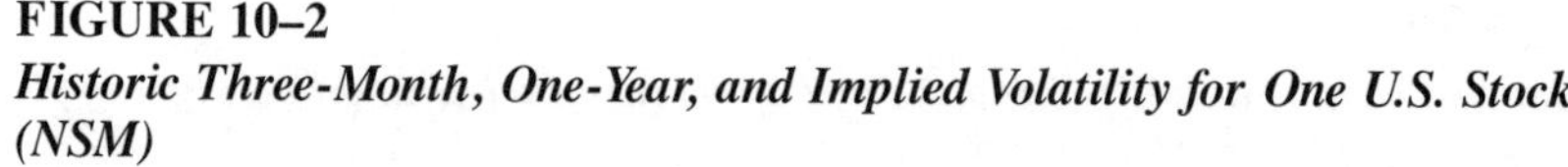

FIGURE 10–2
Historic Three-Month, One-Year, and Implied Volatility for One U.S. Stock (NSM)

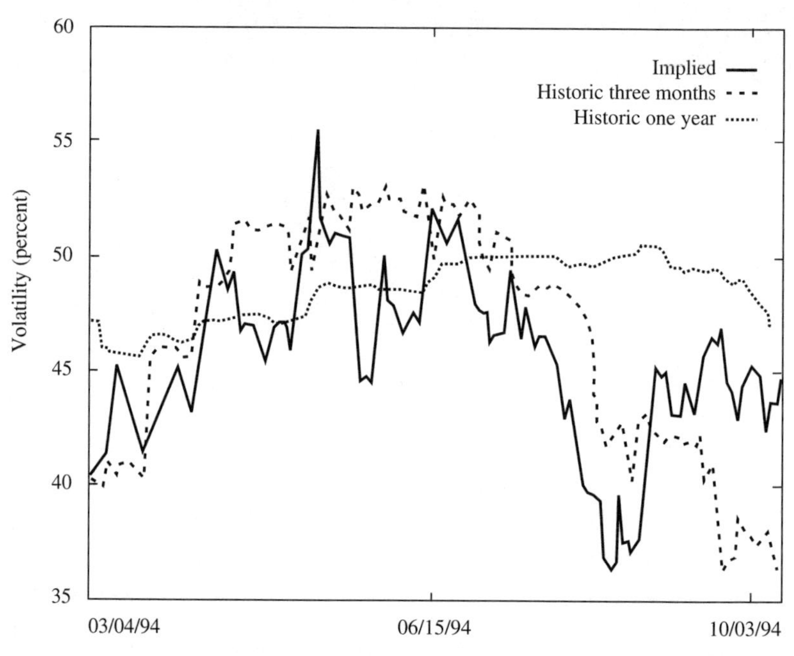

underlying price when volatility exceeds 100 percent. As Figures 10–1 and 10–2 demonstrate, such volatilities are not uncommon. A volatility-insensitive structure is much more likely to be affordable, and offers the kind of leverage that option buyers often desire.

Generic Pricing

Stock prices are easily available to investors, as are the prices of listed options. Over-the-counter options, especially those with single-stock underlying, have to be priced on a case-by-case basis. An investor has to call a dealer to inquire about the price before making a trading decision. Volatility-insensitive structures allow an unusual situation in which the price of the product does not depend on the identity of the underlying.

With such a product, a salesperson can quote a uniform price to a customer, who can then choose the underlying stock without the need to verify the price.

Duration Insensitivity

Volatility-insensitive structures are, by the nature of the process underlying stock price moves, also duration insensitive. The Ito process, and by consequence the value of any derivative product, is almost invariant to a transformation of the form

$$\sigma \rightarrow \alpha \cdot \sigma, \qquad T \rightarrow T/\sqrt{\alpha}$$

where σ is the volatility and T is time to expiration. The symmetry is precise if interest rate (r) and dividend yield (d) are zero. It is still a good approximation for $r \cdot T,\ d \cdot T \ll 1$. It is also possible to correct for interest-rate and dividend yield drifts by striking options relative to the expected future value of the underlying. That practice, common in fixed-income derivatives, can be used as easily for equity derivatives.

Time to expiration, unlike volatility, is rarely uncertain. Structures insensitive to time to expiration are useful because they may apply with little modification to both short- and long- term options. On the short-term end, such a structure is still valuable, while on the long end it remains affordable.

STRUCTURES

Plain Options

Before embarking on a discussion of volatility-insensitive structures, we will briefly examine the volatility sensitivity of plain puts and calls. Figure 10–3 shows the relation between underlying volatility and theoretical option premium for a one-year ATM call. In this and other examples, unless we indicate otherwise, we assume a risk-free interest rate of 6 percent and dividend yield of 3 percent (both continuously compounded). Over a benchmark range of 15 to 60 percent volatility, the option premium changes by a factor of 183 percent.

FIGURE 10–3

Theoretical (Black-Scholes) Option Price versus Volatility for an at-the-Money European Call Option

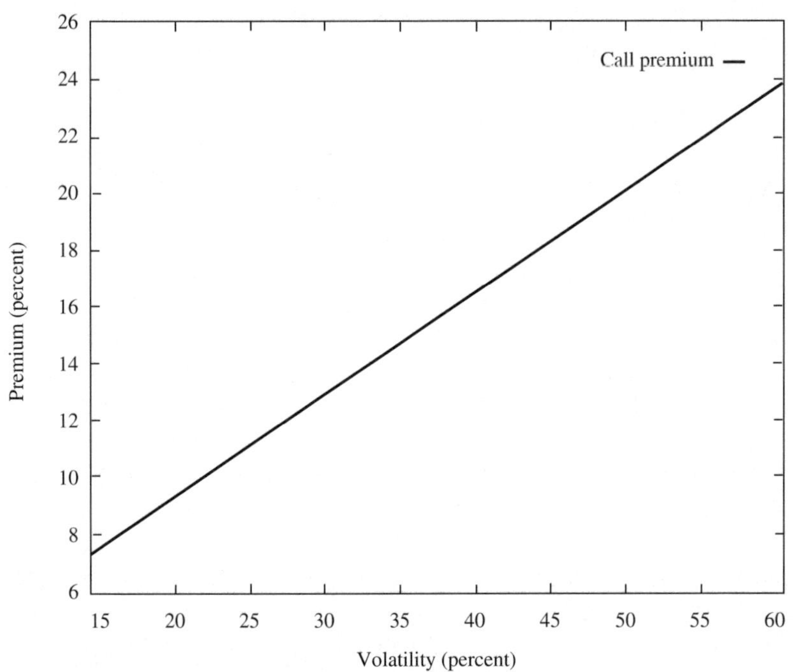

Here and hence we use time to expiration of one year, interest rate of 6 percent, and dividend yield of 3 percent, unless otherwise noted.

Synthetics

Trivial examples of complete volatility-insensitive structures have long been known to options traders. These are synthetic long and short positions. A synthetic long position can be created by buying a call and selling a put, both with the same strike and expiration dates (Figure 10–4). The value of a synthetic long, much like a futures contract, depends on interest rates, time to expiration, and dividend yield, but not on the volatility of the underlying stock.

In practice, one important reason that people buy synthetic shorts is to gain short exposure to unborrowable stocks. Under such circum-

FIGURE 10–4
A Synthetic Long Position Created by Combining a Long Call with a Short Put

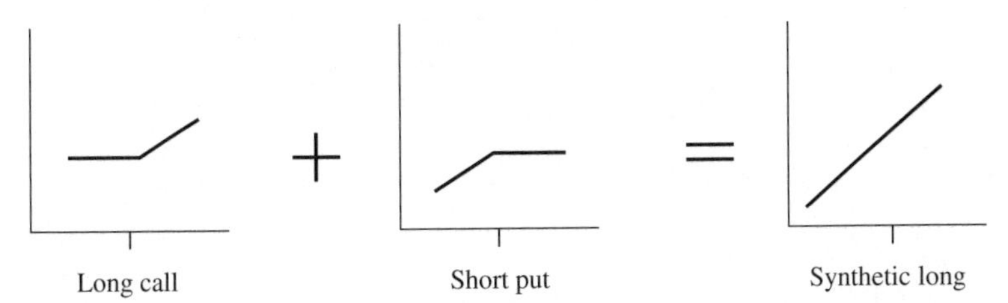

The call and the put have the same strike price. Here and in Figures 10–5 and 10–6, the horizontal axis represents underlying price, while the vertical axis represents the value of the structure at expiry.

stances, one should expect to pay an additional premium for the privilege of gaining such short exposure. In the listed option markets, puts would then trade at higher implied volatility than calls, violating the put-call parity.

Note that synthetics remain completely insensitive to volatility over time. They also remain insensitive to volatility regardless of any moves in the underlying price. One way of explaining the total volatility independence is by noting that the structure involves both buying and selling volatility. The volatility exposure from the purchase and the sale always cancel each other exactly.

Collars and Spreads

By relaxing the requirement that both put and call have the same strike price, a synthetic long or short position becomes a collar (Figure 10–5). Collars are often used in conjunction with a long position in the underlying stock. When one combines a long-stock with a short-collar position (Figure 10–6), one is left with a spread—long exposure to the underlying over a limited price range, and full protection beyond that range. The investor is buying a put to protect his or her downside, and finances the put by writing a covered call. Such collars are particularly popular because strike prices can be chosen such that the entire structure

FIGURE 10–5
A Collar Position Created by Combining a Long Call with a Short Put

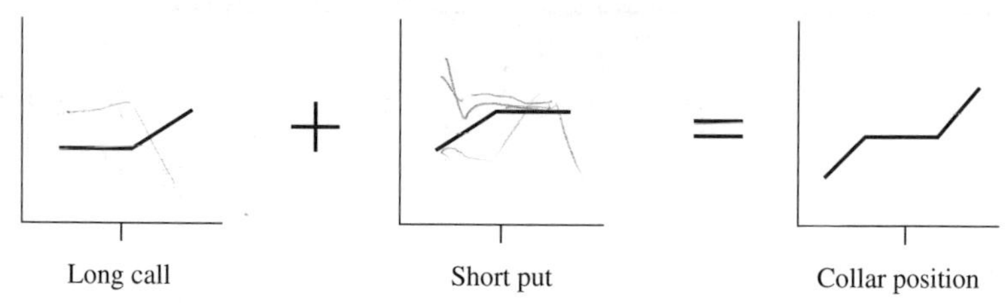

The call and the put have different strike prices.

FIGURE 10–6
A Spread Position Created by Combining a Long-Stock with a Short-Collar Position

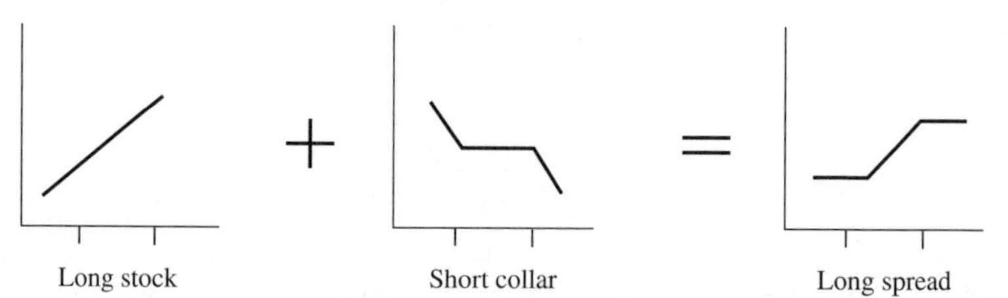

The same spread position can be created by combining a long call with a short call of a higher strike price.

is "costless" in the sense that no premium changes hands initially. The combination of a long stock position with a short collar is identical to a bullish spread, which can be obtained by buying one call and selling another call at a higher strike.

Because a collar (or spread) involves both the buying and selling of volatility, it is much less sensitive to it than an ordinary option. Figure 10–7 shows the dependence on volatility of a one-year 100- to 110-percent call spread. Over the 15 to 60 percent volatility range, the premium on such a spread changes by less than 13 percent.

FIGURE 10–7
Theoretical Price versus Volatility of a 100- to 110-Percent Call Spread

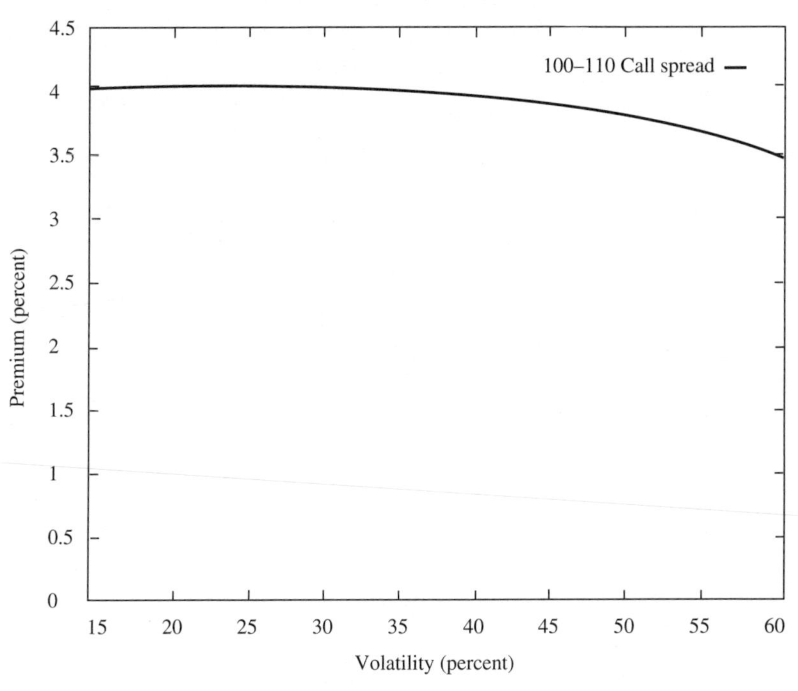

Barrier Options

Barrier options are discussed elsewhere in this book (see Chapter 8). In this section we only discuss the barrier options that pay no rebate. A special class of rebate-paying barrier options is discussed in the next section.

Barrier (knock-in and knock-out) options can be divided into two general categories. The two categories are very different in terms of both their risk-management properties and their volatility sensitivity. It should be noted that knock-in and knock-out options are related, much like puts and calls. The combination of a knock-in and a knock-out with the same parameters is just an ordinary option. Being long a knock-in option is the same as being long an ordinary option and short a knock-out option.

FIGURE 10–8
Theoretical Delta versus Stock Price at Various Times to Expiration

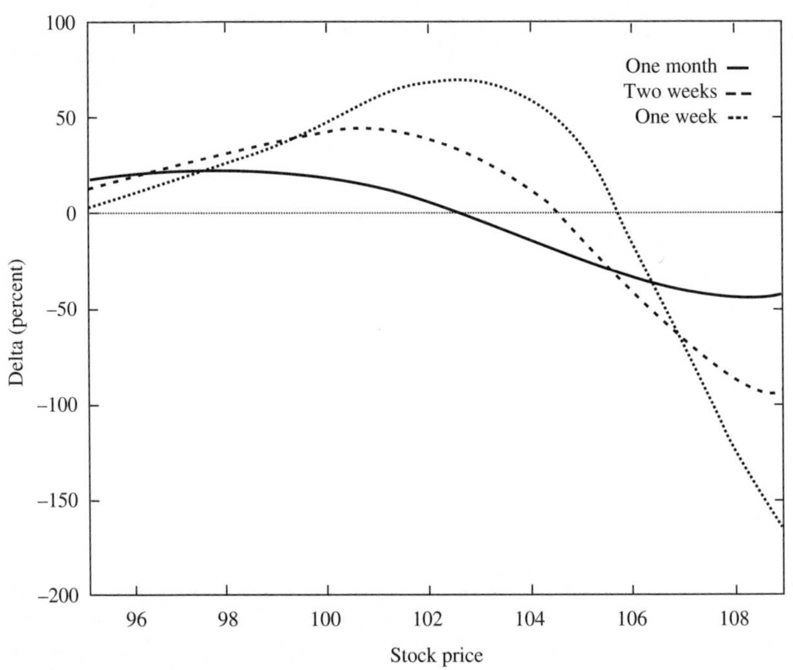

The option is a knock-out call struck at 100 percent with a barrier at 110 percent. We assume stock volatility of 20 percent and continuous sampling.

If the barrier is in-the-money (above the strike price for calls, below it for puts), the option value can be arbitrarily sensitive to underlying price. Delta for such an option could become arbitrarily large (Figure 10–8). Hedging (not just rehedging) would become impossible. In practice, such a scenario creates great temptation for market manipulation, as a small move in underlying price could have great financial consequence. Such options are typically quite sensitive to volatility, although options that knock out in-the-money could be volatility insensitive over a narrow volatility range (Figure 10–9).

When the barrier is out-of-the-money, delta never goes much above 100 percent, although it could change discontinuously when the price

FIGURE 10–9
Theoretical Price versus Volatility for an at-the-Money Knock-Out Call with a Barrier at 150 Percent

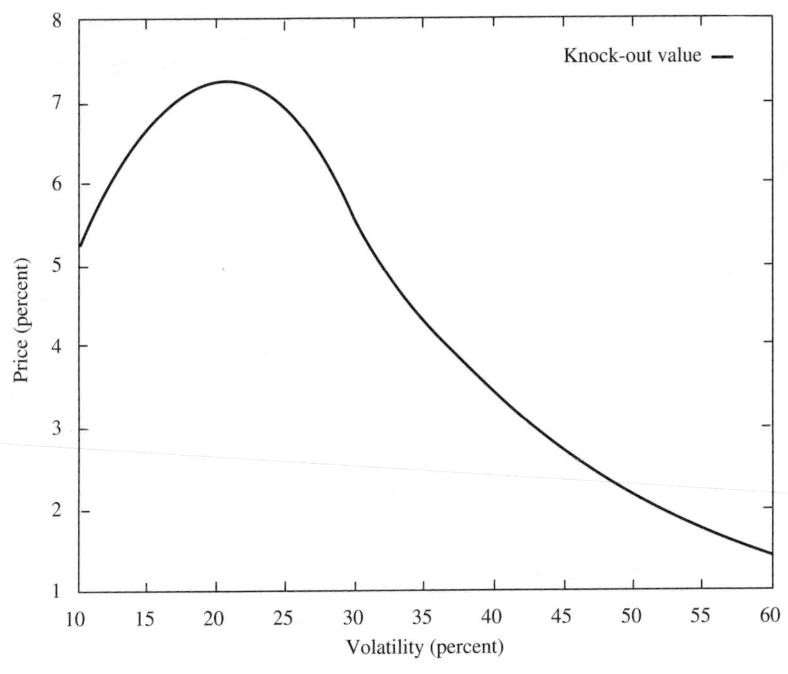

crosses the barrier. Options that knock in far out-of-the-money tend to be particularly sensitive to volatility. The underlying has to make two (rather than one) large moves: first for the option to knock in, and then for it to end up in-the-money (Figure 10–10).

By contrast, options that knock out when out-of-the-money are quite volatility insensitive. The large value of the ordinary option when the underlying has high volatility is offset by the relatively high probability of the option's knocking out. The optimal choice of barrier level depends on the type (put or call) of the option, time to expiration, interest rates, dividend yield, and the volatility region over which minimal sensitivity is desired. Figure 10–11 shows the dependence of the optimal barrier level on interest rates. Figure 10–12 shows the dependence on volatility

FIGURE 10–10

Theoretical Price versus Volatility for an at-the-Money Knock-In Call with a Barrier at 80 Percent

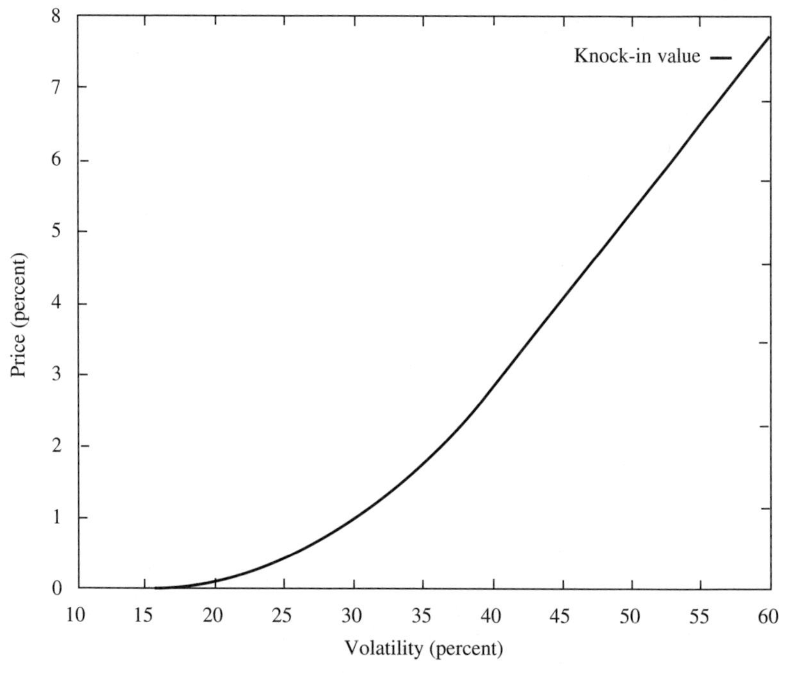

of the value of a knock-out option with an optimally chosen knock-out level. The maximal variation over the 15- to 60-percent volatility range is less than 4 basis points.

One important point to consider is that the theoretical values calculated above assume continuous sampling of underlying price. Some knock-out contracts are defined so that a knock-out event only takes place when the closing price for the day passes the barrier. While no analytic formula exists for calculating the value of such an option, it can be approximated using a simulation.

Even when the contract is defined to include continuous sampling, one has to take into account that in practice, some of the volatility of financial instruments takes place either at off-hours or at such times when, due to

FIGURE 10–11
Optimal Barrier Level versus Interest Rates for an at-the-Money Knock-Out Call

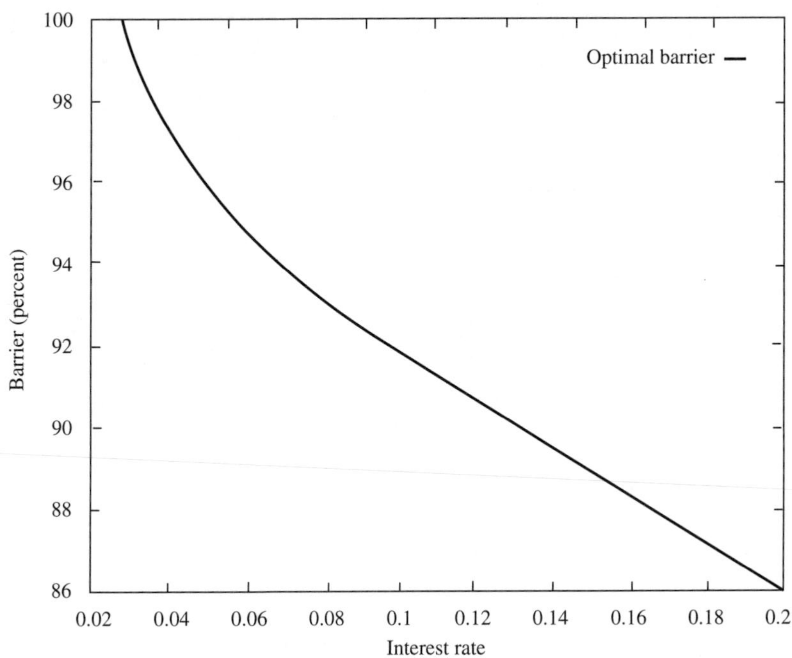

Optimal level is defined as the barrier level at which the spread between maximum and minimum option values over the 15- to 60-percent volatility range is minimized.

suspension of trading, hedging is not possible. The extreme case where virtually all price-moves occur when no trading is possible (e.g., between close of one day and open of the following day) is indistinguishable from daily (rather than continuous) sampling. In practice, of course, only a fraction of the stock's volatility takes place at such times.

Exploding Options

Exploding, or automatic-exercise, options are spread options with the additional feature that as soon as the underlying price reaches the cap

FIGURE 10–12
Option Value versus Volatility for a Knock-Out at-the-Money Call Option with an Optimal Barrier at 95.7 Percent

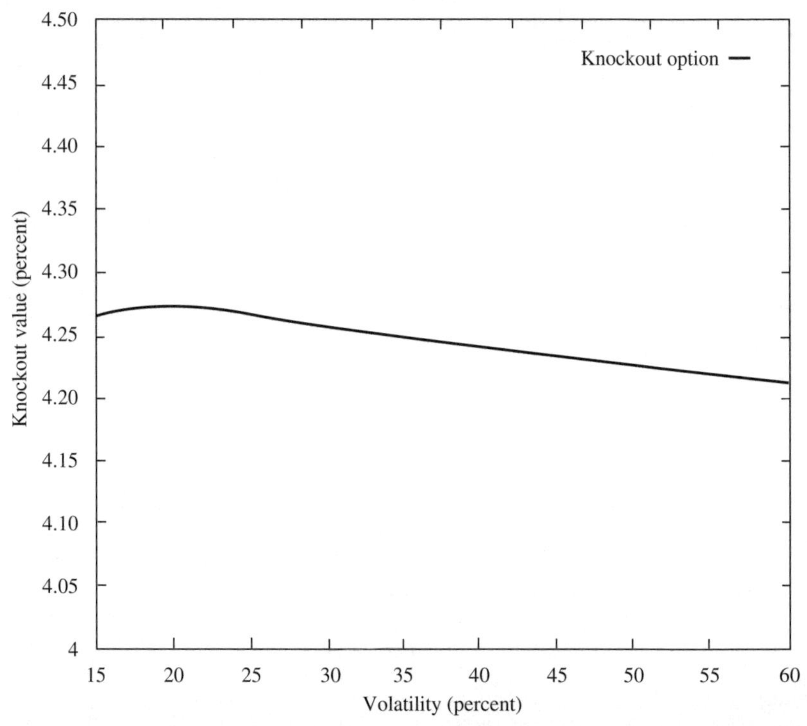

(floor for puts), the option is automatically exercised. Such an option may be evaluated by observing that it is effectively the sum of a knock-out option with a barrier at the cap, and a binary knock-in option, which pays the maximum in-the-money amount as soon as the barrier is crossed (Figure 10–13).

The nature of an exploding option depends on the interplay between the barrier level X, volatility, and time to expiration. In region (A), $X \gg \sigma \cdot \sqrt{t}$, the price is unlikely to reach the cap, and the structure is effectively a plain option, and accordingly is quite sensitive to volatility.

FIGURE 10–13

Value of an Exploding Option, and Its Knock-Out and Binary Knock-In Components, as a Function of Stock Price

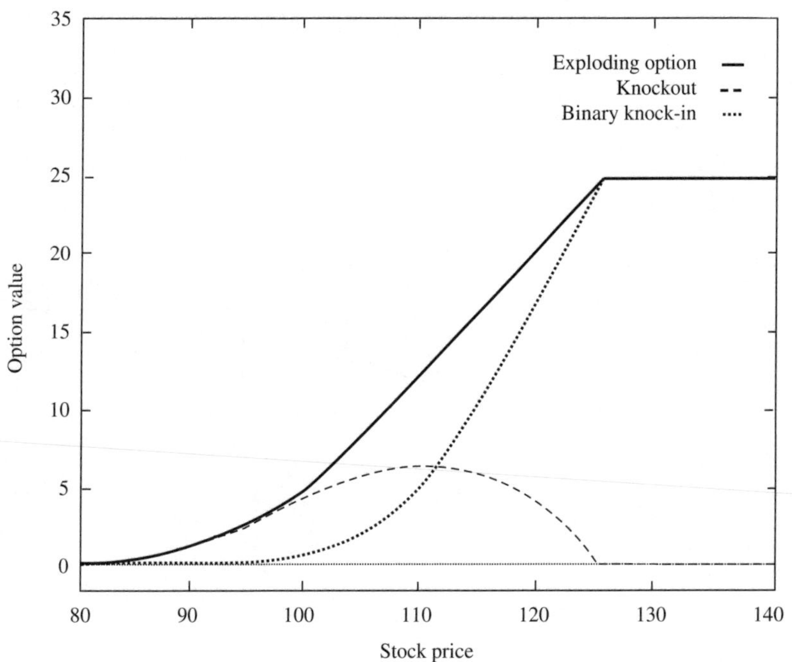

In each case the strike price is 100, the barrier is at 125, the time to expiration is 3 months, and the underlying volatility is 20 percent.

In region (D), $X \ll \sigma \cdot \sqrt{t}$, the barrier is very likely to be hit, the option value is close to the maximum payout, and is consequently volatility insensitive. Figure 10–14 compares an exploding option, an ordinary option, and a capped (spread) option over a wide range of volatilities.

Exploding options are useful because they allow a relatively large premium to be paid while keeping the maximum cash-settlement amount capped. Exploding options may be generalized by adding several checkpoints such that whenever the underlying price reaches a checkpoint, the

FIGURE 10–14

Value of a Plain Call, a 100- to 110-Percent Capped Call and an Exploding Option with a 110-Percent Barrier over a Wide Range of Volatility Values

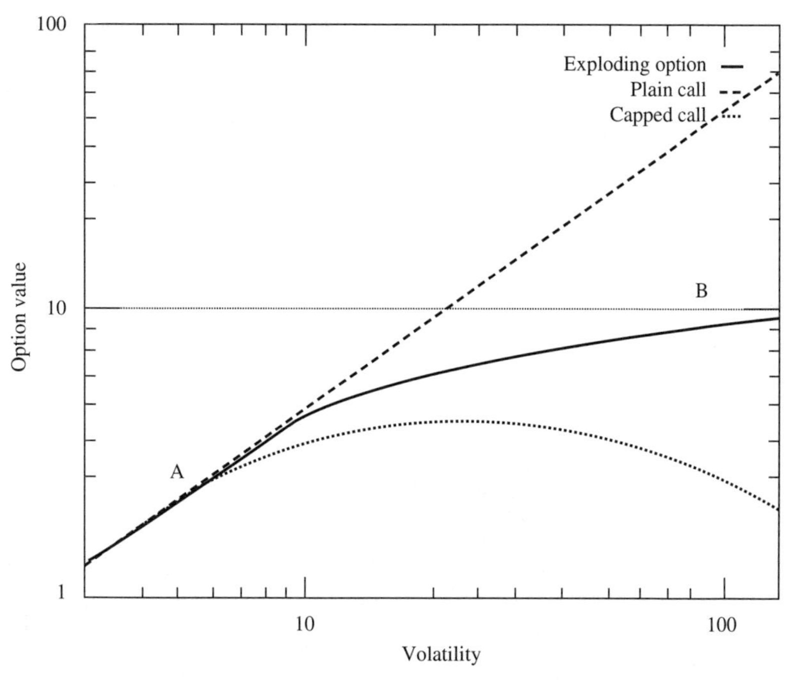

buyer locks in the then in-the-money amount. After such an event, the final payout may still grow, but cannot drop. A call option with strike K and checkpoints at C_1, C_2, . . . , C_n is the same as a combination of knock-out options KO(K, C_1, $C_1 - K$) + KO(C_1, C_2, $C_2 - C_1$) + · · · + KO(C_{n-1}, C_n, C_n, $- C_{n-1}$) where KO(K, B, R) is a knock-out option with strike K, barrier B, and rebate R. In the limit where the checkpoints are arbitrarily close to each other, the structure becomes a lookback option, where the final payout depends on the maximum (minimum for puts) price during the lifetime of the option.

Multiple-checkpoint options (and by extension lookback options) are more valuable, but generally share the same characteristics of exploding

FIGURE 10–15
Option Value versus Volatility for Various Options

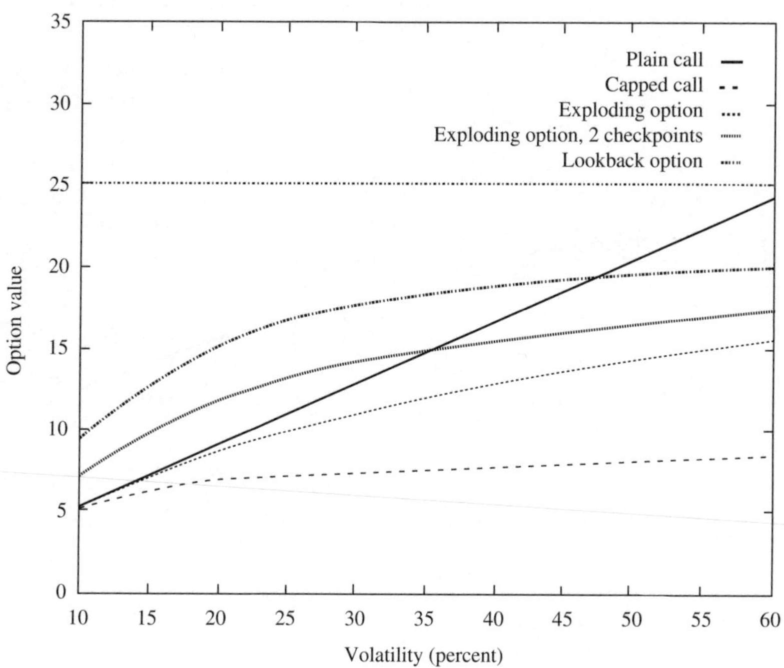

All options are at-the-money calls. All options except the plain call are capped at 25 percent.

options. Figure 10–15 shows the dependence of a checkpoint option on checkpoint frequency.

Custom-Designed Derivative Structures

Even without resorting to exotic options, a very high degree of volatility insensitivity can be achieved by taking a properly chosen combination of ordinary options. For example, the 100- to 110-percent call spread discussed above may be made much more volatility independent by selling

FIGURE 10–16

Option Value versus Volatility for an Ordinary and a Fine-Tuned 100- to 110-Percent Call Spread

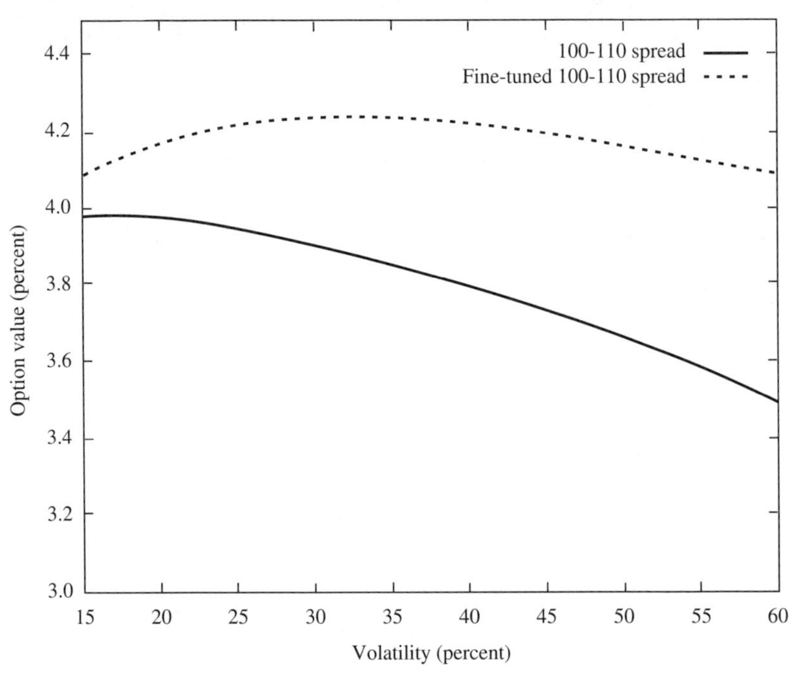

only 0.95 110-percent calls for every 100-percent call purchased. Figure 10–16 shows the dependence on volatility of the original and the modified spread. The appropriate factor can easily be calculated using the following formula:

$$\frac{\text{\# of 110\% calls}}{\text{\# of 100\% calls}} = \frac{\text{vega[100\% call]}}{\text{vega[110\% call]}}$$

If we have several options $C_1, C_2, \ldots, C_n$, each of which has volatility-dependent vega $V_n(v)$, we can create a combination structure $C_1 + C_2 \cdot x_2 + \cdots + C_n \cdot x_n$ with vega of zero at $n-1$ volatility levels $v_1, v_2, \ldots, v_{n-1}$ by solving

$$\sum x_i \cdot V_i[v_i] = 0$$

FIGURE 10–17

Option Value versus Volatility for a Fine-Tuned 100- to 110-Percent Spread and for a Fine-Tuned 100–110–120 Percent Spread.

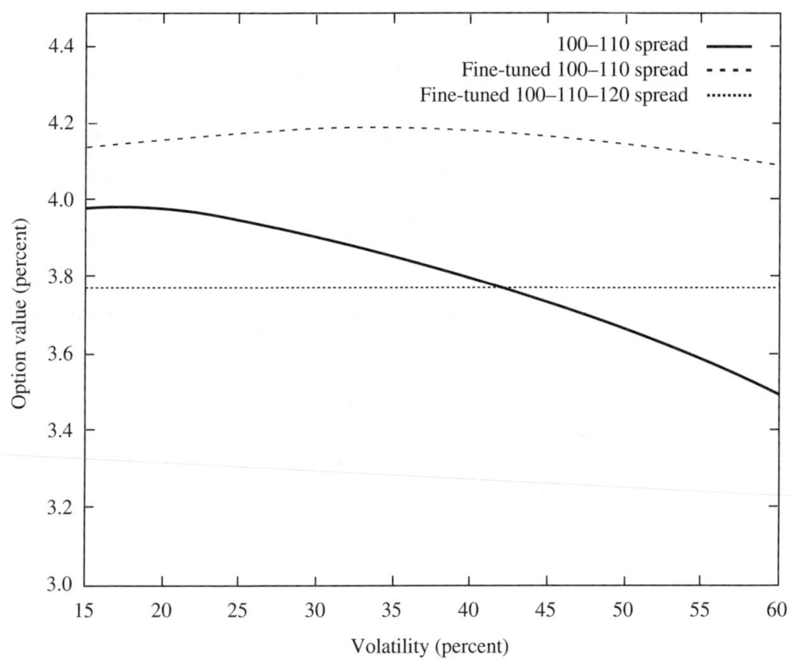

The value of the fine-tuned 100–110–120 percent spread changes by about 1.3 basis points over the 15- to 60-percent volatility range.

for the various x_i. Figure 10–17 shows the effect of creating an appropriate combination by adding another call, with 120-percent strike price.

SUMMARY

Volatility-insensitive structures are useful in a variety of situations where volatility is either unknown or uncertain. Examples of such situations include recent IPOs, small and/or unknown stocks, or options on unknown underlyings. Even when volatility is not completely unknown, volatility-insensitive structures may allow tighter pricing.

TABLE 10–1
Comparing Volatility Sensitivity of Various Derivative Structures*

Type	*Volatility Sensitivity*	*Terms*	*Relative Variation over 15% to 60% Volatility*
Plain Call	High	100% strike	183%
Synthetic	None		0
Collar	Medium	100% and 110% strikes	13%
Barrier	Very High	100% strike, 90% knock-in	2450%
Barrier	Medium	100% strike, 90% knock-out	40%
Barrier	Very Low	100% strike, 95.7% knock-out	0.9%
Exploding	Medium	100% strike, 110% cap	44%
Lookback	Medium	100% strike, 125% cap	66%
Custom Designed	Low	100%–110% strike combination	2.7%
Custom Designed	Very Low	100%–110%–120% strike combination	0.4%

*All structures have a one-year duration, and assume a 6-percent interest rate and a 3-percent dividend yield.

We have explored several types and combinations of plain and exotic options that allow a reduction of volatility sensitivity (see Table 10–1). Plain calls and puts are quite sensitive to the volatility of the underlying asset. Synthetic long or short combinations are totally independent of volatility. Collars and spreads are well known, and offer significant reduction of volatility sensitivity over plain calls and puts.

Knock-in barrier options can be very sensitive to volatility if the knock-in level is out-of-the-money. Knock-out barrier options with the barrier out-of-the-money have naturally low volatility sensitivity. Exploding, checkpoint, and lookback options allow a reduction of volatility sensitivity relative to plain calls and puts, while providing for significantly higher premiums than simple spreads. Finally, by fine-tuning either barrier level or relative weights of ordinary options, one may design structures that have very low volatility sensitivity.

PART III

PRICING AND MODELING

Chapter Eleven

Overview of Modeling Techniques

Jeffrey L. McIver
Director of Financial Engineering
Infinity Financial Technology, Inc.

INTRODUCTION

This chapter is a discussion about the theory and techniques required by a solution to an option valuation problem. The intent is to frame the option modeling problem with an outline of the financial and theoretic underpinnings so that the solution methodologies become more motivated and meaningful. It turns out that the process of solving a particular option valuation problem often requires that the financial engineer assume several distinct roles and view the problem from several different angles, simply because option valuation in general is very complicated and because it touches on many different disciplines. One such role entails casting the pricing problem into a financially coherent and arbitrage-free framework where some financially meaningful quantity or quantities which drive the optionality, are modeled as random variables. Another role certainly involves translating the financial picture into a well-formed mathematical representation, and in turn, mapping the mathematical formulation into a numerically oriented algorithm that can lead to a solution of the pricing problem. The final role that must often be shouldered is that of implementor of the algorithm, where one must pay attention to performance issues, error analysis, and the sundry implementation tricks of financial engineering.

This chapter will frequently interchange the concepts of an option, exotic or not, and a contingent claim. An option usually implies a choice of some kind: *I am selling you the right but not the obligation to purchase an equity on such and such a date at such and such a price.* Occasionally, however, the optimal exercise of an option is just assumed and written into the contract, as in: *I am selling you the maximum of zero or the difference between the opening price of this equity and such and such price.* Both hypothetical contracts are thought of and modeled as options even though one does not really involve choice. An exotic option may as well be thought of as a contingent claim where either the optimal payoff is contractually specified or, if a choice is involved, one assumes the choice is exercised optimally (although calculating that optimal can be difficult). Solving option valuation problems is really just solving general contingent claim valuation problems.

A typical contingent claim will have a payoff that depends in a possibly complicated way on one or more market prices, indexes, or rates. All reasonable, modern treatments of contingent claim valuation involve modeling the underlying prices or rates as stochastic random variables and calculating a fair value within that framework. One never tries, for example, to forecast the variable and estimate an option price from the forecast, or to statistically analyze historical payoffs to decide on an option price. The reason why this forecasting approach does not work is that it is not rooted in trading and hedging activities, while the arbitrage-free pricing approach explicitly addresses the problem with these issues in mind. The randomness of the rate or price in turn will force the amount, and sometimes the timing, of the claim's payoff to be random. The first step in option modeling is to choose what financial variable or variables are meaningful to the claim and to quantify their stochastic behavior within an arbitrage-free framework. An arbitrage is a way to make money risklessly, and since the real world does not allow arbitrages (at least not very big ones for very long), a contingent claim valuation model had better not allow one either. Arbitrage-freeness must be imposed on the mathematical models using theoretic arguments from finance, something we discuss below.

For example to illustrate the process, theory, and valuation techniques, let's outline a very simple albeit somewhat nonstandard option valuation problem. Say we wanted to value a claim that pays **H** dollars at time **T** if the opening price **S** for an equity on that date is over **K** (it is $\mathbf{S_0}$ now), or else pays nothing. This is called a binary option (all or nothing) that only depends on the terminal value of the equity price. As options go, the non-path-dependent binary option is simple enough that we can use it as an example but not so common that it is too well-known to be useful. Let's say the equity will pay no dividend, and the interest rate for time **T**, continuously compounded, is **R**. The obvious choice of the driving stochastic random variable is the stock price **S**, since it determines the payoff and value of the option. Standard practice would have us model this equity price as a geometric Brownian motion

$$dS = \mu S dt + \sigma S dz, S(0) = S_0$$

where μ is the assumed drift (or expected growth), σ is the volatility of the equity price, and where we have assumed we have estimated their values from historical analysis or implied them from the market. The drift of the option μ is the growth of the stock price that we objectively (in the world of actual prices) would expect to observe. This drift term and the stochastic equation imply the forward price $\mathbf{S_t}$ has a specific probability distribution $\boldsymbol{P}$, or measure, for every time **t**; we will refer to this measure $\boldsymbol{P}$ as the *objective* probability measure of **S**.

The binary option payoff is characterized by the terminal condition:

$$B(S_T) = \begin{cases} H \text{ if } S_T \geq K \\ 0 \text{ if } S_T < K \end{cases}$$

These two equations map the financial problem into a mathematical representation; however, they do not as yet impose arbitrage-freeness on the model. As a preview of what implications this imposition will have on valuation, let's step ahead to how we would represent the value of this binary option.

Operationally, applying arbitrage-freeness to our toy binary option model has two implications: (1) we do not use μ for the drift of our dividendless equity price, but instead use the interest rate **R** as the drift; and (2) we value the contingent claim as the expectation of the discounted (at rate **R**) stochastic cash flow. There is a another impact that imposing arbitrage-freeness makes, which appears more like a notational change (we will put a hat on the Brownian motion), but we will return to why we do this later.

The stochastic process for **S** is now

$$dS = R \cdot Sdt + \sigma Sd\tilde{z},\ S(0) = S_0$$

and the formulation for the value of our binary option is the following equation:

$$\text{Value} = \tilde{E}\left[e^{-R \cdot T}\int_0^{\infty} B(S_T)dS\right]$$

The first thing to note is that this presentation of the binary option value is actually already very general; there is nothing in the Value formula that links this formulation of value to a binary option except the terminal option payoff function **B(·)**. If we change the payoff function to something much more arbitrary, the formulation and presentation of value would remain the same. For instance, if we replace the payoff **B(·)** with the following payoff function in the formula for Value, we would just be pricing an ordinary call option on **S**.

$$Call(S_T) = \max(S_T - K,0)$$

THE MATHEMATICS OF ARBITRAGE-FREENESS

The more profound financial question associated with a mathematical representation of option value is, "How does one make the valuation problem arbitrage-free?" We noted that there are operational consequences for imposing arbitrage-freeness, and certainly there is a large body of financial literature devoted to the topic of arbitrage-freeness (see, for example, the bibliography given in [D]). At best, we can only hope to scratch the surface of this subject, but it is important because the underlying theory lends option valuation a sense of unity that is hard to recognize without it.

Within the context of a modeled economy like the one we outlined above for our equity prices **S**, contingent claims (including exotic options) are to be generated by what are called self-financing trading strategies. The idea of a self-financing trading strategy is related to the concept of a replicating portfolio for standard options. A replicating portfolio is a holding of some underlying asset and cash, with the understanding that the relative proportions of the two assets may be constantly rebalanced by trading in and out of the underlying asset. No cash, however, is taken out of or paid into the portfolio. The portfolio and the rebalancing rules are designed so that, at the option's exercise, it can be liquidated to obtain exactly the payoff of the option. The replicating portfolio is so named because it *replicates* the option payoff. Similarly, a self-financing trading strategy for a particular claim is a sequence of trades in the underlying asset(s) meant to replicate the payoff of the contingent claim, with no money taken from or paid in to the trading strategy. Part of the specification of the self-financing trading strategy is the initial portfolio from which the trading rules will replicate the contingent claim payoff.

To get a handle on the mathematics of a trading strategy, imagine that at periodic and closely spaced intervals one has a prescription for trading in a vector of underlying assets including cash. Say at time **t** one buys a vector $\boldsymbol{\theta}(\mathbf{t})$ of extra shares of the assets at the known vector of prices **S** and then waits for the next trading time. By the next trading period the price of the underlying asset will have changed randomly to $\mathbf{S}+\Delta\mathbf{S}$, and the experienced trading gain over the one trading period is $\boldsymbol{\theta}(\mathbf{t}) \times \Delta\mathbf{S}$. Adding up all these trading intervals gives

$$\Sigma\theta(t) \cdot \Delta S_t.$$

Taking limits allows us to represent the change in portfolio value from trading as a stochastic integral of the trading strategy over the vector process **S**.

$$\theta_T \cdot S_T = \theta_0 \cdot S_0 + \int_0^T \theta_t dS(t)$$

Given that a contingent claim can be represented by a self-financing trading strategy, the idea behind modeling arbitrage-free pricing is to forge a link between two concepts: the absence of an arbitrage, and the existence of an equivalent (to $\boldsymbol{P}$) Martingale measure $\boldsymbol{Q}$ for **S** discounted by the risk-free rate **R**. An equivalent Martingale measure is a mathematical object: a measure is a prescription for integrating functions on sets (in this case $\boldsymbol{Q}$ is a probability measure); "equivalent" means it has the same zero-volume sets as the original objective measure, $\boldsymbol{P}$; and "Martingale" is the property that the discounted vector price process **X** for **S**, where each element of **X** is simply the discounted element of S,

$$X_t = e^{-R \cdot t} S_t,$$

has a zero drift coefficient under the measure $\boldsymbol{Q}$. A self-financing trading strategy $\boldsymbol{\theta}$ with respect to $\mathbf{S}$ is also one with respect to $\mathbf{X}$, and for $\mathbf{X}$ the trading strategy's expected trading gains equal zero under the equivalent Martingale measure $\boldsymbol{Q}$.

$$\tilde{E}\left[\int \theta dX\right] = 0$$

As a result, the expected final value of any trading strategy in present value terms will be the integral of that strategy applied to the process $\mathbf{X}$, and by the Martingale property of $\boldsymbol{Q}$ will satisfy

$$\tilde{E}[\theta_T \cdot X_T] = \theta_0 \cdot X_0 + \tilde{E}\left[\int_0^T \theta_t dX(t)\right] = \theta_0 \cdot X_0 = \theta_0 \cdot S_0.$$

This equation says that the expectation under the measure $\boldsymbol{Q}$ of the discounted payoff of the claim, which is equal to today's value of the contingent claim replicated by the trading strategy $\boldsymbol{\theta}$, is equal to the initial portfolio required to replicate the claim. This initial portfolio is simply denoted by $\boldsymbol{\theta}_0\mathbf{S}_0$.

Let us recap what we have discussed. The value today of a (possibly forward) contingent claim is the value of an initial portfolio, plus trading gains or losses that the representing self-financing trading strategy associated to the claim can produce. If there is no arbitrage, then (given some technical conditions) this equivalent Martingale measure $\boldsymbol{Q}$ that we discussed above exists and is unique. If $\boldsymbol{Q}$ exists, then there are no expected trading gains or losses, and the value of the contingent claim reduces to the value today of the initial portfolio required to replicate the claim's payoff. The value of that initial portfolio, however, is nothing but the expectation of the discounted payoff of the contingent claim, where the expectation is taken with respect to the equivalent Martingale measure $\boldsymbol{Q}$ (and NOT the objective measure $\boldsymbol{P}$).

Another way to express that the discounted price process $\mathbf{X}$ is a Martingale under the equivalent measure $\mathbf{Q}$ is to form the process $\mathbf{X}$ times the Randon-Nikodym derivative of $\mathbf{Q}$ with respect to $\mathbf{P}$, and to say this new process is a Martingale with respect to $\mathbf{P}$. A technical lemma, called Girsanov's Theorem, allows one to reflect this as a change in the Brownian process that drives the underlying price process $\mathbf{S}$. The net effect of an application of Girsanov's Theorem is to change the drift term μ of the $\mathbf{S}$ process under $\boldsymbol{P}$, the objective probability measure, to $\mathbf{R}$ under the equivalent Martingale measure Q. This is the origin of the hatted Brownian motion term and the altered drift term in the last section. Once we have made this measure change, theoretic valuation consists of computing the expectation of the claim's discounted payoff. More details and technical conditions for the mathematical embodiment of arbitrage-freeness are included in [D].

While this discussion does give us an outline of the underpinnings of value, in a theoretic sense, it does not shed much light on the mathematical apparatus for *solving* the valuation problem. Certainly, one popular method for computing the value of a contingent claim is by solving a partial differential equation (PDE), but it might not be obvious why this should work. A PDE is an equation in the derivatives of the solution function and is commonly encountered in engineering, applied math, physics, and these days, financial valuation. In fact, the monumental paper of Black and Scholes first presented and solved the standard option valuation problem as a PDE. However, it is less than obvious where and how PDEs materialize in this valuation framework, as it would seem that there is no place in this derivation of financial value for a PDE to be relevant. If "Value" is obtained through an expectation calculation, where does a PDE fit in?

One way to see how a PDE might enter the picture is with a practical financial argument coupled with an application of a important theorem called Ito's Lemma. The idea is that a contingent claim **O(S,t),** which depends on the current underlying asset price **S** and time **t** and which doesn't pay dividends, will instantaneously grow in value at the short-term interest rate **R** under the equivalent Martingale measure Q. As **O(·,·)** depends on the random equity price **S**, its value is also a random variable and follows a diffusion process. The financial argument for no-arbitrage says that, with respect to the Martingale measure (which we have indicated by the hat on the Brownian motion term), the drift term of this process is **R**.

$$dO(S,t) = O \cdot Rdt + O \cdot \Sigma d\hat{z}$$

On the other hand, the analog of the calculus chain rule for stochastic equations, Ito's Lemma, tells us that the drift of **O(·,·)** can be written in terms of the stochastic process for **S**.

$$dO(S,t) = \left(\frac{\partial O}{\partial t} + R \cdot S\frac{\partial O}{\partial S} + \frac{\sigma^2}{2}S^2\frac{\partial^2 O}{\partial S^2}\right)dt + \sigma\frac{\partial O}{\partial S}d\hat{z}$$

Combining these two expressions for the drift term of the claim value **O**(·,·), we get a PDE that **O**(·,·) must satisfy.

$$\frac{\partial O}{\partial t} + R \cdot S\frac{\partial O}{\partial S} + \frac{\sigma^2}{2}S^2\frac{\partial^2 O}{\partial S^2} - O \cdot R = 0$$

This derivation hints at a deeper connection of PDEs and expectations of stochastic variables, and in fact is a beautiful illustration of a fundamental interrelationship between two seemingly different fields of mathematics. A tangible statement of the general relationship between probabilistic expectations and solutions of an associated PDE is given by Kolmogorov's equation. If an Ito diffusion process satisfies the following equation,

$$dX_t = b(X_t)dt + c(X_t)dz$$

and if

$$u(x,t) = E^{X_0 = x}[f(X_t)],$$

then, under some technical conditions the Kolmogorov equation, below, holds.

$$\frac{\partial u}{\partial t} = b(x) \cdot \frac{\partial f}{\partial x} + \frac{c(x)^2}{2}\frac{\partial^2 f}{\partial x^2}$$

Obviously, this result employs a sizable amount of mathematical machinery, but it does point to the close connection of PDEs to expectations. The reader is referred to [O] for more details.

The value of a contingent claim has a theoretic underpinning as an expectation of its discounted payoff with respect to a particular measure that makes every asset price (minus dividends) grow on average at the same rate. Exotic option valuation, a.k.a. contingent claim valuation, comes down to calculating what that expected discounted payoff is. One of the most powerful conceptual methods of viewing that expectation calculation is to restate it in terms of a PDE and boundary conditions. In this format all of the analytic and numeric machinery that has been developed to solve these sorts of PDE problems can be brought to bear on our valuation problem.

We now turn to the practical and traditional methods used to solve the valuation problem. It is important, however, to keep in mind that fundamentally we are calculating the expected value of a random variable.

This perspective will be echoed when we discuss analytic and Monte Carlo methods.

EXCURSIONS IN SOLUTION SPACE

Now that we have discussed the financial modeling and mathematical ramifications of the contingent-claim valuation problem, we turn to valuation techniques. Certainly, analytic solutions of the equivalent PDE problem (as Black and Scholes provided in their original paper), or a direct analytic derivation of the expectation, are highly prized ways to solve the valuation problem. Analytic solutions do not have the troubling nuances that numeric methods have, and analytic solutions can be derived and verified completely independently of any software implementation. Analytic solutions, however, are the exceptions and not the general rule in the zoo of exotic options. This should not be a surprise, considering that it is far easier to describe an option, and therefore describe the implicit boundary conditions that a certain PDE must satisfy, than it is to write down an explicit analytic solution of that PDE.

Analytic Solutions

Nonetheless, analytic answers are useful not only because they afford efficient ways to price particular options, but also because they serve as benchmarks on which other, more numerically based methods, can be calibrated. Analytic valuation formulas come either from solving the valuation PDE with its boundary conditions, or directly from computing the expectation of the discounted claim payoff under the risk-neutral measure. Both have real and useful applications. We will not go through an example of analytically solving a PDE but instead refer the reader to any good introductory text on PDE methods.

A direct computation of the expectation is sometimes effective in calculating an option valuation formula. For instance, the binary option—which paid an amount **H** if the equity price was above a strike price **K** at time **T**, or paid zero otherwise—is a typical contingent claim whose valuation formula is best calculated directly. The expectation (with respect to the Martingale measure ***Q***) that we need to calculate for the binary option is the following:

$$\exp(-R \cdot T)\int_0^\infty B(S)dS = e^{-R\cdot T}\int_K^\infty H dS$$

As the distribution of **S** at time **T** is lognormal, the log of **S** has a normal distribution given by

$$\log(S) \sim N(\log(S_0) + R \cdot T - \frac{\sigma^2 T}{2}, \sigma^2 T),$$

and here we have made explicit use of the measure $\boldsymbol{Q}$ to express the expectation of the lognormal distribution. The expectation integral becomes

$$e^{-R\cdot T}H\frac{1}{\sqrt{2\pi T}\sigma}\int_{\log(K)}^\infty \exp\left[-\frac{\left(x - \log(S_0) - R \cdot T + \frac{\sigma^2 T}{2}\right)^2}{2\sigma^2 T}\right]dx$$

which reduces by a change of variables to

$$e^{-R\cdot T}H \cdot \mathrm{N}\left(\frac{\log\left(\frac{S}{K}\right) + R \cdot T}{\sigma\sqrt{T}} - \frac{\sigma\sqrt{T}}{2}\right)$$

where $\mathrm{N}(\cdot)$ is the cumulative normal function.

Unlike this exercise with the binary option, analytic expressions for option valuations are sometimes very tedious to obtain. Nonetheless, analytic formulas, when they can be found, are very important both for their immediate use and as validation benchmarks for other methods.

Partial Differential Equation Solutions

While analytically solving a PDE in closed form may be difficult or impossible, numerically solving a PDE using one of the many standard textbook methods is often the solution of choice for contingent-claim valuation problems. Sometimes these solutions, as implemented in the industry, are not really recognized as solving the valuation problem as a PDE. There are at least three variants of PDE solvers that we can briefly outline, but the reader is directed to the voluminous literature for all the details we have left out (for example, see [DB]).

One potentially useful PDE technique, but one that is only infrequently used for financial applications, is known as the "finite element method." It is well-known in the engineering literature, and can be the algorithm of choice for the right problem. It originated as a way to simulate the behavior of structural elements in engineering problems, but the technique can be adapted to a variety of PDEs, including those found in financial problems. The finite element method is probably most useful for European-type problems, where there are few or no intermediate cash flows to model.

Another technique, which is widely used in financial applications, is the "finite difference method." Finite difference schemes are most often implemented on a grid or lattice and involve the direct, numeric estimation of the derivatives in the PDE. Typically, one axis of the grid is time and the other(s) is the relevant financial variable(s). For instance, our binary option problem would have an axis for time axis and one for the equity price extending from zero to some practical upper bound. As the true upper boundary is actually infinity, it might be worthwhile to consider one of the several numeric techniques for handling infinite boundaries. Given a grid, the prescription of the boundary values is straightforward; simply place the (implicitly known) value of the option at each lattice point that lies on the boundary. For example, we know that our binary option has zero value if **S** is zero, regardless of the time. At the upper boundary, the option value is **H** regardless of the time because there the option is sure to mature in-the-money. Finally, along the boundary of the maturity time **T**, the option is worth nothing below the strike **K** and worth **H** above the strike.

Once a prescription for the grid with boundary conditions has been made, there are choices as to how to solve the set of finite difference equations. These equations are the translation of the calculus derivatives terms of the PDE into the discrete framework provided by the grid. So called "explicit" methods for solving the finite difference equations are perhaps the most straightforward approach. These methods can be very fast but often suffer from stability problems and tend to be accurate only to first order in time. "Implicit" methods, on the other hand, are stable, but are somewhat more computational-expensive and are likewise only first-order accurate in time. Methods that mix the properties of explicit and implicit finite difference algorithms, like the celebrated Crank-Nicholson scheme, can marry the stability of implicit methods with second-order accuracy in time.

FIGURE 11–1
Tree-Based PDE Solver

Each node calculates the discounted expected value of the nodes to its right.

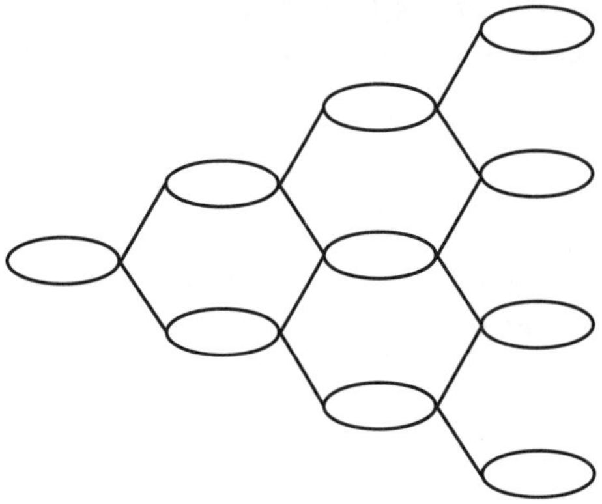

A third and common PDE solution technique used in financial valuation problems is the binomial tree approach (the trinomial tree is similar). Trees are seldom viewed as PDE solvers, even by the people who use them, and there seems to be little interest in them outside of the financial arena. On the other hand, they are easy to implement, easy to understand, and more closely conform to one's intuition of how to value a financial asset than more traditional PDE solvers.

A tree-based PDE solver uses the close relationship between probability problems and the associated PDE that we alluded to above. In its general essence, a PDE solver takes numerically prescribed boundary data and builds out the rest of the solution based on the PDE it is designed to solve. Finite difference methods, for example, do this by simulating the relations of the solution's derivatives in discrete space. In contrast, tree-based models typically build a solution by systematically computing the corresponding discounted expectation (and hence the solution of the PDE) one slice at a time. If the tree is viewed as a fan extending horizontally with the center node to the left, a tree PDE solver calculates the discounted expected value of the claim at each node, based on the connecting nodes to the right of it (see Figure 11–1). This leads to a numeric PDE solver, although it is not necessary to think of the tree approach as such. Using trees allows one to visualize the derivation of the claim value in economic terms, and in that sense is very appealing for financially oriented models. More on tree models and ideas about their implementation can be found in [M].

Sometimes analytic solutions or PDE solutions to the contingent claim valuation problem are simply not available. This can happen if the contingent claim has ingrained path dependencies, which break the connection between the expectation of discounted payoff and a PDE. It is certainly true that some path-dependent claims can be valued as solutions to a PDE, such as European barrier options. However, these cases of path-dependent claim valuations that lend themselves to either an analytic or a PDE solution are usually special cases of "stopped" non-path-dependent processes. Dealing with a general path-dependent claim almost always requires another valuation approach.

Monte Carlo Methods

An alternative approach is to compute the valuation expectation using a family of techniques collectively called "Monte Carlo methods." Briefly, the idea behind Monte Carlo methods is to simulate the pseudorandom events that would affect a claim's payoff and estimate the expectation of the discounted payoff as a statistical average of the simulated events. In one sense, Monte Carlo methods are the most direct way to calculate the theoretic value of a financial claim, since one is literally calculating an expectation. One way to directly apply Monte Carlo methods to our toy binary option example would be to generate a sampling of a random variable that represents the value of the stock price **S** at time **T** under the equivalent Martingale measure $\boldsymbol{Q}$. For those samples that have a simulated stock price over the strike **K**, a payoff of

$$e^{-R \cdot T} H$$

is made, while for those with a simulated stock price under **K** the payoff is zero. If these simulated stock prices reflect the distribution of $\boldsymbol{Q}$, then the value of the option is just the sample mean of the discounted payoffs.

$$\sum_{m}^{N} \frac{\text{PayOff in } m\text{'th simulation}}{N}$$

Most often, Monte Carlo analysis simulates the entire path followed by the underlying asset or rate, since this eliminates the need to have pseudo-random numbers generated from a possibly complicated distribution. Instead, one can generate "infinitesimal" random moves according to the asset's stochastic equation and rely on it to generate an appropriate distribution of the underlying random variable at a boundary (or stopping time). In theory, Monte Carlo analysis can handle any contingent claim, but in practice there are two main problem areas. The first is that Monte Carlo analysis has a difficult time accurately estimating where an optimal early exercise boundary is. This facet of Monte Carlo analysis makes it more difficult to value American-style options, in comparison to other valuation algorithms, such as, a binary tree PDE solver. The second problem area for Monte Carlo methods is more generic; Monte Carlo analysis is slow.

The relatively slow performance of Monte Carlo analysis compared to, for instance, PDE methods, comes from the often large number of simulations required to get a valuation to a required level of accuracy. With Monte Carlo methods, the valuation, which is a sample mean of a set of pseudo-random simulations, is itself a random variable and has a distribution associated with it. The distribution of the mean, which will depend on the distribution of the simulation values, can be approximated as a normal distribution centered on the mean (i.e., the computed valuation) with a standard deviation equal to

$$\text{Standard Deviation of the Mean} \approx \frac{\text{Sample Standard Deviation}}{\sqrt{N}}.$$

This is a pernicious equation. Using 100 times more simulations increases the computational costs 100 times but only increases the accuracy of the valuation result by 10 times.

There are, however, techniques to reduce the computational burden associated with Monte Carlo analysis. One such technique is an approach called "control variates." The idea behind a control variate is to estimate the sampling error of a Monte Carlo method by comparing the unknown value one wants to calculate against a sampled but analytically known and correlated value. For instance, if one is interested in applying a Monte Carlo technique toward valuing the binary call option we discussed above (ignoring the fact that there is an exact analytic expression for the binary call), a control variate for the binary call could be the regular call option. One needs to make an assumption about the statistical correlation σ between the Monte Carlo estimation error of the binary call value and that of the regular call, but often an estimate of unity is sufficiently useful. To apply this control variate in a Monte Carlo valuation of the binary call option with N random samples, record five values:

1. The numeric estimate of the regular call: RC
2. The numeric estimate of the binary call: BC
3. The standard deviation of the mean for the regular call: σ_R
4. The standard deviation of the mean for the binary call: σ_B
5. The analytic regular call value: A_R

Forming the quantity

$$BC - \sigma_B \rho \cdot \left[\frac{RC - A_R}{\sigma_R} \right]$$

is then a better (lower variance) estimate of the true binary call value compared to the raw sampled value BC. This formula has extracted the correlated error information from the known sampling error for the regular call and used it to provide a better estimate for the value of the binary cap. While the reduction in the sampling error for the mean translates into requiring fewer simulations to attain a given level of accuracy, the per-sample cost of this technique is also large. As there is a need to numerically value the "control" variable, each sample is almost twice as expensive to compute.

Another technique to reduce the overall cost of a Monte Carlo calculation is through the use of antithetic variables. The motivation behind antithetic variables is to exploit any intrinsic symmetry and resulting negatively correlated samples that may appear in the generated pseudorandom numbers, the most obvious choice of a symmetry being one induced from flipping the sign of a normal deviate. The reduction in the variance of the calculated mean (and hence in the computation cost) comes from the reduction of the sampled mean when negatively correlated samples are grouped together.

The application of antithetic variables is straightforward. For each generation and use of a normal deviate, the technique calls for the use of the negative normal deviate. Both the original and negative deviates lead to sampled valuations; these two sampled valuations are averaged before being added to the larger set of sampled values. Each sampling is

FIGURE 11–2
Integrating a Linear Function against a Normal Density

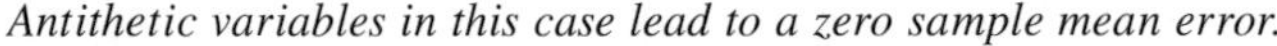

Antithetic variables in this case lead to a zero sample mean error.

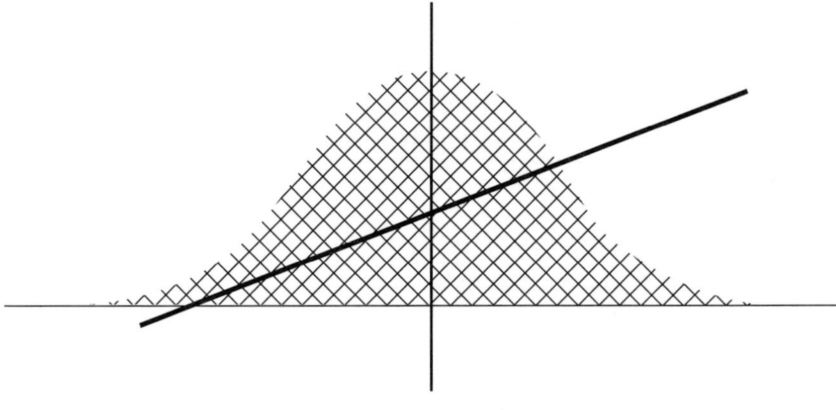

just as expensive to calculate as before, but the antithetic variable technique makes a more efficient use of each sampling by pairing it with a (possibly) negatively correlated value.

A striking example of the gains of the antithetic variable technique comes from integrating a linear function against a normal distribution. Whereas the ordinary sampled mean of this integral would follow a one over square root law, an application of antithetic variables would reduce the sampled variance of the mean to precisely zero (see Figure 11–2). For each positive argument taken from a normal distribution, the antithetic variable will be a negative value, and vice versa. If the integrated function is linear, the positive and negative function arguments will produce offsetting results, and each averaged pair will always return the function's "Y" intercept value. As each pair returns the same averaged value, the sampled mean has zero variance. As a general statement, the use of antithetic variables never hurts a Monte Carlo estimate (provided the pseudo-random number generator is "random" enough) and can often be very useful.

For more general applications of Monte Carlo analysis where the entire path of a random variable is generated, the antithetic variables technique can still be useful. In generating a complete path, some sequence of (usually) normal deviates needs to be generated; the symmetry of the path is induced by changing the sign of each deviate in the sequence. However, here the negative correlation of the variate and the antivariate will generally be much less pronounced and the resulting benefit of using the antithetic variable technique would be similarly reduced.

HANDLING TERM STRUCTURES

The final option valuation topic that we will discuss is the accommodation of term structures in the underlying mathematical models. A term structure can either describe a time-dependent expectation, such as the expectations of a market index that are coming from actively traded futures on the index, or an observation of a curve of related variables, such as an interest-rate curve. In modeling a term structure, there are at least two different approaches to modeling this temporal dependency in an arbitrage-free framework.

The first viewpoint finds wide use in the modeling of interest-rate term structure models where one needs to model all maturities of interest rates (for one market segment) in a consistent manner. These models tend to be quite complicated as one needs to provide a theoretical framework that relates zero-coupon yields of different maturities without allowing arbitrages. This is coupled with the difficulty that, to be useful, the interest-rate term structure models need to conform to an observed curve seen in the market today, implying some type of calibration of the mathematical model to an entire curve of initial data. In this setting, term- structure modeling is often accomplished by allowing the drift and/or the volatility terms in the stochastic differential equation of the underlying variable to be time-dependent functions. These coefficient functions are numerically solved according to the initial data to which the curve must be faithful. This technique is often essential to building certain term-structure models successfully, and the reader is referred to [D] for a discussion of this wide topic.

The other approach to accommodating term structure in the context of a financial model is to distribute the time-dependent behavior among an infinite family of related random variables. For example, in the equity model we described earlier we might assume that all forward positions of the equity price **S** were traded. If we call **F(T)** the forward price traded today of the equity price to be settled at time **T**, then we might expect that the expected forward equity price is just the forward price:

$$\tilde{E}[S(T)] = F(T)$$

If we want to capture this additional observed expected price behavior of **S**, one approach would be to vastly complicate the stochastic equation followed by the one random equity price. Allowing time-dependent coefficients, which must be numerically fit so as to reproduce the forward expectations given by **F(T)**, we could replicate this expected future behavior for a single random process. Instead of this complicated approach, an alternative method would be to form a family of variables $\mathbf{S(t,\tau)}$, with the idea that at time **t** this random variable represents the (unknown) equity price to be observed at time τ (for **t** greater than τ the random variable $\mathbf{S(t,\tau)}$ is undefined). This is a family of random variables indexed by time τ, with each following a stochastic process driven by only one Brownian motion.

$$dS(t,\tau) = \sigma S(t,\tau)d\tilde{z}(t), \quad S(0,\tau) = F(\tau)$$

Each variable in the family is driftless (a Martingale), but each has its own characteristic initial, and therefore expected final, value.

One way to see how this approach to modeling term structure can be useful is to imagine that with our original equity-price equation we asked for the expected first moment and second moment of the average equity price between the present and some time **T** in the future. This calculation, which may seem daunting at first sight, is almost trivial when we construct the term structure of expected behavior from this viewpoint. We would simply formulate the stochastic equation of our equity price as

$$dS(t,\tau) = \sigma S(t,\tau)d\tilde{z}(t), \quad S(0,\tau) = S_0 e^{R\cdot\tau}$$

and note that this does produce the correct time-dependent lognormal distribution for equity price for any future time. The expected first moment of average equity price can be written

$$\tilde{E}\left[\frac{1}{T}\int_0^T S(t,t)dt\right] = \frac{1}{T}\int_0^T \tilde{E}[S(t,t)]dt = \frac{1}{T}\int_0^T S_0 e^{R\cdot t}dt$$

and this integral resolves to

$$S_0\left(\frac{e^{R\cdot T}-1}{R\cdot T}\right).$$

The key observation in the second-moment calculation is that the two distinct random variables $\mathbf{S(t,T_1)}$ and $\mathbf{S(t,T_2)}$ are perfectly correlated up to the minimum of $\mathbf{T_1}$ and $\mathbf{T_2}$. As a result, the second-moment calculation becomes

$$\tilde{E}\left[\frac{1}{T^2}\left(\int_0^T S(t,t)dt\right)^2\right]=\frac{1}{T^2}\int_0^T\int_0^t 2\tilde{E}[S(\tau,\tau)\cdot S(t,t)]d\tau dt.$$

As

$$\tilde{E}[S(\tau,\tau)\cdot S(t,t)]=S_0^2\cdot e^{R\cdot(t+\tau)}\cdot e^{\sigma^2\cdot\tau}$$

we can easily calculate the double integral to obtain the second moment of the averaged equity price,

$$S_0^2\cdot\frac{2}{T^2}\left[\frac{e^{(2R+\sigma^2)T}-1}{(2R+\sigma^2)(R+\sigma^2)}-\frac{e^{R\cdot T}-1}{R(R+\sigma^2)}\right].$$

This moment calculation for an averaged price can be used to obtain analytic approximations for Asian options as, for instance, found in [H]. This approach to modeling term structure information, as a family of related random variables, is not only useful in this regard but also finds expression in the Heath, Jarrow, and Morten term-structure models of interest rates (see [HJM]).

REFERENCES

[D] Duffie, Darrell, *Dynamic Asset Pricing Theory* (Princeton, NJ: Princeton University Press, 1992).

[DB] Dahlquist, Germund, and Ake Bjorck, *Numerical Methods*, (Englewood Cliffs, NJ: Prentice Hall, 1974).

[H] Hull, John, *Options, Futures, and Other Derivative Securities,* 2d ed. (Englewood Cliffs, NJ: Prentice Hall, 1993).

[HJM] Heath, David, Robert Jarrow, and Andrew Morten, "Bond Pricing and the Term Structure of Interest Rates: A New Methodology for Contingent Claims Valuation," *Econometrica*, Vol. 60, No. (January 1992), pp. 77–105.

[M] McIver, Jeffrey, "Tree Power," *Risk* magazine, Vol. 6, No. 12 (December 1993), pp. 58–64.

[MW] Kalos, Malvin, and Paula Whitlock, *Monte Carlo Methods, Volume I: Basics* (New York: John Wiley & Sons, 1986).

[O] Oksendal, Bernt, *Stochastic Differential Equations* (Berlin: Springer-Verlag, 1985).

Chapter Twelve

Volatility Is Not Constant

Robin J. Brenner
Vice President
Merrill Lynch

INTRODUCTION

Largely due to the seminal option-pricing papers of Merton [1973] and Black & Scholes [1973], the field of finance has developed rapidly, growing from a mere subset of economics to an independent field of study with breadth, depth, and sophistication. The substantial rewards for financial innovation available in financial markets have sparked a rapid growth in the types and complexities of financial products available. Since the papers of Merton and Black & Scholes, the range of available financial products has grown from standard call and put options to the large variety of exotic options, the most common of which are covered in this book. In tandem with this growth in available products was an increase in the sophistication of the required analytics. Finance professionals developed the first exotic option pricing formulas by applying many of the known mathematical results for the constant parameter, lognormally distributed asset process used by Merton and Black & Scholes.

While assuming such a price process allowed for the quick development of analytical pricing formulas, the values of exotic options, like knock-outs, can be highly sensitive to deviations from these assumptions. Since knock-out, or barrier, options are a type of *path-dependent* option, their values are particularly sensitive to deviations from the constant-parameter assumptions for volatility and interest rates. In fact, even the prices of nonexotic options are affected by deviations from these two constant-parameter assumptions. Accordingly, the finance profession has seen significant growth recently in the incorporation of interest-rate and volatility *curves* into the pricing of interest- rate-dependent options, from standard bond-options to caps, floors, and swaptions. The tremendous success of models based on the insights of Ho & Lee [1986], Heath, Jarrow, & Morton [1992], and Black, Derman, & Toy [1990] all illustrate this fact.

The purpose of this chapter is to take insights we have gained in modeling nonconstant parameters for the pricing of nonexotic options and apply them to the pricing of exotic options. To demonstrate how to apply these tools, we focus on single barrier knock-out options. The reader can then extend the developments of this chapter to other types of exotic options. The general topic of nonconstant volatility breaks down into three main categories: volatility curves, volatility smiles, and stochastic volatility. This chapter will cover only the first two categories since, due to its complexity, the third category merits a book of its own.

A NUMERICAL EXAMPLE

Before developing any barrier-option pricing techniques, it will be helpful to consider a numerical example, both to form a reference point for discussion and to motivate the pricing techniques developed in this chapter. The example to be used is from Boyle & Lau [1994] and is based on the standard, constant parameter, lognormally distributed asset price process. Boyle & Lau use this example to document the significant numerical problems that are encountered when using a binomial tree to price barrier options. We shall review the results of Boyle & Lau, develop a numerically stable pricing method, and demonstrate the effect volatility curves can have on barrier-option pricing.

In the Boyle & Lau example, the asset price follows a lognormal distribution, the initial asset price equals 95, the barrier level equals 90, the strike price equals 100, the continuously compounded interest rate equals 10 percent, the volatility equals 25 percent, and the maturity equals one year. There are no dividends or cash payouts by the asset. Table 12–1 contains the results for a down-and-out call option using the analytic formulas available in the standard economy. These formulas are discussed in an earlier chapter in this book.

Notice that the delta of the down-and-out call exceeds 1.0. To gain intuition for this result, recall that an option's delta measures the change

TABLE 12–1
Standard Case

Parameter	*Value*
Asset Price	95
Strike Price	100
Barrier Level	90
Interest Rate	10%
Volatility	25%
Maturity	1 year
Down-and-Out Call	$5.9968
Delta	1.120

in the option's price for a small change in the price of the underlying asset. In the example, a small increase (decrease) in the asset price not only increases (decreases) the chances of finishing in-the-money, but it greatly decreases (increases) the probability of the asset price reaching the knock-out barrier. These two effects combine to make the down-and-out call option, at the above parameter values, very sensitive to movements in the spot asset price.[1]

To illustrate the impact of a volatility curve on barrier-option prices, consider two variations of the above example: (1) an increasing volatility curve, and (2) a decreasing volatility curve. In both cases, the average *variance* over the life of the option (i.e., the term volatility) will be kept at 25 percent. For the first case, let the variance start at half its average and increase linearly to 1.5 times its average. This approach results in the standard deviation increasing from a low of 17.7 percent to a high of 30.6 percent. To price this option, the trinomial-based technique described in the next section will be used. Table 12–2 contains the increasing volatility curve results.

Notice that while the delta has increased only slightly, the price of the knock-out call option has increased substantially (nearly $0.46) even

[1]In addition, delta is not a continuous function of the asset price. Clearly, once the asset reaches the barrier, delta equals zero, since the option is knocked out. However, as we approach the barrier from above, delta will not converge to zero, but rather to a value strictly greater than zero. In the example, delta approaches a value near 1.28 as we near the barrier.

TABLE 12–2
Increasing Volatility Curve

Parameter	*Value*
Asset Price	95
Strike Price	100
Barrier Level	90
Interest Rate	10%
Initial Volatility	17.7%
Ending Volatility	30.6%
Term Volatility	25%
Maturity	1 year
Down-and-Out Call	$6.4556
Delta[2]	1.146

though the average variance equaled that of the constant-parameter case—i.e., a term volatility of 25.0 percent. An interesting aspect of the $6.4556 price for the knock-out call is that this price is greater than the price from the constant-parameter formula *for any level of volatility*. To demonstrate this, Table 12–3 contains the values for the constant-parameter model for different levels of volatility.

As Table 12–3 illustrates, the value of the knock-out option reaches a maximum value of $6.11 for volatilities in the range of 16 percent to 17 percent. This value is more than $0.34 below the value obtained from the increasing volatility curve example above. Using the 25 percent volatility's value of $5.9968, the underpricing resulting from not incorporating the volatility curve equates to a 7.65 percent pricing error. Moreover, at no volatility level in Table 12–3 does the constant-parameter-based delta equal the true delta.

Next, consider a decreasing volatility curve by letting the variance start at 1.5 times its average and decrease to half its average. As this case mirrors the increasing-volatility example, the volatility will start at a high of 30.6 percent and decrease to a low of 17.7 percent, with a term volatility of 25.0 percent. Again, we will use the trinomial technique

[2]Delta is computed by standard methods from inside the trinomial tree described in Section III.

TABLE 12–3
Constant-Parameter Model

Volatility	*Down-and-Out Call*	*Delta*
10.00%	5.8524	0.907
15.00%	6.1025	1.041
16.00%	6.1093	1.058
16.25%	6.1100	1.062
16.50%	6.1101	1.065
16.75%	6.1099	1.069
17.00%	6.1094	1.072
20.00%	6.0816	1.100
25.00%	5.9968	1.120
30.00%	5.9067	1.124
35.00%	5.8229	1.117

TABLE 12–4
Decreasing Volatility Curve

Parameter	*Value*
Asset Price	95
Strike Price	100
Barrier Level	90
Interest Rate	10%
Initial Volatility	30.6%
Ending Volatility	17.7%
Term Volatility	25%
Maturity	1 year
Down-and-Out Call	$5.7286
Delta	1.093

described in the next section to price this option. Table 12–4 contains these results.

Table 12–4 demonstrates that a decreasing volatility curve results in a lower value for the knock-out option. Because this value is lower than the maximal constant-parameter price of $6.11, there exists a volatility level at which the constant-parameter formula would give a correct price. From Table 12–3, we can see that this would be a volatility level either below 10.00 percent or above 35.00 percent; both values are far from the 25.00 percent term volatility. For this example, in fact, there are two volatility levels that give this price: 9.00 percent and 41.75 percent. However, the deltas at these two volatilities are quite different, 0.873 and 1.115, respectively.

The results in Tables 12–2 and 12–4, though perhaps surprising, have a very intuitive explanation. In all of the examples, the asset is "drifting" toward the forward price and *away from the barrier*. In the increasing-volatility-curve example, volatility is being moved away from when the asset is, on average, closer to the barrier to when the asset is further away. The lower initial volatility allows the asset to more closely follow its drift and move away from the barrier, thereby reducing the chance of knocking out. The increased volatility near the maturity of the option allows the option a greater chance to finish deep in-the-money at only a moderate increase in the chance of knocking out. In the decreasing-volatility-curve example, the intuitive arguments are the same, but the results are the opposite because we incur the highest volatility when the asset is, on average, nearest to the barrier. This has the effect of increasing the chances of knocking out relative to the constant volatility case, thereby reducing the option's value.

While the numerical example only considered an option that knocked out when it was out-of-the-money, it is also common in today's financial markets to observe knock-out options that knock out when the option is in-the-money. We obtain such an option, for example, by changing the barrier from 90 to 140. For such an option, an increasing (decreasing) volatility curve would decrease (increase) the option's value. As before, shifting volatility to when the asset is close to (far from) the barrier increases (decreases) the likelihood of reaching the knock-out barrier, thereby decreasing (increasing) the option's value.

To demonstrate this, Table 12–5 presents the constant parameter results for a 140-barrier knock-out option against which we can compare the results for the increasing and decreasing volatility curves. Table 12–6 presents the results for the increasing volatility curve, and Table 12–7 shows the results for the decreasing volatility curve.

As Tables 12–6 and 12–7 illustrate, the presence of a volatility curve can significantly affect barrier-option prices when the barrier is in-the-money. Unlike the increasing volatility curve example in Table 12–2, however, there do exist volatility levels for the constant-parameter

TABLE 12–5
Constant-Parameter Model

Parameter	*Value*
Asset Price	95
Strike Price	100
Barrier Level	140
Interest Rate	10%
Volatility	25%
Maturity	1 year
Knock-out Call Option	4.3325
Delta	0.0751

TABLE 12–6
Increasing Volatility Curve

Parameter	*Value*
Asset Price	95
Strike Price	100
Barrier Level	140
Interest Rate	10%
Initial Volatility	17.7%
Ending Volatility	30.6%
Term Volatility	25%
Maturity	1 year
Knock-out Call Option	$4.2157
Delta	0.0675

formula that match the prices in both Tables 12–6 and 12–7. The decreasing-volatility-curve option price of $4.5009 can be matched by using a constant volatility level near 24.30 percent, and the increasing-volatility-curve value of $4.2157 can be matched by a volatility near 25.50 percent. The fact that these two "implied volatilities" are both near the original term volatility of 25.00 percent illustrates that such knock-out options often possess a large amount of vega risk.

TABLE 12–7
Decreasing Volatility Curve

Parameter	*Value*
Asset Price	95
Strike Price	100
Barrier Level	140
Interest Rate	10%
Initial Volatility	30.6%
Ending Volatility	17.7%
Term Volatility	25%
Maturity	1 year
Knock-out Call Option	$4.5009
Delta	0.0845

A TRINOMIAL TREE APPROACH

To motivate the trinomial tree approach, let's first review the work of Boyle & Lau on pricing barrier options with binomial trees. Boyle & Lau demonstrate that in order to accurately measure the probability of hitting a barrier, the tree must have two properties: (1) an "up" move followed by a "down" move (and vice versa) must end up back at the initial value (i.e., a layered tree); and (2) a layer of nodes must fall right on the value of the barrier. Models without these two properties will be inefficient and/or systematically overprice knock-out options due to systematically underestimating the probability of hitting the knock-out barrier.

While it is easy to construct binomial trees that satisfy property (1), property (2) cannot be guaranteed for arbitrarily sized binomial trees. In effect, we cannot always choose the up or down move size such that a layer of nodes falls exactly on the barrier. We simply do not have enough degrees of freedom to accomplish this in a binomial model, for we must match the mean at all times and match the variance at least in the limit. In binomial models, the sizes of the up and down moves are determined once given the volatility and the number of time partitions. Thus, for any given problem, a layer of nodes will fall on the barrier only for

TABLE 12–8
Constant-Parameter Case—Binomial Tree

Time Partitions	*Binomial Down & Out Call*
50	7.2405
75	6.3001
100	7.5045
150	6.5612
200	7.2307
400	6.6505
800	6.6040
1000	6.1002
2000	6.1449
3000	6.0542
4000	6.0998
True Value	**5.9968**

certain numbers of time partitions. Boyle & Lau also establish that the convergence of the binomial price to the true price occurs at an extremely slow rate. So slow, in fact, that simply increasing the number of time steps cannot guarantee accurate pricing. Table 12–8 reproduces Boyle & Lau's binomial tree pricing results for the example from Section II.

As Table 12–8 clearly illustrates, standard binomial trees are not well suited to pricing barrier options. Such trees systematically overestimate the price of knock-out options, converge slowly, and are so unstable that hedge ratios from such a model are very unreliable. Essentially, layered trees—be they binomial, trinomial, or multinomial—will accurately price only those barrier options whose barrier level coincides with one of the layers in the tree.[3] Unfortunately, binomial trees lack the flexibility

[3]Such a result suggests pursuing interpolation schemes based on the prices of barrier options with barriers at the node levels just above and below the desired barrier level. While such approaches do drastically reduce the instability problems exhibited in Table 12–5, they are not as flexible as the trinomial method considered in this chapter.

necessary to construct properly layered trees for arbitrary barrier levels and arbitrary numbers of time partitions.

Noticing the lack of flexibility in the binomial tree, Ritchken [1995] attacked the barrier-option problem using a trinomial tree approach. In trinomial trees, one has the flexibility to adjust the magnitude of the "up" and "down" moves so as to hit the barrier level exactly for any sized tree, and by suitably adjusting the probabilities, one can also match both the mean and variance. To add additional accuracy to this approach for the purpose of pricing standard barrier options, the "middle" node in the tree can be restricted to be a "flat" move, i.e., a move to a node with the same asset price. This creates an additional layered feature to the tree beyond just requiring that up moves followed by down moves (and vice versa) return the initial value. With the middle move restriction, an equal amount of up and down moves together with any number of middle moves gives the initial value.

To describe this approach, we need some notation; let *S(t)* denote the date "t" value of a lognormally distributed asset price with a constant mean and variance, and let B denote the barrier. To simplify the matching of the mean and variance, we will construct the tree on the natural logarithm of the asset price, which, by definition, is normally distributed. To continue defining the necessary notation, let h be the magnitude of the up and down moves and let the middle move be zero, and p_u, p_m, p_d be the probabilities of the up, middle, and down moves, respectively. This notation leads to:

$$\ln(S(t+\Delta t)) = \begin{cases} \ln(S(t)) + h & \textit{with prob } p_u \\ \ln(S(t)) & \textit{with prob } p_m \\ \ln(S(t)) - h & \textit{with prob } p_d \end{cases} \tag{1}$$

$$h = \lambda\sigma\sqrt{\Delta t} \tag{2}$$

$$\lambda = \frac{\eta}{\mathrm{int}(\eta)} \tag{3}$$

$$\eta = \frac{\ln(S(0)\,/\,B)}{\sigma\sqrt{\Delta t}} \tag{4}$$

The term int(x) denotes the integer truncation of "x." The parameter lambda is termed the "stretch parameter" as: (1) lambda is $\geq$ 1.0 and

(2) lambda increases, or stretches, the up and down move size so as to make the tree reach the barrier level exactly. With the above choice for "h," the minimum number of steps needed to reach the barrier equals $|\text{int}(\eta)|$.

By "stretching" both the up and down moves, a layered tree with a layer of nodes on the barrier is constructed. Moreover, by adjusting the stretch parameter, properly layered trees can be constructed for any number of time partitions greater than the minimum needed.[4] By adjusting the trinomial probabilities accordingly, the mean and variance are also matched exactly.

Equations (1) to (4) govern the basic setup when the volatility of the asset is constant over the life of the option. Before presenting the equations governing the trinomial probabilities, it is beneficial to generalize the tree to one that allows for a deterministic volatility curve. To do this, rewrite (2) as:

$$h = \lambda \overline{\sigma} \sqrt{\Delta t} \tag{2'}$$

where

$$\overline{\sigma} = \max_t \sigma(t)$$

By having the up and down move-size be determined by the largest "local volatility" over the life of the option, $\overline{\sigma}$, the trinomial tree can match the highest level of volatility that occurs. If the move sizes were determined by the value of the term volatility, for example, the tree might not be able to match the highest local volatility over the life of the option. The cost of the choice in (2′) is that it is possible that the tree cannot match very low values of the local volatility: for any choice of move sizes, there exist upper and lower volatility levels that the tree cannot match by varying the probabilities. The choice in (2′) helps to solve the upper-bound problem, but, to an extent, makes the lower-bound problem worse. However, with a trinomial tree, the branch farthest from the mean can always be set equal to zero to aid in matching a low volatility level.

---

[4]The minimum number of steps needed is calculated as that needed to reach the barrier in one up or down move when we restrict λ to equal 1.0.

To complete the model, let $\mu(t)$ and $\nu(t)$ equal the time "t" mean and variance of the logarithm of the asset, respectively. To match these values exactly in the trinomial tree, set:

$$p_u = p_d + \mu(t)\Delta t \tag{5}$$

$$p_m = 1 - p_u - p_d \tag{6}$$

$$p_d = .5 * \left[\frac{(\mu(t)\Delta t)^2 + \nu(t)\Delta t}{h^2} - \frac{\mu(t)\Delta t}{h}\right] \tag{7}$$

Since the values for the mean and variance, $\mu(t)$ and $\nu(t)$, are allowed to change over time, the trinomial tree approach has its probabilities changing through time. This gives the tree the ability to price barrier options in the presence of both forward-price curves and volatility curves. This allows the tree to, for example, match a term structure of forward exchange rates and the corresponding standard option volatility curve. With equations (1) to (7), the trinomial tree used to generate the numerical examples in the second section of this chapter can be reconstructed.[5]

To complete the discussion of the trinomial model above, again consider the basic example from Boyle & Lau and the problems of the binomial tree as demonstrated in Table 12–8. Table 12–9 contains the results for the above trinomial tree approach for the constant parameter case. Table 12–9 also compares these results with those of the binomial tree results in Table 12–8.

As Table 12–9 clearly demonstrates, the trinomial-based barrier option pricing technique accurately and efficiently prices the down-and-out call option for all time partitions and produces option deltas that are both stable and accurate. Although only partially illustrated by Table 12–6, the trinomial technique is most accurate for small values of the stretch parameter; the slight mispricing for 75 and 100 time partitions illustrates this point. The large degree of stretching at these time-partition values causes relatively little probability mass to be associated with the up and down moves and more mass to be allocated to the middle move. This

[5]See Brenner [1995] for a more detailed discussion of this technique, its limitations, the constraints imposed by nonnegative probabilities, its application to other types of barrier options, and its generalization to stochastic volatility option pricing.

TABLE 12–9
Constant-Parameter Case

No. of Time Partitions	*Stretch Parameter*	*Trinomial Down & Out*	*Trinomial-Based Deltas*	*Binomial Down & Out*
50	1.32437	5.9955	1.1290	7.2405
75	1.62202	5.9908	1.1283	6.3001
100	1.87294	5.9884	1.1279	7.5045
150	1.14694	5.9981	1.1219	6.5612
200	1.32437	5.9969	1.1217	7.2307
400	1.24863	5.9972	1.1204	6.6505
800	1.05950	5.9973	1.1197	6.6040
1000	1.18455	5.9971	1.1197	6.1002
2000	1.04701	5.9971	1.1194	6.1449
3000	1.02585	5.9970	1.1193	6.0542
4000	1.07687	5.9970	1.1193	6.0998
True Value		**5.9968**	**1.1192**	**5.9968**

leads to an inefficiency in the trinomial tree. Pricing efficiency in any tree-based technique generally requires that the tree match as many moments as possible. While one can match the first four moments in a generic trinomial tree, the introduction of the stretch parameter together with a no change middle move results in the tree generally only matching the first two moments.

The second section of this chapter illustrated how a term structure of volatility can have a significant effect on the pricing of barrier options, and this section demonstrated how to construct a simple trinomial tree to incorporate a volatility term structure into the pricing of barrier options. Implicit in that discussion was the assumption that volatility did not vary across options with different strikes that mature on the same date. The next two sections explore relaxing this assumption.

THE VOLATILITY SMILE

The volatility smile refers to the fact that the implied volatilities for standard options at either in-the-money (ITM) or out-of-the-money (OTM) strikes typically exceed the implied volatility for the at-the-money

TABLE 12–10
Implied Volatility Curve

Strike\Maturity	*1-Month*	*3-Month*	*6-Month*	*12-Month*
.25 Delta Call	14.6%	14.1%	13.4%	13.0%
ATM Forward	14.8%	14.1%	13.4%	12.9%
.25 Delta Put	15.6%	14.7%	13.7%	13.2%

(ATM) option. In many option markets, the volatility smile resembles more of a "smirk," or "skew," as only the implied volatilities of either the ITM or OTM strikes significantly exceed the ATM implied volatility. In equity markets, for example, the implied volatilities for OTM puts (post Oct. 1987) are much higher than the ATM implied volatility, while the implied volatility for the ITM puts is only marginally higher. Essentially, the market assesses a much higher probability of large drops in equity values relative to the Black-Scholes model. In currency option markets, a smile generally prevails, but smirks, or skews, of all types and magnitudes are observed. To simplify the exposition, the term "volatility smile" will hereafter be used to collectively refer to all of the possible types of smiles, smirks, and skews.

Table 12–10 contains a snapshot of the volatility curve for dollar/mark currency options on June 12, 1995. Notice that the strikes of the OTM options are not quoted directly, but indirectly in terms of the Black-Scholes delta of the associated option. This is a common practice in currency option markets. Also, ATM options in this market are defined with respect to the forward exchange rate instead of the spot exchange rate. As is typical in option markets, the volatility curve in Table 12–10 possesses different types of smile patterns across maturity dates. For one-month options, the volatility curve is highly skewed toward a drop in the exchange rate: the OTM put volatility is considerably higher than the ATM volatility, while the OTM call volatility is slightly lower. For both the three- and six-month horizons, this general pattern persists, but it is not as pronounced: the OTM call has the same implied volatility as the ATM options. Finally, at the one-year horizon, we see the classic smile effect emerging, with the implied volatilities of both the OTM call and the OTM put exceeding the ATM value.

At this point, it is helpful to further differentiate volatility curves from volatility smiles in terms of their consistency with a Merton, or Black-Scholes, type economy. Volatility curves are consistent with a slightly generalized version of such an economy if we allow the volatility of the lognormal price process to change deterministically through time. However, assuming an efficient options market, volatility smiles exist because the true distribution of the asset price differs from the lognormal process assumed by the Black-Scholes model—e.g., one, or both, of the tails of the true distribution contain a greater amount of probability mass than a lognormal distribution. Thus, the numerous analytic exotic option formulas derived under the lognormally distributed asset assumption will give incorrect prices and hedge ratios. The question is, how bad are these prices and hedge ratios? For standard options, traders can adjust the volatility parameter and obtain accurate prices and hedge ratios. However, as we saw in the second section of this chapter, such ad hoc adjustments will not always work for barrier options. The third section presented a simple method that allows for the accurate pricing and hedging of barrier options in the presence of a term structure of volatility. To incorporate a volatility smile, though, we must generalize this technique.

As is often the case in option pricing, there is more than one way to incorporate observed anomalies like volatility smiles. Some have proposed matching the smile observed in equities by using different asset-price distributions, such as the constant elasticity of variance (CEV) process of Cox & Ross [1976]. Others have proposed models, such as stochastic volatility and jump-diffusion models, that possess a second source of randomness. The relatively simple approach we will take concerns generalizing the volatility process to one whose functional dependence on the level of the asset price can change; the functional form of how the volatility depends on the level of the asset will be derived so as to fit the volatility smile. Alternatively stated, we will assume that the volatility smile is generated solely due to changes in the level of the asset price and time. Thus, we will assume that the volatility smile can be explained by a "flexible" one-factor model. Therefore, we can still perfectly hedge options with only the asset and a riskless bond. While at first this may sound appealing, the proper way to evaluate such an assumption is by examining the data. If the data reject such an assumption, then exotic option prices and hedge ratios based on such a model will be incorrect.

In equity markets, the time-varying, level-dependent volatility assumption does have some support: as stock prices fall, return volatility, on the average, increases, while return volatility typically decreases when stock prices rise. This is termed the "leverage effect" as drops in stock prices increase the leverage effect of a firm's debt, thereby increasing the volatility of future stock returns. Moreover, such an effect is nonlinear in nature and does not always lend itself to simple approximations like the CEV process. As such, the leverage effect in equity markets provides a theoretical basis for our volatility process assumption. In interest-rate markets, we also see level-dependent volatility: higher interest rate levels lead, on average, to higher volatility levels. While both of these markets do exhibit a degree of level dependence, it is still an open question whether a volatility process with only level dependence and some deterministic component can adequately explain the observed volatility behavior of either equities or interest rates.

Ait-Sahalia [1994] nonparametrically estimated a level-only dependent process for the short-term interest rate and produced results that lead one to doubt such a specification. Because Ait-Sahalia was restricted to a time-invariant process, it is important to ask whether some form of time variation would significantly change his results. Brenner, Harjes, & Kroner (BHK) [1995] partially answer this question. They demonstrate that while level dependence is an important component of short-term interest-rate volatility, the time variation of the volatility's scale parameter is an equally (if not more) important explanatory factor. BHK's results suggest that one-factor models may be inadequate to match the observed interest-rate dynamics that lead to the volatility smile; their results suggest that a stochastic volatility model would provide a better description. In sum, the appropriateness of the one-factor model assumption depends on whether a one-factor process generates the observed smile or whether inferring such a model from the smile constitutes model overfitting, i.e., making a one-factor model consistent with a set of option prices that are actually generated by a multiple-factor process.

While such flexible, one-factor, level-dependent models have at least some theoretical and empirical basis in equity and, perhaps, interest-rate markets, it is hard to argue for such extremely flexible forms in foreign exchange markets. The natural symmetry that exists in foreign exchange markets (we can quote any exchange rate as either domestic currency per foreign currency or foreign per domestic) implies that the volatility dynamics of an exchange rate and its reciprocal must have the same dependence upon level. Unfortunately, there is no guarantee that the implied tree technique would satisfy such a requirement. Thus, the techniques in the next section, if used, are best restricted to markets like equities, where there exists at least some theoretical and empirical support, and not applied to interest-rate and currency markets except with caution. The great danger in using implied trees lies not in the pricing of a book of standard options relative to the set of observed vanilla option prices, but in the pricing and hedging of exotic options. Exotic options by their nature amplify certain aspects of an asset's price generating process, thereby greatly increasing the potential problems caused by incorrect model assumptions.

INCORPORATING THE SMILE WITH A TRINOMIAL TREE

Before discussing how to generalize the trinomial tree described in the third section of this chapter, it is helpful to discuss the more prevalent implied binomial trees recently put forth by Rubinstein [1994] and Derman & Kani [1994]. The basic idea in these papers is that in order to build a binomial tree that has a flexible, level-dependent volatility process, the usual construction of the tree needs to be generalized so as to provide more degrees of freedom. As binomial trees have few components, the only tools available consist of letting the probabilities vary throughout the tree and choosing the placement of the nodes in a convenient way. Rubinstein and Derman & Kani, by drawing upon recent developments in tree design used for the matching of interest-rate curves and their volatilities, provide two related approaches.

Rubinstein's approach uses the usual up and down move sizes, but allows the binomial probabilities to be time and node dependent, i.e., the probabilities of up and down moves are allowed to differ across time steps and across asset values. Such flexibility allows for the construction of a probability structure (i.e., a volatility process) that generates a volatility smile for a given maturity date. Derman & Kani slightly relax the usual move-size assumption (i.e., node placement) to introduce extra degrees of freedom. While Rubinstein focuses on the volatility smile for only one date in the future, Derman & Kani focus on matching an entire sequence of volatility smiles, i.e., a volatility curve across both maturities and strikes. Derman & Kani follow a forward construction technique similar to that used by Black, Derman, & Toy [1990] to construct interest-rate trees consistent with an initial term structure. *As both of these approaches are binomial, they will suffer from the instability problems documented by Boyle & Lau for barrier-option pricing: neither approach can guarantee that a layer of nodes will lie on the barrier for all partition sizes.* (There may exist some variations of these techniques that place a layer of nodes on the barrier and only "approximately" match all the option volatilities.) In spite of this drawback, the methods of Rubinstein and Derman & Kani are still useful, such as in the consistent pricing of an entire book of standard options.

By using the trinomial tree to incorporate a term structure of volatility across both the maturity and strike dimensions instead of the binomial trees of Rubinstein or Derman & Kani, we gain the advantage of always having a layer of nodes on the barrier. For the specifics of incorporating the smile into the trinomial tree, we will follow the approach outlined by Dupire [1994].

Arrow-Debreu Prices

To begin matching a term structure of volatility smiles, European option prices are needed with strike prices equal to all the possible spot asset values and maturities corresponding to the time steps in the tree. Obviously, this entails more option prices than are regularly quoted in the market. To create the required number of option prices, a large number of "synthetic" option prices will be created by interpolating the observed implied volatilities across both strike prices and maturity dates.

Once this set of option prices is computed, the value of the volatility process at each node in the tree can be derived. In practice, however, this is not done, but rather the associated "Arrow-Debreu prices" are computed. Arrow-Debreu (AD) prices are the price today of a very simple security; a security that pays off $1 if a certain node in the tree is reached and $0 otherwise. Such securities form the ultimate set of building blocks for pricing derivatives. The payoffs to all securities, like options, are a linear combination of different AD securities, making security prices just a linear combination of AD prices. Implicit in the price of each AD security is the value of the volatility process; in effect, the volatility process that gives the observed smiles determines the AD prices. Solving for the AD prices is attractive for two reasons. First, established techniques for finding AD prices can be drawn upon.[6] Second, AD prices provide the ability to rapidly price barrier options of different maturities, barrier levels, and strike prices without the need to construct additional trinomial trees. While the recovery of the AD prices constitutes a nontrivial computational cost, it does constitute an efficient method for pricing an entire book of options.

Since the AD prices depend on both the time step and the node, let AD(n,i) equal the AD price for the ith node at the nth time step, where "i" equals the number of up moves minus the number of down moves required to reach a given node. As the notation indicates, at each time step "n" in the trinomial tree, we will need to solve for 2n+1 AD prices, since recombining trinomial trees have 2n+1 nodes at the nth time step. This requires 2n+1 security prices at the nth time step.[7] To illustrate the general method, consider 2n European calls and one European put. The 2n European calls will have strikes that correspond to the value of the asset at each node except the topmost node. The one European put will have a strike equal to the next-to-lowest node value. To complete the notation for this section, let C(n,i) denote the time-zero call price for an option maturing at the nth time step with a strike equal to the asset value at the ith node; let P(n,i) equal the corresponding European put price; let CCF(n,i,j) equal the time step "n," node "i" cash flow associated with the call option with a strike equal to the asset value at node "j"; and let PCF(n,i,j) equal the corresponding put option cash flow. Using this set of options and the expiration day cash flows to each option, the required AD prices can be obtained.

To accomplish this task, proceed *forward* through the tree according to the following algorithm:

1. For the AD price at the top node, AD(n,n), use the AD pricing formula for C(n,n−1). As this option has zero cash flows at all the other nodes, the option value will equal the AD price for this node times the expiration-day cash flow to the option at this node, i.e., AD(n,i) solves C(n,n−1) = AD(n,n) ∗ CCF(n,n,n−1).

[6] See Jamshidian [1991] for a detailed description of the forward induction algorithm used to recover AD prices. This algorithm is commonly used to make spot-rate-based interest-rate models—such as that of Black, Derman, & Toy—consistent with an observed zero-coupon curve.

[7] Not all securities need to be options. In general, one uses the prices of zero-coupon bonds as well.

2. For the AD price at the bottom node, AD(n,−n), use P(n,−n+1), i.e., AD(n,−n) solves P(n,−n+1) = AD(n,−n) * PCF(n,−n,−n+1).
3. Start with node j = (n−1) and proceed sequentially downward to node j = (−n+1). At each node "j," use the value of C(n,j−1) to find AD(n,j). This option will have its value determined by the AD prices and cash flows at the "n−j" nodes above this node in the tree. Since the AD prices are known for each of these "n−j" nodes, the problem reduces to one equation, the AD pricing equation, and one unknown, AD(n,j).

Computing the Probabilities

Given a set of AD prices, the interest rate, and the trinomial tree, the necessary transition probabilities can be recovered. In general, these probabilities will depend on both time and the asset value. Accordingly, new notation needs to be defined for the probabilities, accounting for the time step and the net number of up and down moves. Let $p(n,i,j)$, $j \in \{i - 1, i, i + 1\}$, be the probability of moving from the ith state at time step "n" to the jth state at time step "n+1." Also let $pvf(n)$ be the time-dependent, one time step, present value factor for time step "n" i.e., $pvf(n) = \exp\{-r_n * \Delta t\}$.

To recover the trinomial probabilities, a few basic relationships are used. The first concerns the relationship between AD prices, discount factors, and "risk-neutral" probabilities: the AD price for a given node equals the risk-neutral probability of reaching that node times the discount factor from time zero to that node. The second, known as the "forward equation," is the cousin to the familiar "backward equation" used to price options: the option value at a node is computed by taking a discounted expected value of the values at the nodes one time step ahead. To implement the forward-equation-based procedure, proceed forward through the tree and work on the AD prices in a fashion that resembles a tree in "reverse": time step "n" AD values are used to determine the time step "n+1" value. In the above notation, the forward equation for a trinomial tree equals:

$$\begin{aligned} AD(n + 1,i) = pvf(n) * [&p(n,i - 1,i) * AD(n,i - 1) \\ &+ p(n,i,i) * AD(n,i) \\ &+ p(n,i + 1,i) * AD(n,i + 1)] \end{aligned} \tag{8}$$

FIGURE 12–1

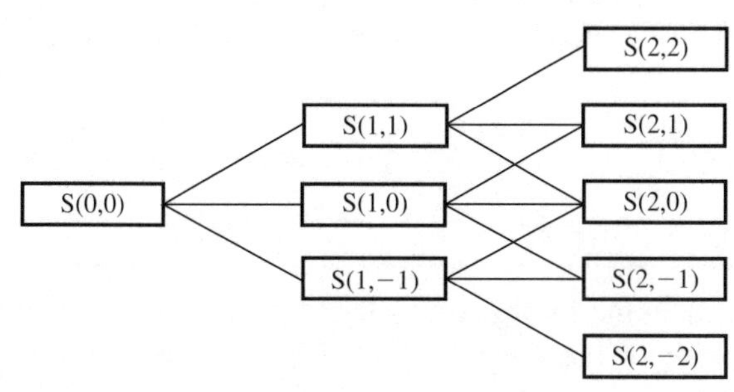

To demonstrate the general algorithm, consider a simple two-step trinomial tree. Figure 12–1 illustrates such a tree, where S(n,i) indicates the asset price at node "i" and time step "n." Use the relationship between AD prices and risk-neutral probabilities to recover the transition probabilities for the first time step; take the AD price at each of the three nodes at the first time step and divide them by the one-time-step discount factor. Thus, the probability of the first down-move is calculated as $p(0,0,-1) = AD(1,-1) / pvf(0)$. Proceeding likewise for the middle and upper nodes gives us $p(0,0,0)$ and $p(0,0,1)$. (See Figure 12–1.)

Given these three probabilities, the probabilities for the next time step can be recovered. The probability of the lowest branch, $p(1,-1,-2)$, is obtained by solving $p(1,-1,-2) = AD(2,-2) / (AD(1,-1)\,^{*}pvf(1))$. To obtain the other probabilities from S(−1,−1), i.e., $p(1,-1,-1)$ and $p(1,-1,0)$, use the fact that these conditional probabilities must sum to 1.0 and that the expected return on the asset must equal the risk-free rate. This forms a system of two equations and two unknowns, allowing us to recover $p(1,-1,-1)$ and $p(1,-1,0)$.

Next, use the forward equation for node S(2,−1) to recover the down-move probability, i.e., $AD(2,-1)$ is a discounted expected value of AD(1,−1) and $AD(1,0)$, and the values of all the necessary variables are known except $p(1,0,-1)$. The remaining two conditional probabilities, $p(1,0,0)$ and $p(1,0,1)$, can be found as the solutions to the same system of two equations and two unknowns as above, but instead emanating from S(1,0). To recover the down-move probability from S(1,1), $p(1,1,0)$, use the forward equation in (8) with the now known values of $AD(2,0)$, $AD(1,-1)$, $AD(1,0)$, $AD(1,1)$, $p(1,-1,0)$, and $p(1,0,0)$. To recover the last two probabilities, use the two-equation, two-unknown procedure as before. By proceeding in a like manner, all of the transition probabilities can be recovered for trinomial trees of any size.

CONCLUSION

This chapter documents the importance of relaxing the constant volatility assumption of the Black & Scholes economy for the purposes of pricing barrier options. For knock-out options where the barrier is out-of-the-money, it was established that the presence of a volatility curve can result in the true price of the option exceeding the maximal value from the constant-parameter knock-out option formula. Moreover, it was demonstrated that the constant-parameter formula can produce significantly different deltas even when matching prices. It was also determined that volatility curves can significantly affect the prices of knock-outs with in-the-money barriers. To incorporate the volatility curves, a trinomial-based pricing technique for knock-out options was developed that produced both accurate prices and deltas. Finally, one possible generalization of the trinomial technique was discussed that would allow it to match the entire volatility smile.

REFERENCES

1. Ait-Sahalia, 1994, "Nonparametric Pricing of Interest Rate Derivative Securities," Unpublished Working Paper, University of Chicago.

2. Black, F., and M. Scholes, 1973, "The Pricing of Options and Corporate Liabilities," *Journal of Political Economy*, 3, pp. 637–654.

3. Black, F., E. Derman, and W. Toy, 1990, "A One Factor Model of Interest Rates and Its Application to Treasury Bond Options," *Financial Analysts Journal*, January-February, pp. 33–39.

4. Boyle, P., and S. Lau, 1994, "Bumping up Against the Barrier with the Binomial Method," *Journal of Derivatives,* 1 (4), pp. 6–14.

5. Brenner, R., 1995, "Pricing Barrier Options with Deterministic and Stochastic Volatility Curves," Unpublished Manuscript, Trading Research Group, Merrill Lynch.

6. Brenner, R., R. Harjes, and K. Kroner, 1995, "Another Look at Alternative Models of the Short-Term Interest Rate," *Journal of Financial and Quantitative Analysis*, Forthcoming.

7. Cox, J., and S. Ross, 1976, "The Valuation of Options for Alternative Stochastic Processes," *Journal of Financial Economics,* 3, pp. 145–166.

8. Derman, E., and I. Kani, 1994, "The Volatility Smile and Its Implied Tree," Quantitative Strategies Research Notes, Goldman Sachs.

9. Dupire, B., 1993, "Pricing and Hedging with Smiles," Paribas Capital Markets.

10. Heath, D., R. Jarrow, and A. Morton, 1992, "Bond Pricing and the Term Structure of Interest Rates; A New Methodology," *Econometrica,* 60, pp. 77–105.

11. Ho, T., and S. Lee, 1986, "Term Structure Movements and Pricing Interest Rate Contingent Claims," *Journal of Finance*, 41, pp. 1011–1029.

12. Jamshidian, F., 1991, "Forward Induction and Construction of Yield Curve Diffusion Models," *Journal of Fixed Income,* 1, pp. 62–74.

13. Merton, R., 1973, "The Theory of Rational Option Pricing," *Bell Journal of Economics and Management Science*, 4, pp. 141–183.

14. Ritchken, P., 1995, "On Pricing Barrier Options," *Journal of Derivatives*, Forthcoming.

15. Rubinstein, M., 1994, "Implied Binomial Trees," *Journal of Finance*, 69 (3), pp. 771–818.

Chapter Thirteen

Valuation of Exotic Options Using the Monte Carlo Method*

By Phelim P. Boyle
Director,
Centre for Advanced Studies in France, University of Waterloo

INTRODUCTION

In recent years the complexity of exotic options has increased enormously, putting more demands on computational speed and efficiency. Monte Carlo methods have proven to be a very useful tool in the valuation of these securities. These methods are also useful in computing the sensitivities of a particular security to various underlying parameters. The Monte Carlo method is attractive because it is usually simple to set up and is very flexible. As exotic options have become more intricate, this is an important advantage. The ever increasing efficiency of computers adds to the attraction of the method. For an overview of recent advances in the application of Monte Carlo methods in finance, see Boyle, Broadie and Glasserman (1995). The purpose of this chapter is to describe the use of the Monte Carlo method in two specific examples that concern the valuation of exotic options. We will use the second example to describe a recent development that leads to an increase in efficiency.

The advantages of the Monte Carlo method include its power and flexibility. The method does have some disadvantages but researchers have made progress in overcoming them. Some exotic options such as

*The author thanks Xiaolin Gu for research assistance and Ken Seng Tan for useful discussions on these topics.

mortgage-backed securities are still cumbersome to calculate under standard Monte Carlo methods. To speed up the convergence, a variety of variance reduction techniques are used. The efficiency of a particular technique depends on the particular problem. Two of the classical variance reduction techniques are the control variate approach and the antithetic variate method. More recently, importance sampling and quadratic resampling methods have been used to value exotic options. In this chapter we will describe the use of a new method based on low discrepancy sequences. This approach is sometimes called quasi-random Monte Carlo.

Until recently, the conventional wisdom was that American-style options could not be valued using the Monte Carlo approach. However Tilley (1993), Grant, et al. (1993), Barraquand and Martineau (1994) Broadie and Glasserman (1995), and Dennis and Rendleman (1995) have all proposed solutions to this problem. Another potential drawback of the standard Monte Carlo method is that the error estimate is probabilistic. In some situations this could be a concern. In standard Monte Carlo simulations the numbers generated by the computer are pseudo-random. This gives rise to the philosophical issue[1] of whether these pseudo-random numbers are truly "random."

In this chapter, we illustrate the flexibility of the Monte Carlo approach by valuing a specific exotic option contract that has some non-standard features. This is an average-price put option based on oil, with the following features. First there is a nonconstant convenience yield, and second the volatility is nonconstant over the contract's life. This contract was issued in mid-January 1991 just before the Gulf War when the situation in the oil markets was quite turbulent. We show how the Monte Carlo method is well suited to this problem.

We also describe a useful recent innovation in the application of the Monte Carlo approach in computational finance. This provides a method of increasing the efficiency of the standard approach. The idea is to use deterministic sequences of numbers that are evenly dispersed throughout the region of integration, rather than random numbers. It can be shown that this leads to quicker convergence. Deterministic sequences with this property are known as low-discrepancy sequences. We describe some recent applications of the method to problems in finance. We also illustrate the use of low-discrepancy sequences in the case of an Asian option.

---

[1]See Zaremba (1968).

THE STANDARD MONTE CARLO METHOD

The basic Monte Carlo approach to option valuation is described by Boyle (1977). Here we review the standard approach to the valuation of a simple European call option. Suppose that the asset price S_t satisfies the stochastic differential equation

$$dS_t = \mu S_t dt + \sigma S_t dB_t$$

where B_t is a standard Brownian motion and μ and σ are constants. The owner of the call has the right to purchase the asset at time T for an amount K so that the value of the option at expiration is $\max[(S_T - K), 0]$. As is well-known, it is convenient for valuation purposes to assume that the asset price follows a related stochastic process: the risk neutral process

$$dS_t = rS_t dt + \sigma S_t dB_t$$

where r is the (assumed constant) riskless rate. Under this assumption $\ln(S_T/S_0)$ is normally distributed with mean rT and variance $\sigma^2 T$. The current price of the call option at $t = 0$ is given by

$$c_0 = E[e^{-rT} \mathrm{Max}(S_T - K, 0)]$$

where the expectation is taken with respect to the risk-neutral density of S_T. This equation leads directly to the Black-Scholes formula by standard integration. We can write the call price in the form

$$c_0 = e^{-rT} \int_{-\infty}^{\infty} [S_T(z) - K]^+ \, n(z) \, dz$$

where n(z) is the standard unit normal density function and

$$S_T(z) = S_0 \exp\left[\left(r - \frac{\sigma^2}{2}\right)T + \sigma z\sqrt{T}\right]$$

We can rewrite the integral as:

$$c_0 = \int_{-\infty}^{\infty} g(z) \, n(z) \, dz$$

Since the call price is now in the form of a definite integral, we can use the crude Monte Carlo method to approximate this integral. We sample N points from the standard normal distribution. The standard error of the estimate will be of the order of $(1/\sqrt{N})$. In practice the types of

TABLE 13–1
Details of Oil Futures Prices and Implied Volatilities for Crude Oil

Contract Month (1991)	*Futures Price (Jan 14, 1991)*	*Implied Volatility*
	$	% p.a.
Feb	27.30	140
March	26.25	125
April	25.25	100
May	24.35	85
June	23.60	75
July	22.90	70
August	22.40	66.7*
Sept	22.00	63.3*
Oct	21.75	60
Nov	21.50	57.5*
Dec	21.30	55

*Obtained by interpolation

problems in which we are interested are of much higher dimension, due either to the presence of several assets and/or path dependency. Our first example illustrates path dependency.

VALUATION OF AVERAGE-PRICE OIL OPTIONS BEFORE THE GULF WAR

Just prior to the outbreak of the Gulf War in mid-January 1991, oil markets were in a very disturbed state. There was great uncertainty about the future supply of oil in the face of the impending hostilities. This uncertainty was reflected in oil option prices at that time. Indeed the implied volatility of the 2-month contract reached 140 percent. In Table 13–1 we provide details of the oil futures prices as well as the implied volatilities at that time.

We consider the valuation of an average price put option to be described more fully below. The valuation date is assumed to be January 14, 1991. Note from Table 13–1 that the futures prices exhibited a strong downward trend at this date. The contract used an average price, which was to be computed using monthly reset dates. The first term in the average was to be the price of the April 1991 futures contract at March 21, 1991. The averaging period started on March 21, 1991, and continued to November 20, 1991. The average was to be based on the arithmetic average of the front month's futures price throughout the averaging period. Thus there were nine reset points with the first one two months and one week from the valuation date. The remaining reset points occurred at monthly intervals. The option strike price was $20.

Most of the standard programs for average-price options assume stationary volatility and a constant convenience yield. In this case neither assumption is valid. Both the convenience yield and the volatility varied over the lifetime of the contract. This example will illustrate the flexibility of the Monte Carlo approach in coping with nonstandard assumptions.

At this stage we introduce some notation. We assume that the current spot price of the asset is S(t). Suppose that the averaging takes place over the future (spot) asset prices at times

$$(t + T_1)\ (t + T_2) \ldots (t + T_n)$$

We assume that the time between the reset points is constant and equal to **h**. In our example h is one month. Hence:

$$T_2 = T_1 + h$$

$$T_n = T_1 + (n - 1)h$$

We assume that the riskless interest rate is constant and equal to *r*. The convenience yield *y* is defined by $y(t, t + u)$ where $o < u < T_n$. Let $F(t, t + T_i)$ denote the current futures price for a futures contract with delivery at time $(t + T_i)$. From the usual cost of carry equation

$$F(t, t + T_i)\, e^{\int_0^{T_i} y(t,\, t + u)\, du} = S(t)\, e^{rT_i}$$

Since we only have monthly futures prices, we approximate the convenience yield by a piecewise constant function. It is taken to be constant between reset dates. Given market data as in Table 13–1 we can solve for the convenience yield over the different monthly subintervals. Notice that the convenience yield behaves like a nonconstant dividend yield. We denote the convenience yield as follows:

$$y(t, t + u) = Y_1 \qquad 0 \le u < T_1$$

$$y(t, t + u) = Y_2 \qquad T_1 \le u < T_2$$

$$y(t, t + u) = Y_3 \qquad T_2 \le u < T_3$$

$$\cdot\cdot \qquad \cdot\cdot$$

$$y(t, t + u) = Y_n \qquad T_{n-1} \le u < T_n$$

In the sequel we shall use the notation $F_i = F(t, t + T_i)$ to simplify the notation.

In a similar way, we can use the series of implied volatilities to compute the volatility that operates during each future month. Here again we are assuming constant volatility between the reset points. We use the following notation for these volatilities:

Time Interval	Volatility
$[0, T_1)$	σ_1
$[T_1, T_2)$	σ_2
..	..
$[T_{n-1}, T_n)$	σ_n

Let us denote the implied volatilities in Table 13–1 by the symbol v. For example, if v_2 is the implied volatility for $[0, T_2)$, the connecting relation with σ_1 and σ_2 is

$$(v_2)^2 T_2 = (\sigma_2)^2 (T_2 - T_1) + (\sigma_1)^2 T_1$$

Notice that the expected value at time t of $S(t + T_i)$ under the risk-neutral measure is

$$E_t[S(t + T_i)] = S(t)\, e^{rT_i}\, e^{-\sum_1^i Y_j(T_j - T_{j-1})} = F_i$$

To use the Monte Carlo method to value an average price put option in this case we generate a set of future oil price paths under the risk-neutral measure. Suppose $\{z_1, z_2, \ldots z_n\}$ is a set of independent unit normal variates. This sequence is used to generate one particular path as follows. The asset price $S(t + T_1)$ for this path is

$$S(t + T_1) = S(t) \exp\left[\left(r - Y_1 - \frac{\sigma_1^2}{2}\right)T_1 + \sigma_1 z_1 \sqrt{T_1}\right]$$

The next price on the path, $S(t + T_2)$ is generated from $S(t + T_1)$ as follows (recall $h = T_2 - T_1$):

$$S(t + T_2) = S(t + T_1) \exp\left[\left(r - Y_2 - \frac{\sigma_2^2}{2}\right)h + \sigma_2 z_2 \sqrt{h}\right)$$

Proceeding in this way, we can generate an entire path and since we know the asset values at the reset points, we can compute the average for this path. Given the average, we determine the terminal value of the put option for this path. We repeat this process for all the paths and find the expected value of the terminal put by taking the arithmetic average over the number of simulation runs. We then discount this expected value to obtain an estimate of the value of the option. We can also find the standard error of the estimate in the usual way.

When we applied this procedure to value the average-price put considered in this section, the Monte Carlo estimate of the price was 2.468, with a standard error of .003 (based on 100,000 simulation runs).

THE USE OF LOW-DISCREPANCY SEQUENCES

In this section we describe the use of low-discrepancy sequences in providing an efficient procedure for the valuation of multidimensional integrals. The key idea is simple. Assume we have just a one-dimensional integral. We can transform the range of integration to [0, 1]. To estimate this integral it is better to use equally spaced points rather than random points. It can be shown that a deterministic sequence suitably chosen will always outperform a random sequence. Hence if we preselect the points in a deterministic way so that they are more or less uniform, we will achieve efficiency gains. The idea can be generalized to higher dimensions. The discrepancy[2] is a measure of the uniformness of a sequence of points, and the lower the discrepancy the more evenly spaced the points are. Low-discrepancy sequences are sometimes known as quasi-random sequences, but this is an unfortunate choice of name since these sequences are deterministic and not at all random.

In this section we describe briefly how this approach works and review some of the recent applications. Spanier and Maize (1994) provide

---

[2]The lower the discrepancy the more uniform the series. For example in the one-dimensional case the sequence of N points that has the lowest discrepancy in [0, 1] is

$$x_n = \frac{2n - 1}{2N} \qquad n = 1, 2 \ldots N$$

a recent overview of these methods, and Neiderreiter (1988) provides an in-depth analysis of low-discrepancy sequences.

There are several examples of low-discrepancy sequences. These are often based on number-theoretic approaches. For example, the Halton sequence[3] is defined by expressing each integer in terms of a prime base and then inverting the coefficients about the decimal point to obtain a number in the interval [0, 1]. In the one-dimensional case we can obtain Halton sequences for each prime r. The jth Halton number $H_r(j)$ is obtained by first expressing j in terms of base r

$$j = \sum_{i=0}^{m} a_i(j)\, r^j$$

Then we perform a radical inversion of the digits to obtain $H_r(j)$

$$H_r(j) = \sum_{i=0}^{m} a_i(j)\, r^{-i-1}$$

We can extend this idea to higher dimensions to produce points in the hypercube $I^s = [0, 1]^s$.

There are several ways to generate multidimensional low-discrepancy sequences. These include Faure sequences, Sobol sequences, Niederreiter sequences, Hammersley points, and others. For a review see Bratley and Fox (1988) and Niederreiter (1988). Joy, Boyle, and Tan (1994) describe how to use Faure sequences to value different types of exotic options. Birge (1993) uses both Halton sequences and Hammersley points to evaluate a standard call option. Paskov (1994) uses both Sobol sequences and Halton sequences to evaluate mortgage-backed securities. Paskov's work involves the evaluation of integrals with dimensions up to 360, and he finds that Sobol sequences are the most efficient and that the use of low-discrepancy sequences outperforms the conventional pseudorandom sequences (i.e., standard Monte Carlo) approach for these types of problems. The general conclusion of these papers is that low-discrepancy sequences are superior to standard Monte Carlo for the applications considered.

Low-discrepancy sequences lead to deterministic error bounds. In principle this is an advantage over standard Monte Carlo estimates, which have probabilistic error bounds. The key result in the area is the

---

[3]See Halton (1960) or Press et al. (1992).

Koksma-Hlawka[4] theorem, which bounds the error in terms of the product of two factors. One is related to the smoothness of the integrand and the other to the uniformity of the sequence of points used to estimate the integral (the so-called discrepancy of the sequence). In practice there are difficulties associated with computing this bound, and the bound is normally much too wide to be of use. For a discussion of error bounds see Paskov (1994) and Joy, Boyle, and Tan (1994).

VALUATION OF ASIAN OPTIONS USING LOW-DISCREPANCY SEQUENCES

We now use low-discrepancy sequences to estimate the value of an Asian option. In this case the payoff of the contract at maturity is based on the average of the underlying asset value over some finite number of points. For simplicity, we consider the valuation of the contract at inception. We compare three approaches to the valuation of this contract. First, we use the standard Monte Carlo approach. This approach provides us with standard errors. We see from Table 13–2 that we need a high number of simulation trials to obtain a low value (around .01) for the standard error. If we want to reduce the error by a factor of 10, we need to perform 100 times as many simulations. We also used Faure's method of generating the low-discrepancy sequences. The procedure is described in Joy, Boyle, and Tan (1994). (See also Faure [1982]). Joy, Boyle, and Tan (1994) also describe an efficient algorithm for inverting the cumulative normal density function. Finally we used Sobol sequences to evaluate the option. Note that the low-discrepancy sequences have faster convergence than the standard Monte Carlo method.

One disadvantage of the low-discrepancy approach is that the theoretical error bound is often too wide to be of practical value. One approach is to run crude Monte Carlo in conjunction[5] with the use of low-discrepancy sequences. We can use the error bound from the crude Monte Carlo to assess the accuracy of the low-discrepancy approach. This would work best if an institution had to value the same type of security very frequently. We could compute in advance the number of low-discrepancy points required to generate a given level of accuracy.

---

[4]See Spanier and Maize (Theorem 1.1).

[5]The programs are actually very similar. We just need different routines to generate the points at which the integral is evaluated.

TABLE 13–2

Five-Week Asian Option with Six Rest Points—Comparison of Standard Monte Carlo Approach with Two Sets of Low-Discrepancy Sequences: Faure Sequences and Sobol Sequences

Asset Price : 100
Strike Price : 100
Volatility : 50% p.a.
Risk-free rate : 9% p.a.

Number of Trials	*Crude Monte Carlo (Standard Error)*	*Faure Sequences*	*Sobol Sequences*
100	3.685 (0.642)	3.876	3.254
400	3.765 (0.298)	3.590	3.531
1,600	3.652 (0.137)	3.618	3.584
9,600	3.590 (0.056)	3.605	3.609
38,400	3.587 (0.028)	3.611	3.612
153,600	3.605 (0.014)	3.612	3.612
614,400	3.606 (0.007)	3.612	3.612

Furthermore, since these points are deterministic we, need only generate them once and then store them for subsequent use.

CONCLUSION

This chapter discussed the use of the Monte Carlo method in the valuation of exotic options. First we discussed the classic Monte Carlo approach. This is a versatile method and we demonstrated its flexibility with an example in which the parameters of the distribution were non-stationary over the option's lifetime. We also discussed some new work in speeding up the convergence of the Monte Carlo method by using low-discrepancy sequences rather than random sequences. These sequences have the property that the points are distributed quite evenly over the unit interval or unit hypercube. Each new addition to the sequence preserves this property so that no matter when we stop adding points the existing points are evenly distributed. These sequences in general provide better approximations than the traditional random sequences (or pseudo-random sequences). These methods have already been successfully applied to a variety of problems in computational finance.

REFERENCES

Barraquand, J., and D. Martineau (1994), "Numerical Valuation of High Dimensional Multivariate American Securities," *Digital Paris Research Report 30,* Digital Equipment Corporation, Paris Research Laboratory, 85, avenue Victor Hugo, 92563 Rueil-Malmaison Cedex, France.

Birge, J. R. (1992), "Quasi-Monte Carlo Approaches to Option Pricing," Working Paper, Department of Industrial and Operations Engineering, University of Michigan, Ann Arbor, MI.

Bratley, P., and B. L. Fox (1988), "ALGORITHM 659: Implementing Sobol's Quasi-Random Sequence Generator," *ACM Trans Math Software,* 14, 88–100.

Broadie, M., and P. Glasserman (1995), "Pricing American Style Securities Using Simulatic" Working Paper, Columbia University

Boyle, P. P., Broadie, M., and P. Glasserman, (1995), "Monte Carlo Methods for Security Pricing," Working Paper, Columbia University (to appear in *Journal of Economics Dynamics and Control*)

Dennis P., and R. J. Rendleman (1995), "Pricing Financial Claims Subject to Interest Rate Risk and Default Risk," Working Paper, Kenan-Flager Business School, University of North Carolina, Chapel Hill, NC 27599-3490.

Faure H. (1982), "Discrépance de suites associées à un système de numération (en dimension s)," *Acta Arithmetica,* 41, 337–351.

Grant D., D. Vora, and D. Weeks (1993), "Path Dependent Options: Extending the Monte Carlo Approach," Working Paper, Anderson Schools of Management, University of New Mexico, Albuquerque, NM.

Joy C., P. P. Boyle, and K. S. Tan (1995), "Quasi-Monte Carlo Methods in Numerical Finance," Working Paper, University of Waterloo, Waterloo, Ontario, Canada.

Niederreiter, H. (1992), "Random Number Generation and Quasi-Monte Carlo Methods," CBMS-NSF, 63, SIAM, Philadelphia, PA.

Paskov, S. P. (1994), "Computing High Dimensional Integrals with Applications in Finance," Technical Report CUCS-023-94, Department of Computer Science, Columbia University, New York.

Press, W. H., S. A. Teukolsky, W. T. Vetterling, and B. P. Flannery (1992), *Numerical Recipes in C, The Art of Scientific Computing,* 2d ed., Cambridge University Press.

Spanier, J., and E. H. Maize (1994), "Quasi-Random Methods for Estimating Integrals Using Relatively Small Samples." *SIAM Review,* Vol 36, No 1, pp. 18–44.

Tilley, J. A. (1993), "Valuing American Options in a Path Simulation Model," *Transactions of the Society of Actuaries,* XLV, pp. 499–520.

Zaremba, S. K. (1968), "The Mathematical Basis of Monte Carlo and Quasi-Monte Carlo Methods," *SIAM Review,* 10, pp. 310–314.

PART

IV

RISK

Chapter Fourteen

Visualizing Risk

By Jack W. Mosevich
Senior Partner
Harris Investment Management

STANDARD HEDGING AND RISK EVALUATION TECHNIQUES

Almost all textbooks and articles dealing with hedging and risk measurement of derivatives present instantaneous measures represented by Greek letters. These are first- or second-order partial derivatives, which measure the change in value of a security or a portfolio for a small instantaneous change in one underlying variable. The resulting values represent the risks of the portfolio relative to the underlying variable and are used as hedging parameters to calculate offset positions. They are also utilized to synthetically replicate a position in a derivative using the underlying security.

The Greeks, as we shall refer to them, are essential to those who must hedge positions continuously. Since their applications have been discussed in other publications, we will assume that readers are familiar with how they are utilized. For reference purposes, the following are the standard Greek measures:

Delta $$\Delta = \frac{\partial P}{\partial S}$$

Gamma $$\Gamma = \frac{\partial \Delta}{\partial S} = \frac{\partial^2 P}{\partial S^2}$$

Kappa (also Vega, Zeta) $$\kappa = \frac{\partial P}{\partial \sigma}$$

$$\text{Rho} \quad \rho = \frac{\partial P}{\partial r}$$

$$\text{Omega } \Omega = \frac{\partial P}{\partial q}$$

$$\text{Theta} \quad \theta = \frac{\partial P}{\partial t}$$

where

P = the current price of the option
s = the current price of the underlying security
t = time to expiry of the option
r = risk-free rate
q = income
σ = volatility

Note that some authors define θ as the change in P over a one-day period and κ as the change in P due to a one-percentage-point change in σ.

It is well known and intuitively clear that the use of these parameters alone is not adequate for representing the risk of a position in options, especially when the position is to be held for a period of time. We are all aware of the fact that even standard options behave in nonsymmetrical, nonlinear fashions and that their risks are multidimensional. Hence it is obvious that such risk cannot be represented by a single vector of numbers at one point in time.

Further, exotic options are even more nonlinear and multidimensional, so we need to explore additional tools for the evaluation of their risks both at the security level and at the portfolio level. One approach is visualization, the subject of this chapter.

VISUALIZATION OF RISK WITH VIRTUAL REALITY

The first step in the hedging and risk management of option positions is to evaluate the exposure of a portfolio, through time t, to those factors that effect its value, such as S, r, q, σ.

Instantaneous exposure is measured by the Greeks. Another powerful approach is to utilize simulation and scenario analysis to measure risk or to compute offsetting positions. A natural means of visualizing the position is with interactive computer graphics, which have recently been incorporated into a powerful approach known as *virtual reality*. Virtual reality (VR) incorporates interactive graphics with human/computer interaction. The computer generates scenes; the user is immersed and interacts with the scenes. Many dimensions can be represented with 3-D (or three-dimensional) graphs, moving icons, sound, and color. Simulation is often incorporated.

We have currently applied only part of this technology (the graphics and immersion) to the subject at hand. The software ExoticOp!® supplied with this book has an optional module that utilizes some of the capabilities of VR as described below. Note that we can view not only the risk of the position but the profiles of the Greek parameters too, if so desired.

The benefits of such an approach are obvious, namely that one gets a global view of risk, which is not possible from a vector of parameters. This permits us to see potential loss and gain through time and relative to all other factors. Viewing the evolution of the Greek parameters can provide valuable insights for both short-and long-term horizons.

EXAMPLES

We can demonstrate the power of visualization by examining the following simple portfolio of three-month options on U.S. T-bond futures:

Short	100	96 Puts
Long	50	98 Puts
Long	50	102 Calls
Short	100	104 Calls

The current futures price is set at 100, we set $r = 5$ percent, and all options are assumed to be European. Figure 14–1 represents the current P/L and exercise P/L of this position.

The light bands above and below the current P/L curve represent the effects on the current P/L due to $\pm$ 3 percent changes in implied volatility.

We will now demonstrate several attributes of this position that the Greek parameters cannot measure. First consider time decay. If the futures price stays at 100, it is true that time decay is in the holder's favor, so for a while we make money at the predicted rate of θ per day. However, after a while θ becomes negative and profits start to be given back.

FIGURE 14–1

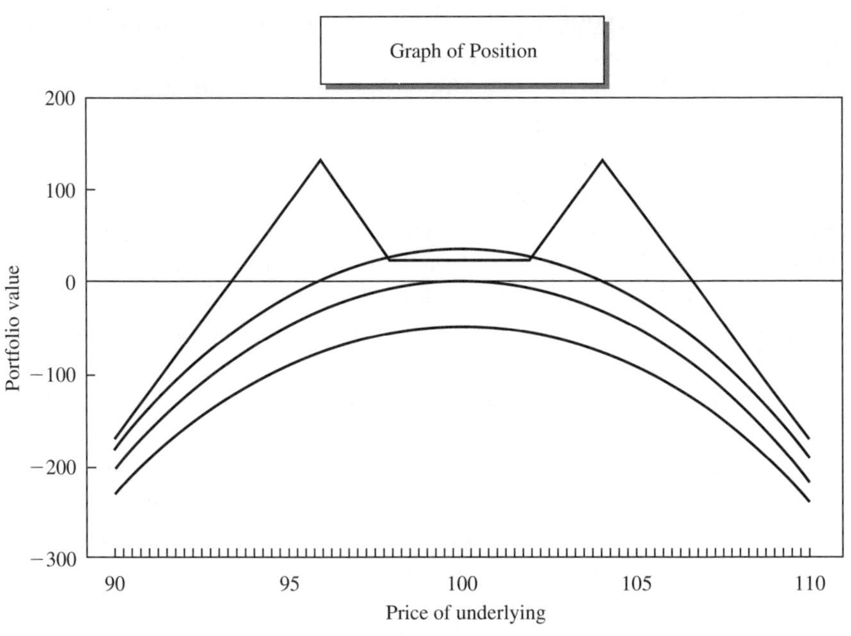

Alternatively, if the underlying futures dropped to, say, 94, we ride a very swift profit-path up one of the "peaks"; here θ is positive and increasing. A view of the position in three dimensions quickly shows how the P/L can evolve through time much more effectively than a table of θ values (see Figure 14–2). This picture is only valid, of course, if σ, ρ, and τ are constant.

Next we examine exposure to implied volatility. Figure 14–3 is a plot of P/L through time while holding the current futures price fixed at 100. Notice how the P/L rises until 20 days before expiration and then starts decreasing. Of even more interest is the behavior of exposure to implied volatility: in the period from 15 to 25 days before maturity, an increase or decrease in volatility reduces the value of the portfolio. Such a situation is called a "volatility pocket" and is not possible to describe with any value of κ. The reason for this behavior is that the options all respond differently to volatility.

FIGURE 14–2

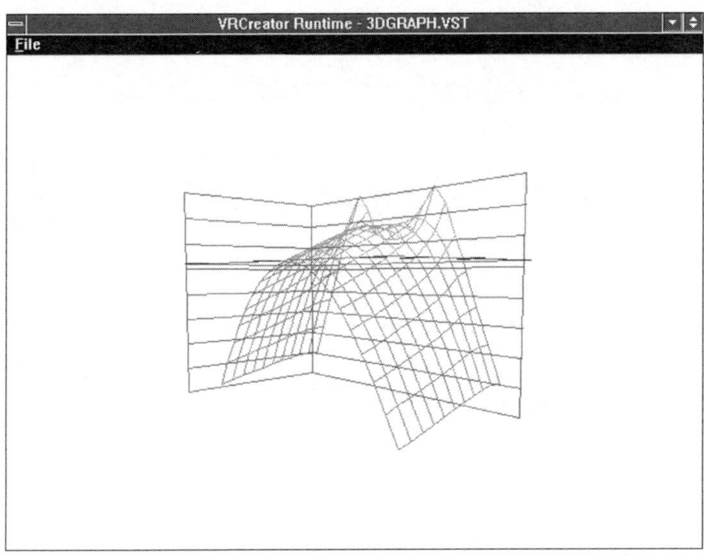

The same view, Figure 14–4, with the futures price set at 104, is totally different and no strange volatility behavior occurs.

The use of graphics gives insights into the position that are not given by parameters. For example, the 3-D graph in Figure 14–2 shows the maximum possible profit attainable with this position. Thus if the market value is near the peak, we should probably liquidate or hedge to lock in this profit as the probability of achieving much more profit is very low and the losses can be quite large. If, on the other hand, the market has moved against us, we can evaluate the odds of time decay working in our favor to bail us out.

It is very enlightening to view the Greek parameters through time and versus the prices of the underlying security. The following figures show Δ, Γ, and κ for our example. We can see how and where changes occur, which will be useful to know as the portfolio ages. Note that the graph of κ alone does not reveal the risks shown in Figure 14–3. Figures 14–5, 14–6, and 14–7 show Δ, Γ, and κ of the portfolio through time and across S.

FIGURE 14–3

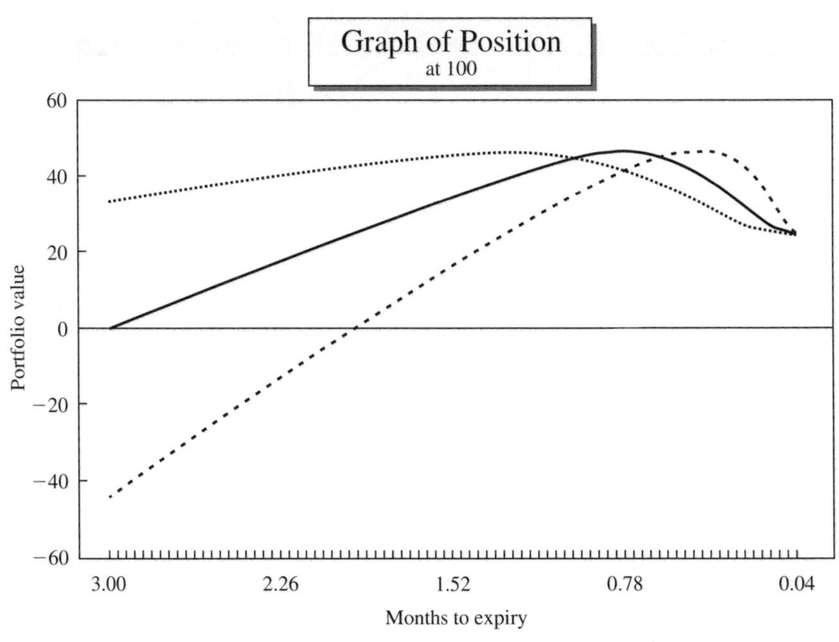

VISUALIZING EXOTIC OPTIONS

The path dependence and special payoff features of exotic options offer real challenges to risk evaluation. Visualization may not be a panacea, but, as we show through the following examples, by being able to explore various attributes of a position a great deal of insight can be gained. In fact it is hard to imagine an alternative means of understanding a position.

Figure 14–8 is a 3-D graph of the P/L of a "step," which is the position created by being long one binary call at a strike of 90 and short one binary call with a strike of 110. Figure 14–9 is a graph of τ and Figure 14–10 is a graph of θ.

The next example is from *Risk* magazine (September 1994). In their article "Forever Hedged," Derman, Ergener, and Kani synthetically approximate an up-and-out barrier with a series of European calls.

FIGURE 14–4

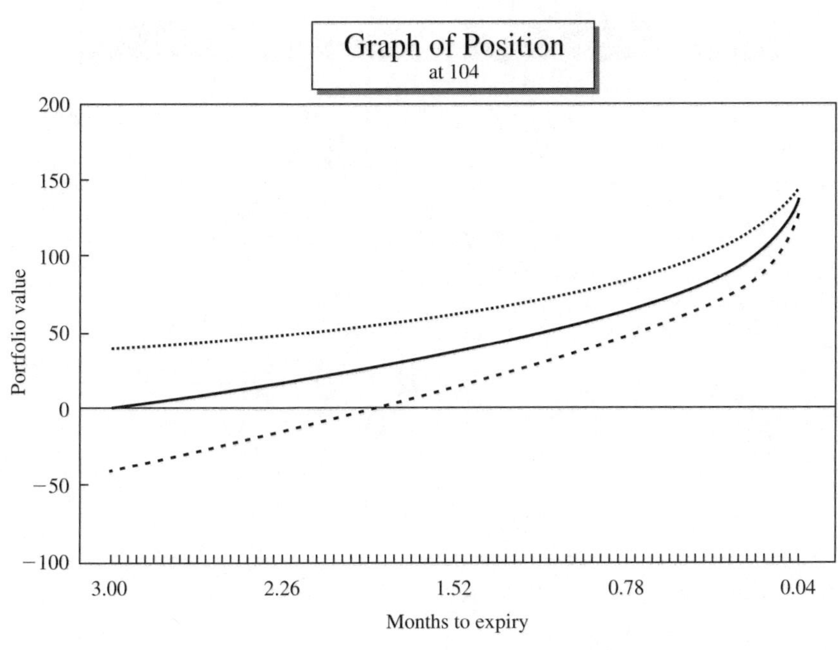

Specifically an up-and-out call with a strike of 100 and barrier of 110 is approximated by the following:

0.16	120.00	Call	11 Apr. 95
0.25	120.00	Call	11 Jun. 95
0.44	120.00	Call	11 Aug. 95
0.93	120.00	Call	11 Oct. 95
2.79	120.00	Call	11 Dec. 95
−6.51	120.00	Call	11 Feb. 96
1.00	120.00	Call	11 Feb. 96

If we create a portfolio consisting of the above calls and short one barrier, then it should be reasonably flat through time and price S. Figure

FIGURE 14–5

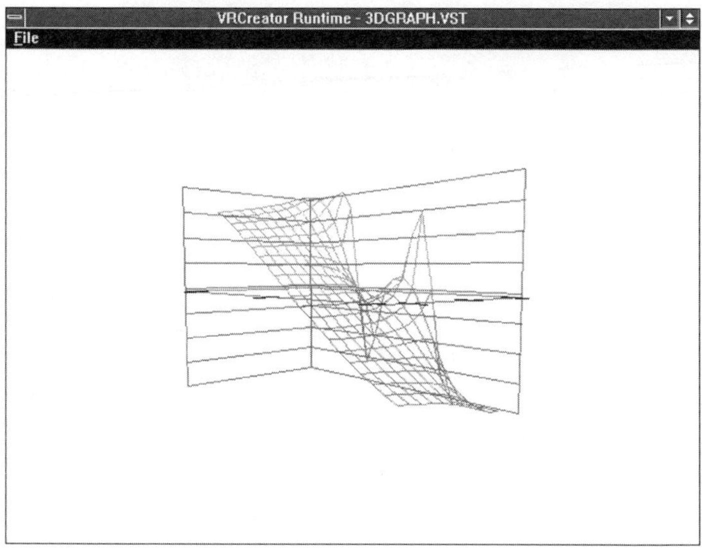

14–11 shows the P/L. Over most values of time and S the position is a good approximation.

FURTHER APPLICATIONS

Besides passive visualization, the real power of VR will occur from user interaction with scenes and the use of simulation. For example, a trader may wish to evaluate the effects of volatility changes through time by generating a future volatility path and seeing the actual portfolio value evolve. Alternatively, if a particular situation is visualized, one can fly to a region on the P/L surface and be presented with the values of variables there that are behind the situation. Multiple dimensional visualization is also possible, whereby the speed or color of moving symbols represents exposure at various places on the risk profile, due to underlying variables. The software ExoticOp!®, a sample of which is supplied with this book, has a module that will allow one to duplicate the above examples as well as to evaluate portfolios of many types of exotics using the emersion capability of VR.

FIGURE 14–6

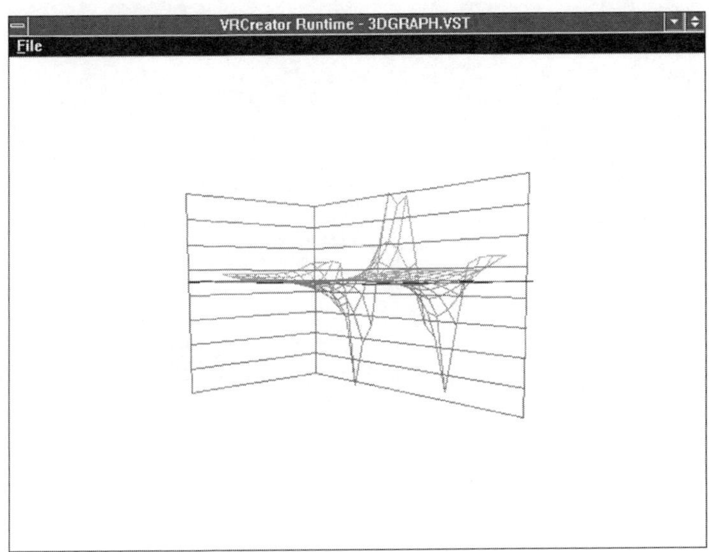

FIGURE 14–7

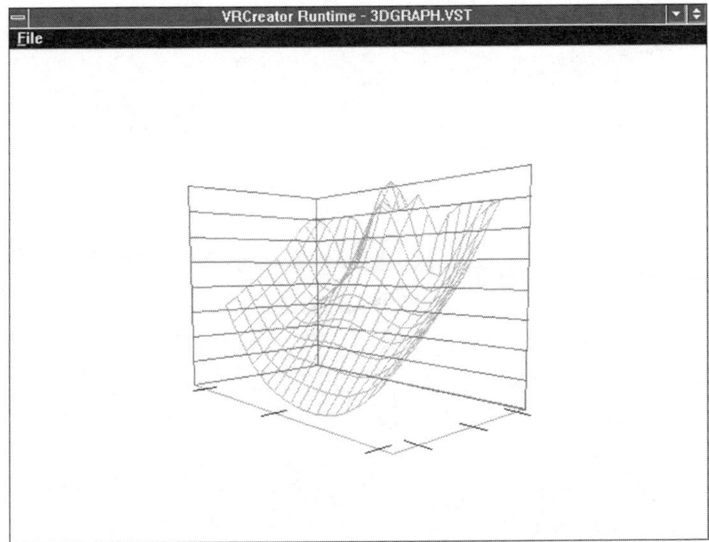

FIGURE 14–8

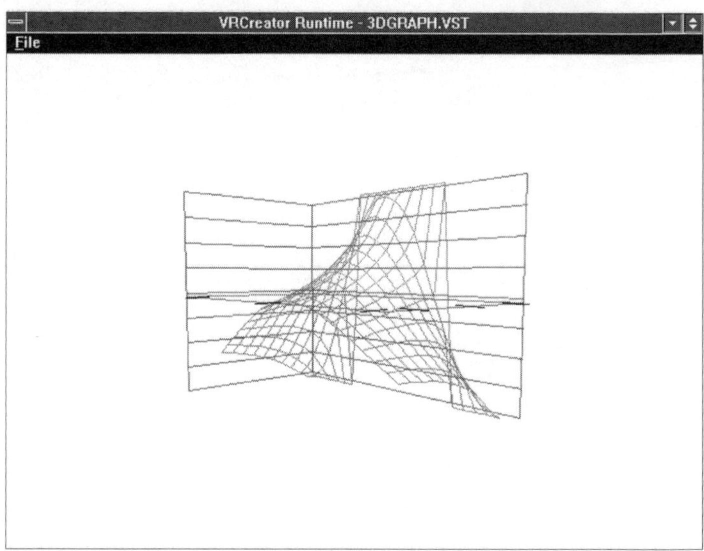

FIGURE 14–9

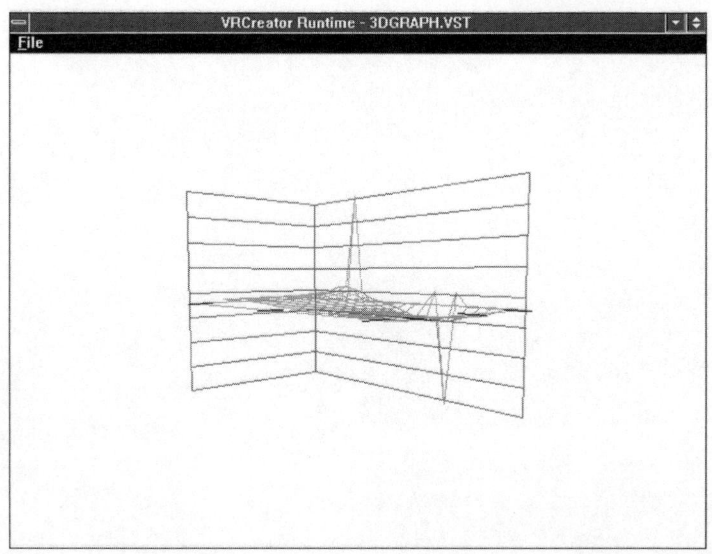

FIGURE 14–10

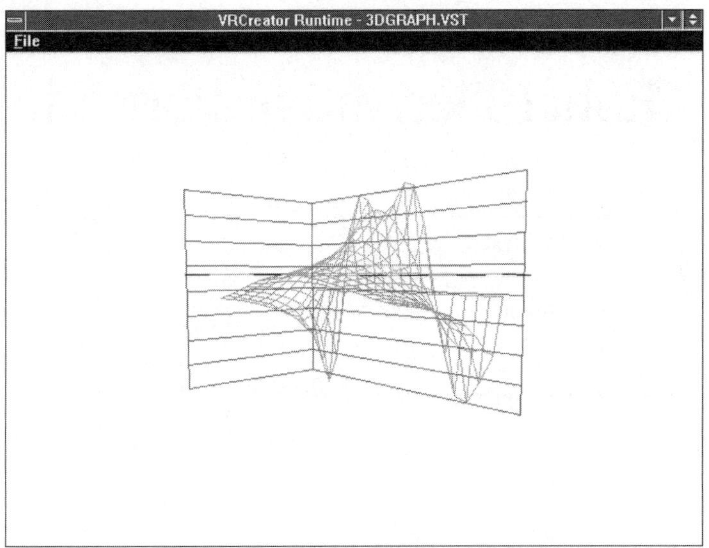

FIGURE 14–11

Chapter Fifteen

Risk Management for Global Derivative Portfolios*

By Robert Geske
Professor of Finance,
University of California, Los Angeles
CEO and Chairman
LOR/Geske Bock Associates

INTRODUCTION

To do a good job of risk management, one must understand the risks to be managed. Some individuals think markets will rise, some think they will fall, and some think they will not change; but probably the most dangerous individual is the one whose belief carries great conviction. I think it was Keynes who suggested that there are two types of investors: (1) those who do not know which way markets will move, and (2) those who do not know that they do not know which way markets will move. It is this hubris that often leads to trouble.

Traders put risk on the firm's balance sheet and this risk is managed by internal controls. In the simple world of good guys and bad guys, there are good and bad traders and good and bad controls. Of the four possible combinations, it is obvious that the best situation is good traders and good controls, while the worst is bad traders and bad controls. However, it is less obvious to the senior manager whether good traders and bad controls are better or worse than bad traders and good controls.

When the firm's portfolio contains derivatives, all of the problems of managing a portfolio are magnified. It is not simply the leverage inherent

*Thanks to Richard Baskin and Brian Dvorak for helpful comments.

in the derivative that magnifies the risk-management problems, but also how exotic or unique the derivatives are. The risk is global because today the interconnected over-the-counter (OTC) financial markets are the world's most integrated, largest, and most rapidly growing. This chapter considers some important issues in global risk management for derivative portfolios.

OBJECTIVES OF RISK MANAGEMENT

A key risk-management objective is to *eliminate surprises.* A current situation of no surprises does not mean that in the future the situation will remain the same. Since the future is uncertain, the elimination of surprise is a task that requires continuous analysis, which hopefully produces useful and timely reports.

In order to produce these beneficial reports, the risk manager must understand the company's and trader's objectives. Typical objectives of a dealer book are to (1) earn the bid/ask spread; (2) maintain a deal inventory; (3) control the risks and retain the deal profitability; (4) take proprietary positions within prescribed limits. The products in a global book may include underlying and derivative positions in interest rates, currencies, equities, and commodities.

What does management need to know? The obvious concerns are the risks to which the firm is exposed. Without this knowledge, protection is impossible. If the exposures all had linear sensitivities, protecting against them would be relatively easy. However, with derivatives the exposure changes are usually very nonlinear. Nonlinearity implies that Gamma is important because Gamma measures the rate of the rate of change, or how quickly the positions in a protected portfolio can accelerate and become unprotected.

Many international groups have recently offered written recommendations about what management needs to know in order to control global risk. All of these groups have suggested that management consider the difference between current risk and potential or future risk. This requires some type of forward-looking scenario analysis. For those interested in gathering these written reports, a brief list for correspondence to some of these recommenders follows: the Group of 30, CFTC, SEC, OCC, GAO, NAIC, BIS, IOSCO, ICI, AICPA, FED, Bank of England, Bundesbank, MOF, Bank of Italy.

RISK REPORTS

What does management need to know from as few reports as possible? While much could be said about this, there are a few obvious pieces of required information: (1) sources of cash-flow revenue; (2) sources of risk; (3) interactions between the sources of revenue and the sources of risk; (4) checks on compliance with the agreed-upon risk limits; (5) assessment of the hedge effectiveness; (6) clear distinction and revelation of current and future risk. It is the potential risk that is the most difficult because it requires analysis of the uncertain future.

Sources of Revenue and Risk

To place the sources of revenue and risk in the context of the somewhat outmoded asset/liability terminology, the sources of revenue are the assets and the hedges are the liabilities. The mismatch, or the inability of the hedges to protect against the risks of the assets, is called the gap. Today this terminology is considered archaic because to control the sensitivities of the highly leveraged derivatives, the "Greeks" have been introduced. The Greeks, namely Delta, Gamma, Vega, Theta, Rho, etc. provide the minimum understanding necessary to control the risks of a derivatives portfolio.

These sensitivities are defined very briefly as follows: *Delta* measures the rate of change in value with respect to a change in the underlying source of risk. *Gamma* measures the rate of change of Delta (or the rate of the rate of change in value) with respect to a change in the underlying source of risk. *Vega* measures the rate of change in value with respect to a change in the volatility of the underlying source of risk. *Theta* measures the rate of change in value with respect to a change in calendar time. *Rho* measures the rate of change in value from future expected cash flows with respect to a change in the discount rate.

The sources of risk are many; some might say they are uncountable. While this may be philosophically true, a good risk manager must begin the enumeration. Below is a partial list of sources of risk, separated into those that are either more or less easily quantified and thus differentiable:

More-quantifiable risks. P&L, interest-rate, currency, equity, commodity, market gaps, volatility, correlation (cross markets/risks), hedging, liquidity, basis, spread, modeling, curve construction (including interpolation and extrapolation), contract, concentration, counterparty, call and prepayment, reinvestment, credit, capital, bankruptcy, country, etc.

Less-quantifiable risks. Systemic, political, personnel, audit, regulatory, tax, legal, knowledge, technology, FASB, data, systems, etc.

Measurement of Current Risk and Exposure

Risk equivalents can be computed using the calculus of partial derivatives. For example, the reference rate Delta of an interest-rate cap can be found by taking the derivative of the cap with respect to the relevant forward rate. Note that this partial derivative will depend on the forward-curve construction, the specific model used to value the cap, the measure of the volatility of the relevant forward rate, the time to the specific forward rate, and the measure of the discount rate. Sensitivities to all these assumptions and measurements can be analyzed. All these sensitivities can be matched as closely as possible in order to obtain a portfolio that has reasonable profit for the relevant risk.

Hedge effectiveness is necessary in order to earn a reasonable profit for the relevant risk. The differences between these risk equivalents for the assets and their hedges is the exposure to that portion of a source of risk. For example, the Gamma exposure to changes in the yen exchange rate can be known and offset. However, if the Gamma exposure is to an exotic contract with less liquidity or a one-sided market, then the risk-offset problem is much more difficult and requires understanding of the relevant "building blocks" that constitute the exotic.

Mismatches in each of the measured risk equivalents for each source of risk are termed "risk exposures." The P&L is typically at the center of focus and concern about mismatches or exposures. Thus, the P&L effect of each of these exposures can be analyzed and reported.

The objectives of hedge effectiveness for P&L management can be simplified to the following three: (1) P&L variations are small; (2) P&L variations oscillate in a random manner about zero; (3) there is no trend in cumulative P&L variations. Obviously a negative P&L trend would be worse than a positive trend, but a positive trend might suspiciously imply extra reward without commensurate risk (i.e., continually beating the market).

Measurement of Future Risk and Exposure

Potential risk is obviously a question to which senior management needs an answer. However, the answer to this question is more difficult to obtain. Simply stated, management wants to know how the portfolio P&L will be *expected* to change under realistic example scenarios: (1) interest rates go up 200 basis points; (2) volatility of the S&P 500 triples; (3) correlation between the yen and dollar halves; etc. Not only does management need to know what the "smart guys" expect to happen, but what errors or sensitivities are embedded in their expectations. It takes considerable hubris for the "smart guys" not to know that their model might not always be appropriate.

The italicized word, "expected," is important in understanding different methods of approaching potential risk. One unrealistic way to consider the future is to ask what happens if one of the above scenarios occurs with certainty, or with probability equal to 1. In other words, what if management is certain that interest rates will rise 200 basis points? This analysis can be done by changing the inputs and then marking-to-market the portfolio. If management is not certain that this scenario will occur, several scenarios could be tried.

A well-understood and a more elegant and rigorous method of generating the future scenarios is with Monte Carlo analysis. In a Monte Carlo simulation, the probability distributions of the sources of risk are used to create realistic future scenarios which produce a distribution of portfolio values. The Monte Carlo analysis can be implemented to satisfy important economic constraints on no arbitrage, interest-rate parity, consistent future distributions of the sources of risk, etc.

The Monte Carlo generated distributions of future portfolio values can be used for a variety of applications such as: (1) value at risk (VAR), (2) credit exposure, (3) liquidity risk, (4) return on capital (ROC), (5) risk-adjusted return on capital (RAROC), (6) capital requirements, (7) counterparty risks, (8) country exposures, (9) netting effects, (10) worst-path analysis, (11) best-path analysis, (12) risk decomposition to each source of future risk, etc.

A key difference between simple scenario analysis (up and down 100, 200, 300 bp) and more-complex Monte Carlo scenario analysis is that with Monte Carlo the future is not arbitrarily specified by the trader, risk manager, accountant, or regulator. Instead, all future paths are selected by the probability distributions of the underlying sources of risk. A drawback is that Monte Carlo is more complicated to understand and implement. There is no reason not to do both. However, Monte Carlo seems to be the choice of the sophisticated players, the rating agencies, and the reserve banks, so it may eventually become the standard of the marketplace.

CONCLUSION

Modern global risk management is indeed a challenging problem that requires clever people to produce useful analyses and timely reports. The risk management reports must cater to both internal and external audit needs. However, it is important to recognize that the takers of risk generally have more at stake (and more hubris) than the observers of risk. In order to satisfy the concerns of both, systems should capture at least all externally required risk measurements. Good internal risk managers will generally have systems that capture much more than the external audits require.

However, there are classic principal-agent problems between senior firm managers, their traders, risk managers, auditors, accountants, and regulators. For example, the captured-regulator hypothesis suggests that regulators may actually work on behalf of the corporations that they were appointed by the public to regulate. Another conflict is that while the traders and risk managers are both internal employees of the firm, the risk manager is external to the trader. While this independence is necessary, it is also troublesome because of conflicting interests. Perhaps if a more encompassing definition of a "good trader" is one with risk controls, then it is not possible to have a "good trader" with bad risk controls.

Responsible senior management recognizes that whoever has the most money can hire the cleverest people to measure and report the firm's risk. Thus, it is their job to level the playing field so that the risk managers have similar quality of people and technology as do the traders. Senior management must obtain the best information possible.

Appendix

EXOTICOP!©
THE EXOTIC OPTIONS PORTFOLIO MANAGER

Sample Disk Installation Guide

The diskette attached to the *Handbook of Exotic Options* is designed to let you experiment with portfolios of exotic options. The disk contains a sample version of our program, "ExoticOp!, The Exotic Options Portfolio Manager." This Windows program can be installed on IBM-compatible PCs (a math co-processor and 8 megabytes of RAM are recommended) in just a few minutes.

INSTALLATION

To install the program on your PC, perform the following steps:

1. Get into Windows by typing **WIN**.
2. Choose **File** from the Program Manager window. This can be done either with the mouse or by pressing the **Alt** key together with the **F** key.
3. Choose **Run** from the File options. Again, do this either with the mouse or by pressing the **Alt** key together with the **R** key.
4. Enter either **A:\SETUP** or **B:\SETUP** into the command line.
5. Press **Enter**. The computer will start installing the software.
6. Follow the prompts until software installation is complete.

OVERVIEW

This software can be used to quickly, accurately, and efficiently price and find the risk profile of a portfolio of exotic options. Closed-form

---

formulas are used wherever possible. In other cases, quick numerical algorithms are utilized.

More than thirty different types of options are included in the package. The software comes complete with a large number of help screens to aid the user.

INITIATION AND EXECUTION

To operate, simply click on the ExoticOp! icon in Windows. The main screen of the program pops up.

Choose an Underlying

The first step is to specify to the program whether the underlying is an equity, a currency, or a commodity. This is done with the mouse by pointing to the **Underlying** menu and choosing the appropriate type of security.

Choose a Compounding Frequency

Next, specify the interest-rate compounding convention used: annual, semiannual, or continuous. This is done with the mouse by pointing to the **Compounding** menu and choosing the appropriate type of compounding.

Details of Underlying

On the top half of the main screen, you will be asked to fill in the details pertaining to the underlying. These are listed here with examples:

Today's Date	15-Jan-1994
Interest Rate	6%
Spot Price	50
Dividend Rate	2%
Volatility	15%

These details will be incorporated into all options.

Frozen Variables

Since this is a sample disk, we have frozen the value of some of the variables. In particular, the following values have been preset:

Spot Price	50
Interest Rate	6%
Volatility	15%

All other variables may be changed by the user.

Unrestricted Program

The unrestricted program is available for sale from Super Computer Consulting Corporation. It also has many other optional features, such as connections to real-time feeds and 3D virtual reality graphics capability. With the optional 3D module, the user can instantly plot the graph of any variable (portfolio price or Greeks) with respect to the time and price of the underlying.

Portfolio

The central part of the screen is the portfolio area. To add an item to this area, choose the type of option from the following broad categories (note that each broad category may be further divided into subcategories):

American
European
Risky European
Chooser
Collar
Compound
Barrier
Gap
Binary
Lookback

Average
Quanto
Underlying

Choose the appropriate folder. A special screen appears in which the user can type and select the particulars of the option. You may also select the **Help** menu bar on the upper right-hand side, which tells you in detail about the option. Two types of help are available: **information** and **payout**. **Information** gives detailed information about the option type. **Payout** describes the payout function at expiry.

Each option has particular fields to be filled. Do not forget to fill in the quantity of options bought. If you are selling options (or writing them), put in a negative number. Other fields may be required; however, this depends on the type of option.

When finished entering the particulars of the option, press **ADD**. This action adds the current option to the working portfolio and replaces the screen in the background. If you change your mind, press **CANCEL**, and the current option will not be added to the portfolio.

After all options have been entered, press the **Price** button on the main screen. This will cause the price of the portfolio and all its derivatives to be computed.

Background

Note that the background of the computed fields appears green immediately after the computation. This indicates that the results are consistent with the screen being displayed. However, if any of the parameters are changed or modified, the results are no longer consistent with the portfolio displayed, and the background changes to red.

Errors

In case of errors in the input data, the program flags the first option with an error. An appropriate message is displayed.

FILE FUNCTIONS

Save As . . . . Save the portfolio just created to a file **example.por** by choosing the **Save As . . .** option from the Portfolio menu and typing the name of the file.

Read. At a later time, one can read a portfolio which has been saved to disk. Choose **Read** from the portfolio menu.

Save. **Save** allows the user to save an existing portfolio which has been modified.

New. The **New** function deletes all positions in the portfolio.

PORTFOLIO FUNCTIONS

Delete. Choose an option and press **Delete**. This will delete the option position from the working portfolio.

Edit. Choose an option and press **Edit**. The correct sheet will come to the foreground and allow you to modify the details of the option. When you are done, press **Add**. If you change your mind, press **CANCEL**. The option will remain unmodified.

NAVIGATION

There are several ways to navigate between screens:

1. Choose the relevant tab using the mouse.
2. From the menu bar, choose **View** and then the appropriate screen.
3. Use the hot keys. For example, **CTRL+B** displays the barrier option screen while **CTRL+Q** displays the Quanto option screen. The hot keys are listed under the **View** menu bar.

EXAMPLE

Suppose that on 15-Jan-1995, the interest rate was 6%. A trader constructs a portfolio on a stock which is currently selling at $50 whose dividend is 2% and whose volatility is 15%. Rates are quoted on a semi-annual basis. The contents of the portfolio are:

Long 4 European A-T-M Call Options with expiry 1-Sep-1995.
Short 3 Regular Choosers with Choice date 15-Aug-1995, Expiry 15-Sep-1995 and strike 49.

To enter this position, follow these steps:

1. Start the program.
2. Initialize by choose **File** from the menu bar and choosing **New**.
3. Choose **Underlying** type: Equity.
4. Choose **Compounding** frequency: Semiannual.
5. In **Today's Date** field enter 15-Jan-1995.
6. Do not modify the **Interest Rate** field as it is already set at 6%.
7. Do not modify the **Volatility** field as it is already set at 15%.
8. Do not modify the **Spot Price** field as it is already set at 50.
9. Enter 2% into the **Dividend** field.

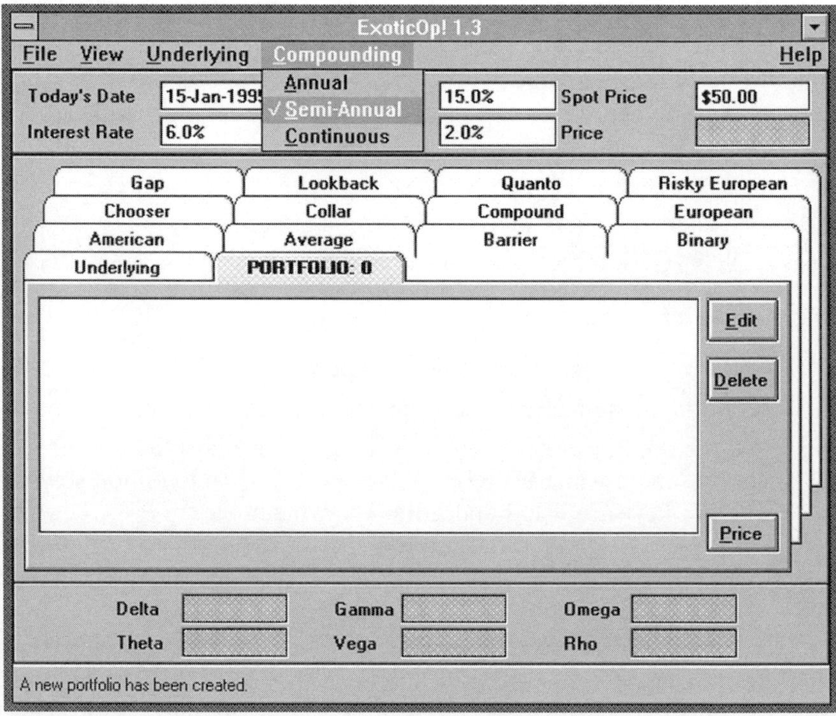

The program has now been set up. Note the notation **Portfolio: 0**, which appears on the portfolio tab. This shows that the portfolio has no positions in it. We now add the various option positions.

1. Press the **European** folder tab.
2. The **European** option screen appears.
3. Enter the quantity as 4.
4. Enter the strike as 50.
5. Enter the expiry date as 1-Sep-1995.
6. Set the **Call** button on (the **Put** button turns off automatically).

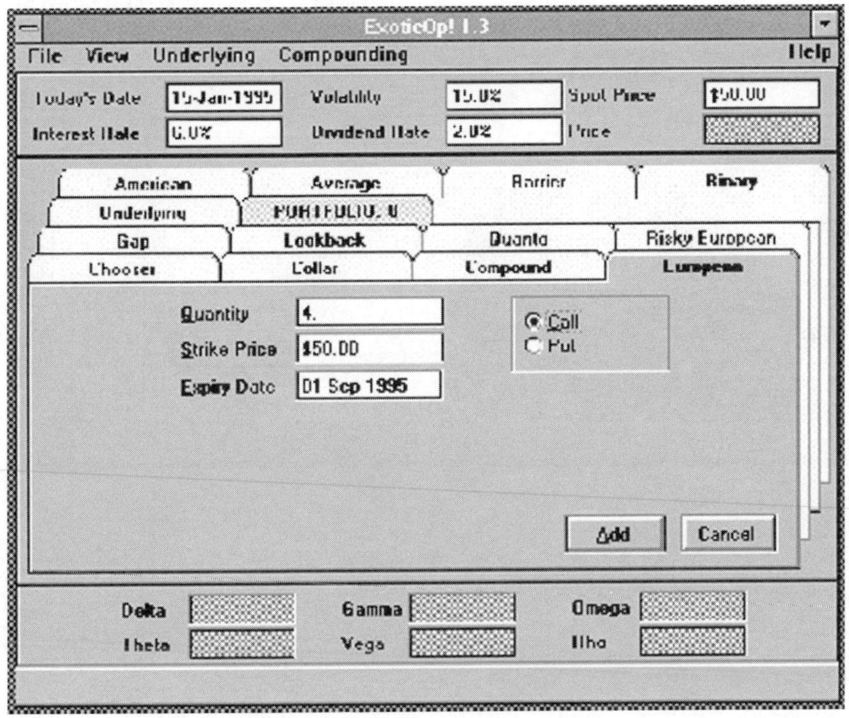

7. Press **ADD**.
8. The **Portfolio** screen now appears in the foreground with the European position entered.

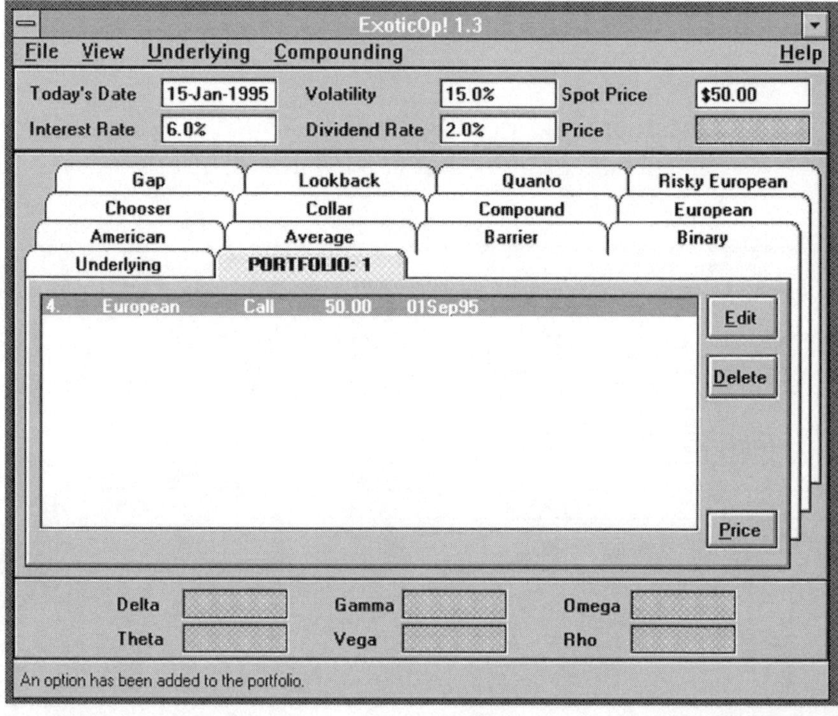

Note the notation **Portfolio: 1** on top of the portfolio tab. This shows that a single position has been entered.

The first options position should appear in the white area in the center of the screen. Next, add the chooser position:

1. Press the **Chooser** tab.
2. From the **Type** menu, on the right hand side, select "Regular."
3. Enter the quantity as −3 (negative three).
4. Enter the choice date as 15-Aug-1995.
5. Enter the strike as 49.
6. Enter the expiry date as 15-Sep-1995.

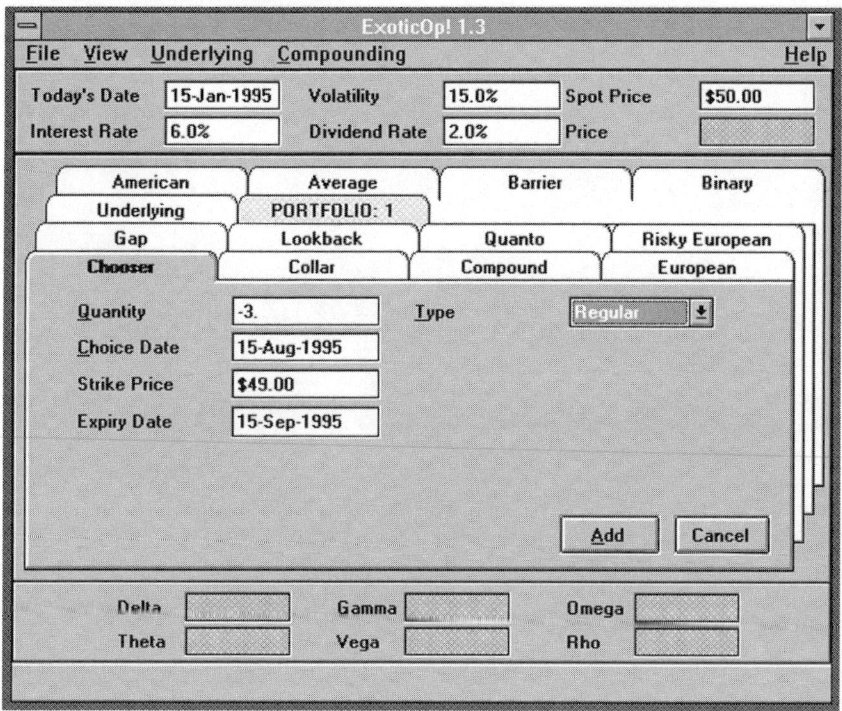

7. Press **ADD**.
8. The portfolio screen appears in the foreground. Note the notation **Portfolio: 2** which indicates that two positions have been entered.

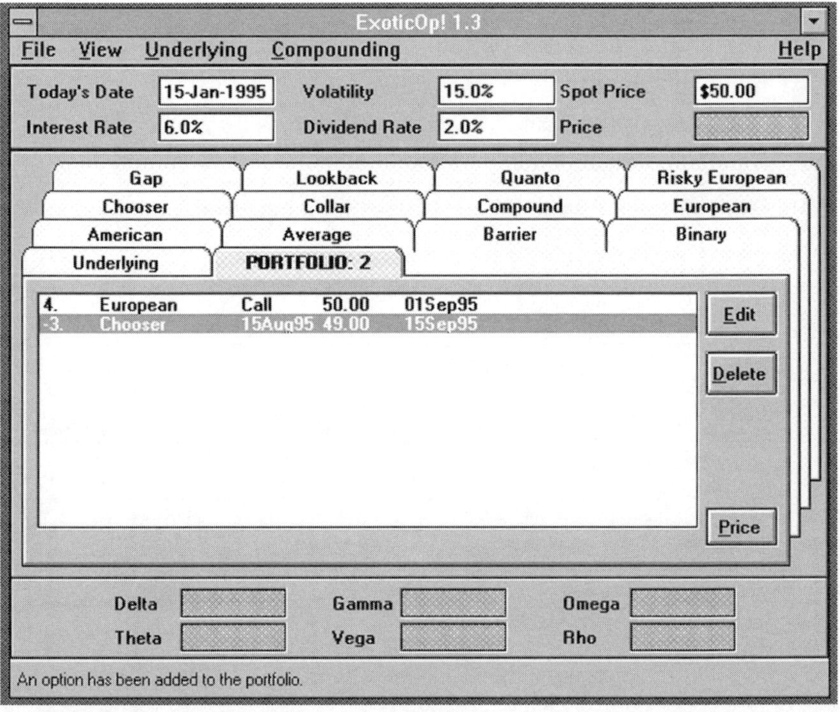

At this stage, we can price the portfolio by pressing **Price**. The price of the portfolio will appear as well as its Greek parameters:

1. Delta: The first derivative with respect to spot price.
2. Gamma: The second derivative with respect to spot price.
3. Omega: The third derivative with respect to spot price.
4. Theta: The first derivative with respect to time (Time decay).
5. Vega: The first derivative with respect to volatility.
6. Rho: The first derivative with respect to interest rates.

In this example, the price of the portfolio is negative, indicating that our short position is more valuable than our long position.

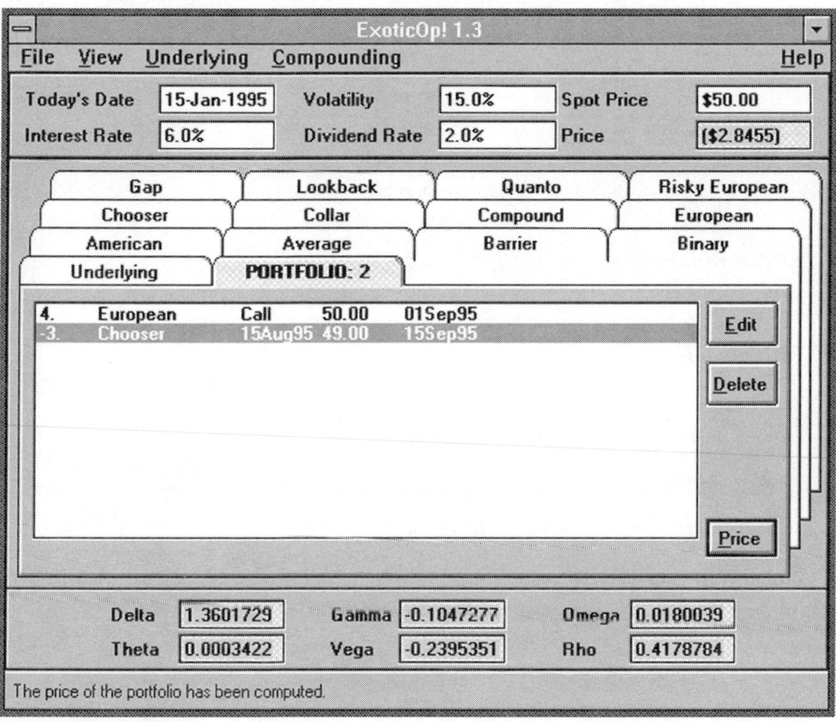

ON-LINE HELP

The program has extensive on-line help facilities. **F1** is your **Help** key. Pressing **F1** or choosing **Help** from the menu bar from any option screen displays the appropriate help document. For example, here is a display of the beginning of the **Help** document for the **Barrier** option.

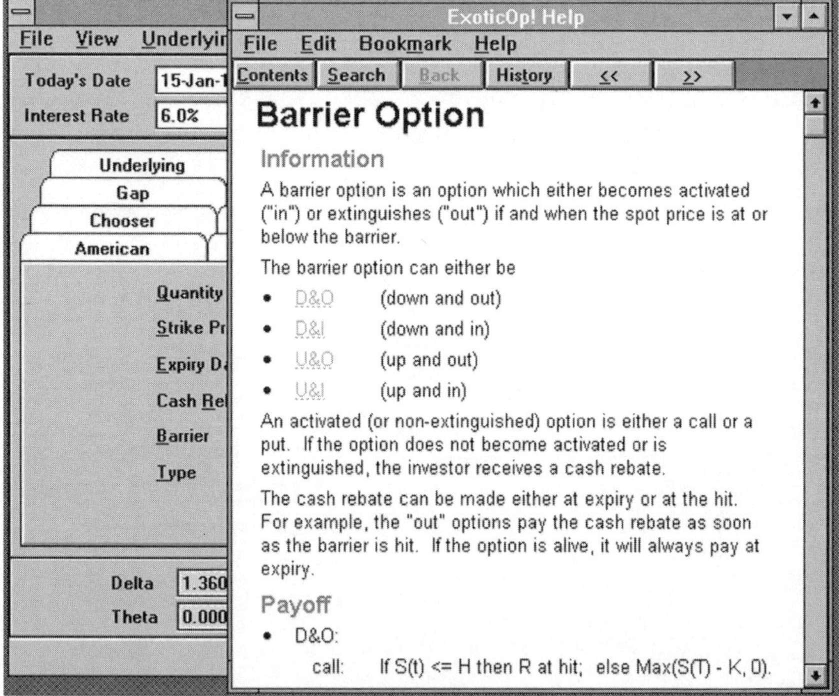

The **Help** documents can be printed. Choose **File** from the **Help** menu bar and then choose the **Print** option.

SCENARIO ANALYSIS

Use ExoticOp! to analyze hypothetical situations as they pertain to your portfolio's value and hedging parameters. For example, what would be the price of the portfolio in the preceding example one month later if dividends were to change to 8%? Change the fields Today's Date to 15-Feb-1995 and Dividend Rate to 8%. Note that the background of the computed fields changes to red. Press the Price key again. Note that new prices and hedging parameters are computed and the background changes to green.

Index